THE ISLAMIC INTELLECTUAL TRADITION IN PERSIA

THE ISLAMIC INTELLECTUAL TRADITION IN PERSIA

Seyyed Hossein Nasr

EDITED BY
MEHDI AMIN RAZAVI

CURZON
PRESS

First published in 1996
by Curzon Press
St John's Studios, Church Road, Richmond
Surrey, TW9 2QA

Typeset in Times by Excel Books, New Delhi
Printed in Great Britain by
T J Press Limited, Padstow, Cornwall

British Library Cataloguing in Publication Data
A catalogue record for this book is available from the British Library

Library of Congress in Publication Data
A catalog record for this book has been requested

ISBN 0 7007 0314 4

Contents

PART IV : PHILOSOPHERS-POETS-SCIENTISTS

PART V: LATER ISLAMIC PHILOSOPHY

PART VI: ISLAMIC THOUGHT IN MODERN IRAN

Acknowledgements

I would first and foremost like to express my gratitude to Seyyed Hossein Nasr for his generous cooperation and invaluable advice regarding many aspects of this work. The present collection of essays could not have been completed without his assistance. I also wish to thank the author for granting me the permission to use the articles included.

I would also like to thank Marylynn Aminrazavi for her numerous editorial suggestions and also her comments on my translations of several articles of this volume. I would especially like to thank Harriet L. Brennan for taking a personal interest in the project and her administrative help and suggestions as well as Cindy A. Toomey.

Finally, I wish to thank various publishers for their permission to use articles and chapters that had previously appeared in their publications.

A number of the works cited in this volume have had later editions with some revisions in them. I have not listed such works in the text but their latest editions are as follows:

1. *Three Muslim Sages,* Lahore: Suhail Academy, 1988.
2. *History of Islamic Philosophy,* Trans. Liadain Sherrard, London: Routledge and Kegan and Paul, 1993.
3. *Ideals and Realities of Islam,* San Fransisco, Harper Collins Publishers, 1994
4. *Science and Civilization in Islam,* New York: Barnes and Noble, 1992
5. *Sohrawardi. Oeuvres Philosophique et Mystiques,* Vol. III, Tehran: The Institute for Cultural Studies, 1993.
6. *An Annotated Bibliography of Islamic Sciences.* With W. Chittick Vol.III, Tehran:, The Institute for Cultural Studies, 1991.
7. *Islam and the Plight of Modern Man,* Lahore: Suhail Academy, 1988.
8. *Islamic Life and Thought,* Lahore: Albany (N.Y.), State University of New York Press 1981.

For more information concerning the latest edition of Seyyed Hossein Nasr's publications see: *The Complete Bibliography of the Works of Seyyed Hossein Nasr: From 1958 Through April 1993.* (ed.) M. Aminrazavi and Z. Moris, Kuala Lumpur: Islamic Academy of Science of Malaysia, 1994.

Introduction

The essays collected in this volume were written over many years by Seyyed Hossein Nasr on the Islamic intellectual tradition in Persia. These writings, which were scattered among numerous journals and collections, have been brought together into a single volume, thereby making it more accessible for the general reader. The essays gathered here provide us with a major study of philosophical activities in Persia since their inception. Moreover, they bear witness to a life devoted to scholarship and are essential for a better understanding of the general intellectual history of Islam and the contributions of Persian philosophers.

Over a lifetime of scholarship, Seyyed Hossein Nasr has dealt with almost every facet of the spiritual and intellectual tradition in Persia and its contributions to the Islamic world. Having demonstrated the remarkable consistency and persistence of philosophical themes in Persia, Nasr presents a world view whose pivotal point has been the quest for the Eternal.

Nasr's attempt to discern the contributions of Persian philosophers has taken him on a journey from Iran to the West and back. Having carried out his early education in a traditional setting, Nasr came to the West where he pursued his studies first in physics and geology and later in both the history of science and philosophy. [1] Following the completion of his graduate work at the Massachusetts Institute of Technology and Harvard, his quest for the *sophia perennis* led him back to Iran where he began to study philosophy and *ḥikmah* (theosophy) with some of the traditional masters while he taught at Tehran University. Among his teachers were 'Allāmah Muḥammad Kāẓim 'Aṣṣār, 'Allāmah Sayyid Abu'l-Ḥasan Qazwīnī, and 'Allāmah Sayyid Muḥammad Ḥusayn Ṭabāṭabā'ī, with whom he studied for over twenty years. Nasr's association with these and a number of other traditional philosophers left an indelible mark upon his philosophical orientation. His earlier familiarity with the works of such traditionalist metaphysicians in the West as R. Guénon, F. Schuon, and A. Coomaraswamy had uniquely qualified him to carry out comparative work in metaphysics.

Upon his return to Iran in 1958, Nasr found himself in an intellectual milieu which ranged from certain jurists who identified philosophy as *kūfr* (heretical) to modernists who regarded the force of traditional philosophy as dwindling and advocated Western philosophy, in particular the ideas of Marx, Sartre and Heidegger. Nasr provided a response to such challenges, not by engaging in a direct dialogue with the propagators of Western philosophy, but by showing the richness of the tradition in Islamic philosophy and reformulating traditional philosophical doctrines in a language modern man could understand. For Nasr, "no philosophy which ignores both revelation and intellectual intuition and thus divorces itself from the twin sources of transcendent knowledge can hope to be anything but a disrupting and dissolving influence in Islamic society."[2]

Nasr views philosophy not as a mere rational activity but as a quest for the Eternal, resulting from a longing within every man to find his original abode. Philosophizing for Nasr, therefore, is the process of reminding ourselves of the forgotten truth and the task of philosophy is to bring about recollection and to reacquaint ourselves with our true related to selves. Having defined philosophy as a sacred activity related to, the *philosophia perennis* Nasr tells us that its aim is unveiling the truth, which for him is God. Philosophy therefore, becomes a quest for Divine Wisdom or what Nasr calls "*theosophia*", [3] the rightful activity of the intellect and not the merely rational activity of a discursive nature.

Since Nasr sees philosophy as a means by which one can remember God, he sets out to do a type of philosophizing which, properly speaking, can be called "philosophical anthropology." A philosophical study, Nasr argues, should not only be limited to its discursive aspects but should include the study of the manifestations of the sacred. Human existence, therefore, is fundamentally a spiritual journey and one must engage in a spiritual hermeneutic (*ta'wīl*) through which the act of remembrance takes place. In light of this view, Nasr comments on many facets of Islamic life and thought, be they art or architecture, music or philosophy, not to mention Sufism, which he regards as the heart and soul of Islam.

Nasr believes in a particular interpretation of philosophy which for him is none other than "theosophy" (*ḥikmah*). He argues that a synthesis of reason, intellectual intuition and the living of a "philosophical life" which embraces the practical aspect of wisdom within the context of tradition can lead to the attainment of the ultimate Reality. *Ḥikmah* for Nasr is that tradition of philosophy which began with the teachings of the prophet Idrīs, identified by classical Muslim authors with Hermes, and passed through different civilizations, in particular the Persian, Egyptian and Greek. This tradition reaches its climax in Persia with the teachings of Suhrawardī and his school of *ishrāq* and later in Mullā Ṣadrā's transcendental theosophy (*al-ḥikmat al-muta'āliyah*). This type of wisdom is based on intellectual intuition as true wisdom rather than knowledge that is attained by rationalistic philosophy only. Nasr calls this tradition *philosophia perennis* and argues that it was kept alive by those sages who had experienced the Divine Truth. According to Suhrawardī's school of illumination, *ishrāq,* the synthesis of rationalistic philosophy and intellectual intuition, resulting from inner purification and ascetic practices, leads to the knowledge of the ultimate Reality.

For Nasr, as for Suhrawardī, rationalistic philosophy is a necessary exercise provided it is accompanied by inner purification and intellectual intuition. It is noteworthy that the mystical narratives of Suhrawardī were edited and introduced by Nasr for the first time. For Nasr therefore, the Persian intellectual tradition especially as it blossomed in the Islamic period is a clear example of perennial wisdom (*jāwīdān khirad*), which led to one of the most prolific and rich philosophical traditions. This philosophical tradition, alive today and practiced in Iran as well as in the Indo-Pakistani sub-continent, is a living testimony that an authentic philosophical tradition remains above the temporary philosophical concerns which change with time.

The hands of destiny brought Nasr, the traditional proponent of Islamic philosophy, to the West. His audience both of Muslims who live in the modern world, and of modern men of post-Renaissance secular society with a bleak view of the "Middle Ages", has to some extent determined the texture of Nasr's scholarship. Unlike academic philosophers, who are concerned with specific arguments, the crux of Nasr's work is first to introduce the pre-Renaissance *Weltanschauung* of the traditional world in general and Islam in particular, and second, to provide an Islamic response to the challenges of the modern world. His works on this subject are numerous and profound.

First and foremost, Nasr is a metaphysician and an ontologist. He is primarily concerned with Being, and his analysis of all other aspects of Islam takes place in light of his understanding of the reality of Being. He is not a philosopher in the rationalistic sense of the word, and his philosophically oriented works, though they do not follow the traditional classifications (metaphysics, logic, epistemology, etc.), contain a structure as a whole. To begin with, he extensively deals with the ontological foundation on which Islam is established. Whatever the subject of his treatise might be, he always begins with a treatment of its ontological foundation, for he knows well that every thought has its roots in a particular ontology. His exposition of the "sacred ontology" is often poetic, depending on the content of the work in question. Nasr uses the teachings of the grand masters of Islamic philosophy from Ibn Sīnā, Suhrawardī and Mūllā Ṣadrā, to Sabziwārī, precisely to demonstrate how the Islamic view of Being embraces every facet of Islamic life and thought. For Nasr, the ultimate Being, God, has an all-embracing nature; whether the subject of a philosopher's analysis is art or science, ultimately one is speaking about Him.

In our various conversations, I have inquired why Nasr does not become engaged in rationalistic philosophy of the sort which some of his teachers have practiced. To this he has answered: "My intention is to introduce traditional metaphysics of Islamic philosophy to the modern world. Hopefully, the future generation of scholars will take on the task of offering the analytically oriented works much needed in this field."

Despite Nasr's answer, I believe there is a more profound reason for his lack of interest in adopting a more rationalistic approach to the fundamental problems of philosophy. Nasr does not believe that existential questions can ultimately be solved through reason alone, but that the answer lies in a combination of contemplation, rationalization and intellectual intuition. In fact, Nasr's way of doing philosophy is the key to understanding his solutions to the enduring questions of philosophy. In this regard, Nasr tells us that the continuity of Islamic philosophical thought is an indication of the perennial truth which has enabled him, as well as his predecessors, to experience and expound upon the same source of inspiration.

As for teaching philosophy in the Muslim countries, Nasr takes a cautious approach, emphasizing the need for an awareness of how Islamic philosophy should be studied before other schools of philsophical thought are introduced. "In teaching philosophy," Nasr says, "Islamic philosophy should be made central and other schools of philosophy taught in relation to it."[4] He advocates the teaching of not only such medieval Christian and Jewish philosophers as St. Bonaventure, Duns Scotus and Maimonides, but also the continuation of these trends as reflected in the works of such figures as E. Gilson, H.A. Wolfson and D. Hartmann.

Nasr is less enthusiastic about advocating the teachings of modern

Western philosophy since the secular and often atheistic character of Western intellectual thought is inconsistent with the spirit of Islamic life and thought whose primary concern is the attainment of the truth. On the subject of comparative philosophy, Nasr argues that a discipline based on permanence cannot be engaged in a dialogue with a philosophical tradition with undergoes a paradigm shift every few decades. The result of such an encounter, if it did take place, would be nothing but a superficial comparison which would wither away once the focus of Western philosophy is changed.

The essays collected here represent a small part of an extraordinary, prolific scholarship over a period of four decades. They bear witness to a life devoted to the analysis and interpretation of Islamic life and thought in general and Persian intellectual heritage in particular. This volume complements Nasr's numerous other writings both in Persian and other European languages on Islamic philosophy and its propagators in Persia.

Where necessary, I have translated essays originally written in Persian by Seyyed Hossein Nasr to further enhance the coherency and inclusiveness of the volume with regard to various aspects of the Islamic intellectual tradition in Persia.

* * *

The first section of the present work is devoted to an examination of philosophy in Persia as a living tradition whose beginning can be traced to pre-Islamic Persia. The cosmology of pre-Islamic and Islamic Persia, as well as the historical developments of intellectual modes of thought, are presented here. Finally, philosophical activities in modern Iran and the place of Sufism, with which Persians have had a long love affair, are examined.

In the second section, the founders of Islamic philosophy in Persia and their contributions to further enrich Persian culture are discussed. The place and ideas of such figures as Fārābī, Ibn Sīnā, Bīrūnī and Rāzī are presented as well as their roles in shaping the fabric of intellectual thought for the next thousand years.

Section three is devoted entirely to Suhrawardī, the master and founder of the school of illumination (*ishrāq*) in the 6th century A.H./ 12th A.D. who, according to Nasr, marked a turning point in the history of philosophy in Persia. Presented here is a demonstration of how Suhrawardī, by reconciling the philosophies of Plato and Aristotle, as well as that of Pythagoreans, Hermeticism, neo-Platonism and the wisdom of ancient Persia within the context of Islamic gnosis gave philosophy in Persia a new direction and maturity, one whose zenith can be seen in the works of Mullā Ṣadrā and the School of Isfahan.

One of the major contributions of Seyyed Hossein Nasr to the revival of philosophical interest in Persia was to introduce writings of Suhrawardī and, in particular, his Persian writings which influenced some of the younger generation of philosophers. Also, modernized Iranians found in Suhrawardī the solution to what they perceived to be the dichotomy of Islam and the ancient Persian culture and religion which is identified with the glory of the Persian Empire.

The fourth section is devoted to certain figures who can be classified as independent thinkers, some of whom, such as Qūṭb al-Dīn Shīrāzī, Rashīd al-Dīn Faḍallāh and Khayyām , were scientists as well as philosophers. They also were a bridge between Suhrawardī's era and the philosophically prolific period of the Safavid dynasty from the 9th/15 to the 11th/17th century.

The fifth section of the present work deals with the golden era of Persian philosophical activities stretched over a two-hundred year period. The articles contained here present a historical and philosophical review of the most prolific philosophical movement in Persia which came to be known as the "School of Isfahan." Nasr meticulously provides us with a picture of this philosophically unique period which began with Mīr Dāmād and came to its fruition in the works of the greatest metaphysician of Persia, Mullā Ṣadrā. The transcendental theosophy (*ḥikmat al-muta-'āliyah)* of Mullā Ṣadrā was once again revived by the sages of the Qajar period, especially Mullā Hādī Sabziwārī, and became the source of inspiration for Iranian philosophers in the modern period.

Islamic philosophy in modern Iran is the subject of the final section of the present work. Nasr's views on the philosophical activities during the 50s and 60s in Iran, and the interaction of traditional Islamic philosophy with certain aspects of Persian intellectual thought in the modern world, are given.

Following Nasr's detailed mosaic of the history and development of philosophy in Persia, the work is brought to an end with a postscript which presents what Nasr considers to be the substance of philosophy in Persia, the Eternal *Sophia.* The longing and yearning of man for *Sophia Perennis,* Nasr tells us, is that existential yearning which, as Rūmī says, turns men into a "reed through whom Thou speaketh" and "a lyre which thou plucketh."

Mehdi Amin Razavi

NOTES

1. For more information on Seyyed Hossin Nasr's life and work, see: *The Works of Seyyed Hossein Nasr Through His Fourthieth Birthday,* compiled by William Chittick, Salt Lake City, University of Utah Press, Monograph No. 6, 1977. For an updated version of this work consisting of Nasr's works until 1993 see *The Works of Seyyed Hossein Nasr Through His Sixtieth Birthday,* compiled by Z. Moris and M. Aminrazavi, Kuala Lumpur, The Malaysian Academy of Science, 1994.
2. S.H. Nasr, "The Teaching of Philosophy" in *Philosophy, Literature and Fine Arts,* London, Hodder and Stoughton, 1982, p. 5.
3. Nasr's usage of this term should be understood in its etymological sense, that is, Divine Wisdom; it is not related to the movement in England and the U.S. called The Theosophical Society.
4. Ibid., p. 10.

PART I

ISLAMIC THOUGHT AND PERSIAN CULTURE

1

Mysticism and Traditional Philosophy in Persia, Pre-Islamic and Islamic*

To speak of philosophy (in its traditional sense) and mysticism and gnosis in their original sense which in Arabic and Persian are (*taṣawwuf* and *'irfān*) during the long span of Persian history, is to speak of tradition,[1] of continuity, of transcendent principles and of forms of wisdom of celestial origin. It is also to speak of two distinct spiritual worlds, the Mazdean and the Islamic, governed by different spiritual principles yet related in many ways because they issue from the same Divine Origin and also because of certain profound morphological resemblances between them. The question of the relation between the sapiental doctrines and methods of spiritual realization during these two phases of Persian history cannot be solved solely in the light of an historicism blind to the genius of both Mazdaism and Islam and of necessity impervious to the transcendent dimensions wherein resides the most profound relationship between them. To deny the transcendent and archetypal world as the origin of certain doctrines, forms, images and symbols which are manifested in both these worlds, is to overlook the main causal nexus between them. It is to search in the shadows, in the historical and purely horizontal relationships in time, for a reality which resides in the luminous world of the spirit above time, although it has manifested itself in different times and places.

---

* This article originally appeared in *Studies in Comparative Religion,* (Autumn 1971),: 235-240 and also the *Journal of the Regional Cultural Institute* (Iran, Pakistan, Turkey) 5 (Winter 1972) : 13-18. A revised version of this essay appeared in *Commemoration Cyrus.* Vol. 1, Hommage Universel, E.J. Brill, 1974, pp. 261-67. The substance of this article was presented at a conference in the International Congress of Iranology held in Shiraz, 10th-15th October 1971, in conjunction with the 2500th anniversary of the founding of the Persian Empire. The theme of the Congress was the continuity of Persian culture.

The study of the religion, philosophy and mysticism of the different epochs of Persian history is synonymous with the study of the traditions[2] mainly Zoroastrian and Islamic, which have dominated various phases of that history. Although these traditions are of different natures and structures, they are related most of all by the fact that they are authentic traditions and not something else, that is, they are messages from the world of the Spirit differing in their outward form but united in their inner essensce.[2] The emphasis upon the inner unity of traditions has in fact been one of the characteristics of the world view of the religious elite throughout Persian history and as every student of comparative religion knows some of the most sublime and beautiful expressions of the "transcendent unity of religions" are to be found in Persian Sufi poetry from 'Aṭṭār and Mawlānā Jalāl al-Dīn Rūmī to Hātif Iṣpahānī.

The result of this traditional character of the different epochs of Persian history, which distinguishes all of it from the anti-traditional character of modern civilization, is an emphasis upon the spiritual world, the orientation of human life towards the life beyond, a sensitivity to earthly beauty as an image of the beauty of paradise, and so many other spiritual attitudes which run throughout the periods of Persian history. Besides elements of historical borrowing and the ethnic continuity which certainly exists along with all that such a continuity implies, the main stream of continuity that is observed in Persian history in the domain of religion, mysticism and philosophy is due more to the similarity between the "vertical" causes of the traditions in question than just to the continuation of a series of "horizontal" and historical factors. It is as if a series of flashes of lightening were to illuminate the earth continuously in such a way that were one to neglect the source of the light, one would simply observe a continuous lighting of the earth one moment after another.

* * *

With this image in mind and also considering certain elements of purely historical borrowing and continuity that have certainly existed on the side, we now turn to a few basic doctrines and themes which have appeared in one form or another in the religion, mysticism and philosophy of Persia throughout its history and which characterize the intellectual and spiritual life of the Persians in its totality.

Let us begin with the concept of the Divinity itself. In both Zoroastrianism and Islam, despite the difference in accent in the two cases and the dualism of the one that can be contrasted with the unitary emphasis of the other, there is a definite similarity in the concept of the Divinity as a transcendent principle that stands above creation and is distinct from it. The subservience of the material order to a spiritual principle and the created nature (in the theological sense) of this order which sets limits to it in both time and space is shared in Mazdaism and Islam, in contrast, let us say, to the Greek cosmologies where an indefinite repetition of cycles beyond a limited boundary is emphasized, at least in the general philosophical interpretations of these cosmologies as they have reached us. For the Persians, throughout their history, the material universe has been conceived as bound in both time and space, as having an alpha and an omega, both of which are themselves above the created order and belong to the realm of Divinity.

Closely connected to the theological conception of creation is the belief in its goodness which has been emphasized by Zoroastrianism and Islam, although not of course by Manichaeism. In Zoroastrian cosmogony the material order was created by Ahura-Mazda but Ahriman did not create a corresponding material world of his own in the way that he created the order of demons. Likewise in Islam creation is considered as a domain of reality which plays a definitely positive role in human life, for, in referring to the world, the Quran says, "Verily we did not create this vain" (*mā khālaqnā hādhā bāṭilan*). The Persian joy for life and appreciation of the beauties of the created order in both the sensuous and the spiritual sense is closely related to the emphasis placed upon the positive role of the created or natural order in man's religious life by the two major religious traditions that have dominated Persian history, namely the Mazdean and the Islamic.

Life on this earth has also been considered to possess an ultimate meaning beyond this world in all of the religions that have dominated Persia. Of course one might say that all religions in general emphasize the importance of human actions in view of man's final end. But the Iranian religions have a conception of human action, morality, final judgement and eschatology as related to man's life on earth that is more akin to the teachings of the Semitic religions than to what is found in the religions of India and the Far East. Not only the concept of the created order but also that of man's life in this world and its relation to the worlds above presents a constancy and permanence throughout Persian history made possible by the repetition of certain teachings of the different religions that have ruled over this land. In Islam, no less than in Zoroastrianism, the effect of both good and evil upon the soul of man and their role in moulding the soul in such a way as to influence its posthumous life is very much emphasized, and constitutes one of its central teachings.

Naturally, this conception of human life in which actions have an ultimate value in the eyes of God is closely related to the belief in the Day of Judgement emphasized so majestically in the Quran and mentioned also in Zoroastrian sources. Even details of the "landscape" of the other world presents certain similarities in the two religions, especially in the image of the bridge over hell, without there being the least question of historical borrowing. Likewise, the belief in a saviour before the Final Judgement is common to Islam and Zoroastrianism as it is of course to other religions as well.[3] Especially in Shi'ite Islam belief in the coming of the Mahdī, who is the Twelfth Imam, and the effect of this belief upon daily religious life can be closely compared with the Zoroastrian belief in Saoshyant and the idea of "expectation" which is contained in certain Zoroastrian teachings. Other elements of eschatology and concepts of hell and paradise (which in both European languages and in Arabic in the form "*firdaws*" is derived from Avestan) present striking similarities and reveal the common origin of all these teachings in the single luminous source of all revelation.

As far as the *imago mundi* is concerned, again there are profound morphological resemblances and sometimes historical borrowings as in the case of the seven *keshvars* of the ancient Persians which found their way into the *Shāhnāmah,* the writings of Bīrūnī, Yāqūt and other Muslim sources.[4] In cosmology also there are similarities that derive most of all from the traditional view of the cosmos based upon the notion of hierarchy and grades of being. Throughout his history, the Persian has always seen himself in a universe composed of multiple states in which he stands at the bottom of a scale leading in an ascending and sacred order (therefore a true hierarchy) to the Divinity. This hierarchic conception of reality with all its artistic as well as social and practical implications is one of the most profound features of the very structure of the soul of the Persian as it has been moulded over the ages by the religious and cultural forces at play in his life.

This hierarchic order is of course inseparable from the angelic order that stands between man and God. Of the older religions, none has emphasized the angelic world and its purely spiritual character as much as Zoroastrianism, which could in fact be called in a sense a "religion of angels" rather than directly of God. Islam also places a great deal of emphasis upon angels and belief in the angels is a part of the definition of *īmān* or faith. As a result of this correlation in emphasis upon the angelic world, the Persian has lived throughout his history in a world always dominated, ordered and controlled by spiritual or angelic substances belonging to the higher levels of being. He has always been aware that this world and man's life in it are the shadow of the angelic world, that they are transient and ephemeral yet reflect the abiding beauty of paradise. In art as well as in philosophy and theosophy—where in the *ishrāqī* school Suhrawardî even incorporated Mazdean angelology into his Islamic scheme[5]— the dominion and power of the angelic world is so great that it can hardly fail to be noticed by any perceptive student of things Persian.

* * *

Despite the presence of these and many other themes, doctrines and symbols that are common between the Mazdean and Islamic traditions, there is a contrast observable in the relation between religion, philosophy and mysticism during the pre-Islamic and Islamic periods of Persian history. During the pre-Islamic period, philosophy, in its traditional sense, was contained completely within the bosom of religion. If we search for the sources of the *sophia* or *khirad* of the ancient Persians which in fact the Greek philosophers and sages sought, we would be mistaken to expect to find works like the *Metaphysics* of Aristotle or even the *Dialogues* of Plato, that is, works similar to those belonging to a period of Greek history when religion, philosophy and science had become separated from each other. In ancient Persia, as in all other Oriental civilizations, the separation between religion and philosophy that one observes in ancient Greece and Rome and again in post-medieval Europe never took place except in rare cases which remain of secondary importance. If we search for the "philosophy" of the ancient Persians or for what Suhrawardī called the *khusrāwānī* theosophy (*ḥikmat-i khusrawānī*) we must delve into such religious works as the *Bundāhishn* and the *Shkand gumānīk vichār* and be aware of the oral teachings which must certainly have existed along with the written texts. We should not search for works similar to the books of the Greek philosophers and then, when we are not able to find them, consider such works as having existed but having later been destroyed.

During the Islamic period the situation is certainly different. Islamic philosophy, although definitely of an Islamic character despite its having taken over elements of older traditions,[6] developed as an independent discipline and school within Islamic civilisation and was not contained, especially during the early centuries, within any of the theological or mystical schools. It is only later, after the attacks of Ghazzālī against the Peripatetic school and the rise of the school of Illumination or *ishrāq*, that philosophy or theosophy becomes wed to the theological and mystical schools to a certain extent. But even in the case of Mullā Ṣadrā, the great Safavid sage of Shiraz who achieved the final synthesis of philosophy, mysticism, theology and religious law, a clear distinction remains between the different schools within Islam. The school of *Ḥikmat* has remained throughout the Islamic period a distinct discipline within the Islamic intellectual universe. The relation of philosophy to religion during the Islamic period, therefore, presents a contrasts with what one finds in the pre-Islamic period despite certain profound morphological resemblances alluded to above.

The case of mysticism is the opposite of that of philosophy. During the pre-Islamic period, the distinctly mystical schools and disciplines such as the religion of the Magi or the "mysteries" of Mithra were distinct from Zoroastrianism although of course even within Zoroastrianism there must have existed an esoteric teaching. In the Islamic period, however, mysticism is nearly identical with the inner dimension of Islam known as Sufism,[7] and also exists within Shi'ism. There has never been during the Islamic period a genuine mystical school in Persia outside of the matrix of Islam and mysticism in all its forms has been connected in one way or another with the inner and esoteric dimension of Islam. There is, therefore, again a reversal of relationship between mysticism and religion during the pre-Islamic and Islamic periods in comparison with the situation of philosophy. Yet, many of the profoundest themes concerning man's quest after the Divine are repeated throughout the history of this land with almost the same language in such a manner as to remind man of the eternal nature of both the mystical quest and its goal.

Because it was destined to be the last religion and the seal of the prophetic cycle, Islam possesses a unique power of assimilation and synthesis. This characteristic enabled Islam to remain fully itself and yet allow the Persians not only to participate in its life and to contribute fully to its elaboration but also to enable them to contemplate in its vast firmament the shining stars of the most profound elements of their ancient religious and spiritual past, a past which far from dying out gained a new interpretation and became in a sense partly resurrected in the new spiritual universe brought into being by the Islamic revelation.

NOTES

1. By tradition we do not mean custom or habit but principles of celestial origin and their applications in time and space along with the sacred forms, rites and doctrines which make the realization of these principles possible. Tradition, therefore, corresponds to religion understood in its most universal sense. See the numerous writings of A.K. Coomaraswamy, R. Guénon, F. Schuon and T. Burckhardt.

2. See F. Schuon, *The Transcendent Unity of Religions,* trans. by P. Townsend, London, 1948; and S.H. Nasr, *Sufi Essays,* London, 1972.
3. See H. Corbin, *En Islam iranien,* vol. I, Paris, 1971.
4. See H. Corbin, *La Terre céleste et corps de résurrection,* Paris, 1961, pp. 40ff; and S.H. Nasr, "La Cosmographie en Iran pré-islamique et islamique" *Arabic and Islamic Studies in Honour of Hamilton A.R. Gibb,* Leiden, 1965, pp. 507-24.
5. See H. Corbin, *En Islam iranien,* vol. II, Paris, 1971; and S.H. Nasr, *Three Muslim Sages,* Cambridge (U.S.A.), 1964, chapter II.
6. We have discussed this matter extensively in many of our writings; see *Three Muslim Sages,* introduction and chapter I; also S.H. Nasr, *An Introduction to Islamic Cosmological Doctrines,* Cambridge, U.S.A., 1964, Introduction.
7. See F. Schuon, *Understanding Islam,* trans. by D.M. Matheson, London, 1963, chapter IV; S.H. Nasr, *Ideals and Realities of Islam,* London, 1966, chapter V, and S.H. Nasr, *Sufi Essays.*

2

Cosmography in Pre-Islamic and Islamic Persia:
The Question of the Continuity of Iranian Culture*

A civilization finds its coherence and continuity in remaining faithful to its governing spiritual principles. Continuity means essentially attachment to transcendent and immutable principles, which have formed the basis of all traditional societies. Therefore, to search for continuity in a civilization is to seek these principles along with their applications in the domain of contingency. Regarded in this manner the history of Persia is characterized by both continuity and discontinuity. It is discontinuous because it is marked by two periods, in each of which a distinct set of religious and spiritual principles has been dominant. The first period may be considered to stretch from the time of the migration of the Iranian tribes onto the Iranian plateau to the coming of Islam, and the second from the time of the integration of Persia into the Muslim world to the present day. Moreover, each of these periods is marked by phases in which different spiritual forces have been dominant.

The pre-Islamic period began which the early pre-Zoroastrian Aryan religion, a religion which bears many similarities to Hinduism and which was followed by the reform of the historic Zoroaster and the establishment of his creed. This second phase was in turn followed by the rise of Mithraism in its new form, as a distinct religious movement rather than just devotion to Mithra, the re-establishment of Zoroastrianism as the state religion by the Sassanids, the rise of Manichaeism and the integration of ideas drawn from different sources into Zurvanism and the

* This essay was written originally in French and appeared as "Cosmographie en I'Iran pré-islamique et islamique: le problème de la continuité dans la civilization iranienne", *Arabic and Islamic Studies in Honor of Hamilton A.R. Gibb,* Edited by G. Makdisi, Leiden: E.J. brill, 1965, pp. 507-24. It was later translated by the author into English as "Cosmography in Pre-Islamic and Islamic Persia". Tehran: The Cultural Committee for the Celebration of the 2500th Anniversary of the Founding of the Persian Empire, 1971, (Monograph).

Sassanid religion in general.[1] Likewise, the Islamic period can be divided into the time of the domination of Sunnism, lasting until the Mongol invasion,[2] and that of the rise of Shi'ism, beginning with the conversion of Sulṭān Muḥammad Khudābandah and culminating in the establishment of Shi'ism as the state religion under the Safavids. Moreover, each of these two periods, the pre-Islamic and the Islamic, is in itself a unity and totality. Mithraism, Manichaeism and Zurvanism all spring from the same Zoroastrian or more generally speaking the same early Aryan background, and Sunnism and Shi'ism are two different interpretations of the same truth and in no way destroy the inner unity of Islam.

Yet despite the obvious discontinuity between these two periods there are also certain basic elements of continuity. The first of these is the "substantial" and "horizontal" continuity of the people of the Iranian plateau over the millenia and all that this ethnic continuity involves in the way of mental and psychological inheritance and various racial characteristics, as well as languages, effects of climactic conditions, etc.[3]

There is, moreover, also an "essential" and "vertical" continuity between Zoroastrian and Muslim Persia which is due to the fact that all traditions descend from the same transcendent source and therefore have common spiritual principles. Furthermore, Islam, coming at the end of the present cycle of humanity, sees it as its duty to affirm rather than deny the revelations before it, i.e., to re-establish what had "existed" primordially and continues to exist in the nature of things. Islam therefore possesses a great power of absorption and synthesis which permitted it to integrate into its view Alexandrian and Hindu wisdom as well as many elements from pre-Islamic Persia. One can see so clearly how pre-Islamic Persian art motifs became Islamicized and how the most important political element of continuity in Persia, i.e., monarchy, to whose 2500th anniversary the present essay is devoted, became integrated into Shi'ite political theory—for which, until the appearance of the Mahdī, the best form of government for the protection and preservation of the *Sharī'ah* has been considered by many to be a kingship. This synthetic power of Islam along with the common celestial archetypes from which all revelations are derived form the major spiritual bonds of unity between the two periods of Persian history. In more than one instance the spirituality of Islam has been, to quote L. Massignon, the light by means of which Iran "has contemplated the visible universe through the illuminated prism of its ancient myths".[4] One can add that the cosmological sciences or the "Lesser Mysteries" of both Alexandria and Zoroastrian Persia came to life once again in the light of the "Greater Mysteries" of Islamic gnosis.

Of the many threads unifying Zoroastrian and Muslim Persia, we have chosen to discuss cosmography, i.e., the representation of the manifested cosmos in its many levels from the angelic to the material worlds, and we have selected a few passages from the vast storehouse of wisdom which exists concerning this subject to illustrate not only certain ideas borrowed historically and integrated into the Muslim perspective but also the presence of certain transcendent archetypes which manifest themselves whenever and wherever the conditions for their manifestation are suitable. The cosmos has a reality in all its visible and invisible aspects which is independent of any individualistic subjectivization. All traditional cosmographies, therefore, must account for the hierarchy of being in essentially the same manner, although they may use different language, just as every civilization has a name for the sun simply because the sun exists and reveals itself to all. Moreover, there are certain archetypal numbers[5] which, being necessary polarizations of Unity, manifest themselves in all traditions. Thus we see the numbers represented by the twelve signs of the Zodiac, the seven planets and archangels and the four elements in Zoroastrianism as well as the pentad in Manichaean cosmogony repeated in the twelve Imams of Twelve-Imam Shi'ism, the seven Imams of the Ismā'īlīs, the five Imams of the Zaydīs and the four caliphs of the Sunnis.[6] These archetypal numbers as well as other cosmological symbols in turn play a major role in creating similarities between Islamic and Zoroastrian cosmographies.[7]

The sources of Zoroastrian cosmography consist mostly of Sassanid Pahlavi texts in which elements of Zurvanism are distinctly present. The Avesta itself is mostly liturgical and only in the *Yashts* are there references to the various elements, the heavens and the earth. The most important Zoroastrian cosmological treatises which have survived are the *Bundahishn,*[8] assembled during the Sassanid period from the earlier *Dāmdāt Nask* now lost, the *Mēnōkē Xrat,* which is the essential text of Zurvanism, the *Rivāyāt* and the *Dēnkart,* the last of which contains elements of Greek ideas—such as the four elements and natures of Empedocles: hot, moist, cold and dry—integrated into Mazdaism.[9]

The Zoroastrian idea of creation posits a twelve thousand year period of struggle between Ormuzd and Ahriman, each millenium of which is presided over by one of the signs of the Zodiac. During the first three thousand years the spiritual world is created and during the next three thousand years the material world along with the evil forces of Ahriman. The following three thousand years mark the eruption of the power of Ahriman into the world and his overrunning it, and the last three thousand years the revelation of Zoroaster and the final triumph of the forces of light at the time of the general resurrection of the world.[10] In Pahlavi texts like the *Greater Bundahishn* in which Zurvanite doctrines play an important role the world comes into being from Zurvān, or Infinite or Boundless Time, and Vāy, or Infinite Space. Both Zurvān and Vāy are in principle above the dualism of good and evil.[11] From the Infinite Zurvān come into being Ormuzd and Ahriman and through them "Zurvān of the Long Dominion" or cosmic time as well as Spihr or finite space.[12] From the infusion of the will of Ormuzd into the Endless Form, which is the spiritual creation and the prototype of nature, the material cosmos comes into being.

According to the first chapter of the *Greater Bundahishn,* Ormuzd, after making a pact with Ahriman, created the cosmos, beginning with the spiritual or angelic world and then proceeding to the visible universe.[13] Ahriman, seeing that his opponent had created the world, in turn brought into being a hierarchy of demons to oppose the angels, but did not create a counterpart material world. The Universe, therefore, consists of three domains: the angelic and demonic domains and material creation.

At the top of the hierarchy of cosmic beings and first in the order of creation are the archangels, *Ameshāspands (Amesha Spentās)*, who are purely spiritual beings above the material universe. In descending order they are Vohuman, Artvahisht, Shaθrēvar, Spendarmat, Hurdāt and Amurdāt and along with Ormuzd himself they form a heptad.[14] Ormuzd also created a hierarchy of angels called the Yāzātās below the Ameshaspands whose number according to the *Yashts* is legion. They are both spiritual and material; one day of each month is devoted to one of them and they guard and preserve the order of the world.[15] The hierarchy of arch-demons includes Akōman, Indar, Sāvul, Nānhaiθi, Taric and Zēric, who along with Ahriman form a heptad opposed to the celestial hierarchy. Moreover Ahriman also created a host of lesser demons who oppose the forces of light in the world.

Below the angelic world and above the demonic lies material creation, which, because of its materiality, preserves a certain neutrality with respect to the forces of good and evil, although it is essentially good since it was brought into being by Ormuzd. The first material creation was the sky, consisting of the stations of the Ameshaspands, the Sun, the Moon, the fixed stars, the planets and the clouds, stations which along with that of Endless Light, the place of Ormuzd, form another heptas.[16] The sky, which is egg-shaped, contains all creation; it is made from a crystal from which water is brought into being. After water the earth is created, round but with an even surface,[17] and then the first plant, from which all other plants grow. After the plants cattle come into being from the Primal Bull, the first animal in creation, and after the animals Gayōmarth, the Primordial Man, from whose seed mankind is generated. This sixfold order of creation, consisting of the sky, water, earth, plants, animals and men is completed by the creation of fire, "whose brilliance is from the Endless Light, the place of Ormuzd".[18]

Aside from this account of the creation and hierarchy of the cosmos in the *Greater Bundahishn,* there is another account in the *Rivāyāt* which is of great interest. According to this latter source, creation comes from the Macrocosmic Man, the Spihr, who is also the archetype of man. The sky is created from his head, the earth from his feet, water from his tears, plants from his hair, the Bull—the symbol of the animal kingdom—from his right hand, fire from his mind and the first man, Gayōmarth, from his seed.[19] Man, therefore, while coming at the end of creation is also its archetype and source.

The world in which man lives, i.e., the earth and its surroundings, is made of the four elements, fire, air, water and earth, fire being the direct presence of the spiritual world in the material. The Zoroastrians considered the elements as sacred and made extensive use of them in their worship. In fact several *Yashts* are devoted to the elements.[20]

As for the earth itself, which is considered as round, the Avesta divides it into six regions of *kishvars* which along with the central region form a heptad.[21] The whole of dry land is surrounded by a vast ocean called *Frāxkart* the ωkεvvos of the Greeks. The seven *keshvars,* which form a circle around a center, are presented as follows:[22]

		E		
		Savahī		
	Vourubarsti		Fradaδafsū	
N		Xvaniraθa		S
	Vidaδafsū		Vurujrδstī	
		Arazahī		
		W		

Fig. 1

The world is centered about the cosmic mountain, called Harā and later Alborz, which was the first mountain to be created.[23] The stars, sun and moon circle about it, the sun shines from it upon all the lands of East and West, and the throne of Mithra is placed upon it, where there is no night or darkness.[24] It symbolizes therefore the totality of the cosmos as well its center and the *axis mundi.*

In the cosmos whose anatomy we have sought to describe the invisible and the visible worlds are closely related, each terrestial (*gētīk*) being having its transcendant (*mēnōk*) counterpart in the spiritual world, whose theurgy and reflection it is here on earth.[25] Each species in this world has its own angel and celestial counterpart just as every man has his own *frahvarti.* Among the archangels, Vahuman is the angel of cattle, Artvahisht of fire, Shaθhisht of metals, Spandarmat of earth, Hurdāt of water and Amurdāt of plants. Likewise each of the lesser angels or Yazatas is the guardian of some order of terrestial existence: Ābān of water, Drvāspā of animal creation, Rāmā Hvāstra of air, Sroasha of the sleeping world, Māh of the moon and Hvarekh shaēta of the sun.[26] The cosmos, therefore, despite its division into the spiritual and physical domains, is essentially a unity, the visible being the reflection and theurgy of its transcendant and immutable counterpart, the spiritual reality or Platonic idea which in Zoroastrianism is identified with the angelic order.

In Islamic cosmography the anatomy of the Universe presents itself in the same basic outline as is seen in Zoroastrianism but in the language of the Quranic revelation and according to the unitary perspective of Islam. Islam revealed what had always been the mystery of mysteries, i.e., the transcendant Unity of the Principle and the consequent unicity and interrelatedness of all orders of cosmic existence. Essentially the Islamic view is based on the absorption of all finite beings into the Infinite, all multiplicity into the One, so that to say *Lā ilāha illa'Llāh* is to say that there is no reality but the Absolute Reality. Yet from the point of view of contingency one may legitimately speak of a cosmos which, although nothing but the shadow of the Principle or in the language of Sufism the Breath of the Compassionate (*nafas al-raḥmān*), is also an image of its Divine Source whose unity it reflects on its own plane. As the master of Islamic gnosis, Muḥyī al-Dīn ibn 'Arabī writes in the *Futūḥāt al-makkiyyah,* "The world consists of the unity of the unified whereas the divine Independence resides in the unity of the Unique".[27] As we turn to the writings of some of the Muslim authors, restricting ourselves to Persia and its surrounding territory, we see the reappearance of earlier concepts and the repetition of the same archetypes and ideas not because of historical borrowing but because such ideas are inherent in the nature of things. But all these concepts are viewed from the Islamic unitary perspective.

In Islam creation is considered as having been brought into being by the Divine Word *kun,* "Be!": God said "Be!" and there was. The Universe is therefore a direct consequence of the Divine Act. It is united with its Principle by its being as well as by the intelligence manifested in the cosmic domain. The Muslim authors, following the Quran, have all emphasized this point although each may have concentrated upon a certain aspect of the question of the generation and effusion of multiplicity from Unity. For example the famous fourth/tenth century historian, Mas'ūdī, makes use of earlier symbolic imagery when he writes: "When God wanted to undertake the work of creation He made come out of water a vapor which rose above it and formed the sky. Then He dried the liquid substance and transformed it into an earth which He then divided into seven parts".[28]

The eighth/fourteenth century Sufi 'Abd al-Karīm al-Jīlī, the author of the well-known Sufi treatise *al-Insān al-kāmil, The Universal Man,* amplifies the same symbolism in speaking of creation as follows:

"Before the creation God was in Himself, and the objects of existence were absorbed (*mustahlak*) in Him so that He was not manifested in any thing. This is the state of 'being a hidden treasure' or, as the Prophet expressed it, 'the dark mist above which is a void and below which is a void', because the Idea of Ideas is beyond all relations. The Idea of Ideas is called in another Tradition 'the White Chrysolite, in which God was before He created the creatures.' When God willed to bring the world into existence, He looked upon the Idea of Ideas (or the White Chrysolite) with the look of Perfection, whereupon it dissolved and became a water; for nothing in existence, not even the Idea of Ideas, which is the source of all existence, can bear the perfect manifestation of God. Then God looked on it with the look of Grandeur, and it surged in waves, like a sea tossed by the winds, and its grosser elements were spread out in layers like foam, and from that mass God created the seven earths with their inhabitants. The subtle elements of the water ascended, like vapour from the sea, and from them God created the seven heavens with the angels of each heaven. Then God made of the water seven seas which encompass the world. This is how the whole of existence originated".[29]

Jīlī also considers the creation of the Universe with respect to the Universal Man, who is at once the archetype and the final goal of creation. As he writes,

"The Universal Man is the pole around which revolve the spheres of existence from the first to the last; he is unique while existence lasts.... However, he embraces different forms and reveals himself through different religions in such a way that he receives multiple names....

"Know that the Universal Man carries within himself correspondences with all the realities of existence. He corresponds to the superior realities through his own subtle nature and to the inferior realities through his gross nature.... His heart corresponds to the Divine Throne. And besides, the Prophet has said that the heart of the believer is the throne of God. His self corresponds to the divine Pedestal, his spiritual state to the Lotus Tree of the Extreme Limit, his intellect to the supreme Kalām, his soul to the Guarded Tablet, his corporeal body to the elements, his receptivity to the Hylé.... etc".[30]

The superior and inferior realities to which Jīlī refers are actually the various orders of angelic, subtle and physical existence. Like Jīlī, who uses such Quranic terms as the Divine Pedestal and the Lotus Tree of the Extreme Limit, the Muslim authors writing on the angelic world also drew most of their terminology from the Quran.[31] The cosmic realities are basically the same as those represented in Zoroastrianism because, being an intrinsic aspect of the total truth, these realities must manifest themselves in one way or another in every tradition. But the symbols used by the Muslim and especially Sufi authors, like the Pen (*qalam*), the Tablet (*lawḥ*), the Pedestal (*kursī*), the Throne (*'arsh*) and the hierarchy of the angels are naturally derived from the language of the Quran.[32]

A popular account of Muslim angelology appears in the famous cosmographical work of Abū Yaḥyā Qazwīnī, *'Ajā'ib al-makhlūqāt*.[33] According to Qazwīnī at the height of the angelic hierarchy stands the Spirit or *Rūḥ,* the mover of all the heavens, surrounded by the four archangels, Isrāfīl, Jibra'īl, Mīkā'īl and 'Izrā'īl. Isrāfīl carries the Divine Command, gives life to beings and governs the elements and compounds. The Guarded Tablet (*al-lawḥ al-maḥfūẓ*) is located between his eyes. Jibra'īl is the angel of revelation and directs the power of anger (*ghaḍab*) with which all beings repel their enemies. Mīkā'īl is the giver of bounty and the angel who guides the growth of creatures toward their perfection. Finally 'Izrā'īl is the angel of death who brings motion to rest and takes the soul back to its original abode after death.[34]

Below these archangels, who lie above the visible cosmos, there are the seven angels of the heavens, who include in descending order Ismā'īl, symbolized by the figure of a cow, Shamā'īl, symbolized by an eagle, Sā'id, symbolized by a vulture, Ṣalṣāfīl, symbolized by a horse, Kalkā'īl symbolized by a beautiful maiden, Samkhā'īl, symbolized by a bird having a human head, and Barmā'īl, symbolized by the human figure. Below this order lies the order of the guardian angels who direct the life of beings on earth. Each human being has two angels, one of the right side and one of the left, who are his link with the angelic world.

The invisible hierarchy appears in a somewhat different guise in the writings of the fifth/eleventh century Ismā'īlī philosopher and poet

Nāṣir-i Khusraw. Beginning with the principle that whatever exists in the visible world is the effect of some reality in the invisible, he reaches the conclusion that there must be seven angelic orders to correspond to the seven planets.[35] These orders are, according to him, the Principle (*ibdā'*); the intellectual substance (*jawhar-i 'aqlī);* the collection of intellects (*majmū'-i'aql*); soul (*nafs*); majesty (*jadd*), identified with Jibra'īl; victory (*fatḥ*), identified with Mīkā'īl; and imagination *(khayāl*), identified with Isrāfīl.[36] This order in turn is made to correspond to the seven prophets: Adam, Noah, Abraham, Moses, Jesus, Muḥammad and the Lord of the Resurrection (*khudāwand-i qiyāmat*).[37]

The hierarchy of being appears in yet another light in the *Kitāb al-mujlī* of the ninth/fifteenth century Sufi and Shi'ite doctor, Ibn Abī Jumhūr, who is one of the important figures of Shi'ite gnosis.[38] In his view the chain of being consists essentially of six degrees corresponding to the six days of creation, these degrees being the Divine Essence (*Dhāt*), the world of unicity or the first determination of the essence (*wāḥidiyyah*), the world of pure spirits (*al-arwāḥ al-mujarradah*), the intellectual souls (*al-nufūs al-'āqilah*) or the world of psychic substance (*'ālam al-malakūt*), the visible world (*'ālam al-shahādah*) or the world of the kingdom (*'ālam al-mulk*) and the totality of existence (*al-kawn al-jāmi'*) which is the Universal Man (*al-insān al-kāmil*).[39]

The visible world, moreover, consists of eleven heavens: the *Primum mobile (falak al-aṭlas*), the heaven of the fixed stars, Saturn, Jupiter, Mars, the sun, Venus, Mercury, the moon, and the spheres of fire, air, water and earth. The sun occupies the middle position and corresponds to the heart (*qalb*) of the Universe.[40] The acts of God on the microcosmic level pass from the Divine Essence to the Spirit, from the Spirit to the heart, from the heart to the imagination (*khayāl*) and from the imagination to the sensible domain. Likewise in the macrocosm every act passes through these same stages: from the Spirit (*rūḥ*) to the soul (*nafs*) to the cosmic imagination to the forms or "ideas" (*ṣuwar rūḥāniyyah*) of the heavens and earth and finally to the world of the elements.[41] The 'arsh' or Divine Throne is like the human brain, the universal soul (*al-nafs al-kullī*) like the inner heart and the visible world like the visible heart of man. So it is that the sun, the heart of the Universe, is the giver of cosmic life as the heart is the center of life in the human body. And so it is that Christ, whose special miracle was to bring the dead back to life is symbolically identified with the "fourth heaven", which is the heaven of the sun.

Ibn Abī Jumhūr, like most other Muslim authors on cosmology, lays great stress upon the concepts of the Throne and the Pedestal, and the Pen and the Guarded Tablet, derived from traditional Islamic sources. He identifies the Throne with the Pen as well as with the Universal Intellect and the *Primum mobile.* Likewise he identifies the Pedestal with the Guarded Tablet as well as with the Universal Soul and the heaven of the fixed stars. And yet he adds that from another point of view the Universal Intellect is the ink, the Universal Soul the Pen and the elements and bodies in the cosmos the paper upon which the Pen brings things into existence.[42] Nature (*al-ṭabīʻah*) is itself one of the faculties of the Universal Soul, a faculty which governs and controls the whole world, from the highest heaven to the center of the earth. It rules over the four natures, which in turn govern the elements[43] (Fig. 2).

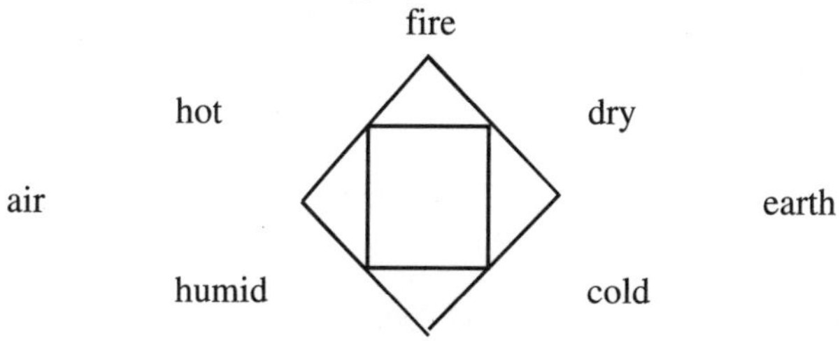

Fig. 2

As another example of Muslim cosmography we consider another Persian Shiʻite author, Sayyid Ja'far Kashfī, a sage and ascetic of the Qajar period. In his *Tuḥfat al-mulūk*, Kashfī analyzes the anatomy of the Universe in terms of two hierarchies of angels and demons deriving respectively from the Divine Compassion (*raḥmah*) and the Divine Anger (*ghaḍab*), so that the unitary point of view is preserved in spite of the cosmic duality of two opposing forces.[44] All Divine Compassion reaches the Universe through the Universal Intellect, which is identified with the Spirit of the Seal of the Prophets (*rūḥ-i khātam al-nabiyyīn*), i.e., the Prophet Muḥammad, upon whom be blessings and peace; and all Divine Anger through ignorance (*jahl*), which is identified with the Spirit of the Wretched (*rūḥ-i khātam al-shaqiyyīn*), i.e., Satan. There are eighteen worlds in both the hierarchy of light and of darkness, in the following order:

The Worlds of the Intellect	*The Worlds of Ignorance*
Universal intellect (*aql-i kull*)	Universal Ignorance (*jahl-i kull)*
Universal Spirit (*rūḥ-i kull*)	*ṭanṭām*[45]
Universal Soul (*nafs-i kull*)	inferno (*jahannam*)
Universal Nature (*ṭabīʻat-i kull*)	the barren wind (*rīḥ-i ʻaqīm*)

materia prima (jawhar-i habā')	dust (*tharā*)
Universal Form (*shikl-i kull*)	the sea of 'Aqbūs (*baḥr-i 'aqbūs*)
Universal Body (*jism-i kull*)	fish (*ḥūt*)
Throne (*'arsh*)	rock (*ṣakhrah*)[46]
Pedestal (*kursī*)	bull (*thawr*)
the seven heavens[47]	the seven earths
the sphere of fire	the sphere of earth
the sphere of air	the sphere of water

Between these two hierarchies lies the sphere of the zephyr, which is the place of the generation of man, animals, plants and minerals, all of which lie between the two worlds of light and darkness.[48] These beings, which symbolize the totality of terrestial existence, form therefore the third order of creatures in the Universe, situated between the two opposing cosmic hierarchies (Fig. 3).

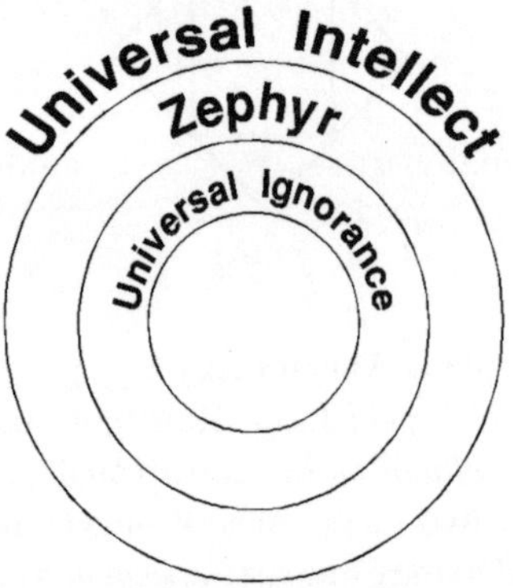

Fig. 3

Before terminating our review of Muslim cosmography we must also consider the "horizontal" and terrestrial division of the world as envisaged by the Muslim geographers. From the beginning, under the influence of Greek authors like Ptolemy but perhaps even more directly under that of pre-Islamic Persian conceptions of the world, Muslim authors divided the earth into seven regions or climates and seven seas, all surrounded by an ocean in the form of a circle which engulfed the whole world. Moreover, following earlier Persian and Greek and indirectly Babylonian examples, they connected the climates with the seven planets and the twelve signs of the Zodiac, thereby uniting heaven and earth and showing that all things below are an image of their heavenly counterpart.

We find the climatic division of the world fully developed by Mas'ūdī. As he writes,

"The division of the seven climates is as follows. First climate: the countries of Babel, Khorasan, Ahwaz, Mosul and Jibal; the signs of the Zodiac for this climate are Aries and Sagittarius and the planet, Jupiter. Second climate: Sind, India and the Sudan; the sign of the Zodiac is Capricorn and the planet, Saturn. Third climate: Mecca, Medina, the Yemen, Ṭā'if, the Hijaz and the intermediary countries; the sign of the Zodiac is Scorpio and the planet, Venus the auspicious. Fourth climate: Egypt, Ifriqiyyah, the lands of the Berbers, Spain and the provinces contained within; the sign of the Zodiac is Gemini and the planet, Mercury. Fifth climate: Syria, the countries of Rūm (Anatolia) and Mesopotamia (al-Jazīrah); the sign of the Zodiac is Aquarius and the planet, Mars. Seventh climate: the lands of Dā'il and China; the sign of the Zodiac is Libra and the planet, the sun".[49]

A picture of the world that is even more striking than the latitudinal division into strips followed by other Muslim geographers is the scheme given by Abū Rayḥān Bīrūnī, the celebrated fourth/tenth century scholar and scientist, in his *Kitāb taḥdīd nihāyāt al-amākin*.[50] This scheme, with a central province and six surrounding regions (see Fig. 4), bears a striking resemblance to the already mentioned seven *keshvars* of the ancient Persians, from which it was almost certainly derived. Bīrūnī made use of the knowledge of the Greeks and of other Muslim geographers, but integrated it into this pattern derived from Sassanid sources.

The seven climates and seas and the creatures living upon the earth are closely related to the angelic world, for each being in this world is guided by an anglic being for whom it is a theurgy.[51] As Mīr Abu'l-Qāsim Findiriskī, the remarkable Safavid Sufi, wrote in his well-known *qaṣīdah*,

"Heaven with these stars is clear, pleasing and beautiful",
"Whatever is there above has below it a form.
"The form below, if by the ladder of gnosis
"Treads upward, becomes the same as its principle".[52]

So for Muslims, as for the pre-Islamic Persians, the terrestial order is the image of the celestial by which it is governed and whose reality it reflects. Whether employing the philosophical term "nature" or the religious term "angel" the Muslim authors consider the order of the world to derive from a power or set of powers which descend from the celestial domain and upon which all earthly existence depends.

In this survey of Persian cosmography in the pre-Islamic and Islamic periods we chose to discuss certain ideas which show the "vertical" as well as "horizontal" continuity between the two periods. We have seen how in angelology, despite the difference in terminology, the reality described in the two traditions is nearly the same and how in certain instances there is even formal resemblance.[53] Of course the metaphysical background into which the cosmological sciences are integrated is not the same, the view of Islam being the emphasis upon the Divine Unity which absorbs all contingencies, from the particle of dust to the highest archangel, and the view of Zoroastrianism the cosmic duality of good and evil or light and darkness.

There are instances of direct borrowing by Muslims from the earlier sources as seen in the sevenfold division of the world into *keshvars* and the many motifs adopted by the illuminationist sages or *ishrāqīs* from their older compatriots, whom they call the "Pahlavi sages" (*ḥukamā' fahlawiyyūn*). There are also instances where the same archetypes are repeated: the numbers seven and twelve, the cosmic mountain *Qāf* and the governing of the terrestial world by angelic substances. Moreover, in certain cases, as in that of Kashfī, the Zoroastrian tripartite division of cosmic reality into the world of light or angels, the world of darkness or demons and the neutral world of terrestial existence between the two is directly repeated, although here there is no implication of any dualism whatsoever, the two opposing orders both deriving their being from the Divine Attributes.

In Persia, where Islam was destined providentially to replace the Sassanid religion, as in other lands where it spread, this final revelation of the present cycle of humanity came not to negate but to affirm and to integrate into itself whatever elements could be absorbed into its unitary point of view. So it was that in the Islamic cosmos, the Persians could contemplate many of the Zoroastrian myths and symbols in the light of Divine Unity and in a universality which has the power to embrace all elements of the Truth, of no matter what origin, into its fold.

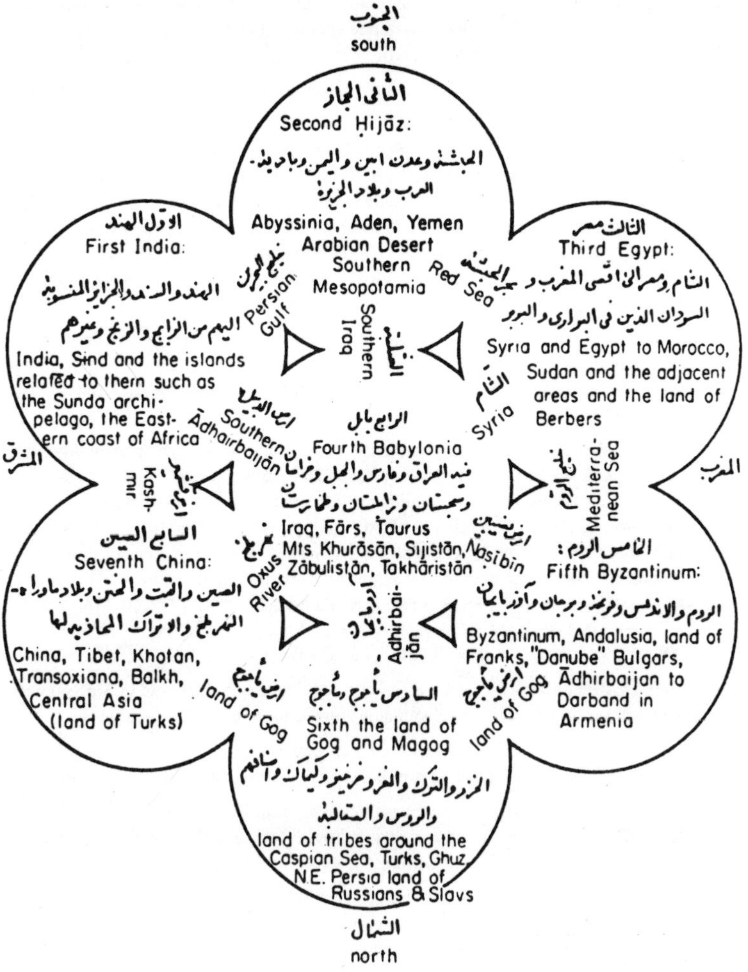
الجنوب
south
Second Ḥijāz:
Abyssinia, Aden, Yemen
Arabian Desert
Southern
Mesopotamia
First India:
India, Sind and the islands
related to them such as
the Sunda archi-
pelago, the East-
ern coast of Africa
Persian Gulf
Red Sea
Southern Iraq
Third Egypt:
Syria and Egypt to Morocco,
Sudan and the adjacent
areas and the land of
Berbers
Syria
Southern Ādhairbaijān
Fourth Babylonia
Iraq, Fārs, Taurus
Mts. Khurāsān, Sijistān,
Zābulistān, Takhāristān
Kash-mir
Mediterra-nean Sea
المشرق
المغرب
Nasibin
Seventh China:
China, Tibet, Khotan,
Transoxiana, Balkh,
Central Asia
(land of Turks)
Oxus River
Fifth Byzantinum:
Byzantinum, Andalusia, land of
Franks, "Danube" Bulgars,
Ādhirbaijan to
Darband in
Armenia
Adhirbai-jān
land of Gog
Sixth the land of
Gog and Magog
land of Gog
land of tribes around the
Caspian Sea, Turks, Ghuz,
N.E. Persia land of
Russians & Slavs
الشمال
north

Fig. 4

NOTES

1. See H.S. Nyberg, "Questions de cosmogonie et de cosmologie mazdéene", *Journal Asiatique*, vol. CCXIX, 1929, p. 2 ff.; A.V. Jackson, *Zoroastrian Studies,* New York, 1938, chap. I. Regarding the religion of the Sassanid period Nyberg writes as follows in the above article: "La religion sassanide vivante est le résulat d'une fusion précoce entre le mazdéism et le zervanism" (p. 125).

2. During this phase of Sunni domination exception must be made of the fourth/tenth century when most of Persia was ruled by the Shi'ite family of the Būyids.

3. Of course with the spread of Islam Persia became closer to the Arabs just as Europe was "Hebrewized" to some degree by becoming Christian. Moreover, the coming of Islam did bring a number of Arabs as settlers into Persia; the descendants of the Prophet have played no small role in the intellectual and social life of Muslim Persia. Despite this fact, however, the ethnic continuity of the Persian people is undeniable, even if the early Aryan invaders were in turn invaded by a series of foreign peoples, including the Greeks, Arabs, Turks and Mongols.

4. L. Massignon, *Salmām Pāk et les prêmices spirituelles de l'Islam iranien,* Paris, 1934, p. 11. Cited also in conjunction with the works of Suhrawardī by H.Corbin in his prolegomena to Suhrawardī, *Oeuvres philosophiques et mystiques*, Tehran-Paris, 1952, p. 98.

5. Here "number" must be understood in the Pythagorean sense as a "personality" and "quality" and not as the pure quantity of modern mathematics. "Whilst one obtains ordinary number by addition, qualitative number results, on the contrary, from an internal or intrinsic differentiation of principal unity; it is not added to anything and does not depart from unity. Geometrical figures are so many images of unity; they exclude one another, or rather, they denote different principal qualities..." F. Schuon, *Gnosis: Divine Wisdom*, trans. by G.E.H. Palmer, London, 1959, p. 113, n. 1. In addition to this work see H. Keyser, *Akroásis*, Stuttgart, 1947, pp. 17 ff. and Faber d'Olivet, *Les Vers dorês de Pythagore,* Paris, 1813, pp. 187 ff.

6. Since Muslim cosmology is closely connected with angelology and in Shi'ism with "imamology", these numbers also play a significant role in cosmography.

7. In as much as Zoroastrianism was the major pre-Islamic religion of Persia we have devoted most of our attention to it rather than to Mithraism and Manichaeism.

8. There are two *Bundahishns,* known as the Lesser or Indian and the Greater or Iranian *Bundahishn,* for which the *Zātspram* is a kind of guide which clarifies some of its obscurities. See R.C. Zaehner, *Zurvan, A Zoroastrian Dilemma,* Oxford, 1955, p. 81.

   The *Greater Bundahishn* has been translated into English by B.T. Ankelesaria, *Zand-Akāsīh, Iranian or Greater Bundahishn,* Bombay, 1956, and the Indian *Bundahishn* by E.W. West in the *Sacred Books of the East* series.

9. For the sources of Mazdaean cosmology and cosmography see H.S. Nyberg. *op. cit.*, p. 5.

10. See A.V. Jackson, *op. cit.,* pp. 110-115, and H.S. Nyberg, *op. cit.,* pp. 29 ff.

11. For a detailed account of Zurvanite cosmogony and cosmology see R.C. Zaehner, *op. cit.,* pp. 106 ff. The figure of Zurvān, which goes back to the earliest period of antiquity, is essentially a quadriform, of which one of the more important kinds consists of the sun, the moon, the signs of the Zodiac and Zurvān. Another famous quadriform is the Manichaean Zurvanite Zurvān, light, power and wisdom, to which Ibn Nadīm refers

to in his *Al-Fihrist*, edited by G. Flugel, Leipzig, 1871-2, vol. 1, p. 333, as Allāh, *nūruhu, quwwatuhu* and *ḥikmatuhu*; the four elements are also Zurvān's earthly reflection. In these quadriforms Zurvān himself appears among his own parts. This is due to a general old Iranian habit of including a thing as the completing member of its own parts. See H.S. Nyberg, *op. cit.,* p. 55 and M. Reitzenstein, *Das iranische Erlösungsmysterium,* Bonn, 1921, pp. 154 ff.

12. As Zaehner mentions, in the *Zātspram* Zurvān becomes incarnated in Spihr, which is considered as the body of the Universe. Spihr is the "Vāy of the long Dominion", which stands in the same relation to Vāy as cosmic time to Zurvān.

13. In Zoroastrian doctrines as in *ishrāqī* wisdom in Islam the border between the spiritual and the material worlds is set at the heaven of fixed stars, the boundary between the visible and the invisible, not at the heaven of the moon as in Aristotelian cosmology.

14. See Zaehner, *op. cit.,* p. 135; Jackson, *op. cit.,* pp. 42 ff.; B. Geiger, *Dia Amesa Spentas ihr Wesen und ihre ursprungliche Bedeutung,* Wien, 1916, and I. Pour-Davoud, *Adabiyyāt-i mazdayasnā, Yasht-hā*, vol. I, Bombay, 1928, pp. 69-96.

15. Among the most important of these Yāzātās are the *Fravashis* or *Fravartis*, a vast army of spirits who are the guardian angels of the souls of men. They exist in heaven before man's birth and unite with the soul after death. To them the nineteenth day of the month and the first month of the year were devoted.

16. This order seems to place the moon and the sun above the heaven of the signs of the Zodiac. This apparent mistake is probably due to the symbolism of light so important to Zoroastrianism. The descending stations of the sky symbolize degrees in which the original light decreases in intensity. It is therefore, natural to place the more luminous sun and moon above the stars.

17. From various Zoroastrian texts one can arrive at either a round or a disc-like figure of the earth.

18. Zaehner, *op. cit.*; p. 135.

19. *Ibid.*, p. 136. This account bears a striking resemblance to the account in *Ṛg-Veda* X. 90 of the creation of the Universe from the body of Purusha and as we shall demonstrate later to the Sufi concept of the Universal Man (*al-insān al-kāmil*).

20. For example the *Ābān Yasht* is written in praise of water and the *Rām Yasht* in praise of air.

21. The seven *keshvars* are mentioned in the *Tīr Yasht*; see Pour-Davoud, *op. cit.*; p. 361.

22. See E. Hertzfeld *Zoroaster and His World,* Princeton, 1957, p. 680. The idea of a round earth surrounded by an ocean is an ancient one shared by the various branches of the Aryan people. The *keshvars* are defined as follows: "Auf der ostlichen Seite [von Qavirāç] ist das Keshvar Çavai, im westen das Keshvar Arzai—zwei Teile—auf der Südseite die Keshvars Fradatafsh und Vidadafsh— 2 Teile—auf der Nordzeite die Keshvars Vorhast und Vorjarst — 2 Teile; das in der Mitte ist Qavirāç und Qavirāç begreuzt das Meer, denn ein Teile dieses Meeres... Ferakhkart ist herungeschlungen zwischen Vorharst and Vorjarst ist ein hohen Berg, gewachsen, denn von einem Keshvar in's andre kann man nicht geben." F. Justi, *Handbuch der Zend-sprache,* Leipzig, 1864, p. 81.

23. I. Pour-Davoud, *Adabiyyāt-i mazdayasnā,* vol. II, Bombay, 1931, pp. 324 ff.

24. Pour-Davoud, *op. cit.*, vol. I, pp. 429, 451 and 577. The cosmic mountain is a universal

symbol which appears in nearly all traditions. It is the Mt. Meru of the Hindus, the Olympus of the Greeks and the *Qāf* of the Muslims.

25. See Nyberg, *op. cit.*, pp. 29 ff.
26. For the name of some of these angels and their theurgies see Jackson *op. cit.*, chap. V.
27. See. T. Burckhardt, *Clé spirituelle de l'astrologie musulmane,* Paris, 1950, p. 47.
28. Mas'ūdī, *Les Prairies d'or,* trad., par C. Barbier de Maynard et Panet de Courteveille, Paris, 1861, vol. I, p. 47.
29. R.A. Nicholson, *Studies in Islamic Mysticism,* Cambridge, 1921, pp. 121-22.
30. 'Abd al-Karīm al-Jīlī, *al-Insān al-kāmil,* Cairo, n.d., chap. *"al-bāb al-muwaffī sittīn fi'l-insān al-kāmil",* p. 131. See also *De l'Homme universel*, trad. par T. Burckhardt, Lyon, 1953, p. 23. The correspondence with the account given above from the *Rivāyāt* is quite clear.
31. Of course this is not always the case. For example Shaykh al-ishrāq Shihāb al-Dīn Suhrawardī, the founder of the *ishrāqī* school in Islam, makes use of Zoroastrian angelology considering the first archangel to be Bahman, the first Ameshaspand of the Zoroastrians. See the prolegomena of H. Corbin to Suhrawardī, *Oeuvres philosophiques et mystiques.* We have not entered here into a discussion of the very complex scheme of angelology in Suhrawardī's writings, which bears a direct relation to Zoroastrian angelology, as it has been amply treated in this work. In any case Muslim cosmology and the angelology to which it is closely related are derived for the most part directly from the Quran.
32. See Ibn 'Arabī, *La Sagesse des prophètes,* trad. par T. Burckhardt, Paris, 1955, pp. 37 and 108.
33. This work has been published many times in Arabic and Persian and in German by F. Wüstenfeld, *Cosmographie,* Göttingen, 1848-49. Our references are to the Tehran lithographed edition of 1283.
34. *'Ajā'ib al-makhlūqāt*, pp. 33-41.
35. Nāṣir-i Khusraw, *Kitāb-jāmi' al-ḥikmatayn*, ed. by H. Corbin and M. Mo'in, Tehran-Paris, 1953, p. 109.
36. As pointed out in the "Études préliminaires" by Corbin (pp. 93-94), this pentade bears much resemblance to the pentade of Manichaean cosmogony.
37. *Ibid.*, p. 112. As revelation has a cosmic as well as a social aspect the coming of Islam implied also an Islamization of the cosmos in which Islam was to breathe. So we find Nāṣir-i Khusraw comparing the angelic order with the prophets of the Abrahamic tradition, or Jīlī, in his *al-Insān al-kāmil,* making the prophets correspond to the planets, starting with Adam, whose dwelling place is the moon. See R.A. Nicholson, *op. cit.,* pp. 122-23.
38. Ibn Abī Jumhūr was particularly instrumental in introducing the doctrines of Ibn 'Arabī into the cadre of Shi'ism.
39. *Kitāb al-mujlī*, Shiraz, 1329, p. 171.
40. Ibn Abī Jumhūr follows closely the cosmography of Ibn 'Arabī. See Burckhardt, *La Clé spirituelle,* pp. 8 ff. The eleven heavens of which Ibn Abī Jumhūr speaks apparently begin from above the sphere of water and exclude water and earth as heavens.

41. *Kitāb al-mujlī*, p. 473.

42. It should not be surprising if various Muslim authors or even the same author give different meanings to the same word in different places. Cosmology is not logic and various cosmic entities take on different meanings depending upon the context and point of view from which they are studied, without there being any basic contradiction.

43. *Kitāb al-mujlī,* p. 475. Ibn Abī Jumhūr follows the tradition of Jābirean alchemy in which the natures are the principles of the elements rather than the Aristotelian school in which the natures are only qualities of the elements and depend upon them for their subsistence.

44. Sayyid Ja'far Kashfī, *Tuḥfat al-mulūk,* Tabriz, 1273, chapter two (*al-ṭabaq al-thānī*).

45. This and some of the following proper names are the traditional Muslim designations of various worlds and forces of evil.

46. *Ṣakhrah* is also the name of the evil genius who stole the ring of Solomon.

47. The seven heavens and the seven earths are derived directly from the Quran, LXV, 12.

48. The similarity of this scheme in its general outline to the cosmography of Dante is obvious although of course the details differ greatly.

49. Mas'ūdī, *op. cit.,* pp. 181-82.

50. See A.Z. Validi Togan, "Biruni's Picture of the World", *Memoirs of the Archaeological Survey of India,* vol. 53, 1937-8, p. 61.

51. This idea, which bears close resemblance to the beliefs of the Zoroastrians, is accepted by all the *ishrāqī* sages after Suhrawardī and discussed by many of the Safavid authors like Mullā Ṣadrā and Mīr Dāmād.

52. See R. Hidāyat, *Riyāḍ al-'ārifīn*, Tehran, 1316, p. 277.

53. As already mentioned we did not even discuss here the angelology of Suhrawardī, the founder of the school of *ishrāq,* which is a direct adaptation of Zoroastrian angelology. This subject has been fully treated by H. Corbin and by ourselves in Part III of be present book.

3

The Tradition of Islamic Philosophy in Persia and its Significance for the Modern World*

The subject of the present paper is one which, it would seem, involves all men, for man, being a thinking being, cannot avoid thought. In whatever society he lives he is forced to think and meditate upon the nature of things. It is possible to put a false way of thinking in place of a true one, but, in any case, it is not possible to be against thought itself, especially since this point of view, when analyzed and dissected, is found to be itself a certain way of thinking. Man cannot, therefore, escape from thought and reflection, and this is true today in the Islamic world in particular as well as in the East in general, where men live in a special situation resulting from the encounter with Western civilization as a result of which a new awareness and evaluation of their own intellectual tradition has become an urgent call and, in fact, probably very much a matter of life and death. In Persia the best proof of this fact is that during the last decade, despite all that has been done in many modernized circles to turn away from purely intellectual matters and to become concerned solely with the practical and the pragmatic, there still can be seen a new kind of awareness of the Islamic philosophical tradition, even among some of the members of the younger generation.

In this discussion the expression "philosophical tradition" (*sunnat-i falsafi*) has been employed for the reason that the use of the term "tradition" itself, which has become current in Persian recently, is an indication of the present intellectual situation in the Islamic world. There are two factors to consider. First, the word tradition (*sunnat*) in its present sense in Persian does not have an antecedent in classical Arabic or Persian usage. The concept which the word evokes today has not existed in the

* This essay was originally written in Persian and appeared in *Ma'ārif-i islāmī*, No.8, 1969, pp. 33-42. The article was later translated by William Chittick înto English and published as "The Tradition of Islamic Philosophy in Persia and its Significance for the Modern World". *Iqbal Review*, 12 (October 1971): 28-49.

same way within the Islamic intellectual heritage where the word *dīn* has always meant tradition in its universal sense; but in fact this particular word, *sunnat*, has not been employed here without a definite reason. Its usage today in Persian, even in such expressions as "traditional decoration", "traditional food", or "traditional music", etc. points up a two-sided reality. It shows that to a degree the modernized generation in Persia as elsewhere in the Islamic world has to a certain extent fallen out of its own intellectual and cultural tradition and thus is able to reflect upon it from the "outside". In the same way, in a recent cultural seminar held in Tehran it was suggested that the very fact that the word culture (*farhang*) has come into use in Persian today as a result of European influence shows that the unity of culture that existed traditionally in Persia is disappearing. Today usually one begins to speak about "culture" only when one no longer possesses its real substance.

In reality, man can look at himself as a pure object only when he has come out of his own mould. Thus the very fact that today people concern themselves with the "philosophical tradition" of Persia shows that, as a result of contact with Western civilization and in general the transformations which have taken place in the world during the past fifty years, certain modernized Persians at the present time look upon their own past "objectively" as a past "tradition" outside of themselves.

The second factor involved in the use of *sunnat*, which is one of vital importance and concern, is that the development of the West during the past fifty years, after 400 years of revolt against tradition by European civilization, has made obvious, at least to the intellectual élite, the paramount importance and absolute necessity of tradition. This intellectual movement first began in France with a remarkable figure named René Guénon, but now talk of tradition is much more widespread, and some Persians are aware of this development. The very fact that the foundations themselves of a given civilization are crumbling and civilization faces dissolution makes the necessity of keeping up the tradition and of living according to it ever more obvious in the eyes of the élite. Although the general spiritual decadence of the modern world has gone on with ever greater speed during the past century, the need for tradition and interest in its presentation have become much more keenly felt than during the past century, although genuine interest in this matter has remained of necessity confined to a few.

Hence the recent use of the word tradition (as *sunnat*) in the Persian language, which has probably multiplied ten times over the last twenty years, is, indirectly at least, the result of a transformation which has appeared within Western civilization and has forced some people to turn their attention toward and respect intellectual tradition, whether or not they have been connected with tradition themselves. For example, in the nineteenth century Western art critics considered the anonymity of artists, writers or creative personalities in the East as a weakness, while today no one would be able to deny the value of Eastern art merely because the name of the artist and creator of a work of art is unknown. If anything, the bitter experience of this century has demonstrated to men of perspicacity that the respect for genuine tradition, tradition in its universal meaning as a reality that unites man with his Divine Origin and source and not custom or convention, is absolutely necessary even for the modernists touched by the spirit of the West. The Persians and other peoples of the East are not an exception to this rule. Only the preservation of tradition can help them preserve the coherence and meaningfulness of their lives. They can no longer appeal to the West as excuse to destroy their own tradition if they are at all aware of what is going on in the modern world.

Tradition in the present context does not mean something which passes or dies, for only that is dead which has no value for man at a given moment. As long as a society's past has value and meaning for it, the society is alive, and this "life" and "death" itself fluctuate over the ages. For example, from the appearance of Mithraism in the third century B.C. until the nineteenth century twenty-three centuries went by, and until the twentieth century, twenty-four centuries. Thus Mithraism should be more forgotten and "dead" in Iran now than during the last century, while in fact this is by no means the case. Today because of the rise of nationalism coming from the West, the modernized Persians pay a great deal more attention to Mithraism than they did in the past century. That is why when we speak about tradition in culture and more particularly in metaphysics and philosophy, we are not speaking only of a temporal relationship. Plato is just as alive today as he was in the fourth century B.C., while Renouvier, whose works were probably being read more than those of any other French philosopher in the year 1890, has now faded into the shadows of history. It can thus be said that an intellectual and metaphysical tradition is always alive in a world that lies above time and space. As long as a nation is alive and the roots of its culture continue to be norished from the spring of its own traditional cultural life, tradition is like a storehouse from which nourishment is drawn according to the nation's needs at different moments of its history.

In consequence to speak of the intellectual tradition in Persia linked organically with its past is to speak of a living intellectual school, whether the doctrines concerned be that of an individual like Suhrawardī, who lived seven centuries ago, or Ibn Sīnā, who lived ten centuries ago. The time span involved makes no difference. These and other Islamic philosophers and sages are alive and belong to the present moment of the life of Persians and other Muslims in general, for whom the Islamic intellectual tradition is alive.

But what is the essential nature of this philosophical tradition? Is it limited to Iran? And if so, what are its characteristics?

Here we meet with the extremely important problem of the continuity or lack of it between two chapters in the history of Persia, that is, the pre-Islamic and the Islamic periods. The former of these is itself worthy of a profound discussion, although we cannot concern ourselves with it at the present moment, for here our purpose is not to deal with historical roots, but rather with the analysis and evaluation of doctrines and ideas.

Without doubt a certain kind of profound intellectual tradition of a "philosophical" or rather theosophical type did exist in pre-Islamic Persia, but within the total world view of the religious traditions, such as Manicheanism, Mithraism and above all Zoroastrianism, themselves. This combination of wisdom and the religious world view is itself the outstanding characteristic of all the traditional civilizations of Asia, or those civilizations which have taken a set of divine principles as the source for all of their activity, modes of thought and way of life.

After the rise of Islam this "philosophical" tradition of the pre-Islamic period became integrated into Islamic intellectual life along with other intellectual legacies. As a result a kind of stage of world-wide dimensions was prepared by Islam, in which the Persians could play an active role. Other ideas and schools of thought, especially Greek philosophy—which itself probably has a profound connection in its origin with the ancient Persian Egyptian and Indian traditions—; concepts which originated in Mesopotamia and India and certain other elements, played their own significant role in the rise of Islamic philosophy. But more important than all else was the religion of Islam, which provided the background against which and the principles by which all of these intellectual currents and ideas were brought together, resulting in the formation of Islamic philosophy.

Many Europeans, unfortunately, because of their strongly prejudiced views concerning ancient Greece, have never admitted that other civilizations also possessed an intellectual tradition of value and originality, as can be seen in most of their appraisals of Pre-Islamic Persia. This prejudice, combined with a large number of other factors, has prevented the importance of the wisdom of ancient Persia and even to a greater extent the significance of Islamic philosophy from becoming clear. As a result the West has neglected to study the tradition of Islamic philosophy in its entirety and because of the great influence that Western writings exercise upon modern Muslims, this has harmed the Muslims and particularly the Persians themselves, for in reality Iran has always been the principal homeland of Islamic philosophy and it was mostly here that the tradition of Islamic philosophy continued after the 6th/12th century. If one reflects upon the fact that so many Islamic philosophers hailed from Iran and then considers Iran's geographical area and population as compared to those of the whole Islamic world, the significance of Iran as the center of Islamic philosophy becomes clear.

Another important point to be considered is that in the modern period Persians have occupied themselves less with writing works on "philosophy" in the modern European sense than the contemporary scholars of other Islamic countries, who have written works in Arabic, Urdu, Turkish and English (especially in India and Pakistan). This apparently negative fact has a very positive reason, which is the profundity and deep-rootedness of traditional philosophy in Iran. The mere fact of the existence of an authentic and original intellectual school has made the presentation of unfounded and insubstantial "philosophies" and ideas which ape the West more difficult. Nowadays, because of the prejudice which exists in certain circles, resulting in lack of attention to the philosophy of Islamic Persia and a great deal of this prejudice is the fault of the Muslims themselves—a truncated and in fact ludicrous concept of Islamic philosophy has taken form in the minds of the modern educated classes of Muslim countries. This fact has placed them at a crossroads which, from the point of view of the future development of Islamic society in general and Persian society in particular and their future intellectual life, is of extreme importance.

In order to remain a healthy being man has basically no choice but to have a certain direct awareness of himself, and if he also observes other beings he always views their personality in the light of his own existence. In fact from the metaphysical point of view all beings in the cosmos display man's existence. Ordinary men see their fallen nature in other beings, while the man who has reached that degree of spiritual development and transcendence which frees him from the chains of his own ego and the limitations of his own soul sees his spiritual essence reflected in the world about him. In any case seeing others in oneself and oneself in others is reached by way of the knowledge of self. This also holds true for cultures, in the sense that a culture must have direct knowledge of its own past. It is true that historical and social developments, contact with other civilizations etc., bring about a certain kind of new understanding of the past, but a culture can never remain healthy and strong by the sole means of seeing its own reflection in the mirror of other cultures.

It is now becoming ever more clear that the problem of the necessity of direct self-knowledge is of serious proportions for all Asian societies and especially the Muslim world. For in so many Muslim lands modernized people now seek to look at themselves from the point of view of the West. Of course, this type of perspective is not prevalent among the common people; rather; it is to be seen especially among the so-called "intelligentsia".

The best proof of this assertion is in the field of art, which, as a concrete phenomenon, can better serve as an example. It is well known that during the last century, before Europeans began to recognize the value of the Persian miniature, the Persians themselves did not have much interest in maintaining this artistic heritage or preserving the precious results it had produced. In the same way until a few years ago there was no interest in Iran in Qajar style paintings, and most of these paintings were to be found hanging on the walls of coffee-houses. But recently, when the real value of these works was recognized by certain European art critics and the Qajar style was designated as an important school of art, those same apparently lowly paintings found their way from humble coffee-houses to exhibitions halls and are bought and sold at tremendous prices. Such a revival in the appreciation of any nation's art as the result of the application of purely foreign standards shows that in a certain sense the culture of that nation has become unstable in the eyes of those who have fallen under foreign influences and that this class lacks confidence in its own cultural identity. If this continues and spreads, the nation will become afflicted by severe disorder within its social structure and the society, like a mentally ill person who experiences a double personality, will become schizophrenic. Within Islamic society, on the one hand, there will exist people on the lower levels who will not yet feel strange and alien within their own society, while on the other hand there will be individuals on the higher levels who will feel alien to, and completely cut off from, the rest of society, thus causing a kind of disharmony and breach to appear within the community. This is a disorder which has already afficted to a greater or lesser degree all Asian societies and is making more difficult for them the possibility of correctly evaluating and judging what comes from the outside, that is, foreign cultures and in particular the civilization of the West.

That is why one can say that for the East in general and for the Muslim world in particular a new awareness and understanding of the nature of their own philosophical and intellectual traditions is not just an academic question. Rather, it is one which involves their future existence, in the sense that for a nation to know where it wants to go it must first know where it is, and this is tied to a complete awareness of its own intellectual past.

However this may be, today in the Islamic world, in most university circles and among those people who are acquainted with modern Western culture, dependence upon the research and even propaganda of some Westerners concerning Islamic thought and philosophy determines the views held by most students of the philosophical tradition of Islam. Moreover, the fact that most members of the intelligentsia of the East are acquainted with the world and with themselves from the point of view of the West has resulted in their feeling a certain insecurity concerning their own intellectual past. This does not mean that all of the studies of the orientalists have been carried out because of ulterior motives or on the basis of ill intentions; on the contrary, one can be certain that a considerable number of these studies have been free of any such stains. But in any case, the researches of the orientalists have been made at best with an eye on the requirements of Western civilization—which, of course, arc not those of the Oriental civilizations.

It must further be pointed out that, as any careful study will show, the shadow of the nineteenth century, when orientalism became established as a university discipline, is still upon us today. If Western thought at that time had accepted the originality and value of a civilization other than its own, it essentially would have destroyed its image of itself and ceased to be what it was during that period. This vital point bears repetition: today in the Persian language it is said that a particular nation is "civilized", or possesses no "civilization". The word which is employed, *tamaddun,* is a literal translation of the French term used by the Encyclopaedists of the eighteenth century. In the nineteenth century Western thought finally led to the "fall" of the absolute "into time". In fact, Hegel, who finally brought this about, and philosophers like him considered nineteenth century Western civilization to be the final and ultimate goal of man's history, and indeed, to be "civilization" as such. It is true that this view has now been rejected, but in the last century it was to a large degree prevalent and it still has supporters in certain schools.

This type of outlook could not accept that other cultures were truly original and "civilized", unless they were so far from the course of

Western civilization and so "exotic" that a certain appreciation of their worth would in no way harm the West—as was the case, for example, with the civilizations of Tibet and Japan, whose recognition in no way prejudiced the deeper motives underlying the researches of the majority of orientalists. But when there was talk of the civilization of Islam and in particular when the problem of thought and intellectual activity was put forward, the subject become much more delicate. The heart of the matter is here: if the orientalists were to accept that a civilization other than the Western had come into being and been of value independently of the culture and civilization of the West, all the bases upon which European philosophy stood at that time would have assumed a relative character. For, in fact, at that time there was no other "absolute" for the countries of Europe to rely upon than what had come to be known as Civilization with a capital C. Christianity had lost its absolute character in the seventeenth century, so that without this new pseudo-"absolute" the foundations of Western civilization would have been destroyed. That is why in their studies and analyses of Islamic civilization most Western scholars have until recently cut off their discussions with the sixth/twelfth and seventh/thirteenth centuries. In most general cultural studies and those dealing with intellectual history all the later phases of Islamic philosophy, Sufism and theology as well as astronomy, mathematics and medicine are neglected almost systematically.

The problems outlined above have been complicated by a number of political movements in the East in the form of nationalism. For example, theer is the case of Arab nationalism in its intense form, where, in order to show that Islamic civilization declined when the Persians and Turks were dominant, some Arab nationalists have discussed and confirmed in their writings the thesis of the sudden curtailment of Islamic intellectual activity which Western authors had advanced, and in this way they have made use of this idea for political purposes. The result of all of these factors has been to make the knowledge of their own culture difficult for modern Muslims, and all of them suffer because of this ignorance.

Even in an area like Persian literature, for example, a careful investigation will show that the greater part of the aversion and lack of interest displayed by modernized scholars in Iran today with respect to the literature of the Safavid period and the Persian literature of the subcontinent is a result of the relatively incorrect evaluation and appraisal of this literature by the first Western scholars who wrote on Persian literary history. This evaluation has brought about a change in the taste of a large number of Persians concerning even their own literature, despite the internal and national character of this subject.

A similar situation exits to a greater or lesser degree in a large number of other fields. Within Islamic civilization this is particularly harmful in every way, for one of two things is true. Either we must accept that during a period of seven or eight hundred years Muslims did not think or possess any form of intellectual activity—and if so, then how would it be possible for such activity to return to life after seven centuries? Or, on the contrary, we must accept that we have had an intellectual tradition—and in this case we must recover the resources of our own tradition and base ourselves on the foundation provided by them.

A country like Iran, which possesses a rich and ancient civilization and culture, faces a much more complicated situation *vis-a-vis* its own intellectual traditions than a country which culturally and geographically has just recently come into existence. Whatever the meaning of such a shallow statement might be, 'entering the twentieth century' in the sense of accepting Western civilization, is quite an easlier matter for such a newly established nation and can probably be accomplished, at least from an economic point of view, by bringing together a few of the necessities and luxuries and the external manifestations of contemporary life. But movement and change in a civilization which is solidly buttressed by the heritage of the past is something else. Unlike a country built upon a completely new foundation such a civilization cannot remain oblivious to its own culture. It must bear its weighty legacy wherever it goes or else remain an incomplete being. Moreover, nations of this type are themselves charged with a mission, which in reality is the guidance and leadership of all men in the twentieth century in the light of their living intellectual and spiritual tradition. They cannot simply follow the dangerous course of Western civilization with their hands folded especially considering the fact that the present century is one with a thousand imperfections and deficiencies, and that, if it continues upon its present course, it is hopeless to expect that civilization in its present form will last another century.

The historical mission of societies in which tradition still survives *vis-a-vis* the modern world is to take seriously their own intellectual and spiritual tradition, and this in fact is something which thoughtful men throughout the world expect of them. European civilization, which in the nineteenth century, because of its absolutist view of Western thought, did not want to accept that the civilizations of the East possessed any originality or foundation of their own, has today put relativity in place of that "absolute". European thought has become relative for Westerners themselves and for the same reason we meet with contradictory value-systems within Western civilization. Whether they want to or not, the more thoughtful elements of this civilization are now forced to accept that the civilizations of the East do possess a certain value and originality in themselves.

Thus it is that the "intelligentsia" of the Eastern traditions finds itself at an extremely difficult crossroads. In Iran, for example, being "Westernized" (*farangī-ma'āb*) at the time of Akhundov was different from what it became at the time of Taqīzādah, and today it is different from what it was then, these three aspects of the same phenomenon displaying tremendous divergences among themselves. Taqīzādah's name is mentioned on purpose, for the life which he lived is a perfect illustration of the developments and changes which have taken place within the intellectual currents of a single nation over a period of almost a century, during which he himself expressed several different views concerning the civilization of the West, thus showing how the mental climate among the "intelligentsia" of Iran and most other Muslim lands has changed.

Today an individual Muslim—especially since, as has been pointed out, Islamic civilization is one of the three or four Oriental civilizations which from this point of view possess an intellectual mission for the modern world—cannot erase from his mind his own civilization and culture as easily as he did in the past decades; for the mere mention of the fact that traditional philosophical thought exists in Islam and more particularly in Persia places him face to face before the question of upon what other intellectual premisses he wishes to base himself in order to forget his own authentic and original mode of thought, when Western modes of thought are themselves crumbling.

Here it must be hoped that the light that has come from study and research in East and West concerning the thought and philosophical tradition of Iran—and which will certainly grow brighter in the coming years—will to a degree illuminate the way for the future intellectual development of Iran and the Islamic world in general. In other words, when young Muslim intellectuals observe, for example, that the *Sharḥ-i manẓūmah* of Ḥajjī Mullā Hādī Sabziwārī has recently been translated into English,[1] they will not be able to maintain the same attitude toward the Islāmic intellectual tradition as did the "intelligentsia" of the past generation. Thus, the awareness which is just beginning to appear around the world concerning the Islamic philosophical tradition in Iran is itself one of the basic elements which will help determine the future intellectual development of the Islamic world.

It must now be asked what this intellectual tradition is in itself. First of all, as has been indicated, the intellectual tradition of Islam with its widespread and extensive roots is in many ways unique in the world:

among classical civilizations it is only the Islāmic that truly possesses an international and world-wide foundation, for this foundation came into being from the encounter of Chinese, Persian and Indian, Greek and Alexandrian elements as well as the intellectual heritages of most of the other ancient civilizations of the world along with, of course, the Quranic sciences and branches of knowledge themselves. The mode of thought which appeared as a result reached its first stage of perfection with Ibn Sīnā; afterwards great theologians, such as Imām Muḥammad Ghazzālī and Imām Fakhr al-Dīn Rāzī, opened up a new direction, and a further stage was reached with the appearance of the School of Illumination (*ishrāq*) founded by one of the greatest intellectual figures of Islam, Shyakh al-Ishrāq Shihāb al-Dīn Suhrawardī. Later stages in the development of this tradition were brought about by the synthesis of gnosis (*'irfān*), philosophy and theology leading to the flowering of these intellectual movements in the Safavid period with Mīr Dāmād and Mullā Ṣadrā, whose school has continued to the present day. These are some of the developments which appeared within Islamic thought over the centuries, and it is precisely this chain of thought which we have in mind when we speak of the "Islamic philosophical tradition".

Unfortunately, because of lack of extensive research, the particularities of much of this tradition are unknown to us, for at the very least most of the thousands of books written in this field must first be studied. But a few of the basic principles which can be seen throughout the various stages of the intellectual life of Islam and in particular in Iran are manifestly clear. Here it is hoped to compare and contrast these principles with the prevalent thought-patterns of the modern world and the problems which modern science and philosophy have placed before man.

The first and most important message of the Islamic philosophical tradition, which more than all others has drawn the attention of the most penetrating of modern scholars, is that this "philosophy" cannot be learned but must be "realized". Philosophy in the East is not just a school of thought and an academic discipline; it is also something that must be combined with a "wayfaring", and an inner transformation of man's being. In other words, as first taught, most of all by Suhrawardī, in Islam becoming a philosopher (*faylasūf*) or traditional theosopher (*ḥakīm*) is joined to the attainment of spiritual and moral perfection.

It is well enough known that one of the elements that has caused the tragedy of modern man is the complete separation between knowledge and ethical principles, in the sense that at the present time there is no relationship whatsoever between moral and spiritual perfection and scientific progress. This itself is the source of immediate danger, even causing one of UNESCO's experts to remark a few years ago, "I wish we were back in the age of the alchemists when science was only in the hands of the elite, and they kept it secret"; for disseminating science in man's present situation is like putting a sword in the hand of a drunken sailor.

Today every "forward" step which man takes in reality widens the gulf between what he is and what he thinks. That is why we are regrettably faced with a severe crisis resulting from the application of the practical aspects of modern science, as is observed, for example, in certain negative and harmful consequences of modern medicine and biology. Thus a complex problem is placed before us: why does the application of science, which apparently is based upon experiment and the observation of nature, cause man to fall into violent conflict with that same nature, so that it has even become possible that in the end man and nature will be destroyed? Again, this difficult and perhaps insoluble dilemma of modern man derives basically from the split between science and wisdom in general on the one hand and science and spiritual and moral perfection on the other.

To understand why the situation has come to this crisis it is necessary to cast a glance at the history of Western thought and to search for the cause of the separation of Western science and metaphysics. It is true that this separation produced certain positive results and led to the appearance of new branches of science, but its negative aspect is much greater and has resulted in the disappearance of any satisfactory universal point of view. Thus, in the words of one of the greatest physicists of this century, we have a physics, but no natural philosophy which can integrate it into a more universal form of knowledge. Then again, further difficulties are caused by the sort of caricature of natural science which has come into being in the humanities and social sciences in the form of the ludicrous imitation of seventeenth century physics, that is, the constant reduction of quality to quantity and the drawing of a few curves to explain psychological and social phenomena.

Today, then, man is faced with an exceedingly dangerous situation and a chasm which has destroyed the unity of his existence. Today in a Western university, as well as those of the East which imitate Western models, a student is obliged to study the humanities, natural sciences and mathematics together. In other words, he comes out of his physics class and enters one on literature, and from there he goes to classes on art, and from there to classes on the doctrines and history of religion, without there being any significant relationship between his studies in these fields. This has brought about a kind of "hardening of the arteries", which we in the East must never be negligent of or try to imitate. If we do not take preventive measures and do not attempt to find an immediate solution, within one or two generations we shall be afflicted by the same disorder that has now overtaken the societies of the West and which cannot be any means by taken lightly: separation between wisdom and science, between morals and science and between complete disarray and discontinuity within science itself and more particularly separation between the humanities and the natural sciences, and most of all aversion toward traditional philosophy and metaphysics (leaving aside the few traditionalists alluded to above) which arose out of European history when after Leibniz genuine metaphysics was forgotten. What is called metaphysics today in the West is not true metaphysics except for what is found in the writings of traditional authors like R. Guénon and F. Schuon. Metaphysics in its true sense must always be connected with a way of union with the Truth, whereas the so-called metaphysics in Western philosophy is made up for the most part of expenditure of breath and, ultimately, simply mental noises, as Western philosophy itself has been referred to by a contemporary sage.

Moreover, true metaphysics, as it has existed in Islamic civilization, in the bosom of traditional theosophy (*ḥikmat*) and gnosis (*'irfān*), has produced significant scientific results and has been the mother of the traditional sciences. For this reason also the intellectual tradition of Islam is extremely valuable as a guide for today's world. Islamic civilization is the only one which has been able to produce a mathematician of the highest calibre, who was also a competent poet. It is true that one or two of the symbolist poets of France knew mathematics, but they were never great mathematicians and only knew mathematics as an academic discipline, while, as far as we know, throughout the whole history of science only Khayyām was both a great poet and an eminent mathematician. In addition, probably half of the great scientists of Islam followed gnostic doctrines, such man, as Ibn al-Bannā' al-Marrākushī, the last great mathematician of the Western lands of Islam, who was himself the spiritual master (*shaykh*) of a Sufi order; or Quṭb al-Dīn Shīrāzī, or even people like Khwājah Naṣīr al-Dīn Ṭūsī and Ibn Sīnā, both of whom had strong inclinations towards Sufism and gnosis.

Here it might be asked what sort of intellectual life was able to bring together in the mind of one person logic and gnosis, or allow a person to write a book like *The Theosophy of the Orient of Light* (*Ḥikmat al-ishrāq*, by Suhrawardī), the first part of which is among the most accurate criticisms ever made of Aristotle's formal logic, and the second part one of the most entrancing discussions of gnosis in Islam. How is it possible for these two modes of thought to be integrated together without any sense of contradication? It is here that the uniqueness of the philosophical tradition of Islamic Persia shows itself quite clearly. The other civilizations of Asia, like the Buddhist and the Hindu, gave birth to a pure gnosis of the highest order which in many respects is comparable to that of Jalāl al-Dīn Rūmī, Ibn 'Arabī and Ḥāfiẓ, but expositions of the exact sciences and mathematics in the framework of gnosis are to be found most of all in the Islamic philosophical and scientific tradition.

Here it is possible to object that the Islamic natural sciences were not like modern science. In a certain respect this is a valid objection, seeing that modern science is transitory and the traditional sciences have a permanent value. But even if we take the point of view of the historical development of science, the scientific activity of each period must be judged according to the culture and civilization that prevailed during it. Today's science also will be rejected tomorrow. Aristotle was the greatest biologist of the fourth century B.C. and Harvey was the greatest physician of the seventeenth century A.D. just as today a particular person is, for example, the greatest contemporary biologist. In the same manner, Khwājah Naṣīr al-Dīn Ṭūsī was just as much a great mathematician and astronomer in his time as Laplace in his and Einstein and Poincaré in our own. Thus the value of scientific thought in itself is not related to the simplicity or complexity of a given period's science. Moreover, when a civilization has been able to place scientific thought within a perspective which includes traditional theosophy and gnosis, this possesses the highest significance for today's world and especially for us who are Muslims, for it is precisely the separation of science from theosophy (*ḥikmat*) and truc metaphysics which has brought the world face to face with today's alarming crisis.

Probably the attention which is beginning to be paid to this aspect of Islamic philosophy in the West derives from the same reason, that is, that on its highest levels this tradition has synthesized reason (*istidlāl*), with all of its most precise requirements and conditions, and illumination (*ishrāq*) and intuition (*dhawq*). Moreover, its expression has never been separated from beauty. A point of basic importance for modern man, with which many scientists have concerned themselves, is that although theoretically modern science does possess an aspect of beauty—to the extent that scientists, especially physicists themselves, are usually attracted to it by the beauty of its theories and speak more of "beauty" than of "truth", presenting a new scientific theory as "beautiful"—when this science is applied, the result is ugliness. In other words, one of the characteristics of industrial and machine-age civilization is ugliness, and for the same reason beauty has come to be considered a luxury and as something more or less superfluous. In non-industrial civilizations, on the other hand, beauty has always existed in every aspect of life.

Over the past few years, as a result of the increase in mental illness and the discord brought about by industrial society, a certain number of people have gradually realized that beauty is not a luxury or something extraneous to life, but one of the necessities for existence. This is a fact which Islamic philosophy and civilization have always confirmed. For example, in the Islamic world various disciplines have been studied by making use of poetry, not merely because it is easier to memorize difficult and complicated subjects with the help of poetical rhythm and harmony: the *Alfiyyah* of Ibn Mālik, the *Manẓūmah* of Sabzīwārī, the *Nisāb* and many other works all illustrate the taste and discernment of a people in appreciating beauty by moulding scientific concepts into poetical form. The attempt to achieve beauty by combining science and scientific explanations with poetry does not derive from the wish to simply demonstrate virtuosity. It is rather one of the most important heritages of the intellectual and philosophical tradition of Islam, impossible to accomplish without recourse to traditional theosophy and gnosis. It is only the gnostic (*'ārif*) who can both produce mathematics and compose poetry. In other words, gnosis is the frontier and only common ground between the two. Until now, without turning to gnosis and achieving, in fact, the spiritual maturity it provides, no one has been able to be the source of original intellectual creations combining both reason and intuition.

The last important characteristic of the Islamic intellectual tradition which we wish to mention here is its universality. It has never been limited to a particular subject, people or location, but has always been concerned with the highest truths of an unlimited nature as well as with mankind and the world as a whole. In fact, one of the characteristics of Islam, which fortified a characteristic which had existed in Persian civilization from ancient times, has been precisely its international and universal perspective. It is well known that Cyrus the Great was the first person to have granted different nations under his rule the right to follow their own way of life and that the Persians were the first people who did not limit the world to their own borders. This aspect of Persian civilization was fortified by the universal perspective of Islam, so that the character of universalism is a strong feature of all Islamic philosophy, especially as it developed in Persia.

A great many people now realize that man's future will probably depend more than all else upon his ability to preserve completely his own religious opinions and beliefs and at the same time to accept the value of those of others. Of course, this is not an easy matter, as is shown, for example, by the fact that the most important barrier standing in the way of Christian thought today is the existence of other religions. This is because Christianity can no longer consider all other religions and faiths to be heathen and astray, as it did in the nineteenth century, when comparative religion first appeared as a field of study. Today as soon as believing Christians see that there are people belonging to other religions and characterized by sincerity and spiritual perfection, they will stand in danger of losing their own faith if they try to ignore the factors which are the cause of that perfection.

Today in the West there is a great deal of interest in the study of the history and comparison of religions. It is hard to believe, but apparently the number of students studying comparative religion in American universities is greater than that in many other fields, and is increasing every day. This extraordinary interest is due to the fact that, as Western civilization spreads and cultural barriers are broken down by the external aspects of modernism, Western man's need for immediate standards by which to judge the values of other cultures increases, and without a universal perspective from which to understand the truths of other religions the danger of losing his own faith always threatens him. In the Islamic world and in most of the other countries of the East this problem is still hardly perceptible, except in the case of a very small number of people who have had an extremely close acquaintance with the West and have passed through the stages of anguish, hope and despair of the Western intelligentsia. Nevertheless, this is undoubtedly the most important spiritual problem in today's world and in the future will be even more perceptible in the East. Its solution is far more difficult than sending two or three men to the moon, for it involves the faith of billions of human beings.

Let the problem be expressed quite clearly. How is it possible, for example, for a person to remain a Christian and truly accept, with complete sincerity, the truth of Islam? Or how is it possible for a person to be a Muslim and yet accept the verities of Buddhism and Christianity? In the future this problem will be felt everywhere with the same seriousness as it is felt today by a few young people in the best universities of the West. American youth do not, for example, study a text on Buddhism without motivation, but rather as the result of a deep need of which many people in the East are probably not aware. That everyday in the West new centers are opened at the universities for the study of comparative religion, or Islam or Hinduism, is not for the most part because, in the manner of the nineteenth century, people want to find out about the nations of the East in order to be able to rule them better; rather, it is because of a spiritual and "existential" need on the part of an important section of the Western intelligensia.

The very life and existence of a reflective and thoughtful student today in the West demands that he become acquainted with the cultural, religious and philosophical values of others. He must either accept their validity and see his own standards become relative, or reject them; he must either live in confusion and without orientation, or try to find another solution. In any case he is forced to undergo a crisis which is probably the most pressing and urgent intellectual problem which man will face in the future, along with the battle between tradition and anti-traditional or secularist tendencies.

In this situation Islamic philosophy again possesses a massage of the utmost importance. Persians in particular are all familiar with the poetry of the Muslim gnostics and Sufis, especially Rūmī, who turned their attention to the unity of religions and held that God's message has been sent to all. The verse of the Noble *Quran,* "Every nation has its messenger" (10:48, Arberry's translation), is likewise a reference to this subject, and no holy book has proclaimed the universality of revelation as much as *Quran*. The doctrine of the inward unity of religions became particularly developed and refined in Iran, located geographically as it was between the Mediterranean world and India. That is why today the Muslims of Persia possess without their even knowing it consciously not only a philosophy of religions but a "theology" of religions in the Western sense. The possibility of understanding a variety of intellectual, gnostic, philosophical and religious systems and modes of thought exists within their own philosophical and gnostic tradition.

In one way the above point can be observed in the works of Suhrawardī, who combined the philosophies of ancient Persia and ancient Greece within the framework of Islamic gnosis and brought into being such works as *Alwāḥ-i 'imādī* and *'Aql-i surkh* which in a certain way sublimate and transform the epic narratives of pre-Islamic Persia into mystical recitals. In another way we see this perspective, as indicated above, in the works of Rūmī, in particular in his *Mathnawī,* and in the poetry and writings of many other Sufi masters. Modern Persians read and enjoy these works as poetry, and often they unfortunately "profit" from them in a sort of inverse manner by deriving from them a kind of relativity in the face of all *Sharī'ite* injunctions. But the worth of this heritage is much greater than shallow people would understand, for it can be a guide for Muslims in the future to "be themselves" without negating the tradition of others. More particularly it can be of special service to a number of countries besides Persia, whether to the East, where the two religions of Hinduism and Islam face each other, or to the West, where friction exists between Islam and Christianity and even more between Islam and Judaism. This also, then, is one of the great characteristics of the Islamic philosophical and gnostic tradition of Iran, which in the future can be a great intellectual aid for the Islamic world in general if not for the world as a whole.

To summarize, the purpose of the present paper has not been to analyze in detail difficult philosophical and gnostic concepts, but rather to point out the general lines of the philosophical tradition of Islamic Persia. The most notable feature of this tradition is that philosophy in its true sense belongs to those possessing a spiritual quality, that is, philosophy in the sense of the ancient Pahlavi wisdom (*khirad*) and the traditional theosophy (*ḥikmat*) of Islam, or that philosophy which attaches man to spiritual reality and to truth. All men must think, whether they be physicians, engineers or mathematicians. All must first be human beings, then be experts in their own fields. Thus it is that on the general level which we have been considering the traditional philosophy of Persia belongs to all the intellectual classes of society. Therefore, and if we are to have in Iran and in the Islamic world in general a university which has a truly intellectual character, we must make use of our own intellectual traditions as background for all fields of study. This applies *mutatis mutandis* to all aspects of the life of the Islamic world.

Today in the East we are sleeping on hidden treasures. We must first awaken and evaluate them, and only afterwards go on to acquire new knowledge and sciences. Otherwise the modern sciences which we import from the West, even the natural sciences and mathematics, will never be anything but superficial activities without roots, and even if they do take root their roots will dry up and dessicate the existing culture and civilization. New branches must be grafted onto a living tree, but if the tree itself is not alive and strong no new grafts will ever be possible.

Many of those in the East who speak today of science and knowledge and who as a service to science want to eliminate their own culture with its gnostic, philosophical and religious dimension are either unaware of what is happening or are in fact labouring under a greater illusion about the modern world than the Westerners themselves. Islamic culture and more generally the traditions of the East will only be able to respond positively to the impact of the West if they are themselves a living entity. It does happen that they are fortunate enough to still have the possibility of remaining alive as themselves, especially wherever there continues to survive a very original and valuable intellectual tradition. God willing, the coming generation of Muslims, by taking their own spiritual and intellectual heritage seriously, will be able to preserve the Islamic tradition and also cast a light which will illuminate the otherwise dark skies that modern man has brought into being through forgetfulness of the truth which lies in the nature of things.

NOTES

1. By T. Izutsu and M. Muḥaqqiq; Part one of the translation has been published in the Islamic series of McGill University Press. The Arabic text of this work was published by these two scholars in Tehran in 1969.

4

The Significance of Persian Philosophical Works in the Tradition of Islamic Philosophy*

Without doubt Arabic is the most important language of Islamic philosophy and even the Persians, who have produced the largest number of Islamic philosophers, have written mostly in Arabic and produced some of the best known classics of Islamic philosophy in the Arabic language, such as the *Shifā'* and the *Maqāṣid al-falāsifah*. But it is equally true that Islamic philosophical texts in Persian constitute an important corpus without whose study the understanding of later Islamic philosophy as it developed in Persia and the Indo-Pakistani subcontinent would be impossible. Moreover, even in the case of some of the earlier figures who wrote in both Arabic and Persian, men like Ibn Sīnā and Ghazzālī, the totality of their message cannot be understood without taking into consideration their Persian writings. There are even figures in both the earlier and the later centuries of Islamic history who wrote mostly or completely in Persian, such as Nāṣir-i Khusraw and Afḍal al-Dīn Kāshānī, and who are usually left out of consideration in most of the general histories of Islamic philosophy precisely because of the language in which they expressed their ideas. Of course Turkish and Urdu are also of some importance for certain philosophical texts written during the past two or three centuries, but the use of Persian goes back over a thousand years and the Persian language must be considered along with Arabic as a main language in which the Islamic intellectual sciences were expressed in Persia itself as well as in the subcontinent and even to a certain extent in the Turkish world.

Because the modern Western approach to Islamic philosophy developed within a scholastic tradition in which knowledge of Islamic philosophy was limited to Arabic texts, the tendency has continued in the

---

* This essay was published in *Essays on Islamic Philosophy and Science*. Edited by G. Hourani, Albany: State of New York University Press, 1975, pp. 67-75.

Occident to ignore the considerable corpus of Islamic philosophy written in Persian.[1] Only during the past few years has attention been paid to this body of writing, and gradually important philosophical works in Persian by such men as Ibn Sīnā, Nāṣir-i Khusraw, Suhrawardī, Afḍal al-Dīn Kāshānī, Naṣīr al-Dīn Ṭūsī and others are beginning to see the light of day. The field is, however, still a virgin one. Much remains to be done even to discover the titles of all the Persian philosophical texts, and much more to edit and publish them.[2]

The fact that Persian was destined to become an important intellectual language in Islam is difficult to explain in terms of purely historical factors. The "asymmetry" in the matter of language which one sees in early Islamic history, namely both Islamization and complete Arabization of the lands of *dār al-islām* west of Arabia, and Islamization but only very partial Arabization east of Iraq, left room for the rise of modern Persian as an Islamic language. Once Islam developed a unified civilization with two centers of culture, one Arabic and one Iranic, Persian was bound to develop as a language of intellectual discourse especially since the Persians were themselves so active in the intellectual sciences (*al-'ulūm al-'aqliyyah*) and contributed so much even to the development of Arabic prose in science and philosophy. As Persia gradually became independent of the caliphate from the fourth/tenth century onward, the Persian language began to develop rapidly in both poetry and prose, and from that early period scientific and philosophical works appeared in Persian which laid the foundation for the more lucid and successful Persian philosophical texts of subsequent centuries.

The earliest prose works of the Persian language, which belong to the fourth/tenth century, deal with either religious subjects, especially commentaries upon the Quran and Sufism, or with those branches of the intellectual sciences which are only partly related to Islamic philosophy. Such early prose works in Persian as *Kitāb al-mu'ālajāt al-buqrāṭiyyah* of Aḥmad ibn Muḥammad Ṭabarī, the physician of Rukn al-Dawlah the Dailamite, and the *Hidāyat al-muta'allimīn fi'l-ṭibb* of Abū Bakr Ajwīnī Bukhārī, one of the students of Muḥammad ibn Zakariyyā' Rāzī[3] deal with medicine but contain sections that belong also to natural philosophy. From another angle, some Sufi works of the same period, such as the *Nūr al-'ilm* of Abu'l-Ḥasan Kharraqānī, are also concerned with certain metaphysical themes closely related to *falsafah*.[4]

At the end of the fourth/tenth and the beginning of the fifth/eleventh century Persian philosophical works properly speaking began to appear. The Ismā'īlīs, whose intellectual center continued to be Persia even when the focus of their political activity became Egypt, produced some of the earliest philosophical works of the Persian language. The commentary of Abū Sa'd Muḥammad ibn Surkh Nayshāpūrī upon the philosophical poem (*qaṣīdah*) of Abu'l-Haytham[5] and the Persian version of the *Kashf al-maḥjūb* of Abū Ya'qūb Isḥāq Sijistānī[6] belong to these early years. Shortly after this period Nāṣir-i Khusraw, that most neglected theologian and philosopher, wrote all of his philosophical works in Persian. His *Jāmi' al-ḥikmatayn, Zād al-musāfirīn, Wajh-i dīn, Safar-nāmah, Khān al-ikhwān* and *Gushāyish wa rahāyish* represent, along with Ḥamīd al-Dīn Kirmānī's masterpiece in Arabic *Rāḥat-al'aql,* the peak of development of Ismā'īlī philosophy of the Fatimid school.[7]

During this same period there also appeared the first Persian works of the Peripatetic school, initiated by Ibn Sīnā's epoch-making *Dānish-nāma-yi 'alā'ī*, which is the first systematic work of Peripatetic philosophy in Persian.[8] Although it did not succeed in establishing the Persian language immediately as an instrument for the expression of *mashshā'ī* philosophy, because some of its technical expressions remained somewhat forced, this work marks the beginning of a process which reached its peak two centuries later with Suhrawardī and Ṭūsī. The *Dānish-nāmah* is important not only as a document in the history of the Persian language but also as revealing certain aspects of Ibn Sīnā's thought not to be discovered so easily in his Arabic Peripatetic works. Chief among these is the very manner of discussing the question of being, since in Arabic there is no copula between the subject and the predicate while in Persian such a copula does exist. Moreover, the very possibility of using the word for being in Persian (*hastī*), in addition to the Arabic *wujūd* and *mawjūd*, made it possible for Ibn Sīnā to be fully aware of the important distinction between being as a state and being as an act. Later Persian philosophers were also to draw advantage from this possibility; for example, we observe Mullā Ṣadrā referring to *hastī* even in the middle of an Arabic work to make fully clear the basic difference between the state and the act of being.[9] This important development in ontology in Islamic philosophy and its relation to problems of semantics must be traced back to a large extent to the *Dānish-nāmah* and the attempt made by Ibn Sīnā to discuss ontology in two languages which possess a completely different grammatical structure.

A series of Persian works appeared during Ibn Sīnā's lifetime or shortly thereafter which are attributed to him but which most probably are translations of his Arabic works by his immediate disciples and the followers of his school. This collection includes such treatises as the

Ẓafar-nāmah, Ḥikmat al-mawt, Risāla-yi nafs, al-Mabda' wa'l-ma'ād, al-Ma'ād, Ithbāt al-nubuwwah, Risālah dar aqsām-i nufūs, Risāla-yi iksīr, Qurāḍa-yi ṭabī'iyyāt, Risālah dar ḥaqīqat wa kayfiyyat-i silsila-yi mawjūdāt wa tasalsul-i asbāb wa musabbabāt, 'Ilm-i pīshīn wa barīn, Risāla-yi 'ishq, Risālah dar manṭiq,[10] the Persian translation of *al-Ishārāt wa'l-tanbīhāt*[11] and the Persian translation and commentary upon *Ḥayy ibn Yaqẓān.*[12] The sudden appearance of all these works belonging to the school of Ibn Sīnā in Persian was certainly instrumental in spreading the influence of the master of Muslim Peripatetic philosophy in Persia beyond the circle of traditional philosophers, who also knew Arabic, to a wider audience embracing nearly all classes of men interested in learning and at the same time familiar with the Persian language.

The Seljuq era was a golden age for Persian prose. During the period there appeared the great Persian prose masterpieces of Sufism such as the *Kashf al-maḥjūb* of Hujwīrī, the *Asrār al-tawḥīd* of Abū Sa'īd, the works of Khwājah 'Abdallāh Anṣārī, the Persian translation of the *Risālat al-qushayriyyah* and the monumental esoteric and gnostic commentary upon the Quran, the *Kashf al-asrār of* Mībudī, all important indirectly in the later development of theosophy (*ḥikmah*). As for Sufi works of this period which directly influenced later schools of *ḥikmah*, the writings of Ghazzālī and 'Ayn al-Quḍāt Hamadānī must especially be mentioned. In the West Ghazzālī's Persian works have never received the careful study they deserve. His *Kīmiyā-yi sa'ādat* and *Naṣīḥat al-mulūk*, both in Persian, influenced centuries of Muslims concerned with ethics and politics, while his Persian *Letters* (*Mukātabāt*) contain keys to the solution of many delicate aspects of his thought. Some of his works such as the *Ayyuha'l-walad* are Arabic translations of an original Persian work, in this case the *Farzand-nāmah.* There is even an important Persian work of Ghazzālī on eschatology (*Zād-i ākhirat*) which has remained completely neglected and unedited until now.

As for 'Ayn al-Quḍāt, his *Tamhīdāt, Risāla-yi jamālī* and *Nāmah-hā*, all in Persian,[13] mark an important phase in the development of the intellectual expression of Sufism which found its full perfection in the hands of Ibn 'Arabī and members of his school. This type of writing naturally influenced later schools of Islamic philosophy in most of which gnosis (*'irfān*) was a major constitutive element.

As for philosophy proper, it suffered an eclipse during the Seljuq period and fewer philosophical works were written in either Arabic or Persian at this time than either before or after. Nevertheless, important philosophical works were composed in mature and lucid Persian during this period. Khayyām not only translated the Arabic *Khuṭbat al-gharrā'* of Ibn Sīnā into Persian but also wrote several independent Persian philosophical treatises of which the *Risāla-yi wujūd* is particularly noteworthy.[14] There also appeared cosmological and cosmographical compendia in Persian of philosophical importance of which *Nuzhat-nāma-yi 'alā'ī* of Shāhmardān ibn Abi'l-Khayr and *Kayhān-shinākht* of Qaṭṭān Marwazī may be mentioned.

The most important Persian philosophical corpus of this period belongs not to the Peripatetic school but to the new school of Illumination (*ishrāq*) founded by Suhrawardī.[15] The thirteen Persian treatises by Suhrawardī, the authenticity of two of which had at one time been disputed by some scholars but is now beyond question, are among the most outstanding masterpieces of the Persian language.[16] In a Persian that is at once lucid and extremely rich in symbolic imagery, Suhrawardī wrote works dealing with subjects ranging from logic and natural philosophy to symbolic and mystical recitals. Suhrawardī succeeded not only in opening a new intellectual dimension in Islam but also in developing the possibilities of the Persian language for the expression of a whole range of subjects from the most rigorous debates of logic and metaphysics to the most poetic descriptions of the spiritual transmutation of the human soul. Like *ishrāqī* theosophy itself, which is a bridge between the world of logic and the ecstasy of spiritual union, the Persian language developed by Suhrawardī became a most powerful instrument for the expression of all types of philosophical and theosophical ideas contained in the Islamic intellectual tradition ranging from the logical to the purely esoteric and gnostic.

Suhrawardī's schoolmate in Ispahan, Fakhr al-Dīn Rāzī was, like Ghazzālī, a theologian opposed to *falsafah,* but also like Ghazzālī and perhaps even more than he, he became deeply influential in the later development of Islamic philosophy. Rāzī wrote several treatises in Persian such as the *Jami' al-'ulūm*, which is a compendium of the sciences, *Risālah dar uṣūl-i 'aqā'id* on the principles of religion and *Risālat al-kamāliyyah* on *Kalām.* His works are typical of a tendency at this time to write not only philosophy but also *Kalām* in Persian, a tendency that was to continue strongly during later centuries when Shi'ite *Kalām* entered the scene and gradually replaced the Ash'arite school in Persia.

A major corpus of prime importance for Persian philosophical prose that appeared just at the end of the sixth/twelfth and beginning of the seventh/thirteen centuries is the treatises of Afḍal al-Dīn Kāshānī, known popularly as Bābā Afḍal, who was both a *ḥakīm* and a Sufi. He was a relative of Naṣīr al-Dīn and influenced the philosophers who came after the Mongol invasion in more than one way. Afḍal al-Dīn is the author of thirteen treatises along with several letters and answers to various questions, in Persian of a very high quality.[17] The treatises combine views of the Peripatetic school with those of Sufism and Hermeticism and are characteristic of the later development of Islamic philosophy in Persia in which different schools were gradually synthesized. The writings of Bābā Afḍal, along with those of Suhrawardī, represent the summit of philosophical prose in Persian in which intellectual discourse of the highest order is expressed in a language of the greatest clarity and beauty.

With the coming of the Mongols and throughout the Timurid period, a large number of works on philosophy continued to appear in Persian. The central figure in the revival of the intellectual sciences after the Mongol invasion, Khwājah Naṣīr al-Dīn Ṭūsī, wrote numerous philosophical works in Persian such as *Aqsām al-ḥikmah, Baqā'-i nafs, Jabr wa ikhtiyār, Rabṭ al-ḥādith bi'l-qadīm, al-'Ilm al-iktisābī,* as well as two important ethical works, the well-known *Akhlāq-i nāṣirī*[18] and the less well-known *Akhlāq-i muḥtashimī*.[19] His student and collaborator, Quṭb al-Dīn Shīrāzī, is the author of *Durrat al-tāj,* the most voluminous compendium of Peripatetic philosophy in Persian.[20] Of course important works were also written in Arabic by both Naṣīr al-Dīn and Quṭb al-Dīn as well as other members of their school such as Dabīrān Kātibī Qazwīnī, author of *Ḥikmat al-'ayn,* and Athīr al-Dīn Abharī, who wrote the famous classic *Kitāb al-hidāyah* which became a standard text for the study of philosophy for many centuries. But Persian texts of high literary and doctrinal quality appeared parallel with the Arabic texts and are characteristic of the school of Naṣīr al-Dīn.

From the seventh/thirteenth to the tenth/sixteenth centuries, during the least known period of the development of Islamic philosophy in Persia, important works continued to appear in Persian, only a small part of which has been studied so far. A significant landmark of this period is the treatises of Ṣā'in al-Dīn ibn Turkah who lived in the eighth/fourteenth century and who wrote nearly forty treatises in Persian which foreshadow the final synthesis between the *mashshā'ī, ishrāqī* and *'irfānī* schools achieved by Ṣadr al-Dīn Shīrāzī in the tenth/sixteenth century.[21] These treatises have been neglected until now even in Persia itself and only after their edition and publication, which is under way, will they gain the popularity they deserve among an audience that is more extensive than the few who are acquainted with manuscript material in this field.

A second important corpus of works of this period in Persian is the writings of Jalāl al-Dīn Dawānī who of course like Ibn Turkah, Quṭb al-Dīn, and Suhrawardī also wrote in Arabic. Of his Persian works the *Akhlāq-i jalālī,* modeled upon the *Akhlāq-i nāṣirī* is well known in the West mostly because of its popularity in India and its translation into English during the past century. But he also wrote a number of works in Persian dealing with *Kalām* and Sufism as well as philosophy.[22] His writings, like those of Ibn Turkah, display the tendency to synthesize the different schools of Islam, in his case mostly *Kalām* and philosophy.

Strangely enough with the advent of the Safavids, which marked the establishment of a national state in Persia, the use of the Persian language in the intellectual sciences diminished rather than increased. Mīr Dāmād, the founder of the "School of Ispahan"[23] wrote only one philosophical work in Persian, the *Jadhawāt*, although he composed some fine Persian poetry. The greatest *ḥakīm* of this age, Ṣadr al-Dīn Shīrāzī, also wrote only one major work in Persian, the *Si aṣl,*[24] the rest of his numerous doctrinal treatises being in Arabic. Only among the later Safavid figures such as Mullā Muḥsin Fayḍ Kāshānī, the author of *Kalimāt-i maknūnah*, 'Abd al- Razzāq Lāhījī, the author of *Gawhar-murād,* and Qāḍī Sa'īd. Qummī, the author of *Kalīd-i bihisht* do we find again a greater interest in writing in Persian although even in these cases most of their works were in Arabic. Kāshānī and Lāhījī, however, were also important poets of the Persian language and in fact expressed much of their metaphysical teaching in didactic poetry. Altogether during the Safavid period the Indian subcontinent was perhaps the most active arena for Persian prose in the field of the intellectual sciences, while in Persia itself there was a definite decrease in the usage of philosophical and scientific Persian in comparison with the periods either before or after.

During the Qajar period there was a marked renaissance of Persian prose and a return to writing philosophical works in Persian although Arabic remained the main language of the traditional sciences. During the Qajar period, especially from the time of Nāṣir al-Dīn Shah when Tehran became the center for the study of traditional philosophy, a movement began to translate major works of the Islamic sciences, and particularly philosophy, into Persian. Several works of Mullā Ṣadrā for example were translated from Arabic at this time[25] in a movement that resembles somewhat the work of the fifth/eleventh and sixth/twelfth centuries to translate Ibn Sīnā and other masters into Persian. Parallel with this movement, many of the outstanding *ḥakīms* of the day wrote major works in Persian. Ḥājjī Mullā Hādī Sabziwārī, the best known figure of his day in *ḥikmah*, wrote one of his major works, the *Asrār al-ḥikam* in Persian[26] and also composed several independent treatises on *ḥikmah* in that language.[27] Mullā 'Abdallāh Zunūzī wrote two major treatises mostly on eschatology entitled *Lama'āt-i ilāhiyyah* and *Anwār-i jaliyyah* in Persian,[28] while his son, Mullā 'Alī Zunūzī, who was perhaps the most original *ḥakīm* of his day, wrote all of his works, of which the *Badāyi' al-ḥikam* is the best known, in Persian. This tendency continued into the Pahlavi period among traditional *ḥakīms* as can be observed in the writings of such masters as Sayyid Muḥammad Kāẓim 'Aṣṣār, Sayyid Abu'l Ḥasan Rafī'ī Qazwīnī and 'Allāmah Ṭabāṭabā'ī, all of whom write in both Arabic and Persian.

The vast majority of Persian philosophical texts written in Persia itself as well as in the subcontinent and Turkey remain unedited and have been only rarely studied. The few works mentioned here are only the summits of a few mountain peaks. The rest of the range remains hidden beneath clouds which only careful and patient scholarship can gradually disperse until the complete anatomy of the range becomes visible. Practically every library catalogued recently in Persia has revealed important manuscripts in this field that had not been known before. These texts invite the talents of scholars who must perform the often thankless task of editing these works so as to make them available to a larger audience.

The vast body of philosophical and theosophical works in Persian is an integral part of the Islamic intellectual heritage without a knowledge of which many chapters of the history of Islamic philosophy and the sciences will remain completely obscure. Moreover, this body is of the utmost significance for the present-day intellectual life of Persia, Afghanistan, and even Tajikistan and the Muslims of the subcontinent because it is these works—more than those in Arabic read by fewer people in these lands today—that can influence the direction of thought and life of the Muslims of these areas in the future. The rich intellectual heritage of Islam, which alone can provide the necessary weapons to combat the deadly influences of secularism and modernism, is naturally most easily accessible to the Persian-speaking world through works written in its own language. For the general public with a modern education in these lands whose knowledge of classical Arabic has unfortunately become limited, these texts provide the most direct avenue of access to that "paradise of wisdom" which came into being in the bosom of Islam and which is a most precious heritage for all Muslims. As for scholars and specialists in the field of Islamic philosophy, this Persian corpus is a necessary supplement to the basic Arabic works. Without it the vast panorama of the Islamic intellectual sciences cannot be completely seen, a panorama which was destined to be depicted mostly in Arabic but also to a significant degree in Persian, although many ethnic groups contributed to its execution.

NOTES

1. Even in Persia itself the traditional courses on Islamic philosophy are taught to this day from Arabic texts which are usually read by the master and then commented upon in Persian. That is why the major effort to publish texts of Islamic traditional sciences including philosophy (which we use throughout this paper in its traditional Islamic sense of *ḥikmah* and not in its profane meaning) in lithographed editions during the past century in Persia was concerned for the most part with Arabic texts and only a few Persian texts appeared at that time. Only during the present generation, with the decrease in knowledge of Arabic among people with modern education, has the importance of Persian texts in keeping Islamic philosophy alive for these classes become fully realized and an effort begun during the past few years to edit the Persian texts. See S.H. Nasr, "Islamic Philosophy in Contemporary Persia; A Survey of Activity During the Past Two Decades," Middle East Center, University of Utah, Monograph, 1971; also Part VI of this volume.
2. The systematic catalogues of different Persian libraries that have appeared during the past few years under the care of such men as M.T. Danechpazhuh, A.N. Monzavi, Ibn Yūsuf, 'A. H. Ḥā'irī, Ṣ'A. Anwār, A Gulchīn Ma'ānī, have brought to light many important manuscripts. See A. Monzavi, *A Catalogue of Persian Manuscripts,* 3 vols. (Tehran: Regional Cultural Institute, 1969-70); and the pioneering work of C. A. Storey, *Persian Literature, A Bio-Bibliographical Survey, 1927-58.*
3. Edited by Jalāl Matīnī, who is a specialist in 4th/10th and 5th/11th century Persian prose, Mashhad, 1344 (A. H. Solar).
4. In his *Tārīkh-i adabiyyāt dar Īrān,* 3 vols., Tehran, 1342 on, Dr. Ṣafā has listed many of the philosophical, scientific, theological and Sufi works in Persian up to the Mongol invasion.
5. H. Corbin, ed., *Commentaire de la Qasida Ismaélienne d'Abu'l Haitham Jorjani* (Tehran-Paris, 1955).
6. H. Corbin and M. Mo'in, eds. *Kashf al-Mahjub* (Tehran-Paris, 1949).
7. For a history of this much too neglected school see S. H. Nasr, "Philosophy," in *Cambridge History of Iran,* vol. 4, ed. R.N. Frye 1975 and H. Corbin (with the collaboration of S.H. Nasr and O. Yahya), *Histoire de la philosophie islamique,* vol., 1 , Paris, 1964, pp. 110 ff.
8. The metaphysics and natural philosophy of this work were edited by A. Khurāsānī, Tehran, 1315; and S.M. Mishkāt, Tehran, 1331; and M. Mo'īn, Tehran 1331 (A. H. solar).
9. See the introduction of H. Corbin to Mullā Ṣadrā, *Kitāb al-mashā'ir (Le Livre des pénétrations métaphysiques),* Tehran-Paris, 1964.
10. Most of these works were published by Anjumān-i Athār-i Millī in Tehran on the occasion of Ibn Sīnā's millennary celebrations, the majority edited by Ghulām Ḥusayn

Ṣadīqī. See S.H. Nasr, *An Introduction to Islamic Cosmological Doctrines,* Cambridge, 1964. pp. 296-97.

11. Edited by E. Yarshater, Tehran, 1333 (A.H. solar).
12. H. Corbin, ed. and trans, *Avicenne et le récit visionnaire,* vol. 2 Tehran-Paris, 1954.
13. See 'A. 'Uṣayrān's edition of 'Ayn al-Quḍāt, *Tamhīdāt,* Tehran 1341 (A.H. solar); and 'A. Monzavi and 'A. 'Uṣayrān's edition of his *Nāma-hā*, Tehran, 1348 (A.H. solar).
14. See the *Rasā'il* of Khayyām, ed. by M. Awistā, Tehran 1338 (A.H. solar), and *Kulliyyāt-i āthār-i fārsī-yi Ḥakīm 'Umar-i Khayyām*, ed. by M. 'Abbāsī, Tehran, 1338 (A.H. solar).
15. On the significance of this corpus see S.H. Nasr, "The Persian Works of Shaykh al-Ishrāq Shihāb al-Dīn Suhrawardī", chapter 13 of this volume.
16. We have edited this complete corpus as *Les Oeuvres persanes de Sohrawardī,* Tehran-Paris, 1970.
17. Edited by M. Minovi and Y. Mahdavi as *Muṣannafāt*, 2 vols., Tehran, 1331-37.
18. This best known of Muslim works on philosophical ethics has been a main text in the educational curriculum of generations of Persian and Muslims of the subcontinent. See G.M. Wickens, trans., *Nasirean Ethics,* London, 1964.
19. Edited by M.T. Danechpazhuh, Tehran, 1339.
20. Most of this vast work was edited by S.M. Mishkāt, Tehran, 1317-20.
21. These treatises have been edited for the first time by Ṣ 'A. Mūsawī Bihbahānī and I. Dībājī and are being printed by the Tehran University Press.
22. Most of these were edited by I. Wā'iẓ Jawādī in different numbers of the bulletin *Taḥqīq dar mabda'-i āfarīnish*. He is now planning a complete edition of Dawānī's Persian works in a single volume.
23. See S.H. Nasr, "The School of Ispahan", in *A History of Muslim Philosophy*, ed. M.M. Sharif vol. 2, Wiesbaden, 1966, pp. 904 ff.
24. Edited by S.H. Nasr, Tehran, 1340.
25. See for example the translation of Mullā Ṣadrā's *Mashā'ir* by Badī' al-Mulk, edited by H. Corbin in *Le Livre des pénétrations métaphysiques* (*Kitāb al-mashā'ir*).
26. Edited by A. Sha'rānī, Tehran, 1380 (A.H. lunar).
27. Edited by S.J. Āshtiyānī, *Rasā'il* (Persian and Arabic), Mashhad, 1970.
28. Currently being edited by S.J. Āshtiyānī.

PART II

EARLY ISLAMIC PHILOSOPHY

5

Why Was al-Fārābī Called The Second Teacher?*

> Poi ch' innalzai un poco più le ciglia,
> Vidi' l maestro di color che sanno,
> Seder tra filosofica famiglia.
>
> When I looked up, I saw that the
> 'teacher' of those who 'know' is
> sitting amongst the children which
> philosophy has created.
>
> (Dante, *The Divine Comedy*)[1]

For centuries in the East as well as the West, Aristotle has been referred to as the 'First Teacher' (*al-Mu'allim al-Awwal*), and al-Fārābī the 'Second Teacher' (*al-Mu'allim al-Thānī*).[2] In Islamic literature also from the 10th and 11th centuries onwards, al-Fārābī was regularly referred to as the 'Second Teacher' and Aristotle the 'First Teacher'.[3] These titles have gained such fame that often the meaning of the term 'teachers' in these instances is not questioned. Why is it that in both cases the teachers of these 'teachers', who were founders of philosophical schools before them, or such learned men as Pythagoras and Plato on one hand, and al-Kindī on the other hand, were never called 'teachers'? In our view the meaning of the term 'teacher' that has been used in referring to Aristotle and al-Fārābī by Muslims is so profound, and its significance for the contemporary world so fundamental, that it is worth delving into this matter to see why al-Fārābī was called the 'Second Teacher' and Aristotle the 'First'.

To begin with, it is necessary to mention that the title of 'teacher' was given to Aristotle by the Muslims and not by the Greeks, and that the use

* This essay was originally written in Persian and published in the journal of *Adabiyyāt wa 'ulūm-i insānī*, Year 22, No. 2, 1975, pp. 14-19. This essay was translated by Mehdi Aminrazavi into English and published as "Why Was Fārābī Called the Second Teacher", *Islamic Culture*, Vol. 59, No. 4, Oct. 1985, pp. 357-64.

of this title, particularly by the Western philosophers (as it appears in the famous poem of Dante at the beginning of this article), is due to the influence of the Islamic intellectual tradition upon the West. The title of 'teacher' in this particular context is directly related to the Islamic view of science and knowledge, whose origin cannot be attributed to Greek sources. When one looks at the Islamic sources, both old and new, it can be seen that there are different accounts as to the meaning of the word 'teacher', and reasons why al-Fārābī has been referred to as the 'Second Teacher' have been offered. These references may be summarized and divided into four categories:

1. There are those who say that since al-Fārābī was the most learned philosopher after Aristotle, and since he was a great commentator of the 'First Teacher', he was called the 'Second Teacher'. Among the advocates of this view, one can name Muḥammad Luṭfī Jum'ah, the contemporary Egyptian writer, and the Dutch scholar T. J. de Boer.[4] The main objection to this theory is that its advocates do not explain why Aristotle himself was called the 'First Teacher'. Also, if the criteria for granting of this title was that one must be a commentator or have a distinguished position in philosophy, then why was Ibn Rushd the greatest Muslim commentator of Aristotle in history, or Ibn Sīnā, the most distinguished Peripatetic philosopher in history, not called the 'Second Teacher'?

2. A number of scholars, from earlier generations and contemporary alike, consider the granting of this title to al-Fārābī to be because of his mastery of logic. They even claim that Aristotle's title as the 'First Teacher' is due to his success in the discovery of formal logic. In his famous *Prolegomena to the Study of History,* Ibn Khaldūn has referred to this view. He states:

> The leading representative of these doctrines, who presented the problem connected with them, wrote books on them as (the subject of) a systematic science, and penned the arguments in favour of them as far as we presently know was Aristotle of Macedonia, from Macedonia in Byzantine territory, a pupil of Plato and the teacher of Alexander. He is called "the first Teacher", with no further qualification. It means "teacher of Logic", because logic did not exist in an improved form before Aristotle. He was the first to systematize the norms of logic and to deal with all its problems and give a good and extensive treatment of it. He would, in fact, have done very well with his norm of logic if (only) it had absolved him of responsibility for philosophical tendencies that concern metaphysics.[5]

Among contemporary scholars this view is also common.

Ibrahim Madkour, one of the foremost authorities on al-Fārābī's philosophy, has frequently sugested that generally the title of 'teacher' is related to the field of logic, because logic is the foundation for the teaching of all sciences.[6] However, this cannot be the only reason since the great masters of logic after al-Fārābī did not attain such a title, and, as will be pointed out, Mīr Dāmād who was not specially known as a logician came to be known as the 'Third Teacher'.

3. There are those scholars, such as al-Najjār, who maintain that al-Fārābī's title can be attributed to his success in establishing a new school of philosophy [7] and they even consider him to be the first Muslim philosopher. The significance of al-Fārābī in the history of Islamic philosophy and his contributions to Peripatetic philosophy in its historical context are obvious. This fact by itself is not, however, sufficient for calling him the 'Second Teacher' since there have been other eminent figures, such as Suhrawardī, who have founded philosophical schools, and since al-Kindī, prior to al-Fārābī, founded Islamic philosophy as we know it, yet, such figures were not called *mu'allim.* Therefore, neither being in the forefront of a philosophical school, nor the cause for the establishment of a philosophical school can be the only reasons for al-Fārābī having been given the title of 'Second Teacher'.

4. Finally, one has to speak of the theory that is set forth by some historians and writers, such as Ḥajjī Khalīfah, [8] a theory which has been accepted by certain contemporary scholars such as Zia Ülken[9] and Muḥammad 'Alī Mutarjim Tabrīzī, the author of *Rayḥānat al-adab.*[10] They believe that because al-Fārābī has commented upon and corrected the texts of Aristotle's works, calling his own work the 'second teaching', he has been called the 'Second Teacher'. Undoubtedly this view is not to be dismissed and is worthy of serious consideration. However, it can be asked, why were the writings of Aristotle called the 'first teaching' and himself the 'First Teacher'? Furthermore, why was Mīr Dāmād called the 'Third Teacher' whereas he produced no 'third teaching'? Because of these questions, we conclude that this theory is also not satisfactory or convincing.

Having discussed the views of many previous and contemporary scholars, we may now consider a definition that is accepted by many of the great contemporary traditional scholars of Iran. According to this definition, the term 'teacher' in this particular context refers to a person who, in fact, determines the limits and boundaries of the sciences and the methods and means of attaining knowledge, and who also classifies them in such a manner that the unity of the various branches is preserved.[11] The preservation of this unity is crucial because of its relation to the concept of unity in Islam. The branches of the sciences in Islam are interrelated like the branches of a tree all of which are connected to its trunk which in the case of the Islamic sciences is the Quranic revelation. By looking at Aristotle's and al-Fārābī's role in the classification of the sciences and the various scientific methodologies in the Greek and Islamic traditions, respectively, the validity of this view becomes even more apparent.

Aristotle was not the first Greek philosopher or scientist, but he was the first to formulate and apply a scientific methodology based on his logic. He also began to classify the sciences and created unity amongst the various branches of the sciences. In the case of Islam al-Kindī and his students began to write logical treatises before al-Fārābī, and al-Kindī himself wrote an important treatise on the classification of the sciences called *On the Types of Sciences (Fī aqsām al-'ulūm)*;[12] yet it was soon forgotten. Such attempts were of an exploratory nature and were not as yet in such a state as to influence Islamic civilization widely. This, however, was not the case with al-Fārābī. As the distinguished contemporary scholar on al-Fārābī, Muhsin Mahdi, has indicated on numerous occasions, al-Fārābī was in fact the 'father of logic' in Islam. It is in the light of the meaning of logic in the Islamic sciences that he should be viewed as the founder of a systematically formulated methodological approach to the sciences. Al-Fārābī is also the author of the well-known book on the classification of the sciences called *Fī īḥṣā' al-'ulūm* that became famous not only in the Islamic world but also in the West, and was influential in the development of curriculums in Western universities.[13] This book marked the beginning of the efforts of a large group of Muslim thinkers to organize and classify the sciences and subsequently to create harmony between 'reason' and 'faith', or philosophy and religion. These attempts were later followed by such well-known figures as Ibn Sīnā. Ikhwān al-Ṣafā' (who were the authors of the well-known treatises known as the *Rasā'il*), Khwājah Naṣīr al-Dīn Ṭūsī, and finally Mullā Ṣadrā. As can be seen, the particular significance of this work amongst other writings of al-Fārābī is evident as some of the oldest historical sources and the works of many eminent Muslim scholars of the present day testify.[14]

Whether one studies the works of al-Fārābī on logic, which are the foundation of science and serve as the introduction to sciences in Islamic civilization, or his book *Fī īḥṣā' al-'ūlūm,* one sees that both are concerned with the verification and definition of various modes of 'knowing', the relation between the sciences which originate from these modes of 'knowing', and the relation of these sciences with different aspects of Islamic thought.

With respect to the unique spirit that dominates over Islamic civilization and thought, which sees all their aspects in reference to the fundamental principle of unity, and which seeks to express and manifest this principle in various facets of human life,[15] it is obvious that what al-Fārābī did in Islam, as Aristotle had done before him in Greece, was so fundamental from an Islamic view that it became necessary to refer to each of these figures by a special title. Aristotle, therefore, from an Islamic perspective, was called the 'First Teacher' and this title then went beyond the borders of Islamic civilization to the West.

The later history of Islam confirms this view since no one received the title of 'teacher' although sciences were expanding in an astonishing manner up to the Mongol and even the Safavid periods. When, for the first time, Twelve-Imam Shi'ism became a dominant force in Persia, a new chapter was opened in the history of Islam.

In this new situation, and in the light of the new Shi 'ite religious unity, Mīr Muḥammad Dāmād was able to revive and reorganize the philosophical and intellectual sciences by establishing the 'School of Isfahan'. It was as a result of this achievement that he received the title of 'teacher', and was called the 'Third Teacher' (*al-Mu'allim al-Thālith*) and not as a result of his being a great philosopher. In his works he refers to Ibn Sīnā as the 'partner in mastery', while he calls al-Fārābī the 'partner in education'.

The commemoration of al-Fārābī throughout the world in general, and in Iran in particular,[16] provides an opportunity to view him as an example for model contemporary Muslim thinkers. Al-Fārābī lived during a time when, as a result of numerous translations made from various languages and drawn from different cultures, Islamic civilization had come to confront new and different sciences, methodologies and philosophies. He took a fundamental step to bring order to the sciences and create harmony between these sciences and various aspects of Islamic intellectual life as well as the religion itself. By unifying these sciences and relating them to each other as well as to the whole of Islamic thought, he profoundly Islamicized them. Henceforth, they became creative and constructive elements in the citadel of Islam and al-Fārābī was able to prevent the eruption of intellectual chaos and anarchy.

Today, with the dominance of Western sciences within the cultural and geographical borders of Muslim nations, any Muslim who is concerned about the future of his cultural heritage faces a duty similar to that of al-Fārābī. The thinkers of this age, especially those belonging to non-Western cultures, have the responsibility of creating harmony between the branches of the sciences, and also between the sciences and their particular traditions. It is for this reason that al-Fārābī's thought together with his methodological approach is particularly significant for the contemporary generation. The 'Second Teacher' is a thinker whose spirit is alive, and the presence of his influence can still be felt. It might in fact be said that the world of Islam requires more than any thing else a 'Fourth Teacher', [17] who can guide the Islamic world through the maze of intellectual chaos of the contemporary world and to criticize, appraise and finally integrate what is intellectually legitimate in the modern sciences into the Islamic intellectual universe.

It is hoped that the commemoration of the anniversary of the 'Second Teacher' would make this need obvious, and that the necessity of unifying the sciences would become apparent. May the exposition of al-Fārābī's thought and his example help to bring about the appearance of the 'Fourth Teacher'.

NOTES

1. *La Commedia di Dante Alighieri,* Inferno, Canto IV, 129-131 Cambridge, Harvard University Press, 1972, pp. 42-43.
2. In the West such figures as St. Thomas Aquinas and Albert the Great have repeatedly referred to Aristotle as *Magister Primus.* Although there have not been many references to al-Fārābī as the 'Second Teacher' in Latin literature, at various places he *has been* referred to as *Magister Secondus.*

   In the Muslim world almost everyone has given al-Fārābī the title of 'Second Teacher' and in this century a distinguished work on Islamic philosophy (written by Shaykh Muṣṭafā 'Abd al-Rāziq, [Cairo, 1939]) which discusses al-Kindī and al-Fārābī's thought refers to them as the 'Philosopher of the Arabs and the Second Teacher' (*al-Faylasūf al-'arab wa 'l-mu'allim al-thānī).*

   In recent years the contemporary scholar' Isā Ṣadīqī, in his book, *The History of Iranian Culture,* Tehran, 1957, p. 126, indicates that Edward Browne, in his book, *The History of Islamic Medicine,* refers to Ibn Sīnā as the 'Second Teacher'. This view is, however, unfounded, and contrary to the intellectual tradition of Islam and numerous references by Muslim authors throughout the centuries.
3. *Tatimmah ṣiwān al-ḥikmah* of Bayhaqī, Lahore, 1935, p. 20 is the first book in which I have been able to trace the title of 'Second Teacher'. There Bayhaqi says, "He is from Faryab of the Turkistan area, known as the 'Second Teacher' and the distinguished scholars of Islam have called him by that name."
4. "The title of the 'Second Teacher' refers to the highest of *ḥakīms* after Aristotle, whose name was the 'First Teacher'', Muḥammad Luṭfī al-Jum'ah, *History of Islamic Philosophy in the East and the West,* Cairo, 1966, p. 19. "...but his natural powers were applied to the study of Aristotle's writings for which reason the name given him by the East was the 'Second Teacher', that is (the second Aristotle)." T.J. de Boer, *The History of Philosophy in Islam,* translated by E.A. Jones (London, 1933), p. 109.

5. Ibn Khaldūn, *An Introduction to History (the Muqaddimah),* translated from Arabic by Franz Rosenthal, New York, Bollingen, 1958, vol. 3, p. 249.
6. 'He surpassed his teacher [Abū Bishr Matta ibn Yūnus] and, on account of the eminent position he had gained in this field [logic], he came to be called the "Second Teacher". M.M. Sharif (ed.), *A History of Muslim Philosophy,* vol. 1, Wiesbaden, 1963, p. 451.
7. F.M.J. Najjār says, "Al-Farabi was the first Muslim philosopher to head a school and to become known as a teacher." R. Lerner and Mahdi (eds.), *Medieval Political Philosophy, A Source Book,* Glencoe, 1963, p. 22.
8. Ḥājjī Khalīfah, *Kashf al-Ẓunūn,* Leipzig, 1941, vol. 3, p. 999.
9. Ibn Abī Uṣaybi'ah in his book on the biography of Ibn Sīnā refers to a monumental work of al-Fārābī called "The Second Teaching" (*al-Ta'līm al-thānī*). For more information, see H.Z. Ülken, *La Pensé de l'Islam,* trans. G. Duboiset et l'auteur, Istanbul, 1953, p. 381.
10. The title of 'Second Teacher' for al-Fārābī came after Manṣūr ibn Nūḥ al-Sāmānī assigned him to complete and correct the translations of Aristotle's books, and he called his works the 'second teaching'. It was for this reason that he came to be known as the 'Second Teacher'.
11. This view was expressed in the teaching sessions of two of the greatest contemporary *ḥakīms* of Iran, Sayyid Abu' l-Ḥasan Qazwinī and Sayyid Muḥammad Kāẓim 'Aṣṣār, both of whom passed away recently.
12. This important work which was later influenced by al-Fārābī's work made no impact upon the main fields of Islamic scholarship. For more information, see L. Gardet, "Le Problème de la Philosophie Musulmane", in *Mélanges offerts à Etienne Gilson,* Paris, 1959, pp. 261-84.
13. This book under the title of *De Scientiis* was translated into Latin by Domincus Gundisalvi and has influenced such Western thinkers as Peter of Albano. For more information, see M. Alonso, "Traducciones del Domingo Gundisalvo", *al-Andalus,* vol. 12, 1947, p. 298.
14. Ibn Abī Uṣaybi' ah, in his book, *'Uyūn al-anbā',* admires *Fī iḥṣā' al-'ulūm,* and Ibn al-Qifṭī, in his book, *History of the Scientists (Ta'rīkh al-ḥukamā'),* states that this famous book *Fī iḥṣā' al-'ulūm* is on the subject of defining the purposes and that no one prior to him had written or discussed them. Students of the sciences were never without need of it and were guided by it.
15. S.H. Nasr, *Science and Civilization in Islam* (Cambridge, U.S.A., 1968), Introduction.
16. This article constitutes the text of a paper delivered at a conference held in Tehran in 1973 on the occasion of the celebration of the 1000th year commemoration of al-Fārābī (translator).
17. H. Corbin in his works has already referred to the need for a 'Fourth Teacher' and its significance in Islamic thought for the contemporary Islamic world.

6

Ibn Sīnā: A General Survey*

IBN SĪNĀ (Abū 'Alī al-Ḥusayn ibn 'Abdallāh ibn Sīnā, 980-1037), Islamic philosopher, scientist, and physician, known in the West as Avicenna and in the East sometimes as Bū 'Alī (the son of 'Alī) and also as al-Shaykh al-Ra'īs (the foremost among the wise).

Ibn Sīnā was born in the Persian city of Bukhara into an Ismaili family devoted to learning. He exhibited incredible precocity and at an early age mastered the Quran and the religious sciences. By the age of sixteen he was already known as a physician and in that capacity gained access to the royal Samanid library after successfully treating Nūḥ ibn Manṣūr, the Samanid prince. Intense study in this exceptionally wealthy library enabled Ibn Sīnā to master the other sciences, including metaphysics, so that at the end of his life he could mention in his autobiography that he knew no more then than he did at the age of eighteen. He is without doubt the most important self-taught master in Islamic philosophy and medicine, where regular transmission from teacher to student is strongly emphasized.

By the age of twenty-one, Ibn Sīnā had already become a widely known physician and scholar whose services were sought near and far by princes and kings, including Maḥmūd of Ghazna, who captured Bukhara at that time. But Ibn Sīnā had a particular dislike for this famous conqueror, and so departed from his native city to spend the rest of his tumultuous life in various cities of Persia at a time when, as a result of the Turkish migrations, local uprisings, and struggles between local rulers and the central caliphate, Persia and adjacent lands were experiencing a period of continuous disturbance. The physically strong Ibn Sīnā crossed the forbidding desert from Bukhara to the Caspian Sea on foot and survived the arduous journey while his companions perished.

* This essay originally appeared in the *Dictionary of the Middle Ages,* Vol. 2, Collier Macmillan Canada Press, New York 1988, pp. 302-07.

From this exodus onward Ibn Sīnā's life was marked by traveling from one city to another to act as either court physician or, occasionally, government clerk. He traveled for a while in Khorasan, then went to Rayy to one of the Buyid courts, and from there to nearby Qazwin. But neither of these cities provided the necessary support to enable him to have the peaceful scholarly life he was seeking. Therefore, he accepted the invitation of another Buyid prince, Shams al-Dawlah, to go to Hamadan in western Persia. There he gained the favor of the ruler, becoming the prime court physician and even vizier, as a result of which he had to face political intrigues and was once imprisoned.

In 1022, after the death of Shams al-Dawlah and great difficulties that followed for him, Ibn Sīnā left Hamadan and went to Isfahan, where he enjoyed the longest period of tranquillity in his mature life, a period of fourteen years. During this time, in addition to being court physician, he taught regularly at a school that still stands in the old city of Isfahan and composed most of his books. In 1037, while accompanying the ruler 'Alā' al-Dawlah on a campaign, he fell ill and died shortly thereafter from colic in Hamadan, where his mausoleum, reconstructed in the 1950's, in one of the major historical monuments of Persia to this day.

Because of an incredible power of concentration, which enabled him to dictate even the most difficult works on metaphysics while accompanying a ruler to battle, Ibn Sīnā was able to produce an immense corpus despite the unsettled life he was destined to lead. Up to over 220 works have been mentioned as having been written by him, ranging from the monumental *Kitāb al-shifā'* ("The Book of Healing"), which is the largest encyclopedia of knowledge composed by one person in the medieval period, to treatises of a few pages. These works cover nearly every branch of knowledge, from metaphysics to medicine, in conformity with the integrating and at the same time encyclopedic genius of Ibn Sīnā.

The *Kitāb al-shifā'* consists of four books devoted to logic, natural philosophy (*tabī'iyyāt*), mathematics (*riyāḍiyyāt*), and metaphysics (*ilāhiyyāt*). The *Kitāb al-najāt* ("The Book of Deliverance") is a shorter synopsis of the *Shifā'*, while the *Kitāb al-ishārāt wa'l-tanbīhāt* ("The Book of Directives and Remarks") represents the last major philosophical work of Ibn Sīnā and the most personal statement of his philosophical views. His other important philosophical treatises include the *Kitāb al-hidāyah* ("The Book of Guidance"), *'Uyūn al-ḥikmah* ("Fountains of Wisdom"), *al-Mabda' wa'l-ma'ād* ("The Book of Origin and End"), and the *Dānish-nāma-yi 'ala'i* ("The Book of Knowledge for 'Alā' al-Dawlah"), which is the first work of Peripatetic philosophy in Persian, and the visionary recitals *Ḥayy ibn Yaqẓān ("Living Son of the Awake"),*

Risālat al-ṭayr ("Treatise of the Bird"), and *Salāmān wa Absāl* (Salāmān and Absāl), which comprise a cycle wherein is to be found major elements of his "oriental philosophy". Ibn Sīnā also wrote a number of short treatises on the "hidden sciences" and mystical, theological, and religious subjects, including commentaries on the Quran in which he does not display any specific Ismaili tendencies. It is in fact difficult to judge which interpretation of Islam he followed.

The most important scientific works of Ibn Sīnā are the sections on natural philosophy and mathematics of the *Shifā'* and the *al-Qānūn fi'l-ṭibb* ("The Canon of Medicine"), which is perhaps the most famous work in the history of medicine in both East and West. Composed of five books devoted to the principles of medicine, *materia medica,* "head-to-toe" diseases, diseases that are not confined to a specific organ, and compound drugs, this book served as a veritable bible for medicine in the West practically up to modern times, while it continues to be used in India and the Islamic world to this day. Ibn Sīnā also wrote some forty other medical works, including *al-Urjūzah fi'l-ṭibb* ("Poem on Medicine"), which was used by medical students to memorize the principles of medicine and pharmacology.

Ibn Sīnā wrote important treatises on language, grammar, and phonetics and devoted many pages of the *Shifā'* to the study of politics and sociology. He was also an accomplished poet, and many of his poems dealing with philosophical and medical subjects in Arabic and Persian have survived.

PHILOSOPHICAL PERSPECTIVE

Ibn Sīnā marks the peak of Islamic Peripatetic (*mashshā'ī*) philosophy. He brought to completion and perfection the movement begun by al-Kindī, al-Fārābī, al-'Āmirī, and others to harmonize the philosophies of Aristotle and Neoplatonism in the bosom of the unitary teachings of the Quran and in the world of Abrahamic monotheism as it was reasserted through the Islamic revelation. Ibn Sīnā is without doubt the most universal and all-embracing of these Muslim Peripatetics, much more influential in later Islamic history than Ibn Rushd (Averroës), with whom the "Western" interpretation of this school in Spain reached its culmination a century and a half later. Ibn Sīnā placed the seal of his genius upon a grand synthesis that became a permanent intellectual perspective within the Islamic world. Basing himself in the unitary teachings of Islam, he drew from Aristotelian logic and physics, Neoplatonic metaphysics and psychology, and even certain elements of Stoicism and Hermeticism, and constructed a philosophy that marks the beginning of "medieval philosophy" in the Western sense of the term.

Despite being the greatest of the Muslim Peripatetic philosophers, however, Ibn Sīnā was also attracted to a more esoteric and "gnostic" form of wisdom based on inner illumination and the interiorization of the cosmos in the process of the journey of the soul beyond all cosmic manifestation. In his *Manṭiq al-mashriqiyyīn* ("Logic of the Orientals"), the visionary recitals, and other works, he wrote of that wisdom which was at once illuminative and oriental and which was to receive its full elaboration in the twelfth century by the master of the "School of Illumination" (*ishrāq*), Shihāb al-Dīn Suhrawardī.

LOGIC AND LANGUAGE

Along with al-Fārābī and Ibn Rushd, Ibn Sīnā is the greatest of Muslim logicians and the most systematic among them. When he appeared upon the scene, the older school of Baghdad, in which the study of logic was based on the method of writing commentaries upon the *Organon* of Aristotle, had nearly died out, and the new activity of writing independent manuals on logic had not yet begun. Ibn Sīnā stands alone as the link between these two phases. He systematized the earlier work, especially that of al-Fārābī, but Ibn Sīnā's work was not confined to elaboration and systematization. He pondered over the role of logic as at once the tool of philosophy and a branch of it. He provided a detailed theory of hypothetical and disjunctive syllogisms and discussed articulation with respect to both quality and quantity. He elaborated the theory of singular propositions in a manner resembling the Stoics. He also dealt with the theory of logical definition and classification. These and other features of his logic place him as one of the foremost figures in the development of that discipline in the medieval period.

Ibn Sīnā was also keenly interested in the use of language in relation to logic and to philosophy in general. Not only did he make studies on the origin of language and the relation between a word and its meaning, but he tried to elaborate and elucidate a philosophical vocabulary based on his semantic view. While in Arabic he had to rely on the existing technical vocabulary, which he refined in many instances, in Persian he carried out the much more daring task of seeking to create a whole new vocabulary and language to express *mashshā'ī* philosophy for the first time in his other tongue. The *Dānish-nāmah* is an invaluable document from the point of view of the relation between language and philosophical meaning, and is a most important source for the traditional philosophy of language and semantics.

METAPHYSICS AND COSMOLOGY

Ibn Sīnā has been rightly called the first "philosopher of being", for it was he, rather than the Greek philosophers, who placed the study of being (ontology) at the heart of philosophy. As a result of the influence of the monotheistic revelation, namely Islam, within which he lived and breathed and whose tenets he followed, he considered the study of being to be the heart of that highest science which, since Aristotle, has come to be known as metaphysics. It is true that for Aristotle also the study of being was central, but the meaning of this fundamental concept in the work of the two thinkers is quite different. First of all, the concept of existence does not appear as a definite and clear concept in Greek philosophy as it does in Islamic philosophy, especially with Ibn Sīnā. Secondly, Ibn Sīnā distinguishes between necessity and contingency as a fundamental distinction between Pure Being, which is that of God and is very different from the Aristotelian understanding of being, and the existence of all that is other than Him. God is the Necessary Being (*wājib al-wujūd*), while existents are contingent (*mumkin al-wujūd*) and hence rely in a fundamental way upon the Necessary Being, without which they would be literally nothing. Ibn Sīnā also makes the clear distinction between existence and quiddity, which, along with the distinction between necessity, contingency, and impossibility (*imtinā'*), form the backbone of his ontology. In all creatures, existence is added to their quiddity or essence. Only in the Necessary Being are they the same. The medieval Scholastic discussions about essence and existence were heavily influenced by Ibn Sīnā and other Islamic philosophers. It is enough to compare the Greek, Arabic, and Latin texts to see that what distinguishes medieval philosophy from Greco-Hellenistic philosophy is rooted in the Ibn Sīnan and Fārābian discussions of being.

Besides emphasizing the oneness of the Necessary Being in conformity with the unitarian perspective of Islam, Ibn Sīnā also confirms the necessity of the One to give of Itself, to emanate and bring forth manifestation. He bases the creation of the world not only on the Divine Will but also on the Divine Nature. Being both Absolute and Infinite, God cannot but create the world, without which He would not be Creator (*al-khāliq*) as described in the Quran. Hence, there is the first creation or manifestation of the One, which Ibn Sīnā identifies with the Logos or Universal Intellect (*al-'aql*). The Intellect contemplates the One as Necessary Being, itself as contingency, and its existence as necessitated by the One. From these three modes of contemplation there issue the Second Intellect, the First Soul, and the First Heaven, the process continuing until the cosmos is generated. Creation is thus related to contemplation, existence to knowledge.

Ibn Sīnā was well aware of both the Aristotelian and Ptolemaic astronomical systems and described both of them in different works. As far as cosmology is concerned, he adopted the scheme of the nine spheres of Islamic astronomy, based on the Babylonian and Greek, and related the emanation of the Intellect, whose idea was connected to Plotinian emanation of the Intellect and the Souls from the One, to the visible heavens. Ibn Sīnā did not, however, fall into any form of so-called pantheism since he always emphasized the contingency of all that exists, from the Universal Intellect to the dust of the earth, before the One Necessary Being. The Second Intellect in this scheme coresponds to the highest heaven above the fixed stars and the Tenth Intellect to the moon, below which begins the world of generation and corruption. In the sublunar world, form and matter are wed together to constitute bodies, and there is constant change, new forms being impinged upon sublunar matter by the Tenth Intellect, which is thus called the "giver of forms" (*wāhib al-ṣuwar;* Latin, *dator formarum*).

The cosmology of Ibn Sīnā also emphasizes the idea of the chain of being whose origin can be seen in Greek philosophy but which in fact was "completed" for the first time only in the *Kitāb al-shifā'*; herc Ibn Sīnā treated the "three kingdoms" (that is, minerals, plants and animals) fully, complementing the work of Aristotle in zoology and Theophrastus in botany, and integrating the chain within the natural world into the universal hierarchy of existence reaching to the One, who remains transcendent vis-à-vis the chain. Furthermore, in his "oriental philosophy", Ibn Sīnā developed an esoteric cosmology in which the cosmos was not only described in a scientific manner, but was depicted as a crypt through which man has to journey and which he must ultimately transcend. There are in fact certain Latin apocryphal treatises on the journey of the soul through and beyond the cosmos attributed to Ibn Sīnā.

PSYCHOLOGY

Basing himself on Aristotle's *De Anima* and Alexandrian commentators, but also adding elements not to be found in those sources explicitly, Ibn Sīnā developed a faculty psychology based on the relation between the five external and five internal senses. He also classified souls (*nafs*) into the vegetative, animal, and human or rational, each soul possessing certain faculties that are in fact developed fully only in certain species of a particular kingdom. Only in man are all the faculties belonging to all the three souls, which he possesses within himself, fully developed. Ibn Sīnā relates the gradual development of each faculty to the great chain of being, which is based on the fundamental notion of hierarchy and an ever greater degree of perfection as the chain is ascended.

Islamic philosophers such as al-Kindī and al-Fārābī developed the idea of grades and levels of the intellect from the potential to the Active Intellect. This fundamental doctrine, which was known and much debated in the medieval West, received its fullest elaboration in the hands of Ibn Sīnā, for whom the mind receives forms from the Active Intellect and through gradual perfection is able to become united with it.

NATURAL PHILOSOPHY

The contributions of Ibn Sīnā to the various branches of the natural sciences are too numerous to list in any summary study. His most important work in physics was to develop—within the context of the four Aristotelian causes and the theory of hylomorphism—the criticism of John Philoponos against Aristotle's theory of projectile motion. Ibn Sīnā, like Philoponos, believed that in the case of such motion, a power is imparted to the moving body by the cause that puts the body in motion. Moreover, in contrast to Philoponos, Ibn Sīnā asserted that this power, which he called *mayl qasrī* (Latin, *inclinatio violenta*), would not be dissipated in a vacuum. He also tried to provide a quantitative relation between the velocity and weight of such a body. It was this cardinal idea that, through the writings of Peter Olivi and John Buridan, finally resulted in Galileo's impetus theory. The root of the key concept of momentum can thus be found in Ibn Sīnā's critique of the Aristotelian theory of projectile motion.

In geology Ibn Sīnā displayed some of his acumen in observation and experiment by analyzing meteors and studying the process of sedimentation. But his most important contribution was perhaps in the classification of substances and the systematic study of minerals in a section of the *Shifā'* that came to be known in the West as the *De Mineralibus* and was attributed to Aristotle until modern times. Ibn Sīnā also made important studies in botany but almost always in relation to the medical properties of herbs.

MEDICINE AND PHARMACOLOGY

Ibn Sīnā is without doubt the most famous of Muslim physicians. In his work the grand synthesis of the Hippocratic, Galenic, and Dioscoridean, as well as the Indian and Iranian medical traditions reached its most perfect form. The author of the *Qānūn*, which was printed in Latin nearly thirty times before the era of modern medicine and which is still used in the Islamic and Indian worlds, was entitled the "prince of physicians" in Europe, while in the East his fame became so proverbial that he entered into the folk literature of the Persians, Arabs, Turks, and Indian Muslims.

In medicine Ibn Sīnā combined a philosophizing tendency with clinical observation and acumen. He provided a grand framework for medicine by providing a philosophy of medicine based on an inner equilibrium between various temperaments and humors as well as the body and various "souls". He also emphasized the necessity of the ecological balance between the body and the outside environment, which included not only food and diet, whose significance for health he emphasized, but also air and other factors, including even sound. Ibn Sīnā was also a master of psychosomatic medicine and was fully aware of the importance of the health of the mind and the soul for the body.

Ibn Sīnā is credited with the discovery of brain tumors and stomach ulcers. He was the first to diagnose meningitis correctly and realize the contagious character of tuberculosis. He explained cerebral apoplexy and facial paralysis, and was able to distinguish between epileptic seizures and epileptiform hysteria. He studied sterility and sexuality and even proposed surgery for people displaying bisexuality. Besides emphasizing hygiene and preventive medicine, he wrote much on the significance of the correct diet for health, starting with the mother's milk, whose significance for the proper growth of the newly born he underlined. In the use of drugs he emphasized herbs and developed the existing pharmacopeia to an extent that it has served as a foundation for many medical practices to this day in the Islamic world.

INFLUENCE, EAST AND WEST

The philosophy of Ibn Sīnā, although attacked by such Ash'arite theologians as Ghazzālī and Fakhr al-Dīn Rāzī, received renewed support in the thirteenth century from Naṣīr al-Dīn Ṭūsī and survived in the eastern Islamic world long after the decline of Peripatetic philosophy in Muslim Spain following the death of Ibn Rushd. In fact Ibn Sīnan philosophy became a permanent intellectual current in the Islamic world and has had followers to this day. His medical writings, meanwhile, gained universal acceptance throughout the Islamic world and his name became synonymous with Islamic medicine, which is sometimes referred to as (*ṭibb-i Bū 'Alī* (the medicine of Ibn Sīnā). In the contemporary revival of Islamic medicine, especially in India and Pakistan, his influence remains substantial. The figure of Ibn Sīnā is a permanent feature of Islamic thought, arts, and sciences whenever and wherever they are cultivated.

In the West, which came to know Ibn Sīnā as Avicenna (through the intermediary of Hebrew sources), the works of the master began to be translated in Toledo under the direction of Dominico Gundisalvo. The most prominent translators were the Jewish Avicennian philosopher Abraham ibn Dā'ūd, or Avendeuth, and Gerard of Cremona. In the Sicilian school also much attention was paid to Ibn Sīnā, who was translated by Michael Scot. The process of translation of Ibn Sīnā continued throughout the Middle Ages and lasted into the sixteenth century with Andrea Alpego. As a result, much but not all of the *Shifā'* as well as the *Najāt,* the *Autobiography*, the *Qānūn,* and smaller works, appeared in Latin, but none of the "Oriental Philosophy" and such late texts as the *Ishārāt* reached the West.

Although there did not develop a Latin Avicennism in as distinct a manner as Latin Averroism, the influence of Ibn Sīnā is to be seen in nearly all the important later figures of Scholasticism, and he is, after Averroës, without doubt the most influential Islamic philosopher in the West. The direct influence of Ibn Sīnā is to be seen in the Augustians, beginning with Gundisalvo himself, and in the strand of thought that Gilson has called "Avicennian Augustinianism". His influence is also to be seen in William of Auvergne, Alexander of Hales, Albertus Magnus, Thomas Aquinas, and especially Roger Bacon and Duns Scotus, the last of whom starts his study of metaphysics from a position which is close to that of Ibn Sīnā. But, strangely enough, the latinization of Ibn Sīnā meant also the secularization of the Avicennian universe through the banning of angels, who play such an important role in the Avicennan cosmos, and through rejection of his theory of the illumination of the mind by the Active Intellect, which he also identified with the angel of revelation. As a result, the Avicenna who came to be so well known to the Latin West gradually parted ways with the Ibn Sīnā whom the Islamic world looked upon ever more through the eyes of the Suhrawardian philosophy of illumination.

BILIOGRAPHY

Sources. *Avicennae de congelatione et conglutinatione lapidum,* E.J. Holmyard and D.C. Mandeville, trans. (1927); *Avicenna on Theology,* Arthur J. Arberry, trans (1951); *Avicenna Poem on Medicine,* Haven C. Krueger, trans. (1963); *Avicenna's Psychology,* F. Rahman, trans. (1952); *The Life of Ibn Sina,* William E. Gohlman, trans. (1974); *Le Livre de science,* Mohammad Achena and Henri Massé, trans., 2 vols. (1955-1958); *Le Livre* *des directives et remarques,* A. M. Goichon, trans. (1951); *The Metaphysica of Avicenna (Ibn Sīnā),* Parviz Morewedge, trans. (1973); *Die Metaphysik Avicennas,* Max Horten, trans. (1907); *La Métaphysique du Shifā': Livres I à V,* Georges C. Anawati, trans., I (1978); *Psychologie d'Ibn Sīnā,* Jan Bakos, trans., 2 vols. (1956); *A Treatise on the Canon of Medicine of Avicenna,* O. Cameron Gruner, trans. (1930).

Studies. Soheil Afnan, *Avicenna: His Life and Works* (1958); Georges C. Anawati, *Essai de bibliographie avicennienne* (1950); Bernard Carra de Vaux, *Avicenne* (1900); Henry Corbin, *Avicenna and the Visionary Recital,* Willard Trask, trans. (1960); Miguel Cruz Hernández, *La metafisica de Avicenna* (1949); M. T. D'Alverny, "Avicenna latinus", in *Archives d'histoire doctrinale et littéraire du moyen âge,* 36-45 (1961-1970), 47 (1972); Louis Gardet, *La Pensée religieuse d'Avicenne (Ibn Sīnā)* (1951); Étienne Gilson, "Avicenne et le point de départ de Duns Scot", in *Archives d'histoire doctrinale et littéraire du moyen âge,* 2 (1927); Amélie M. Goichon, *The Philosophy of Avicenna and Its Influence on Medieval Europe,* M.S. Khan, trans. (1969); Iran Society (Calcutta), *Avicenna Commemoration Volume,* V. Courtois, ed. (1956); Seyyed H. Nasr, *Three Muslim Sages* (1975) and *An Introduction to Islamic Cosmological Doctrines* (1993); Mazhar H. Shah, *The General Principles of Avicenna's Canon of Medicine* (1966); Roland de Vaux, Notes *et textes sur l'avicennisme latin aux confins des XII-XIII siècles* (1934); G.M. Wickens, ed., *Avicenna, Scientist and Philosopher: A Millenary Symposium* (1952).

7
Ibn Sīnā's Prophetic Philosophy*

Ibn Sīnā was born in year 370 of the Hegira (year 980 of the Christian era) in Khurasan, which along with Baghdad was the most important centre of intellectual activity in the Islamic world during the fourth century (tenth century). By the time he had opened his eyes to this world, such philosophers as al-Kindī, al-Fārābī, Abu'l-Ḥasan al-'Āmirī, and Abū Sulaymān al-Sijistānī had already established the foundations of Peripatetic (*mashshā'ī*) philosophy in Islam. The Mu'tazilite school had already produced its most illustrious representatives such as al-Naẓẓām and Abu'l-Hudhayl al-'Allāf. The Ash'arites, through Abu'l-Ḥasan al-Ash'arī and Abu Bakr al-Baqillānī, had capûtured the centre of the intellectual arena in Baghdad as far as *Kalām* was concerned, and were pressing their attacks against the *falsafah.* Other schools of Islamic philosophy such as the Hermetico-Pythagorean and the Ismā'ilī had produced important figures such as Jābir ibn Ḥayyān and Abū Ya'qūb al-Sijistānī. Sufism of both the Baghdadi and Khurasani schools had been witness to the lives and teachings of such outstanding masters as Junayd, Ḥallāj and Bāyazīd. Likewise, Islamic science had already produced some of its outstanding luminaries such as Muḥammad ibn Mūsā al-Khwārazmī in mathematics and Muḥammad ibn Zakariyyā' Rāzī (Rhazes) in medicine.

Ibn Sīnā was heir to all of these schools and their teachings. He learned their doctrines and assimilated elements from them into his own world view. Moreover, he was influenced not only by those schools which he followed but even by those which he rejected and criticized. In fact his writings reflect not only Peripatetic theses which he developed or Sufi doctrines which he defended, but also the *Kalām,* which he sought to refute thoroughly, especially in its Ash'arite form. The very first chapter of his last masterpiece, *Kitāb al-ishārāt wa'l-tanbīhāt* ("The Book of

---

* This essay originally appeared in *Cultures,* V. 7 (no. 4, 1980),pp. 302-307.

Directives and Remarks") entitled "On the Substantiality of Bodies" (*fī tajawhar al-ajsām)* reflects his concern with the *Kalām* thesis that all bodies are made up of atoms. Ibn Sīnā wrote his numerous works with full awareness of the very rich Isamic intellectual life which had preceded him. He himself was destined to contribute so much to that life that he came to put his seal upon Islamic *mashshā'ī* philosophy for all later periods and his indelible mark upon all of Islamic culture and thought. To this day he remains the prototype of the Islamic philosoper-scientist, that figure who has been at once a logician, metaphysician and man of science, the *ḥakīm* or wise man who has played such a central role in the whole of traditional Islamic education.[1] By the time he died in 428/1037, Ibn Sīnā had already made a permanent mark on both philosophy and medicine and had developed both of these disciplines into a form which was to have extensive influence both within and outside of the Islamic world for the next millennium, and which in fact survives to this day. The relatively brief trajectory of his life upon the plane of time was to have an effect far beyond that short span for he was to open an intellectual perspective of permanent importance for the entire Islamic intellectual tradition.[2]

AN EXTENSIVE BODY OF WORKS

Before dealing with Ibn Sīnā's philosophical ideas, it is important to say something about his works. His prolific pen left some 180 trreatises behind of which many have been lost; another forty works are either attributed to him or to his immediate circle of disciples and may in fact have been his own ideas as collected, transcribed or rewritten by his students. Of these works many are devoted to the sciences, some to purely religious subjects (such as commentaries on the Quran), some to language, grammar, prosody and the like and a major portion to philosophy.[3] A detailed study of this corpus and its content would, needless to say, require a separate work. Nonetheless, what we would emphasize here is that Ibn Sīnā's philosophical thought is to be found not only in what are, strictly speaking, his philosophical works but in the scientific and religious ones as well. His Quranic commentaries, hardly studied seriously in modern times, are an important source of his "religious philosophy", as this category is understood today,[4] while his scientific writings, especially the first book of the *Qānūn (Canon),* are a rich source of his natural philosophy.[5]

As far as the philosophical works themselves are concerned, they fall into two categories: those dealing with *mashshā'ī* or Peripatetic philosophy and those dealing with *al-ḥikmat al-mashriqiyyah* or "Oriental Philosophy". In the first category there are of course the well-known *al-Shifā'* ("The Healing"), his monumental philosophical encyclopaedia and the *summa* of Islamic *mashshā'ī* thought, and its shorter treatises ranging from those of a few pages to texts of one or two hundred pages dealing with more specific themes such as logic, epistemology, the intelligible hierarchy, resurrection, etc. These shorter works are perfectly coherent and in harmony with the content of the *Shifā'* and *Najāt* and differ from it only details and types or methods of demonstration. They prove the assertion made by Ibn Sīnā in his *Autobiography* that he had learned nothing "new" since he was eighteen years old but that the knowledge acquired in youth had become more profound in later life. There is no gradual development in these works as one observes in the case of most modern thinkers who pass through various stages and outgrow their own earlier philosophies. Early in life Ibn Sīnā seems to have reached an intellectual plateau upon which he was to march to the end of his earthly existence. Even the "Oriental Philosophy" was not the result of an evolution which would have led him to gradually go beyond and finally abandon the *mashshā'ī* philosophy, but rather another intellectual dimension which had opened before him and which stood hierarchically above the *mashshā'ī* perspective. The "Oriental Philosophy" did not emerge from the interior development of his *mashshā'ī* philosophy at a more advanced stage, even if almost all of the works in which the ideas of the "Oriental Philosophy" are to be found were written during the last half of his life.

As far as the "Oriental Philosophy" is concerned, it is more difficult to reconstitute the actual texts upon which it was based since the major works on this subject as specified by Ibn Sīnā himself are lost. To a great extent, it is thanks to the brilliant reconstruction of Henry Corbin that the textual basis of this other aspect of Avicennian philosophy has become known.[6] It can be said that of the surviving works of Ibn Sīnā, his last masterpiece, *al-Isharat wa,'l-tanbīhāt* ("The Book of Directives and Remarks"),[7] especially its last three chapters, the three visionary recitals, the *Hayy ibn Yaqẓān* (Living Son of the Awake), *Risālat al-ṭayr* ("Treatise of the Bird") and *Salāmān wa Absāl* ("Salāmān and Absāl") as well as some of the poems and mystical treatises,[8] belong to the corpus of writings related to the "Oriental Philosophy" as does of course the short *Manṭiq al-mashriqiyyīn* ("The Logic of the Orientals"), which is a key for understanding what Ibn Sīnā meant by the often discussed and disputed "Oriental Philosophy".[9]

BEING AND EXISTENCE

To understand Ibn Sīnā's philosophical doctrines, it is necessary to understand the ontology formulated by him. Although the actual term ontology was later attributed to Suarez, the philosophy of *being* was established above all by Ibn Sīnā, who has been called the "philosopher of being" *par excellence,* and the father of ontology as it developed later in both the Islamic world and the West, in spite of the fact that these developments were to move in very different directions in these two worlds during later periods. Certainly the Greek philosophers spoke of being, but the discussion of being as the central concept and concern of philosophy, as found in Latin Scolasticism and what followed in its wake, is based not on the Greek but the Islamic conception of being as developed by the early Islamic philosophers, culminating in Ibn Sīnā.

The earlier Islamic thinkers, breathing in a universe in which God as understood in the Quranic revelation ruled supreme, were already moving in the direction of creating a philosophy based upon the concept and the reality of Being, and sought to interpret Greek philosophy accordingly. They tried first of all to create an appropriate vocabulary using such terms as *aysiyyah,* implying existence (as against *laysiyyah* meaning non-existence), or *inniyyah,* again meaning existence based upon the assertive particle in Arabic *inna,* although there have been those who have claimed that this key term used by al-Fārābī[10] was etymologically derived from the Greek *on* meaning existence. In any case, by the time Ibn Sīnā wrote his philosophical works, the terminology which in fact he crystallized and finalized as the technical vocabulary of Islamic *mashshā'ī* philosophy had been already developed, based on such key terms as *wujūd* (existence and being),[11] *māhiyyah* (quiddity, the Latin term *quidditas* being the direct translation of the Arabic), *wujūd* (necessity), *imkān* (contingency and possibility) and *imtinā'* (impossibility).[12]

The most important distinction made in Avicennian metaphysics is between *wujūd* and *māhiyyah,* the first term denoting both Being and existence and the second essence or quiddity. Although these terms are used by Aristotle in his *Posterior Analytics,* they gain a new significance in al-Fārābī and especially in Ibn Sīnā, who makes this distinction the cornerstone of his ontology. For Aristotle this distinction is not basic because his concern is with existents (*ens*), that is, quiddities which exist in reality and which already possess existence. For Ibn Sīnā, however, it is possible to conceive of quiddities which do not exist and which "receive" existence in the way that the Abrahamic religions conceive of creation and in which the Quran, in particular, speaks of "Be and there was !" (*kun wa yakūn*). The Avicennian world is not the "ontological block without fissure" of Aristotle to use the words of Etienne Gilson [13] but is in need of a principle beyond itself to gain existence.

Ibn Sīnā makes a rigorous distinction between *wujūd* and *māhiyyah* in such a way that there is nothing in the nature of *māhiyyah* to account for existence. Contrary to the view held by Aristotle, we can conceive of the essence or quiddity of a thing completely irrespective of whether that thing exists or not. To quote Ibn Sīnā:

> It often happens that you understand the meaning of "triangle" and yet entertain doubt as to whether it is qualified by "existence" *in concreto* or it is not "existent". This is in spite of your having represented (the triangle) in your mind as being composed of a line and a plane. (In spite of your having represented the triangle in this way) you may still have no notion as to whether it exists or not.
>
> Everything having a "quiddity" becomes actualized, as an "existent" *in concreto* or as a representation in the mind, by all its constituent parts being actually present. So when a thing has an "essence" (*ḥaqīqah*) other than (1) its (i.e. the thing's) being "existent", whether mentally or extra-mentally, and (2) its being constituted by "existence'', "existence" must be something added (i.e. something different, and coming from outside) to the "essence" of the thing, whether it (i.e. that something additional) be inseparable (from the "essence") or separable.
>
> Furthermore, the causes of "existence" are different from the causes of "quiddity". "Being-man" (*insāniyyah*), for instance, is in itself an "essence" and a "quiddity", for which its being "existent" *in concreto* or in the mind is not a constituent element, but is simply something added to it. If it were a constituent element of the "quiddity", it would be impossible that the notion of the "quiddity" be actualized in the mind without being accompanied by its constituent part (i.e. "existence" which is supposed to be its constituent part).
>
> And it would be utterly impossible that the notion of "being-man" should be actualized as an "existent" in the mind and yet there should be doubt as to whether or not there is corresponding "existence" in the external world.
>
> Certainly in the case of man (and in other similar cases), there rarely occurs doubt regarding real "existence". But that is not due to the notion of man; it is due to the fact that we are acquainted with its particulars (i.e. individual men) through sense-perception.[14]

The basic distinction thus made by Ibn Sīnā was complemented by another distinction of a fundamental nature, namely that between necessity (*wujūb*), contingency or possibility (*imkān*) and impossibility (*imtinā'*). There are quiddities which once abstracted by the mind can either exist or not exist without causing a logical contradiction. Such a quiddity which stands equipoised between existence and non-existence is a contingent or possible being once it becomes an existent while that quiddity which cannot but exist is necessary. It is that one quiddity or essence which is none other than Pure Being Itself and which is called Necessary Being (*wājib al-wujūd*), a term used to designate the Divinity by nearly all schools of Islamic thought after Ibn Sīnā.[15] Finally, that quiddity which could not possibly exist because its existence would be logically contradictory is called "impossible being" (*mumtani' al-wujūd*). Only God is Necessary Being while all other existents in the universe are contingent beings. Also since these contingent beings do exist and therefore could not exist, they have gained their existence and also the necessity to exist from an agent beyond and other than themselves, and are therefore called *wājib bi'l-ghayr,* that is, made necessary by other than itself. In this manner Ibn Sīnā established an ontology based on the "poverty" of all things before God and their reliance upon the Source of all being for their very existence, asserting a view very much in conformity with that of Islam.

The question that was soon to arise was the relation between quiddity and existence, if existence is imposed from the outside upon quiddity. In answering this crucial question, Ibn Sīnā used the Arabic term *'āriḍ,* that is, "occurring to", stating that existence "occurs to" or is *'āriḍ* upon quiddity. Since the Arabic word for accident in its Aristotelian sense is *'araḍ,* later commentators not only in Europe but even in certain countries of the Islamic world—including Ibn Rushd (Averroës) himself—misunderstood Ibn Sīnā and thought that he meant by this assertion that existence is an accident in the ordinary sense of the term. For this reason they looked upon Ibn Sīnā as an "essentialist" philosopher whereas nothing could be further from Ibn Sīnā's point of view. As understood so correctly by Mīr Dāmād and Mullā Ṣadrā, Ibn Sīnā believed in the principiality of existence (*aṣālat al-wujūd*) if this later category of Islamic philosophy is applied to Avicennian ontology. Here are Ibn Sīnā's own words concerning the so-called "accidentality" of existence *vis-à-vis* quiddity or essence:

> The "existence" of all "accidents" in themselves is their "existence for their substrata", except only one "accident", which is "existence". This difference is due to the fact that all other "accidents", in order to become existent, need each a substratum (which is already existent by itself), while "existence" does not require any

"existence" in order to become existent. Thus it is not proper to say that its "existence" (i.e. the "existence" of this particular "accident" called "existence") in a substratum is its very "existence", meaning thereby that "existence" has "existence" (other than itself) in the same way as (an "accident" like) whiteness has "existence". (That which can properly be said about the "accident"-"existence") is, on the contrary, that its "existence in a substratum" is the very "existence" of that substratum. As for every "accident" other than "existence", its "existence in a substratum" is the "existence" of that "accident".[16]

In a brief essay such as the present one it is not possible to deal with all the fine features of Ibn Sīnā's ontology. Suffice it to say that upon the foundation briefly outlined above he established an imposing edifice which brought Islamic *mashshā'ī* philosophy to its peak and which has served as foundation and basis even for schools such as those of *ishrāq* (Illumination) and the "Transcendental Theosophy",[17] which opposed many of Ibn Sīnā's theses.

ARC OF ASCENT AND ARC OF DESCENT

Ibn Sīnā's cosmology is closely wed to his ontology. Based on the principle that "from the One only one can issue forth" (*lā yaṣdiru 'ān al-wāḥid illa'l-wāḥid*) he asserts that the First Intellect is emanated from the Necessary Being as the ray of light would emanate from the sun, except that even the First Intellect is contingent in itself, necessity belonging to God alone. The First Intellect (*al-'aql al-awwal)* contemplates the Necessary Being, itself as possible being and itself as a being made necessary by other than itself. From these three modes or aspects of contemplation the Second Intellect, the First Soul and the First Heaven or Sphere are brought into being. The process continues in this manner until the nine spheres of classical astronomy and the cosmic "chain of being" are completed. Below the ninth sphere which is also the sphere of the moon lies the world of generation and corruption governed by the Tenth Intellect which is the "giver of forms" (*dator formarum, wāhib al-ṣuwar),* the source of all the forms in the sublunar world in which everything is composed of the four elements of fire, air, water and earth. The heavens, however, are made of the fifth element, ether, which does not undergo change, generation or corruption.[18]

In the sublunar world there is an ever-increasing complexity in the mixture of the elements, from mineral to plant to animal and finally man, in whom the complexity of the mixture of the elements reaches its peak and from whom also begins the arc of return to the One who is the origin of all the beings in the arc of descent (or the "great chain of being"), ranging from the angel to prime matter and finally to man. Although Ibn Sīnā adopted elements of Aristotelian physics and natural philosophy, Ptolemaic as well as Aristotelian astronomy and the Neo-platonic theory of the emanation of the grades of being from each other and finally from the One, it was he rather than any of the Greek philosophers who finally integrated the three kingdoms into a vast cosmological synthesis. The first work which in fact treats the three kingdoms together and as a whole is the *Shifā',* which combines the zoological and botanical studies of Aristotle and Theophrastus with the study of the mineral world by alchemists and natural historians, to which Ibn Sīnā was to add many elements based on his own reflection, observation and even experimentation.

FROM DISCURSIVE KNOWLEDGE TO ILLUMINATION

In man, a new faculty or soul appears on the stage of the cosmic arena which is called the "Rational Soul" and which, like the other souls, emanates from the Tenth Intellect. This soul is characterized by the power of ratiocination and finally intellection. Man is, therefore, endowed with the possibility of knowing principles and universals in addition to possessing the internal and external senses which he shares with the animals and plants which have animal and vegetative souls. But in most men the intellect is dormant and in a potential state. Through discipline and the acquiring of knowledge, however, it can rise stage by stage until it becomes united with the Active Intellect. The theory of the intellect and its levels developed by Ibn Sīnā on the basis of the well-known treatises of al-Kindī and al-Fārābī on the subject is among the best known aspects of his philosophy and exercised much influence in both East and West.

It is important to remember that for Ibn Sīnā knowledge is inseparable from the illumination of the intellect of man by the Active Intellect and that there is always an aspect of illumination which accompanies every kind of knowledge. The grandeur of man is precisely in being endowed with this intelligence which can ultimately come to know the One and to return to the Necessary Being. But it is also important to note than man is treated in the grand scheme of Ibn Sīnā only after he expounds ontology and cosmology. For example, in the *Shifā',* it is only in the sixth book of the "Natural Philosophy" (*al-tabī'iyyāt*), where he is treating the subjectof the soul (*al-nafs*) or *De Anima* in the Aristotelian sense, that he speaks of man and his "faculties". This is in perfect conformity with the

Islamic perspective which shuns every form of Prometheanism and which sees the greatness of man only in his ability to know the One and to live in conformity with this knowledge.[19]

Ibn Sīnā's philosophy, even in its Peripatetic aspect, was completely integrated into the Islamic perspective and very much concerned with theology as this term is understood in modern western languages. He wrote extensively on the nature of God, the Divine Names and Qualities, determinism and free will and even such specifically religious subjects as eschatology and the meaning of religious rites such as prayers and pilgrimage. Although many of his religious works are not available and those accessible have not been studied carefully, enough is known to attest to the significance of his philosophy for religious philosophy or even theology. In fact Ibn Sīnan philosophy, like all Islamic philosophy, is essentially "prophetic philosophy" and all of its aspects are impregnated in one way or another with religious significance.

Some of Ibn Sīnā's works are also concerned with Sufism. Not only was Ibn Sīnā always attracted to Sufi masters, as reflected in many apocryphal accounts of his meetings with such famous Sufi saints as Abū Sa'īd Abi'l Khayr, but he wrote one of the most intellectually lucid and powerful defenses of Sufism in Islamic history at the end of his *al-Ishārāt wa'l-tanbīhāt* in the chapter entitled "On the Stations of the Gnostics" (*Fī maqāmāt al-'ārifīn).*

Ibn Sīnā's philosophy was of course also very much related to the sciences. In fact he developed a natural philosophy which is still of interest for contemporary science and medicine in search of a world view other than that which has been prevalent since the Scientific Revolution. Ibn Sīnā, like many traditional philosophers, was deeply concerned with the classification of the sciences and the hierarchy of knowledge, and sought to integrate different types of science and modes of achieving knowledge into his vast metaphysical and philosophical synthesis. He used not one but many methods to gain knowledge, ranging from intellectual intuition and illumination to ratiocination, observation and even experimentation, which he carried out in medicine as well as metallurgy. He even occasionally used the syllogism in such a way as to relate it to concrete and individual causes rather than to universal ones, making it an instrument for the inductive rather than the deductive method. This did not mean, however, that he rejected the deductive method or that his "Oriental Philosophy" was simply the substitution of the inductive method in place of the deductive, as suggested by certain modern scholars such as A. M. Goichon. For Ibn Sīnā there was a harmony and hierarchy between methods rather than an either-or attitude which would rely on only one method of knowing, viewed as "*the* scientific method" to the exclusion of others.

The pertinence of Ibn Sīnā's philosophy for science is to be seen not only in physics and the philosophy of nature, but also and especially in medicine. This "Prince of Physicians", as the mediaeval West came to call him, saw the patient as a total being, possessing body, soul and spirit and not as just a living organism. His treatments ranged all the way from giving herbal or mineral drugs to playing music for the patient. He was fully aware of the mutual effect of body and soul upon each other and the relation of the soul to the Spirit and the effect of this relation upon the whole of the human microcosm. He was a master of psychosomatic medicine without in any way neglecting the physical aspect of the science of healing. Ibn Sīnā developed a medicine based on the whole person. He knew the natural potentiality of the body for recovery and believed that the physician should seek the help of the body itself for the treatment of an illness. He demonstrated his knowledge of the power of mind over physical disorders and the power of faith over the mind and its functioning while discovering, diagnosing and treating for the first time such maladies as meningitis. He was the physician of the whole person and developed a philosophy of medicine which is once again gaining attention in the contemporary world where many people are in avid quest of a holistic medicine.

An aspect of Ibn Sīnā's thought which from the beginning of this century has attracted much attention in the West, but which was unknown to the European Middle Ages, is his "Oriental Philosophy" (*al-ḥikmat al-mashriqiyyah*), which because of the nature of Arabic orthography can also be read as *mushriqiyyah* or Illuminationist. Although Ibn Sīnā's major opus bearing this title and other works of a similar nature have disappeared, his *Logic of the Orientals* and other segments can be reconstructed to give an idea of what Ibn Sīnā meant by the "Oriental Philosophy", which he considered to be only for the "intellectual elite" (*al-khawāṣṣ*). As already mentioned, this task of reconstruction was in fact carried out by Henry Corbin who put an end once and for all to the long debate on this issue in orientalist circles.[20] What Ibn Sīnā had in mind was not a harmless addenda to Peripatetic philosophy with an "eastern" flavor in the geographic sense of the term but the reconstitution of that theosophy which is at once illuminative and Oriental, in the symbolic sense of Orient (Orient of enlightenment, rising illumination), a school of theosophy which was finally established a century and a half later by the master of the school of *ishrāq,* Shaykh Shihāb al-Dīn Suhrawardī.[21]

THE VISIONARY RECITALS

The "Oriental Philosophy" of Ibn Sīnā did not change the contours of the *mashshā'ī* cosmos, but it did change its significance. The cosmos, rather than being an external reality to be explained, became a crypt through which the gnostic must journey to the Reality beyond all levels of cosmic manifestation. Knowledge, including logic, became the means of ascending the scales of being and philosophy as wed to spiritual discipline, the road to the ecstasy which comes from that supreme vision depicted with great beauty in Ibn Sīnā's visionary recitals that contain most of what remains of his writings on the "Oriental Philosophy". In the visionary recitals not only did Ibn Sīnā commence a new path in Islamic intellectual life, which was to lead later to the establishment of a new intellectual perspective by Suhrawardī, but the master of Islamic Peripatetics established a new form of philosophical writing in Islam, the recital or narrative which was to be pursued by many Islamic philosophers who came afterwards, including Suhrawardī himself.[22]

The impact of Ibn Sīnā on both the Islamic world and the West was immediate and lasting, while in the sub-continent of India his ideas did not spread until nearly three centuries after his death. Within the Islamic world itself the influence of Ibn Sīnā was to be felt not only in philosophy but also in theology, not to speak of the sciences, with which we are not concerned in this essay. His closest disciples such as Bahmanyār, Juzjānī and Ma'sūmī continued the teachings of the master during the middle decades of the fifth century (eleventh century of the Christian era) but as a result of the ascendency of *Kalām,* the *mashshā'ī* school was soon eclipsed in the eastern lands of the Islamic world for a long period which lasted until the seventh century (thirteenth century). During this period it was in the Maghrib, especially in Andalusia and Morocco, that *mashshā'ī* philosophy flowered. In the fifth and sixth centuries (eleventh and twelfth centuries A.D.) every major philosopher of this area, whether it was Ibn Bājjah, Ibn Ṭufayl or Ibn Rushd (Averroës), was influenced to one degree or another by Ibn Sīnā. This is particularly true of Ibn Rushd, who had a different interpretation of Islamic Peripatetic philosophy than Ibn Sīnā, an interpretation of a more rationalistic nature, that was to influence the West much more than the Islamic world where the influence of Ibn Sīnā was much greater than that of the Andalusian philosopher.

It was in the seventh (thirteenth) century that Naṣīr al-Dīn Ṭūsī undertook to revive the philosophy of Ibn Sīnā by answering the criticisms made by Fakhr al-Dīn Rāzī against Ibn Sīnā and especially the *Ishārāt.* Naṣīr al-Dīn's work *Sharḥ al-ishārāt wa'l-tanbīhāt* ("Commentary upon the Book of Directives and Remarks"), one of the great masterpieces of Islamic thought, resuscitated Ibn Sīnā and the *mashshā'ī* school and enabled this school to survive over the centuries as a living intellectual perspective in the Islamic world, which is still valid to this day. Numerous works of Ibn Sīnan inspiration have appeared since then, ranging from the monumental *Durrat al-tāj* ("The Pearl of the Crown") of Ṭūsī's associate, Quṭb al-Dīn Shīrāzī, to the *Muḥākamāt* ("Trials") of Quṭb al-Dīn Rāzī during the following century, and including the important commentaries on the *Shifā'* by Sayyid Aḥmad 'Alawī and Ṣadr al-Dīn Shīrāzī during the Safavid period.[23]

The influence of Ibn Sīnā was also to be of great importance in Islamic philosophical schools other than the *mashshā'ī.* It is impossible to understand the school of *ishrāq* without full knowledge of Ibn sīnā teachings. In fact the thought of Ibn Sīnā spread into India to a large extent in connection with and in the context of the school of Suhrawardī. The Ismā'īlī philosophy of the Fatimid period was also influenced by Ibn Sīnā as can be seen by the writings of its most famous expositor, Nāṣir-i Khusraw. The Ismā'īlī themselves were fully aware of the philosophical significance of Ibn Sīnā and sometimes referred to Ḥamīd al-Dīn Kirmānī, his contemporary who wrote the most systematic exposition of Fatimid philosophy, as the "Ismā'īlī Ibn Sīnā". Furthermore, nearly all the later Islamic philosophers of note such as Mīr Dāmād in Persia and Shaykh Aḥmad Sirhindī in India were deeply indebted to Ibn Sīnā. And the "Transcendent Theosophy" of Ṣadr al-Dīn Shīrāzī, which gave the Islamic world a new intellectual perspective, cannot be comprehended at all without recourse to Ibn Sīnā's teachings. It is enough to study practically any chapter of *al-Asfār al-arba'ah* ("The Four Journeys") by Ṣadr al-Dīn to realize his debt to the master of Islamic Peripatetics.[24] To this day wherever there is an authentic manifestation of Islamic intellectual life the spirit of Ibn Sīnā is present in one way or another.

Although *Kalām* was opposed to *mashshā'ī* philosophy, it was nevertheless influenced in many ways by it. It is important to note that the most famous attacks of the theologians or *mutakallimūn* against *mashshā'ī* philosophy were in fact directed against Ibn Sīnā, as can be seen in the works of Ghazzālī, Shahrastānī and Fakhr al-Dīn Rāzī. They all felt that by demolishing the thought of the foremost figure among the philosophers of this school, they would also destroy that school. But in this process *Kalām* itself became influenced by Ibn Sīnā's philosophy both in the subjects discussed and certain concepts taken over from the *mashshā'ī* school. Of the latter, of course the most important is the concept of "Necessary Being" which entered into the vocabulary of later *Kalām* and even the general religious perspective of the Islamic community. Moreover, what distinguishes "later *Kalām,*" as Ibn Khaldūn calls it, from the early school of *Kalām* concerns most of all elements related to Avicennian influence. The later *Kalām* is often called philosophical *Kalām* precisely because of the struggle waged by *Kalām* against *falsafah* in general and Ibn Sīnā in particular, a struggle which was to have reciprocal influence on both later *Kalām* and *falsafah.*

Space does not allow us to speak of the mark left by Ibn Sīnā on other Islamic intellectual disciplines, including both doctrinal Sufism (*al-ma'rifah* or *'irfān*) and the principles of jurisprudence (*uṣūl al-fiqh*). Suffice it to say that a close examination of the writings of the masters of Islamic gnosis such as Ibn 'Arabī and Ṣadr al-Dīn al-Qunyawī reveals that these authors, while rejecting most of the theses of the *mashshā'ī* school, nonetheless were definitely influenced by certain aspects of Ibn Sinan teachings. Likewise, an examination of the methods used in *uṣūl,* especially Shi'ite *uṣūl,* which reached its peak of development during the past century, shows the unmistakable mark of Ibn Sīnan logic, which constituted the most developed and systematic exposition of formal logic in the Islamic world and which had a vast influence on nearly every field of knowledge.

In the West, only half a century after its composition, the *Shifā',* known through its partial Latin translation as *sufficentia,* was being taught in Paris. Father R. de Vaux, among others, has quite rightly spoken of a "Latin Avicennism" paralleling the better known "Latin Averroism". The *Summa* of Saint Thomas would be inconceivable without Ibn Sīnā and even more so than the doctrines of the "angelic doctor", the philosophy of Duns Scotus is closely related to that of Ibn Sīnā, who was also deeply influential among Jewish philosophers such as Ibn Dā'ūd. Although the West never knew the "Oriental Philosophy" and the climate of the West became too rationalistic to allow Avicennism to grow as extensively as the rationalistic interpretation given of Ibn Rushd in Latin Averroism, the influence of Ibn Sīnā was nevertheless extensive and profound in mediaeval Europe. In fact he had become so famous that certain treatises of early Christian writers were attributed to him[25] while several anonymous Latin treatises appeared based on his ideas. Furthermore, the *Canon* and other medical works of Ibn Sīnā became very popular and authoritative in the Occident and complemented the philosophical works as channels for the spread of his ideas in the Latin world, an influence which continued even during the Renaissance and up to the Seventeenth Century Scientific Revolution.

THE REDISCOVERY OF IBN SĪNĀ

Much could also be said of the influence of Ibn Sīnan ideas in the lands east of Persia, especially in India. Here, although many of the documents have not been examined, there is ample evidence to show that his impact was not limited to the Muslims of India but that there was an appreciation of his thought and ideas even among certain Hindus. If one day the full story of Islamic intellectual life in India were to be told, Ibn Sīnā would stand as one of its major figures.

Today in a world bewildered by problems of its own making, saddled with schools of philosophy many of which hate rather than love wisdom, and confronted with a science which because of its separation from other forms of knowledge as well as ethics leads to ever greater perils for mankind, contrary to the intentions of its creators, the teachings of Ibn Sīnā appear as one of the great achievements of the human intellect, attracting inquiring minds from near and far. On the occasion of the millenary celebration of his birth, it has been of utmost importance to reacquaint ourselves with the thoughts and teachings of this great master, not only as an episode of intellectual history but as an intellectual perspective of great value for the contemporary world. His works should be studied and his ideas reformulated in a contemporary language so as to become accessible to people all over the globe who are searching for perennial truths but who do not possess the means of deciphering the language in which these truths have been usually couched.

The rediscovery of Ibn Sīnā is of course of particular importance for the contemporary Islamic world where there are many forces which wish to revive the Islamic intellectual tradition but where the richness of this tradition and the absolute necessity of possessing full knowledge of it for confronting the modern world is not always realized and appreciated. May the study of Ibn Sīnā not only help us to illuminate a thousand years of Islamic intellectual life, but also be an aid in casting light upon the problems faced today by all of humanity in both East and West, in both the Islamic world and in that Occident where Ibn Sīnan teachings were received with such enthusiasm a millennium ago.

NOTES

1. See S.H. Nasr, *Three Muslim Sages* (Albany, N. Y., 1975), Chapter I, "Ibn Sīnā and the Philosopher-Scientists", where we have used the term philosopher-scientist for the first time in this context. On the figure of the *ḥakīm* and its significance for Islamic education, see S.H. Nasr, *Science and Civilization in Islam* (Cambridge, Mass., 1968), Chapter I.

2. We will not deal with Ibn Sīnā's biography here. His autobiography as recorded by Abū 'Ubayd al-Juzjānī is found in W.E. Gohlman, *The Life of Ibn Sina. A Critical Edition and Annotated Translation* (Albany, N. Y., 1974). See also S.H. Nasr, "Avicenna" in the *Encyclopaedia Britannica* (Chicago, 1980, 15th ed.), and Nasr: *An Introduction to Islamic Cosmological Doctrines* Chapter XI.

3. On the bibliography of Ibn Sīnā, see Y. Mahdavi, *Bibliographie d'Ibn Sīnā* (Tehran, 1954); G.C. Anawati, *Essai de bibliographie avicennienne* (Cairo, 1950); O. Ergin, *Ibni Sina Bibliografyasi* (Istanbul, 1956); and F. Sezgin, *Geschichte des arabischen Schrifttums,* vols. 3-5 (Leiden, 1970-74).

4. Such works as L. Gardet, *La Pensée religieuse d'Avicenne/Ibn Sīnā* (Paris, 1951), and A.J. Arberry, *Avicenna on Theology* (Londo, 1951) deal with his religious thought but not with the Quranic commentaries in a substantial manner.

5. See O.C. Gruner (trans.) *A Treatise on the Canon of Medicine, Incorporating a Translation of the First Book* (London, 1930) and M.H. Shah, *The General Principles of Avicenna's Canon of Medicine* (Karachi, 1966).

6. See Henry Corbin, *Avicenna and the Visionary Recital,* trans. William Trask (Dallas, 1980) and the original French edition, *Avicenne et le récit visionnaire* (Paris-Tehran, 1952-54, 3 vols.), which contains the original Arabic text of the recitals as well as some ealry Persian translations.

7. Translated by A.M. Goichon, *Le Livre des directives et des remarques* (Beirut-Paris, 1951).

8. Some of these have been edited and translated by A.F. von Mehren in *Le Muséon* in the 1880's.

9. See Nasr, *An Introduction to Islamic Cosmological Doctrines, op. cit.,* pp. 185 ff.

10. This as well as many other key terms of Islamic philosophy were used in the *Fuṣūṣ al-ḥikmah* attributed to al-Fārābī and claimed by some scholars to be by Ibn Sīnā himself.

11. Since there is but a single term in Arabic to denote Being, being and existence, in writing on Islamic philosophy one must be careful how the three terms are used, especially since there is so much confusion in the discussion of ontology in European languages.

12. The technical vocabulary of Ibn Sīnā has been discussed by A.M. Goichon, *Lexique de la langue philosophique d'Ibn Sīnā/Avicenne* (Paris, 1937) and in the more general work of S. Afnan, *Philosophical Lexicon in Persian and Arabic* (Beyrouth, 1969) which is also important for technical terms used by Ibn Sīnā.

13. Referring to Aristotle, Gilson says "substance (is) conceived as an ontological bloc without fissure", *L'Être el l'essence* (Paris, 1948), p. 90.

14. Ibn Sīnā, *al-Ishārāt wa'l-tanbīhāt* (Cairo, 1960), pp. 202-203, translated by T. Izutsu in his introduction to Sabzavari, *Sharḥ-i manẓūmah,* T. Izutsu and M. Mohaghegh, eds. (Tehran, 1969), pp. 62-63. This introduction which is basic to the understanding of Avicennian ontology in later Islamic philosophy as it developed in the Islamic world itself and especially in Persia, has also appeared in Izutsu, *The Concept and Reality of Existence* (Tokyo, 1971). See also Goichon, *La Distinction de l'essence et de l'existence d'après Ibn Sīnā/Avicenne* (Paris, 1937).

15. On this distinction, see Nasr, *An Introduction to Islamic Cosmological Doctrines, op. cit.*, pp. 198 ff.

16. From the *Ta'līqāt* of Ibn Sīnā as translated by Izutsu, *op. cit.*, pp. 110-111.

17. On these schools see Nasr, *Three Muslim Sages, op. cit.*, Chapter II; H. Corbin, *En Islam iranien*, vols. II and IV (Paris, 1970-71); Nasr, *Sadr al-Din Shirazi and His Transcendent Theosophy* (London-Boulder, 1978).

18. On Ibn Sīnā's cosmology see Nasr, *An Introduction to Islamic Cosmological Doctrines, op. cit.*, pp. 236 ff.

19. See F. Schuon, *Understanding Islam*, trans. D.N. Matheson (London, 1979). On the treatment of man in Islamic philosophy, see G. Monnot, "La place de l'homme dans la philosophie islamique", *Revue Thomiste* (Jan.-March 1980, pp. 88-94).

20. See Corbin, *Avicenna and the Visionary Recital* (Dallas, 1980); Nasr, *An Introduction to Islamic Cosmological Doctrines, op. cit.*, pp. 185 ff.

21. See Corbin, *En Islam iranien, op. cit.*, vol. II; Nasr, *Three Muslim Sages, op. cit.*, Chapter II.

22. See Sohrawardi, *OEuvres philosophiques et mystiques*, vol. III, S.H. Nasr ed. (Paris-Tehran, 1977), where we have edited all of Suhrawardī's Persian recitals while those in Arabic, especially *Qiṣṣat al-ghurbat al-gharbiyyah* ("The Story of the Occidental Exile"), which is one of the most important, was edited by Corbin in vol. II of the same series.

23. See Corbin and S.J. Ashtiyani (eds.), *Anthologie des philosophes iraniens depuis le XVII siècle jusqu'à nos jours*, vols. I-II (Tehran-Paris, 1971).

24. See F. Rahman, *The Philosophy of Mulla Sadra* (Albany, N. Y., 1976); Nasr, *Sadr al-Din Shirazi and His Transcendent Theosophy, op. cit.*, pp. 77 ff., where the influence of Ibn Sīnā and his school upon Ṣadr al-Dīn is discussed explicitly.

25. See for example, M.T. d'Alverny, "Une rencontre symbolique de Jean Scot Erigène et d'Avicenne. Notes sur le *De causis primis et secundis et fluxu qui consequitur eas*" in J. O'Meara and L. Bieler, eds., *The Mind of Erigena* (Dublin, 1973, pp. 170-181) which discusses a treatise containing the ideas of Erigena but under the name of Ibn Sīnā. M.T. d'Alverny has spent a lifetime in editing and studying the Latin Ibn Sīnan corpus and in making the extensive influence of the philosopher during the Middle Ages known to the contemporary scholarly world.

8

Bīrūnī as Philosopher*

In the context of classical Islamic civilization the name "philosophy" (*al-falsafah* or *al-ḥikmah)* is reserved for a particular set of disciplines associated with the well-known schools of "Islamic philosophy" such as the Peripatetic (*mashshā'ī*), Illuminationist (*ishrāqī*) and the like, and not other schools, like theology (*Kalām*), which often deal with philosophic ideas but are not officially recognized as "philosophy".[1] Therefore the title of "philosopher" (*al-faylasūf*) is usually reserved for those who are masters of the doctrines of one of these ''philosophical'' schools with all the different ramifications and nuances that various branches of these schools contain. Considered in this light, Bīrūnī has never been classified by classical authors as a "philosopher'', nor associataed with one of the well-known schools of traditional Islamic philosophy. But if we understand philosophy in its more general sense as logical and rational discourse upon the nature of things, then Bīrūnī must certainly be considered as a philosopher of note to be studied for his significance in the general context of Islamic intellectual history and also for the innate value of his intellectual vision. Of course he is still a traditional philosopher, even if not a member of the well established schools, for profane and secular philosophy simply did not exist in Islamic civilization and certainly would not have concerned such a profoundly religious man as Bīrūnī even had it existed.

Bīrūnī was a scientist, scholar, compiler and philosopher for whom the quest for knowledge was held as the supreme goal of human life. He respected knowledge in all its forms and hence sought it wherever and in which ever form possible. He saw in knowledge an almost divine quality

---

* This article was presented on the occasion of the Millenary of Abū Rayḥan Bīrūnī at the Bīrūnī International Congress in Karachi, Pakistan in 1973. This essay also appeared as ''Free Wheeling Philosophers' *Couriers,* (June 1974): 38-41.

very much in conformity with the fundamental tenets of Islam, whose spirituality is "gnostic" in nature, and with the values exalted by Islamic civilization.[2] Hence Bīrūnī, with the universal vision and the remarkable intellectual qualities which he possessed, turned to Greek as well as Persian and Indian sciences, to both the religious Islamic sciences and the intellectual ones. He holds the rather unusual distinction of being at once one of the greatest mathematicians and historians of humanity. And he wrote in nearly every field, from astronomy to pharmacology.[3] But strangely enough, unlike his contemporary scientist Ibn al-Haytham, Bīrūnī has not left behind independent philosophical works of a systematic nature. The only exception among his extant works is the *Questions and Answers* ("al-As'ilah wa'l-ajwibah") exchanged with Ibn Sīnā, which deal with cosmological, physical and philosophical problems.[4] As for his lost works, he apparently wrote three philosophical narratives *'Āyn al-ḥayāt, Qāsim al-surūr* and *Urmuzdyār wa mihryār,* which if found would be very significant, considering the importance of this kind of philosophical narrative romance in the corpus of Ibn Sīnā, Suhrawardī and many other Islamic philosophers.[5]

In order to understand Bīrūnī's philosophical thought, it is therefore necessary to turn to his other writings dealing with history, geography or even astronomy, for in nearly all of these works, one will find elements dealing with philosophy, cosmology and metaphysics interspersed within the main scientific or historical discussion at hand. In the *India* not only does Bīrūnī describe Indian doctrines, but he often comments upon them and offers his own metaphysical and philosophical ideas and interpretations. In his *Chronology of Ancient Nations* profound observations are made about the nature of time and the cycles of human history as well as the origin of the order observed in nature. In *The Determination of the Coordinates of Cities* the origin of science and its classification are discussed as are themes related to the question of the origin and creation of the universe. One could go on in the same vein with his other writings.[6] Moreover, the very fact that he chose to translate into Arabic such a work as the *Patañjali Yoga* shows his intense interest in metaphysical and spiritual matters.

When all of these sources are extracted and studied, it becomes clear that Bīrūnī was neither a Peripatetic, nor a follower of scholastic theology (*Kalām*), nor a disciple of Hermetic philosophy or the Islamic philosophy related to it, nor a member of any of the other established schools of his time. The most noteworthy aspect of his philosophical views is his strong and often original criticism of Aristotelian philosophy, which is reflected in the questions and answers he exchanged with Ibn Sīnā and his student 'Abdallāh al-Ma'ṣūmī.[7] Bīrūnī thus belongs to a series of independent anti-Peripatetic thinkers of the early period of Islamic history who were also scientists, such men as Muḥammad ibn Zakariyyā' Rāzī, whom in fact Bīrūnī both admired and criticized.[8]

Bīrūnī did not oppose all of the teachings of Peripatetic philosophy *en bloc*. Rather, basing himself on firm religious faith in Islam on the one hand and the tool of logic, rational analysis and observation on the other hand, he refuted many of the theses of Peripatetic philosophy, such as the eternity of the world and the possibility of indefinite division of matter. What is important for an understanding of Islamic intellectual history is that such a strong and rigorous criticism of Peripatetic thought did not come from a nominalist or rationalist, as was to happen from the end of the Middle Ages to the 17th century in the West, but that it came from a man like Bīrūnī who was deeply immersed in both the life of faith and metaphysical and cosmological doctrines of Islam and other traditions. It is of great significance for an understanding of the reason for the different paths that Islamic and Christian civilizations were to take at the end of the Middle Ages that one of the foremost critics of the Aristotelian world view in Islam should also be the person who introduced the *Patañjali Yoga* to the Islamic world and one of the few Muslim figures really well versed in the Vedanta.

In order to understand Bīrūnī's philosophical views it is necessary to turn to a few specific subjects. In the question of cosmogony and creation, Bīrūnī rejected violently the idea of the "eternity" (*qidam*) of the world and like the Islamic theologians held that to believe in the eternity of the world is to negate the need for a cause for the world and therefore to negate indirectly Divine Unity (*al-tawḥīd*), which was the principle most dear to Bīrūnī.[9] In fact the whole of Bīrūnī's works can be interpreted as a quest for the realization of unity in various forms of knowledge and planes of existence. It was most of all with the aim of preserving the inviolability of the doctrine of unity that he criticized the Peripatetic view of the eternity of the world in the second of the questions he posed to Ibn Sīnā, and refused to accept the Peripatetic response that an existant needs a cause not because it has a temporal origin, but basically because it is a possible being (*mumkin al-wujūd*) and is therefore in need of the Necessary Being (*wājib al-wujūd*) in order to become actualized and to gain existence. The debate between Bīrūnī and Ibn Sīnā as well as Ma'ṣūmī on this subject concerns one of the most important questions of Islamic philosophy, namely the condition under which something needs a cause. Bīrūnī identified the eternity of the world with its not being created. For him, in contrast to Ibn Sīnā, the "newness" of the universe (the quality of being *ḥādith*) implied its being created (*makhlūq*), and the denial of this "newness" or acceptance that the world does not have an origin in time destroyed the conception of the creation and ultimately the unity of the Creator and his power. Hence in other works such as *The Determination of the Coordinates of Cities* he affirmed clearly his belief in the created nature of the world[10] and tried to provide both scientific and theological reasons for it.

As a result of his vast and varied study of nature, history and various traditional doctrines of time and of the world, Bīrūnī became clearly aware of the qualitative nature of time, of the fact that it is not uniformly stretched out like a mathematical coordinate. He also strongly denied the idea of uniformitarianism so dear to modern geology and paleontology and provided both scientific and philosophical arguments to disprove it.[11] For Bīrūnī time has a cyclic nature, but not in the sense of returning to the same point again, which is a metaphysical absurdity and a modern caricature of the real traditional teaching.[12] Rather, by "cyclic" Bīrūnī understands qualitative changes and correspondences between various elements of time within each cycle. Without doubt his profound study and intimate knowledge of not only the Quranic conception of time, which is based on cycles of prophecy, but also the teachings of the *Puraṇas* and of many other traditions on the meaning of time and history helped Bīrūnī develop perhaps more profoundly than any other Islamic philosopher and scientist the meaning of qualified and cyclic time and its implications for the study of nature and of man.

A basic aspect of Bīrūnī's thought, which is closely related to his treatment of time, concerns the development and becoming of things, which many have by mistake identified with the modern theory of evolution, the latter being no more than a parody of the traditional doctrine of gradation.[13] Bīrūnī was fully aware of the long history of the earth, of the cataclysms which changed mountains into seas and oceans into continents, of the fact that certain species preceded others on earth and that each species has its own life cycle.[14] Pondering over the vast panorama of nature in both time and space and the teachings of various sacred writings on the creation and subsequent history of the universe, Bīrūnī became aware of the basic principle that the development and becoming of things in this world is the gradual unfolding and actualization of all the possibilities that are inherent within each being. Nothing evolves from one form into another as a result of external additions or accretions; rather whatever transformation does take place is no more than the manifestations of possibilities already present in that being. In the same way, what becomes manifested at a particular period of history is no more than the unfolding of possibilities inherent in that particular cycle of time. This principle, which is one of the cornerstones of Bīrūnī's thought and is a crystallization of well-known traditional doctrines, is applied by Bīrūnī to his study of various domains of nature, both animate and inanimate, as well as to history and man.

Being an outstanding physicist, Bīrūnī was deeply interested in the general principles of natural philosophy, in such questions as motion, time and matter, as is again seen in his criticism of Aristotelian natural philosophy presented in the series of questions and answers exchanged with Ibn Sīnā. As far as the nature of matter is concerned, he sided with the Islamic theologians against the Peripatetic view of hylomorphism and supported the atomism of *Kalām,* which was originally formulated by Abū Hudhayl al-'Allāf and other earlier Mu'tazilites. The arguments offered by al-Bīrūnī against hylomorphism and in support of atomism are mostly those of the theologians with certain scientific arguments elaborated and expanded to support the usual logical and philosophical arguments. It is somewhat strange that a scientist such as Bīrūnī should support the view of the theologians concerning the structure of matter, for usually the Muslim scientists believed in the continuity of matter, and even Rāzī, who believed in atoms, posited a form of atomism akin to that of Democritos and not like the atom (*juz' lā yatajazzā*) of the theologians (*mutakallimūn*).[15]

Of paramount importance for an understanding of Bīrūnī's philosophical ideas is his view of knowledge and the methods used for its attainment. Bīrūnī held a view of knowledge which was at once dynamic and static, that is he believed clearly in the gradual development of particular forms of knowledge and at the same time in the immutability of principial knowledge derived from revelation. In his treatment of the sciences he usually dealt with their history and gradual development as is seen so clearly in his *Maqālīd 'ilm al-hay'ah* ("Keys to the Science of Astronomy"), in which the history of the subject preceding Bīrūnī is treated carefully. In fact in addition to being the founder of the discipline of comparative religion or the history of religion he must also be considered as one of the founders of the history of science. Yet, he never lost sight of immutable knowledge, which for him is always found in the revealed scriptures and which provides the matrix for all the human sciences which change and develop.

Moreover, Bīrūnī was the great champion of pure knowledge and its value for the perfection of man. Of course in Islam there has never been the idea of "science for science's sake" as is found in the West. But within the context of Islamic civilization Bīrūnī[16] emphasized the importance of pure knowledge and the pursuit of knowledge for the sake of the perfection of man as against those who stressed the importance of its utility. Of course inasmuch as Bīrūnī spoke within the context of the traditional world view his defense of pure knowledge and the view of those who emphasized its utility met at the highest level, for what can he more "useful" to man than the knowledge which is an adornment for his soul and the means for its attainment of perfection. Bīrūnī himself was aware of these two poles and attitudes involved and in his own writings combined the aspect of pleasure (*lidhdhah*) associated with the attainment of knowledge with its aspect of utility (*manfa'ah*). For him the two were not completely divorced from each other but were complementary in the deepest sense.

As far as methodology is concerned, the most significant feature of Bīrūnī is that he never became the slave of a particular method nor accepted that kind of tyranny of methodology characteristic of so much of modern science. He used different methods in different sciences in conformity with the nature of the science in question. Where it was necessary he used induction, or observation, or experimentation, or deduction or had recourse to intellectual intuition. He was the most exact of scientists without ever being fooled into believing that the methods of experimental science could he applied to the domain of religion or the sciences of man. That is why in Bīrūnī, who in a sense summarizes the whole history of Islamic science, there is no single method but *methods* for acquiring various forms of knowledge in conformity with the innate nature of the sciences in question.

The basic significance of Bīrūnī for the modern world and especially the contemporary Islamic world in fact is not only in that he was the father of geodesy or that he weighed several precious stones and metals carefully or even that he criticized Aristotelian natural philosophy profoundly. Rather, it is most of all in his success in being an outstanding scientist but not only a scientist, in being scientific without being scientistic. It is in being logical without losing sight of the spiritual empyrean, the knowledge of which is not irrational nor illogical but unattainable though logic and reason alone. It is in his remarkable sense of discernment which was able to give each form of knowledge its due, to assign to each element the place to which it belonged by nature, so that he could practice mathematics with the rigour of the greatest of mathematicians and at the same time write of human affairs with a vision that is much more profound than the view of those in the modern world who try to ape the methods of the exact sciences in the field of the humanities and who do not possess a fraction of Bīrūnī's scientific knowledge.

Bīrūnī stands as the model of the thinker who was able to harmonize within his own intellectual vision various forms of knowledge, from the sciences of nature to religion and philosophy. He also stands as proof that it is possible within a traditional world-view to develop and even found various branches of the sciences without becoming enslaved by them and without falling under the deadly influence of belief in the unilateral and tyranizing power of science so prevalent today, a belief whose end cannot but be the stifling of the human spirit and the destruction of the natural environment which serves as support for man's terrestrial journey.

NOTES

1. See S.H. Nasr, "The Meaning and Role of Philosophy in Islam", *Studia Islamica,* vol. XXXVII, 1973, pp. 57-80.
2. On the gnostic nature of Islamic spirituality see F. Schuon, *Understanding Islam,* trans. by D.M. Matheson, London, 1963; Baltimore (Penguin Books), 1972, especially chapters one and four. Also S.H. Nasr, *Ideals and Realities of Islam,* London, 1967; Boston, 1972, chapter I.
3. On Bīrūnī's writings see D.J. Boilot, "L' oeuvre d'al-Biruni: essai bibliographique", *Mélanges Ins. Dominicain du Caire,* 1955, vol. 2, pp. 161-256; also S.H. Nasr, *al-Biruni: An Annotated Bibliography,* Tehran 1352 (A.H. Solar) /1973.
4. See al-Bīrūnī, *al-As'ilah wa'l-ajwibah,* ed. by S.H. Nasr and M. Mohaghegh, Tehran, 1352 (A.H. Solar)/1973.
5. On the significance of the "visionary recital" in Islamic philosophy see H. Corbin, *En Islam iranien,* vol. II, Paris, 1971, pp. 211 ff.
6. See S.H. Nasr, *An Introduction to Islamic Cosmological Doctrines,* chapters 6-10.
7. For an analysis of these questions and answers see the introduction of S.H. Nasr to his edition of the *As'ilah wa'l-ajwibah*; S.H. Barani, "Ibn Sina and Alberuni, a study in similarities and contrasts", *Avicenna Commemoration Volume,* Calcutta, 1956, pp. 3-14; M. Muṭahharī, "Pursish-hā-yi falsafī-yi Abū Huyḥan az Bū 'Alī", *Essays on al-Bīrūnī,* Tehran, 1352 (A.H. Solar) 1973, pp. 54-163; and Y.N. Zavadovskiy,[60] Ibn Sina i ego filosofskaya polemike a Bīrūnī", *TIVAN Uz SSR,* vol. 1, 1953, pp. 46-56.
8. See S. Pines, "Quelques tendances anti-péripaticiennes de la pensée scientifique islamique", *Thalès,* vol. 4, 1940, pp. 210-19.
9. This point is analyzed extensively in Muṭahharī, *op. cit.,* pp. 86 ff.
10. See al-Bīrūnī, *The Determination of the Coordinates of Cities,* trans. by J. Ali, Beirut, 1967, pp. 14-15.
11. See Nasr, *An Introduction. . .* pp. 118-119.
12. For an authentic exposition of the traditional doctrine of cycles see R. Guénon, *Formes traditionnelles et cycles cosmiques,* Paris, 1970.

13. See S.H. Nasr, *The Encounter of Man and Nature, the Spiritual Crisis of Modern Man,* London, 1968, pp. 124 ff.
14. Nasr, *An Introduction. . .* chapter 6.
15. On atomism among Muslims see S. Pines, *Beiträge zur islamischen Atomenlehre,* Berlin, 1936.
16. For the role played by knowledge in all its aspects in Islamic civilization see F. Rosenthal, *Knowledge Triumphant,* Leiden, 1971.

REFERENCES

Bīrūnī, *al-As'ilah wa'l-ajwibah,* ed. by S.H. Nasr and M. Moheghegh, Tehran, 1973.

Bīrūnī, *Chronology of Ancient Nations,* trans. by E.C. Sachau, London 1879.

Bīrūnī, *The Determination of the Coordinates of Cities,* trans. by J. Ali, Beirut, 1967.

Bīrūnī, *India,* trans. by E.C. Sachau, London, 1910.

S.H. Nasr, *An Introduction to Islamic Cosmological Doctrines,* Cambridge (U.S.A.), 1964.

9

Bīrūnī versus Ibn Sīnā on the Nature of the Universe*

In the rich tradition of Islamic Intellectual history there are several instances in which leading thinkers have left in writing the exchanges of ideas and debates which they have carried out with each other on the highest intellectual level.

One of the most important is the series of *Questions and Answers* exchanged between Bīrūnī and Ibn Sīnā (Avicenna) in which Ibn Sīnā's student Ma'ṣūmī, also took part. This series of exchanges stands as a peak of Islamic intellectual history and a key to the understanding of an aspect of Bīrūnī's thought not discussed extensively in his other writings.

The *Questions and Answers* include ten questions pertaining to Aristotle's *De Caelo* (On the Heavens) and eight other questions posed by Bīrūnī himself. These are answered by Ibn Sīnā one by one. Then Bīrūnī once again responds to Ibn Sīnā answers, discussing eight of the first ten and seven of the last eight questions. Finally Ma'ṣūmī answers Bīrūnī once again on behalf of Ibn Sīnā.

There are then altogether two sets of exchanges on some of the most fundamental points of "natural philosophy" between Bīrūnī, the "independent" scientist and thinker, and Ibn Sīnā the most eminent representative of the Islamic Peripatetic (*mashshā'ī*) school, and one of his foremost pupils, Abū Sa'īd ibn 'Alī al-Ma'ṣūmī.

In one question Bīrūnī criticizes the reasons given in Aristotelian natural philosophy for denying that the celestial spheres have gravity or levity. Bīrūnī does not reject the view of Aristotle but criticizes the reasons given to sustain such a view. Moreover, he attacks the Aristotelian thesis that circular motion is innate to heavenly bodies, asserting that

* This essay originally appeared as "Bīrūnī versus Avicenna in the Bout of the Century" in *Courier* (June 1974), :27-29. The French translation appeared in *Maroc Magazin*, 9 Dimanche, 1974, p. 7. This essay has been translated into fourteen other languages.

although the heavenly bodies do move in circular motion, such a motion could be "forced" and accidental while the motion natural to these bodies could be straight.

Ibn Sīnā replies to these objections along the lines of argument presented in standard works of Aristotelian natural philosophy.

In another question Bīrūnī criticizes Aristotle's over-reliance on the views of the ancients and his predecessors concerning the conditions of the heavens without relying upon his own observation. Bīrūnī gives an example of the Hindu description of mountains which he says cannot be relied upon because if one observes them today one sees that they have altered.

Ibn Sīnā reminds Bīrūnī of the difference between mountains which undergo generation and corruption and the celestial bodies which do not do so. Furthermore, he accuses Bīrūnī of having learned this argument from either John Philoponus, who was opposed to Aristotle because he himself was a Christian, or Muḥammed ibn Zakariyyā' Rāzī, who according to Ibn Sīnā should have remained content with medicine and not meddled in metaphysics, in which he had no competence.

Bīrūnī criticizes the Aristotelian denial of the possibility of the existence of another world completely different from the one we know, and unknown to us because it is completely veiled to our senses. He cites as illustration the fact that it is impossible for the person who is born blind to conceive of vision. In the same way there might be other worlds for the perception of which man does not have the necessary faculties. Ibn Sīnā accepts the existence of other worlds which differ from this world but defends the Aristotelian view that there cannot be another world such as this with the same elements and nature.

After these questions which are related to Aristotle's *De Caelo,* Bīrūnī poses eight other questions himself related to natural philosophy.

Bīrūnī, for example, asks how vision is possible. Why can we see beneath water whereas water is an opaque body which should reflect the rays of light at its surface? Ibn Sīnā states that according to Aristotle vision results from the eye becoming affected by the "qualities" of visible colours contained in the air that is in contact with it. According to this theory the problem mentioned by Bīrūnī does not arise since both water and air are transparent bodies that can transmit the colours to the sense of sight, thus making vision possible.

If there is no vacuum either inside or outside this world, Bīrūnī asks, why is it that if the air within a flask is sucked out water rises up in it? Ibn Sīnā answers that this is not due to a vacuum. Rather, a certain amount of the air remaining in the flask contracts as a result of the coldness of the water causing the water to rise within the flask.

If things expand through heating and contract through cooling then why, Bīrūnī asks, does a flask full of water break when the water within it freezes? Ibn Sīnā believes that it is the air which upon being cooled contracts, almost causing a vacuum to be created in the flask, and since that is not possible, causing the flask to break.

Finally, Bīrūnī queries, why does ice float on water while its earthy parts are more than water and it is therefore heavier than water? Ibn Sīnā replies that upon freezing ice preserves in its internal spaces and lattices airy parts which prevent it from sinking in water.

An examination of the questions posed by Bīrūnī reveals their vital significance for the history of science. In Islamic civilization the main school of natural philosophy which served as the immediate philosophical background for most Muslim scientists was the Peripatetic, itself a synthesis of the views of Aristotle, his Alexandrian commentators and certain elements of later Neoplatonism. Ibn Sīnā in his Peripatetic writings represents this main current in its most mature form.

But there was also an anti-Aristotelian current which is of much importance for an understanding of Islamic science, to which the questions of Bīrūnī belong. Some of the anti-Aristotelian elements derived from schools related to the Pythagorean-Hermetic heritage of Antiquity such as the writings of Jābir ibn Ḥayyān and the Ikhwān al-Ṣafā' while others issued from the logical criticism of individual philosophers and scientists such as Muḥammed ibn Zakariyyā' Rāzī and Bīrūnī.

Bīrūnī's criticism of Peripatetic natural philosophy is one of the sharpest attacks on this dominant school. It touches upon the most difficult and thorny problems of Aristotelian physics and for that reason resembles some of the arguments against this form of physics by Renaissance and 17th century scientists in the West, although the point of view of Bīrūnī is very different from that of the Western critics of Aristotle.

10

Nāṣir-i Khusraw: The Philosopher-Poet

Nāṣir-i Khusraw (394-465 to 470, 1004-1072 to 1077), properly Abū Mu'īn ibn Khusraw; distinguished Persian philosopher and poet as well as the most celebrated of Ismā'īlī thinkers.

Life. Born in the town of Qubadiyan near Balkh, Nāṣir-i Khusraw hailed from a small family that was either Sunni or Twelver Shi'ite but definitely not Ismā'īlī. Although he came to be considered a descendant of 'Alī and was often given the title of *'Alawī,* many modern scholars doubt this genealogy.

As a young man he was attracted to the study of various sciences and philosophy as well as that of other religions, which remained a major concern for him throughout his life. He entered government service early on and rose to high positions that allowed him to enjoy the life at court, but at the age of forty-two, his life was transformed by a dream admonishing him, ordering him to awake from the life of forgetfulness and journey to Mecca. Following the directives of the dream, he set out immediately for Mecca in December 1045. The transforming experience of this journey was to come, however, in Egypt, where he formally embraced Ismaili Shi'ism. Remaining in Cairo for six years, he received the title of *ḥujjat* ("proof") before leaving as Ismā'īlī "missionary" *(dā'ī)* to Khorasan.

In Khorasan he encountered fierce opposition, to the extent that his house was attacked, and he was forced to take refuge in the far-off valley of Yumgan, in the mountains of the Hindu Kush, under the protection of the emir of Badakhshan. In this bleak and isolated valley Nāṣir-i Khusraw was to spend the rest of his life. To this day his tomb is a center of pilgrimage for Sunni Muslims, who view him as a Sufi pir, and for the Ismā'īliyyah of the area, who venerate him as an Ismā'īlī sage.

---

* This essay originally appeared as "Nāṣir-i Khusraw" in the *Encyclopedia of Religion,* Vol. 10, New York, Macmillan Publishing Co., 1987, pp. 312-313.

Thought and Work. Nāṣir-i Khusraw's philosophy represents the most complete and mature synthesis of early Ismā'īlī and Faṭimid philosophy and must be considered the final development of the philosophical school that had already produced Abū Ḥātim Rāzī (d. 933/4) and Ḥāmīd al-Dīn Kirmānī (d. after 1020). Nāṣir-i Khusraw was very much concerned with the issues these authors addressed, such as confirmation of the necessity of prophecy as against the views of Muḥammad Zakarīyyā' Rāzī (Rhazes: d. 925) and emphasis upon esoteric hermeneutics (*ta'wīl*) as against both legalism and rationalism. Also, like these earlier figures, he had keen interest in religions other than Islam and followed earlier formulations of Ismā'īlī metaphysics based upon the supraontological principle and the effusion of the intellect, soul, and nature through the process of contemplation.

Many apocryphal works bearing Nāṣir-i Khusraw's name are known, but only the following eight authentic books remain extant:

1. *The Dīwān*—The celebrated metaphysical and moral work based, on the one hand, upon Ismā'īlī philosophical doctrines and, on the other, upon disdain of the world and its pleasures. It also contains some autobiographical material, including the "confessional ode" depicting the dream that transformed his life and beginning with the lines

   O widely read, O globally travelled one,
   (still earth-bound, still caught beneath the sky),
   what value would the spheres yet hold for you
   were you to catch a glimpse of hidden knowledge?

   (trans. P. W. Wilson and G. K. Aavani)
2. *Rawshanā'ī-nāmah* ("The Book of Light")—A poem of some 582 verses dealing with metaphysics and eschatology.
3. *Safar-nāmah* ("Book of Travels")—One of the most famous travel books of the Persian language, which is an important source not only for Nāṣir-i Khusraw's life but also for the contemporary geography and history of Iran and the Arab East.
4. *Wajh-i dīn* ("The Face of Religion")—A major work of Ismā'īlī exegesis of both the doctrines and the practices of religion based upon the method of *ta'wīl*.
5. *Gushāyish wa rahāyish* ("Release and Deliverance")—Answers to thirty questions dealing at once with metaphysics, physics, and religious law.
6. *Khwān al-ikhwān* ("The Feast of the Brethren")—A work written in fairly simple language dealing again with both doctrine and practice of religion and using many earlier works, including some of the author's own lost treatises.

7. *Zād al-musāfirīn* ("Provision for Travelers")—An almost purely philosophical work, including extensive quotations from earlier philosophers such as Rāzī (Rhazes).
8. *Jāmi' al-ḥikmatayn* ("Harmonization of the Two Wisdoms")—Nāṣir-i Khusraw's last work, written in Badakhshan in 1070 and perhaps his greatest philosophical masterpiece. It seeks to harmonize the tenets of Greek, philosophy, especially the thought of Plato and Aristotle, with the teachings of Islam as expounded in Ismā'īlī philosophy. The whole book is a response to a well-known philosophical poem by the tenth-century Ismā'īlī Abū Haytham Jurjānī.

An additional eight books, including *Bustān al-qulūb* ("Garden of Hearts") and *Kitāb al-miftāḥ wa'l-miṣbāḥ* ("Book of the Key and the Lamp"), are mentioned by Nāṣir-i Khusraw himself but are seemingly lost.

Influence. Nāṣir-i Khusraw, although greatly neglected in general accounts of Islamic philosophy, must be considered a major philosophical figure in the history of Islamic thought. His influence in this domain is not confined to later Ismaili thought but extends to later Islamic philosophy in general as it developed in Persia and in certain forms of Sufism. One of the very few Persian poets to be honored with the title of *ḥakīm* ("sage"), he has retained his reputation for centuries. To this day his *Dīwān* remains part and parcel of classical Persian poetry that is read and often memorized from Persia to the borders of China.

BIBLIOGRAPHY

Corbin, Henry, "Nāṣir-i *Khusrau* and Iranian Ismā'īlism." In *The Cambridge History of Iran*, vol. 4, edited by R.N. Frye, pp. 520-542. Cambridge, 1975.

Corbin, Henry, with Seyyed Hossein Nasr and Osman Yahia. *Histoire de la philosophie islamique.* Paris, 1964.

Ivanow, W., *Nasir-e Khusrow and Ismailism.* Bombay and Leiden, 1948.

Nāṣir-i Khusraw. *Kitab-e Jami' al-Ḥikmatain: Le Livre rêunissant les deux sagesses.* Edited by Henry Corbin and Mohammad Mo'in. Tehran and Paris, 1953.

Nāṣir- Khusraw. *Forty Poems from the Divan.* Translated by Peter L. Wilson and Gholam Reza Aavani, with an introduction by Seyyed Hossein Nasr. Tehran, 1977.

Nāṣir-i Khusraw. *Wajh-i Dīn (Face of Religion).* Edited by Gholam Reza Aavani, with an introduction by Seyyed Hossein Nasr. Tehran, 1977.

Nāṣir-i Khusraw. *Naser-E Khosraw's Book of Travels (Safarnama).* Translated by Wheeler Thackston, Jr. Albany, N. Y., 1985.

11
Fakhr al-Dīn Rāzī

LIFE, SIGNIFICANCE OF THOUGHT, AND WORKS*

The intellectual life of Islam after the attacks of Ash'arī and Ghazzālī upon nationalistic philosophy can be largely described as the gradual transition from the rationalism of Aristotelian philosophy toward the intuitive and illuminative wisdom of the *ishrāqīs*[1] and Sufis. Although Islam began to weaken politically and culturally during the later part of the 'Abbasid Caliphate, Muslim thought especially in the Shi'ife world continued the process of divorcing itself from the categories of Peripatetic philosophy. One of the most influential and colourful figures in this movement, who played a major role in the attack against the rationalists, was Fakhr al-Dīn Rāzī, who is considered to be the reviver of Islam in the sixth/twelfth century as Ghazzālī was in the fifth/eleventh.[2] Rāzī is in many ways a second Ghazzālī; in fact, he may without exaggeration be considered to be one of the greatest Muslim theologians.

Abu'l Faḍl Muḥammad ibn 'Umar, known as Fakhr al-Dīn Rāzī and also as Imām Fakhr, Ibn al-Khaṭīb, and *Imām al-Mushakkikīn* (the Imam of the Doubters),[3] was born in Rayy in northern Persia in 543/1149 in a family of scholars who came originally from Tabaristan. His father, Ḍiā' al-Dīn, was a well-known scholar in Rayy and was Imam Fakhr's first teacher. Later, Fakhr al-Dīn studied philosophy with Muḥammad al-Baghawī and Majd al-Dīn al-Jīlī (the latter being also the teacher of Shaikh al-Ishrāq Shihāb al-Dīn Suhrawardī) and theology with Kamāl al-Dīn Simnānī in Rayy and Maraghah, and soon became a master of all the sciences of his time including even the mathematical, medical, and natural sciences.[4]

---

* This essay appeared in *A History of Muslim Philosophy,* Edited by M.M. Sharif, Vol. 1, Wisbaden: O. Harrassowitz, 1963, pp. 642-56.

Having completed his formal studies, Imam Fakhr set out for Khwarazm to combat the Mu'tazilites, and from there journeyed to Transoxiana and was warmly accepted at the courts of the Ghur rulers, Ghiyāth al-Dīn and his brother Shihāb al-Dīn. But this stay terminated soon due to the opposition and jealousy of certain scholars and courtiers. Consequently, Imam Fakhr left the Ghur Court for Ghaznah, where he taught for a while, and finally settled in Herāt where, under the patronage of Khwarazm Shāh 'Ala'al-Dīn, a special school was built for him. There he spent the rest of his life as a teacher and preacher in comfort and honour among a large number of disciples and students who came from all over the Muslim world to study under him. He passed away at the height of fame and glory in 606/1209. [5]

The career of Imam Fakhr is in many ways a repetition of that of Ghazzālī's. Like his great predecessor, he was of the Shāfi'ī school, well versed in all the sciences and philosophy and yet opposed to many aspects of the Greek heritage, a critic of the Muslim philosophers, and drawn towards Sufism.[6] In theology, in which he followed the Ash'arite school, he was certainly influenced by Ghazzālī and Imam al-Ḥaramayn. In philosophy he came under the influence of his compatriot, Muḥammad Zakariyyā' Rāzī, as well as Ibn Sīnā, and in physics his master was without doubt Abū'l-Barakāt al-Baghdādī. Like a series of anti-Aristotelian philosophers before him, Imam Fakhr tried to reconcile religion and rational philosophy by reliance upon ideas derived more from the *Timaeus* of Plato than the *Physics* of Aristotle.[7]

Imam Fakhr's main role in the intellectual life of Islam was to support the orthodox policy of the caliphate of his time to suppress rationalistic philosophy in favour of theology. In the unified view of Islam, politics, religion, and intellectual life have never been divorced, so much so that the political struggle of minorities in the caliphate, whether they were opposed to Arab domination or, like the Shi'ah, to the 'Abbasid caliphate as such, was reflected clearly in the intellectual and religious activities of the period. As the caliphate supported the orthodox Sunni theologians against the rationalists, the philosophers sought refuge in the courts of those minor dynasties that were opposed to the central authority of the caliphs. So we see such figures as Ibn Sīnā and Khwājah Naṣīr al-Dīn Ṭūsī seeking favour of rulers opposed to the authority of Baghdad, and especially of Shi'ah princes.[8] And, on the other hand, there appeared a series of great scholars and sages, mostly theologians and Sufis, of whom the most important were Ghazzālī, Imam Fakhr, and the Sufi masters like Shihāb al-Dīn 'Umar Suhrawardī, who lifted their pen in support of the caliphate and used both theology and Sufism in order to combat rationalistic philosophy.[9] The works of Imam Fakhr were above all else dedicated to this cause. Sunni theology reached its height in his works and weakened considerably with the fall of the 'Abbasid caliphate, which came to an end about fifty years after his death.

The writings of Fakhr al-Dīn Rāzī, of which nearly a hundred are known, deal almost with every aspect of Muslim intellectual life and include all the sciences of his time.[10] Some of these, like the commentary upon the *al-Ishārāt wa'l-tanbīhāt* of Ibn Sīnā and upon his *'Uyūn al-ḥikmah* and the *Mabāḥith al-mashriqiyyah,* are written as criticisms of Muslim philosophers, especially Ibn Sīnā, and on general problems of philosophy.[11] Others deal with the many branches of the intellectual sciences including logic, mathematics, metaphysics, and the natural and the esoteric sciences.

Still another set of books deals with theology, of which the most famous are the *Kitāb al-arba'īn fī uṣūl al-dīn, Lawāmi' al-bayyināt,* and the *Muḥaṣṣal,* a classic among writings on *Kalām*. Fakhr al-Dīn also wrote a large number of works on particular sciences, like the commentary upon the syntax of Zamakhsharī, *Kitāb al-sirr al-maktūm* on astrology and astronomy, *Manāqib al-shāfi'ī* on history, the commentary upon the *Qānūn* or *Canon* of Ibn Sīnā, and many other treatises dealing with medicine, geometry, physiognomy, agriculture, theurgy, etc. Besides these writings, Imam Fakhr composed a large number of works on the purely Islamic sciences of exegesis and jurisprudence, of which the most famous are the *Mafātīḥ al-ghayb,* the voluminous commentary upon the Quran, and *al-Ma'ālim fī uṣūl al-fiqh* on the principles of jurisprudence. Throughout these writings the character of Imam Fakhr as a critic and "doubter" is evident. He criticizes not only the philosophers, but also theologians like Ash'arī and historians like Shahrastānī, whom he accuses of plagiarizing Baghdādī's *al-Farq bayn al-firaq* in his *al-Milal wa'l-niḥal.*[12] Imam Fakhr's particular genius for analysis and criticism is evident in whatever field he turns his attention to, so that in the annals of Muslim thought he has quite justly become famous as one who is a master in posing a problem but not in solving it, in entering into a debate but not in concluding it.

THEOLOGY (*KALĀM*)

Ash'arite theology or *Kalām* began as a reaction against the rationalistic school of the Mu'tazilites, and only gradually developed into a complete science. In the earlier centuries the theologians, following the lead of

Abu'l-Ḥasan al-Ash'arī, tried to use logic, the instrument of their enemies, in order to defend the truths of revelation. From the fourth/tenth century onward, this defence itself became more subtle and systematic, reaching its height in the works of Imam al-Ḥaramain Abu'-l-Ma'ālī 'Abd al-Malik al-Juwaynī, such as the *Irshād* and the *Shāmil.*[13] With Ghazzālī *Kalām* took a new turn; opposed as it was from the beginning to the school of the philosophers, it now began to employ the syllogistic method, intellectual (*'aqlī*) evidence, and certain theses of the philosophers, thus laying the foundations of the school of philosophical *Kalām* of the later theologians.

Imam Fakhr is the greatest master of this later school of theology, surpassing in many ways even the more illustrious Ghazzālī. With Imam Fakhr philosophical *Kalām* reaches its zenith of power and perfection; his works became consequently a continuous source of influence over the later theologians, whether they were Sunnis like al-Ījī and al-Taftazānī or Shī'ahs like Khwājah Naṣīr.[14] Properly speaking, Rāzī must be credited with the foundation of a new school of *Kalām,* and certain writers have even considered him to be the Third Teacher after Aristotle and Fārābī.[15] Actually, he composed works characteristic of both the first period of Muslim theology—marked by a revolt against the philosophers and yet by a dependence upon their methods and even some of their ideas—and the second period, after Ghazzālī, in which theology became a more independent science and lost much of its defensive and apologetic quality. Among the first type of writings one may name *Muḥaṣṣal* and *al-Arabī'n fī uṣūl al-Dīn* and among the second *Asās al-taqdīs* and *Lawāmi' al-bayyināt.*

The theology of Imam Rāzī is marked by the integration of theological themes with other sciences. For example, in his Persian treatise, *Asrār al-tanzīl,* he combines theology with ethics; and in the *Lawāmi' al-bayyināt,* theology with Sufism, giving theology a fragrance of spirituality and beauty not found in most writings. In the sixth chapter of the *Lawāmi'* he gives a detailed and profound discussion concerning *dhikr,* the invocation of one of the Divine Names, which is the basic technique of Sufism. Concerning one of the interior forms of *dhikr* he writes: "The third kind of *dhikr* is that man should contemplate the creatures of God until each particle of the essence of creation becomes a polished mirror before the unmanifested world so that when he looks into this mirror with the eye of wisdom the ray of the eye of his soul will fall upon the world of Majesty. This is a station without end and a sea without limit."[16] In this way Imam Rāzī raises theology to a height approached only by Ghazzālī, far surpassing the usual level of this study.[17]

To understand Rāzī's approach to theology, it is enough to analyse the structure of one of his treatises. We take as an example perhaps the most famous of his theological works, the *Muḥaṣṣal,* which became a classic sourcebook on *Kalām* almost from the moment of its composition.[18] Here, Imam Rāzī divides theology into four parts *(arkān)*: Preliminaries, Being and its divisions, rational theology *(ilāhiyyāt),* and traditional questions *(sam'iyyāt).* The preliminaries include the principles of logic, the sufficiency of demonstration *(dalīl)* to prove the existence of God, and the obligation upon each believer to prove God's existence.[19] The section on Being and its divisions considers the questions of Being and non-Being, attributes of Being, the negation of modes between Being and non-Being, the relation of the One to the many, cause and effect, etc. rational theology which is interlaced with passages from the Quran concerning the Necessary Being. His Attributes and acts and the Divine names. Finally, the traditional questions, which are exclusively scriptural, concern prophethood, eschatology, the Imamate, the faith, and other related subjects. As a whole, therefore, Imam Rāzī's theology combines the transmitted or traditional elements of revelation *(naqlī)* and the intellectual and rational evidence concerning religious and metaphysical questions *('aqlī)* into a science which takes into account the problems of religion while participating in many of the discussions of philosophy.

In the method and problems of theology, Imam Rāzī followed the Ash'arites. As he writes in his *Kitāb al-arba'īn*: 'We (the Ash'arites) believe that God is neither body nor substance, and that He is not in space; yet, we believe that we can see God." But to show his independence of judgment he goes on to assert: "Our companions (the Ash'arites) have given an intellectual reason for the possibility of seeing God, but we have brought twelve objections against it which cannot be answered. Therefore, we only say that we can see God by appealing to transmitted reasoning, i.e. the Quranic text."[20]

Imam Rāzī also criticized Ash'arī on the question of atomism which is such an essential aspect of the Ash'arite theology. Rāzī rejected atomism in his earlier works like the *Mabāḥith al-mashriqiyyah* and wrote his *Kitāb al-jawhar al-farḍ* to refute it, but in later works like the great Quranic commentary, the *Mafātīḥ al-ghayb,* he accepted it once again. (Atomism does not play a major role in his theology as it does in the system of other Ash'arites like Bāqillānī). This change of position occurs also in the rejection of infinity, the void, and the plurality of worlds in the earlier writings and their acceptance in later works like the *Mafātīḥ.*

There are several points in Imam Rāzī's theology which are of special interest in so far as his particular point of view is concerned. One relates to the question of faith in which he joins most theologians in regarding faith as the necessary and sufficient requirement for being saved. Hell is not for those who have committed evil acts accidentally but for the infidels who have no faith. Man is of course responsible for his work but ultimately all is determined by the Divine Will. Imam Rāzī is very emphatic in his determinism and overthrows even the theory of acquisition (*kasb*) of the Ash'arites. His Qurānic commentary is full of arguments for determinism, which he defends more openly and ably than any other theologian. God is the creator of both good and evil, faith and impiety, benefit and injury; all these qualities are decreed by the determination of the Divine Will *(qaḍā' wa qadar).* Yet, none of the Divine Acts can be considered to be inappropriate or blameable since God is the creator and ruler of the world, and whatever He does in His kingdom is His own affair and is as such appropriate.

According to Imam Rāzī, God's Attributes and Names must be interpreted symbolically *(ta'wīl)* in order to be understood. He follows the method of Imam al-Ḥaramayn in applying *ta'wīl* to the Quran, especially to those verses in which God is attributed with such anthropomorphic qualities as sight, hearing, etc. This does not mean that Rāzī tries to overcome the rational difficulties of certain of the principles of faith by *ta'wīl,* as did many of the philosophers. For example, on the question of resurrection, unlike the philosophers who believed only in the resurrection of the soul, Imam Razī asserts that at resurrection God will create for each soul the same body, made of the same elements as those it possessed in this life.

On the question of knowledge and the process of reasoning, Imam Rāzī is of the view that reason is neither the cause of which knowledge is the effect nor the source which produces knowledge. There is an intelligible succession between the two; God creates a reasoning which knowledge follows necessarily.[21] He accords a definite value to the rational faculty; his aim in theology is in fact to create a science which combines and harmonizes reason and revelation, *'aql* and *naql.* In his Quranic commentary he calls those who have succeeded in integrating these two elements the Muslim sages *(ḥukamā' islāmiyyah),* and praises them greatly. His own importance in Muslim theology lies in his success in establishing the school of philosophical *Kalām,* already begun by Ghazzālī, in which both intellectual and revelational evidence played important roles.

PHILOSOPHY

The importance of Imam Rāzī in philosophy lies more in his criticism of the philosophers than in the establishment of a new school. Influenced by the writings of Ghazzālī, he studied philosophy to such an extent that he became a definite master of it. Unlike those theologians who rejected Greek philosophy totally or those Peripatetics who followed it strictly, Imam Rāzī criticized many points of Greek philosophy while accepting certain others. In the introduction to the *Mabāḥith al-mashriqiyyah,* the most important of his philosophical works, he writes: "Our associates belong to two groups: one consisting of those who imitate the Greek philosophers, permit no one to discuss their thought, and take pride in being able to understand their sayings, and the other comprising those who reject all of their ideas without exception. Both of these groups are wrong. We have delved deep into the writings of the previous philosophers and have affirmed the true and rejected the false. We have added certain principles to this philosophy and have put forth some new ideas."[22]

The new ideas of which Imam Rāzī speaks are mostly those pertaining to the rejection of certain basic elements of Aristotelianism and in some cases of Platonism. In the *Mabāḥith* he rejects the Platonic ideas, since in the Ash'arite perspective all higher modes of Being are absorbed in the Absolute. He also criticizes the Platonic notion of knowledge as reminiscence and the idea held by certain Muslim philosophers that light is a body. One of his most important and penetrating discussions involves criticism of the principle that from Unity only unity can issue forth, *ex uno non fit nisi unum,* a principle held by nearly all medieval philosophers. Imam Rāzī puts this view to the test of his severe judgment and criticizes it with his usual genius for analysis. He asserts, on the contrary, that from Unity multiplicity can issue forth, but does not pursue the proof of this assertion very far.

The *Mabāḥith* deals with many other subjects treated in the well-known texts of Muslim philosophy like those of Ibn Sīnā. In each case it is the acute criticism of commonly held Peripatetic notions that is of interest. In his commentary upon the *al-Ishārāt wa'l-tanbīhāt* of Ibn Sīnā, which after the *Mabāḥith* is his most important philosophical work, this type of criticism and doubts about Peripatetic philosophy continue—doubts which his pupil, Naṣīr al-Dīn Ṭūsī, tried to answer in his own commentary upon the *Ishārāt.* Ever since these works were written, nearly every student of Peripatetic philosophy in the Muslim world, especially in Persia, has reached this philosophy through the criticism of Imam Rāzī, so that the thought of Imam Rāzī has become a permanent heritage of Islamic philosophers. His other philosophical works, like the commentary upon the *'Uyūn al-ḥikmah, Lubāb al-ishārāt* and many treatises on logic and metaphysics, are also significant, but his greatest philosophical importance lies in the criticisms and doubts cast upon the principles of Peripatetic philosophy, which not only left an indelible mark upon that school but opened the horizon for the other modes of knowledge like *ishrāqī* philosophy and gnosis, which were more intimately bound with the spirit of Islam.

THE SCIENCES

There have been very few Muslim theologians who have had as much knowledge of the mathematical and natural sciences as Imam Rāzī. His preoccupation with the sciences is itself of great interest, because usually the Sunni theologians and doctors of Law shunned any discipline outside the sphere of the strictly religious sciences. Imam Rāzī, on the contrary, studied all the *awā'il* sciences, that is, the sciences inherited from the Greeks, and was considered by many of his contemporaries to be the greatest authority of his time on them. There is hardly a science in which he did not compose a treatise—although he never occupied himself with the study of nature in the manner of Ibn al-Haytham or Bīrūnī. His main importance in the sciences was in considering their principles and their relation to theology and to the spirit of Islamic revelation.

A field in which Imam Rāzī excelled is medicine, a discipline the mastery of which one hardly expects from a theologian. He wrote several treatises on health, pulse, and anatomy, and a medical encyclopaedia entitled *al-Jāmi' al-kabīr* or *al-Ṭibb al-kabīr* which he never completed. His most important medical work was his commentary upon the *Qānūn* of Ibn Sīnā, which he often criticized, basing himself on the opinions of Galen and the Muslim physicians, especially Muḥammad Zakariyyā' Rāzī. The commentary is sufficient evidence that Imam Rāzī did not learn medicine by reading one or two manuals but studied it thoroughly and was well versed in it. He was in fact famous in Herat for his ability and exactitude in diagnosis.

Imam Rāzī also wrote several treatises on geometry, astronomy, agriculture, politics, history, and comparative religion.[23] Also of interest are his works on the hidden sciences *(al-'ulūm al-gharībah)*, to which he devoted much attention. There remain among his writings treatises on theurgy *(ṭalismāt)*, geomancy *(raml)*, physiognomy *(firāsah)*,[24] astrology, and other similar subjects. It is curious that Imam Rāzī wrote all these treatises, although he was opposed to certain of these subjects like astrology which he attacked throughout his writings.[25] He was, however, more sympathetic to the study of hidden sciences than either the theologians or the philosophers, as is illustrated by his defence of alchemy against the charges of Ibn Sīnā.[26]

Of particular interest to the history of Muslim sciences is the scientific encyclopedia of Imam Rāzī, the *Jāmi' al-'ulūm.*[27] This work offers a good source for the names, definitions, scope, and major principles of the various Muslim sciences. Imam Fakhr begins with a discussion of traditional religious sciences such as theology, jurisprudence, dialectics, comparative religion, inheritance, will and testament, Quranic commentary, and reading of the Quran and *Ḥadīth;* and then passes on to the linguistic sciences dealing with grammar, syntax, etymology of words, prosody and poetic metre, and, after that to history. Having considered the transmitted *(naqlī)* sciences, he devotes the rest of the book to the intellectual *('aqlī)* sciences which include natural philosophy, interpretation of dreams, physiognomy, medicine, anatomy, pharmacology, the science of the occult properties of things, alchemy, theurgy, agriculture, geometry, science of weights, arithmetic, algebra, optics, music, astronomy, astrology, metaphysics, ethics and its various branches, and even chess and other games. Imam Rāzī describes the principles, scope, and major problems of each science. Despite the fact that his discussion is always general and characteristic of an encyclopedist and never penetrates too deeply into any single science, the work is perfect evidence of his vast erudition and encyclopedic knowledge. In this respect Imam Rāzī is similar to the Ismaili and the later Twelve-Imam Shi'ah theologians of the Safavid period many of whom, like Shaykh Bahā' al-Dīn 'Āmilī, took great interest not only in philosophy but also in all the cosmological and mathematical sciences. Imam Fakhr's importance in the Islamic sciences is, therefore, mostly in bringing closer together the theological and cosmoloical traditions which until his time had been far apart, and in studying nature with a view to discovering God's wisdom in creation, as was done by many other Muslim scientists.[28] In this case, as in so many others, he advanced upon a path already trodden by Ghazzālī.

COMMENTARIES UPON THE QUR'ĀN

Imam Rāzī's fame in the Muslim world lies as much in his commentaries on the Noble Quran as in his theological works. He was greatly devoted to the Quran from childhood and studied Quranic commentary with his father. His study of all the other sciences by no means reduced his love for the Quran. As he wrote in old age: "I have experienced all the methods of theology and all the ways of philosophy, but I did not find in them the benefit which could equal the benefit I derived from the reading of the exalted Quran."[29]

Imam Rāzī's Quranic commentaries include the *Tafsīr al-fātiḥah, Tafsīr sūrat al-baqarah, Asmā' Allah al-ḥusnā,* and *Risālah fi'l-tanbīh 'alā ba'ḍ al-asrār al-maw'iẓah fi'l-qur'ān,* which last is a theological commentary combined with Sufi ideas in which metaphysics *(ilāhiyyāt)* is based on the chapter *(sūrah) al-Ikhlāṣ,* prophecy on the chapter *al-A'lā,* resurrection of the chapter *al-Tīn,* and the recording of human actions on the chapter *al-'Aṣr.* The most important of Imam Rāzī's commentaries is the voluminous *Mafātīḥ al-ghayb,* known as the "Great Commentary" *(Tafsīr al-kabīr),* which was collected and organized by Ibn al-Khu'ī and Suyūṭī after his death. This work is the most important theological commentary even written on the Quran. Imam Rāzī makes this also an occasion to expose his encyclopedic knowledge in that he intermingles history, geography, and other branches of knowledge with the commentary of the Quranic text wherever possible. He mentions and praises often in this work the Muslim sages who combine intellectual principles with the principles of Islamic revelation. He also analyses the stories of the Quran and interprets their theological and metaphysical meanings. Despite its volume and the number of topics which do not seem very relevant to the immediate subject-matter, the *Mafātīḥ* is an impressive theological Quranic commentary. In its intellectual interpretation and the combining of *'aql* and *naql,* of reason and authority, and in the understanding of the sacred Scripture it remains one of the major commentaries upon the Quran.

JURISPRUDENCE (FIQH)

Although primarily occupied with theology, Imam Rāzī occasionally devoted himself to jurisprudence as well. The few works like *al-Maḥṣūl fi'uṣūl al-fiqh, al-Ma'ālim,* and *Iḥkām al-aḥkām* bear evidence to his mastery of jurisprudence which he interpreted according to the school of the exgetes. As already mentioned, he belonged to the Shafi'ī school of which he was considered to be one of the *'ulamā'* and authentic interpreters. Imam Rāzī was particularly well versed in the principles of jurisprudence *(uṣūl),* which he treated in a manner similar to theology. This subject has, in fact, never been able to divorce itself from *Kalām,* and is still studied almost as if it were one of its branches. The importance of Imam Rāzī in Shāfi'ī jurisprudence lies more in his contribution to the theoretical principles of *fiqh* than in their actual application embodied in the *fatwās* of the various Shāfi'ī *'ulamā'.*

DIALECTIC, RHETORIC, AND POETRY

Following the example of Ghazzālī, Imām Rāzī became a dialectical theologian and, as his works testify, excelled in dialectics. He was famous for his eloquence in persuasion and argumentation, for the quickness of his intelligence and keenness of wit. These gifts were combined with a rhetorical power which made him the most famous preacher in Herat. Hardly would a scholar dare enter into debate with him; those who took sides against him would soon feel the thrust of his dialectical and rhetorical weapons. The *Munāẓarāt* bears ample evidence of these traits. In its pages one sees Imam Rāzī as a tiger who pounces mercilessly upon his helpless adversary and has little regard for softness in discourse. Much of his energy throughout life was spent in attacking bitterly the small sects which arose against the main orthodoxy, such as the Karrāmiyyah, who probably finally poisoned him.[30] As the *Shaykh al-Islām* of Herat, his main duty was to preach and defend Islam; and he took the opportunity of using his remarkable gifts of rhetoric and dialectic in a manner which made him one of the most famous of Muslim preachers.

Imam Rāzī had also the gift of poetry, and many verses both in Arabic and Persian are attributed to him. As in the case of so many other sages like Khayyām, poetry became for Imam Rāzī the vehicle for the expression of gnosis and the form of "ignorance" which lies above all formal knowledge. In a quatrain in Persian he writes:

> "My heart was never deprived of science;
> There is little of the mysteries that I did not understand.
> For seventy-two years I thought night and day,
> Yet I came to know that nothing is to be known."

SUFISM

There is little doubt that Imam Rāzī was sympathetic to Sufism, especially in later life, when he wrote most of his poems like the one mentioned above. Moreover, many of his works are, like his Quranic commentary, full of Sufi ideas,, and in his *Lawāmi' al-bayyināt* he outlines the degrees of knowledge in a manner very similar to the Sufi treatise of Suhrawardī, *Ṣafīr-i Simurgh.*[31] He is altogether a theologian with sympathies towards Sufism.

What is difficult for us to discover is whether Imam Rāzī was a practising Sufi or not. Certainly Sufism is not so evident in his writings as in Ghazzālī's, and his life, rich in worldly fame and wealth, had none of the ascetic elements of the life of his great predecessor. There is even an extant letter from the master of gnosis, the Andalusian Sufi, Shaykh al-Akbar Muḥyī al-Dīn ibn 'Arabī, advising Imam Rāzī to leave dialectic and discursive thought and try to reach the stage of gnosis and contemplation, telling him that in heaven medicine and geometry will do him little good.[32] Moreover, in his writings as in his life, Imam Rāzī displayed an aggressiveness and fighting quality hardly characteristic of the lives and writings of the Sufis.

Yet, despite all this negative evidence, some of his later writings do show the clear influence of Sufism upon him, and it may be that, because of his social position even after joining the circle of the Sufis, he to a large extent hid his sympathies and affiliations in order to avoid any external opposition. His own poems and his great love for the blind Arab poet Abū ʻAlā' al-Maʻarrī, the gnostic who often appears like a sceptic to the uncritical eye, on whose *Dīwān* he is said to have commented, point to the fact that Imam Rāzī was not an ordinary theologian but knew that there is another form of knowledge, gnosis, which lies above all rational sciences like theology. Whether he actually participated in this knowledge in an effective way, is a question too difficult to answer from either historical evidence or internal evidence from his own writings.[33]

There is a poem of Imam Rāzī which is in itself almost sufficient evidence for his Sufism. In the original Arabic it is so beautiful and effective that hardly any of his biographers has failed to mention it. Written in old age by a man who was the leading scholar and theologian of his day and who enjoyed all the comfort and glory of the life of this world, it is a vivid reminder that beyond the sphere of all human life and knowledge there is another reality which man must seek in order to remain faithful to his own intimate nature. The poem begins with these verses:

> "Our souls fear our bodies as if they want to separate from them.
> The result of our life in this world has been nothing but pain to others and sin.
> For all the discussions and debates of our life
> We have derived no benefit but senseless noise.
> How often have we seen men and kingdoms
> All perish quickly and cease to exist!
> How was their glory once more exalted than a mountain,
> Yet, men perish and the mountain remains the same!"

THE SIGNIFICANCE AND INFLUENCE OF IMĀM RĀZĪ

The many-sided genius of Imam Rāzī, to which the previous pages bear partial witness, makes him one of the most colourful figures in Islam. Following the example of Ghazzālī, by whom he was profoundly influenced and whose retreat in Ṭus he visited, Rāzī spent a life-time in combating the rationalistic aspect of Greek philosophy. Although not of equal stature to Ghazzālī in Sufism and ethics, he, nevertheless, exercised as much influence, especially in theology, as did his more famous predecessor. Possessed of a special gift for posing problems and for analysing philosophical questions, he left an indelible mark upon all later Muslim philosophers, especially upon Khwājah Naṣīr al-Dīn Ṭūsī, his pupil, who was the reviver of Muslim philosophy after Imam Rāzī, and was also the most famous of Shi'ah theologians.

Imam Rāzī's role in Islamic intellectual life, besides establishing the school of philosophical *Kalām* begun by Ghazzālī, was to intensify the attack against Peripatetic philosophy, thereby preparing the way for the propagation of the metaphysical doctrines of the *ishrāqīs* and Sufis who, like Imam Rāzī, opposed the rationalism inherent in Aristotelianism. With the method of doubt in which he was the greatest master in Islam, he analysed and criticized Peripatetic philosophy in a way hardly ever equalled by anyone except Ghazzālī. Yet, he was a theologian also interested in the cosmological, natural, and esoteric sciences.[34] Imam Rāzī played an important role in bringing theology closer to the sciences and even to Sufism, with which he flavoured his theological works. In the centuries when the Muslim world was turning away from Peripatetic rationalism toward modes of thought more akin to its own spirit, Imām Rāzī played a major role in this transformation. He remains as one of the most arresting figures among Muslim theologians, a figure the power of whose thought spread over the whole Muslim world at the very moment when the Mongol onslaught was putting an end to the caliphate, to the survival of which his work was to a large extent dedicated.

BIBLIOGRAPHY

G. Gabrioli, "Fakhr al-Dīn al-Rāzī", *Isis,* 7, 1925, pp. 9-13; L. Gardet and M.M. Anawati, *Introduction à la théologie musulmane,* Librarie Philosophique J. Vrin, Paris, 1948; I. Goldziher, "Aus der Theologie des Fakhr al-Dīn al-Rāzī", *Der Islam,* III, 1912, pp. 213-47; M. Horten, *Die philosophischen Ansichten von Rāzī and Ṭūsī,* Bonn, 1910; *Die spekulative und positive Theologie des Islam nach Rāzī und ihre Kritik durch Ṭūsī,* Leipzig, 1912; P. Kraus, "Les 'controverse' de Fakhr al-Dīn Rāzī", *Bulletin de l'Institut d'Égypt,* t. XIX, 1936-37, pp. 187-214; Y. Mourad, *La physiognomonie arabe et la Kitāb al-Firāsah de Fakhr al-Dīn al-Rāzī,* Librarie Orientaliste, Paul Geuthner, Paris, 1939; S. Pines, *Beiträge zur islamischen Atomenlehre,* A. Heine GmbH., Gräfenhainichen, Berlin, 1936.

Fakhr al-Dīn al-Rāzī, *Asrār al-tanzīl,* lithographed edition, Tehran, 1301/1883; *Fawā'id-i Ghiyāthiyyah,* Maṭba'-i Qāsimī, Hyderabad, 1323/1905; *I'tiqādāt farq al-muslimīn wa'l-mushrikīn*, Maktabat al-Nahḍat al-Miṣriyyah, Cairo, 1356/1937; *Jāmi' al-'ulūm,* Mirzā Muḥammad Khān, Bombay, 1323/1905; *Kitāb al-arba'īn fī uṣūl al-dīn,*

Dairatul-Maarif-il-Osmania, Hyderabad, 1353/1934; *Lubāb al-ishārāt,* Cairo, 1343/1924; *Mafātīḥ al-ghayb,* 8 Vols., Cairo, Maṭba'at al-Amīrat al-Sharafiyyah, 1308/1890; *Muḥaṣṣal,* Maṭba'at al-Ḥusayniyyah, Cairo, 1323/1905; *Munāẓarāt,* Dairatul-Maarif-il-Osmania Hyderabad, 1355/1936; *al-Risālat al-kamāliyyah fi ḥaqā'iq al-ilāhiyyah,* Tehran University Press, 1335 Solar.

NOTES

1. For the definition and desertion of this term refer to the following chapter on Shihāb al-Dīn Suhrawardī.
2. According to a *ḥadīth,* in each century God sends a great sage and scholar into the world to strengthen Islam. Muslim historians, following this *ḥadīth,* have searched during each century for the fittest person to receive this honour.
3. He was given this title because he doubted so many of the views of the previous philosophers and even of the theologians.
4. In the *Wafayāt al-a'yān,* Ibn Khallikān writes that Imam Rāzī was the greatest authority on the Greek sciences *('ulūm al-awā'il)* in his time. The best sources for the biography of Rāzī are Ibn Abī Uṣaybi'ah, *'Uyūn al-anbā',* Ibn al-Qifṭī, *Tārikh al-ḥukamā',* Ibn Khallikān, *Kitāb wafayāt al-a'yān,* Shams al-Dīn Shahrazūrī, *Nuzhat al-arwāḥ wa Rawḍat al-ajrāḥ,* and Ibn Taqī al-Dīn al-Subkī, *Ṭabaqāt al-shāfi'iyyat al-kubrā.*
5. Al-Subkī, *Ṭabaqāt al-shāfi'iyyat al-kubrā,* Maṭba'at al-Ḥusayniyyah, Cairo, 1324/1906, Vol. V, pp. 33-40.
6. Although not a great Sufi figure like Ghazzālī, Imam Rāzī was nevertheless sympathetic towards Sufism, especially in the later period of his life. Subkī, *op. cit.,* p. 35, writes that Rāzī was himself a Sufi, and some of his poems and frequent quotations from the Sufi masters like Ḥallāj and Abū Sa'īd certainly point in this direction.
7. For an outline of the ideas of the group of Muslim thinkers who were influenced by Platonic physics, see S. Pines, *Beiträge zur islamischen Atomenlehre.*
8. It is far from accidental that the philosophy and the sciences which were connected with the Greek heritage flourished especially in the fourth/tenth century when most of the Muslim world was governed by the Shi'ah Buyids and Faṭimids.
9. The opposition of this group to Greek philosophy was primarily against its rationalistic and syllogistic aspects. The cosmological and certain metaphysical doctrines of the Greeks were not only not criticized but were also openly accepted by them. So we see a Ghazzālī using Hermetic symbolism or a Fakhr Rāzī writing numerous treatises on the cosmological sciences related Greek sources.
10. For a bibliography of his works, see Subkī, *op. cit.,* pp. 33-40 and Imam Rāzī's *I'tiqādāt farq al-muslimīn wa'l-mushrikīn,* Maktabat al-Nahḍat al-Miṣriyyah, Cairo, 1356/1937, Introduction by Shaykh 'Abd al-Razzāq, pp. 27ff.
11. Imam Rāzī's pupil, Khwājah Naṣīr al-Dīn Ṭūsī, wrote many works answering his teacher's criticism of Ibn Sīnā and other philosophers.
12. See Fakhr al-Dīn Rāzī, *Munāẓarāt,* Dairatul-Maarif-il-Osmania, Hyderabad, 1355/1936, where he also criticizes certain parts of Ghazzālī's *Tahāfut al-falāsifah* on the motion of the planets. See also P. Kraus, "Les 'controverse's de Fakhr al-Dīn Rāzī", *Bulletin de l'Institut d'Égypt.,* t. XIX, 1936-37, pp. 187-214.

13. For a history of Muslim theology, especially of the Sunni school, see Shiblī Nu'mānī, *Tārīkh 'ilm-i kalām,* tr. M. Fakhr Dā'ī Gīlānī, Rangīn Press, Teheran, 1328/1910, and L. Gardet and M.M. Anawati, *Introduction à la théologie musulmane,* Librarie Philosophique J. Vrin, Paris, 1948.

14. The theological masterpiece, the *Tajrīd,* of Khwājah Naṣīr al-Dīn Ṭūsī, who is the greatest of the Shī'ah theologians, is to a large extent influenced by Imam Rāzī's *Masā'il al-khamsīn.*

15. This title, however, is more commonly given to Mīr Dāmād, the master of theology and philosophy during the Safavid period.

16. Fakhr al-Dīn Rāzī, *Lawāmi' al-bayyināt,* Library of Imām Riḍā, Mashhad, MS. Cat. No. 233.

17. Imam Rāzī, like the Christian theologians, considered *Kalām* to be the queen of the sciences and subordinated all the other rational sciences like philosophy and the mathematical and natural sciences to it.

18. For a more detailed discussion of this work, see L. Gardet and M.M. Anawati, *op. cit.,* pp. 162-64.

19. In all Muslim theology it is considered obligatory upon each Muslim to prove the existence of God according to his intellectual ability. See F. Schuon, "Nature et arguments de la foi", *Etudes Traditionelles,* Vol. 54, Dec. 1953, pp. 344-63.

20. Fakhr al-Dīn Rāzī, *Kitāb al-arba'īn fi uṣūl al-dīn,* Dairatul-Maarif-il-Osmania, Hyderabad, 1353/1934, p. 190.

21. Many theologians before Rāzī considered this relation between reason and knowledge to be custom (*'ādah*), but he explicitly rejects this notion.

22. Fakhr al-Dīn Rāzī, *al-mabāḥith al-mashriqiyyah,* Dairatul-Maarif-il-Osmania, Hyderabad, 1343/1924, Vol. I, p. 4.

23. His historical works include *Kitāb faḍā'il al-ṣaḥābah* and *Kitāb manāqib al-Imām Shāfi'i,* and his work on comparative religion, the *I'tiqādāt farq al-muslimīn wa'l mushrikīn.*

24. See Y. Mourad, *La physiognomonis arabe et le Kitāb al-Firāsah de Fakhr al-Dīn al-Rāzī*, Librarie Orientaliste, Paul Geuthner, Paris, 1939.

25. See *Munāẓarāt,* pp. 20-24.

26. See *Mabāḥith....,* p. 214.

27. This work Imam Fakhr wrote for Khwārazm Shāh Abū al-Muẓaffar ibn Malik al-Mu'aẓẓam. It has always been a popular scientific encyclopedia and was printed in a lithographed edition in Bombay in 1323/1905.

28. Imam Fakhr's writings are full of passages in which he appeals to various natural phenomena as "signs" of the different Divine Qualities and Names. See his *Asrār al-tanzīl,* Teheran, lithographed edition, 1301/1883, pp. 68ff.

29. Ibn Abī Uṣaībi'ah, *'Uyūn al-anbā' fi ṭabaqāt al-aṭibbā',* Maṭba'at al-Wahābiyyah, Cairo, Vol. II, p. 27.

30. There is a story told of Imam Rāzī's opposition to the Ismā'īlīs. He used to attack them bitterly in public, accusing them of having no proofs for their doctrines. One day one of their agents, posing as a student, found Imam Rāzī alone in his library, pulled out a knife and pointed it to his chest saying, "This is our proof." Henceforth, Imam Fakhr

never attacked the Ismailis in public. One day the disciples asked him why he no longer spoke against this group—the group which he had opposed so bitterly before. He replied, "Because I have seen their proof." This story appears in nearly all the biographies of Imam Fakhr which we have already mentioned and is characteristic of his wisdom in public life.

31. See the next chapter on Suhrawardī.

32. See Fakhr al-Dīn Rāzī, *al-Risālat al-kamāliyyah fi'l-ḥaqā'iq al-ilāhiyyah*, Tehran University Press, 1335 Solar, Introduction by Sayyid Muḥammad Bāqir Sabziwārī, p. (kt).

33. There is a story told that Imam Rāzī met the Sufi Najm al-Dīn Kubrā in a gathering and boasted of his religious knowledge and said that he knew a hundred proofs for the existence of God. Najm al-Dīn answered, "Is not each proof due to some doubt? God has placed in the heart of the Sufi a light of certainty which dispels all doubt, so that he no longer has need of proofs." Imam Rāzī hearing this answer surrendered himself to the Shaykh and was initiated into Sufism.

34. It is of great interest that not only in the Muslim world but also in medieval Christianity and in China many of those who preoccupied themselves with the science of nature, like the Taoists, Ikhwān al-Ṣafā', and the Franciscans, were opposed to philosophical rationalism and accepted some form of esoteric and metaphysical doctrine based on intellectual intuition and revelation.

PART III

SUHRAWARDĪ AND THE SCHOOL OF ISHRĀQ

12

Shihab al-Din Suhrawardī *

The intellectual life of Islam and that of Christianity—the two sister civilizations—in the Middle Ages can be compared with each other to a large extent through the role that Aristotelian philosophy played in them. Peripatetic science and philosophy entered the Western world through translations from Arabic in the the fifth/eleventh and sixth/twelth centuries and eventually became dominant to such an extent as to replace the Augustinian and Platonic wisdom of the earlier period only to be overthrown itself by the humanistic rationalism of the Renaissance. In Islam the attack of Sufis and theologians upon the rationalistic aspect of Aristotelian philosophy weakened its hold at the very time when that philosohy was gaining strength in the Christian West and was replaced in the Muslim world by two elements, the doctrinal Sufism of Muḥyī al-Dīn ibn 'Arabī and the *Ḥikmat al-ishrāq*[1] or illuminative wisdom of Shaykh al-Ishrāq Shihāb al-Dīn Yaḥyā ibn Habash ibn Amīrak Suhrawardī,[2] both of which aimed at an effective realization of the "truth" and replaced the rationalism of Peripatetic philosophy by intellectual intuition (*dhawq*).

LIFE, WORKS, AND SOURCES OF DOCTRINES

Shihāb al-dīn Suhrawardī, whose *ishrāqī* wisdom has played such a great role in the intellectual and spiritual life of Islam and especially of Shi'ism, was born in Suhraward, a village near the present city of Zanjan in northern Persia, in 549/1153. He studied at first with Majd al-Dīn Jīlī at Maraghah and later with Ẓahīr al-Dīn Qārī at Ispahan. Having finished his formal studies, he began to travel through Persia, meeting various Sufi masters and benefiting from their presence and teachings. During this period he spent much time in meditation and invocation in spiritual

* This essay appeared in *A History of Muslim Philosophy,* Edited by M.M. Sharif. Vol., I pp. 373-398.

retreats. He also journeyed during the same period through the regions of Anatolia and Syria and acquired great love for the cities of these countries. On one of his journeys, he went from Damascus to Aleppo and met Malik Ẓāhir, the son of Ṣalāh al-Dīn Ayyūbī, the celebrated Muslim ruler. Malik Ẓāhir became much devoted to Shihāb al-Dīn and asked him to stay at his court. It was here that the master of *ishrāq* fell into disgrace with the religious authorities in the city who considered some of his statements dangerous to Islam. They asked for his death, and when Malik Ẓāhir refused, they petitioned Ṣalāh al-Dīn himself who threatened his son with abdication unless he followed the ruling of the religious leaders, Shihāb al-Dīn was thereby imprisoned and in the year 587/1191, at the age of 38, he was either suffocated to death or died of starvation.[3]

Many miraculous features have been connected with the life of Suhrawardī and many stories told of his unusual powers. His countenance was striking to all his contemporaries. His illuminated and ruddy face and dishevelled hair, his handsome beard and piercing eyes reminded all who met him of his keen intelligence. He paid as little attention to his dress as he did to his words. Sometimes he wore the woollen garb of the Sufis, sometimes the silk dress of the courtiers. His short and tragic life contains many similarities to the life of Ḥallāj, whom he quoted so often, and to that of the Sufi writer 'Ayn al-Quḍāt Hamadānī who was to follow a similar career a few years later.

The writings of Suhrawardī are numerous despits his short and turbulent life. Some of them in the libraries of Persia, India, and Turkey.[4] Unlike his predecessors, Ibn Sīnā and al-Ghazzālī, he was never translated into Latin and, therefore, never became well known in the Western world. Yet, his influence in the East can almost match that of Ibn Sīnā, and any history of Islamic philosophy written without mentioning him and the school of *ishrāq* is, to say the least, incomplete. Histories of Muslim philosophy written by Westerners, like Munk and de Boer, usually end with Ibn Rushd because the authors have considered only that aspect of Muslim philosophy which influenced Latin scholasticism. Actually, the seventh/thirteenth century, far from being the end of speculative thought in Islam, is really the beginning of this most important school of *ishrāq*. Suhrawardī's writings came to the East at the same time as Peripatetic philosophy was journeying westward to Andalusia and from there through the influence of Ibn Rushd and others to Europe.

There are altogether about fifty titles of Suhrawardī's writings which have come down to us in the various histories and biographies.[5] They may be divided into five categories as follows:[6]

1. The four large doctrinal treatises, the first three dealing with Aristotelian (*mashā'ī*) philosophy with certain modifications and the last with *ishrāqī* wisdom proper. These works, all in Arabic, include the *Talwīḥāt, Muqāwamāt, Muṭāraḥāt,* and the *Ḥikmat al-ishrāq.*[7]

2. Shorter doctrinal treatises like *Hayākil al-nūr, al-Alwāḥ al-'imadiyyah, Partaw-nāmah, I'tiqād al-ḥukamā', al-Lamaḥāt, Yazdān shinākht,* and *Bustān al-qulūb*[8] all of which explain further the subject-matter of the larger treatises. These works are partly in Arabic and partly in Persian.

3. Initiatory narratives written in symobolic language to depict the journey of the initiate towards gnosis (*ma'rifah*) and illumination (*ishrāq*). These short treatises, nearly all written in Persian, include *'Aql-i surkh, Āwāz-i par-i-jibra'īl, al-Ghurbat al-gharbiyyah* (also in Arabic), *Lughat-i mūrān, Risālah fī ḥālat al-ṭufūliyyah, Rūzī bā Jamā'at-i ṣūfiyān, Risālah fi'l-mi'rāj,* and *Ṣafīr-i sīmurgh.*

4. Commentaries and transcriptions of earlier philosophic and initiatic texts and sacred Scripture like the translation into Persian of the *Risālat al-ṭa'ir* of Ibn Sīnā, the commentary in Persian upon Ibn Sīnā's *Ishārāt wa tanbīhāt*, and the treatise *Risālah fī ḥaqīqat al-'ishq* which last is based on Ibn Sīnā's *Risālat al-' ishq* and his commentary upon the verse of the Qur'an and on the Ḥadīth.[9]

5. Prayers, litanies, invocations, and what may be called books of the hour, all of which Shahrazūrī calls *al-Wāridāt wa'l- taqdīsāt.*

These works and the number of commentaries written upon them during the last seven centuries form the main corpus of the tradition of *ishrāq* and are a treasure of traditional doctrines and symbols combining in them the wisdom of Sufism with Hermeticism, and Pythagorean, Platonic, Aristotelian, and Zoroastrian philosophies together with some other diverse elements. There is little doubt that Suhrawardī is greatly indebted to the Muslim philosophers, especially Ibn Sīnā, for the formulation of many of his ideas. Moreoever, inasmuch as he is a Sufi as well as a philosopher or, more properly speaking, a theosopher,[10] he is in debt, both for spiritual inspiration and for his doctrine, to the great chain of sufi masters before him. More specifically he is indebted to Ḥallāj whom he quotes so often and to al-Ghazzālī whose *Mishkāt al-anwār* played so important a role in his doctrine of the relation of light to the Imam.

Suhrawardī came also under the influence of Zoroastrian teachings, particularly in angelology and the symbolism of light and darkness.[11] He identified the wisdom of the ancient Zoroastrian sages with that of Hermes and, therefore, with the pre-Aristotelian philosophers, especially Pythagoras and Plato, whose doctrines he sought to revive. Finally, he was influenced directly by the vast tradition of Hermeticism which is itself the remains of ancient Egyptian, Chaldaean, and Sabacan doctrines metamorphosed within the matrix of Hellenism and is expressed in the primordial symbolism of alchemy. Suhrawardī considered himself to be the reviver of the perennial wisdom, *philosophia perennis,* or what he calls *Ḥikmat al-khālidah* or *Ḥikmat al-'atīqah* which existed always among the Hindus, Persians, Babylonians, Egyptians, and the ancient Greeks up to the time of Plato.[12]

The concept of the history of philosophy for Suhrawardī and his school is itself of great interest. This school identifies philosophy with wisdom rather than with rational systematization. Philosophy for it does not begin with Plato and Aristotle: rather, it ends with them. Aristotle, by putting wisdom in a rationalistic dress, limited its perspective and separated it from the unitive wisdom of the earlier sages.[13] From the *ishrāqī* point of view. Hermes or the Prophet Idrīs is the father of philosophy, having received it as revelation from heaven. He was followed by a chain of sages in Greece and in ancient Persia and later in Islam which unified the wisdom of previous civilizations in its milieu. The chain of transmission of *ishrāqī* doctrines, which must be understood symbolically rather than only historically, may be schematized as follows:

Hermes
Agathodemon (Seth)

Asclepius	Persian priest-kings:
Pythagoras	Kiūmarth
Empedoeles	Farīdūn
Plato	Kai Khusraw
Neoplatonists	
Dhū'l Nūn Miṣrī	Abū Yazīd Basṭāmī
Abū Sahl Tustarī	Manṣūr Ḥallāj
	Abu'l-Ḥasan Kharraqānī

Suhrawardī

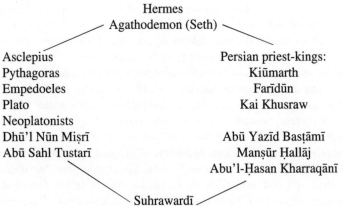

In the introduction to his *Ḥikmat al-ishrāq*. Suhrawardī states explicitly the nature of *ishrāqī* wisdom and its relation to ancient doctrines. As he writes: "Although before the composition of this book I composed several summary treatises on Aristotelian philosophy, this book differs from them and has a method peculiar to itself. All of its material has not been assembled by thought and reasoning; rather, intellectual intuition, contemplation, and ascetic practices have played an important role in it. Since our sayings have not come by means of rational demonstration but by inner vision and contemplation, they cannot be destroyed by the doubts and temptations of the sceptics. Whoever is a traveller (*sālik*) on the way to truth is my companion and a help on this Path. The procedure of the master of philosophy, the *divine* Plato, was the same, and the sages who preceded Plato in time like Hermes, the father of philosophy, followed the same path. Since sages of the past, because of the ignorance of the masses, expressed their sayings in secret symbols (*rumūz*), the refutations which have been made against them have concerned the exterior of these sayings and not their real intentions. And the *ishrāqī* wisdom the foundation and basis of which are the two principles of light and darkness as established by the Persian sages like Jāmāsp, Farshādshūr, and Būzarjumihr is among these hidden, secret symbols. One must never think that the light and darkness which appear in our expressions are the same as those used by the infidel Magi or the heretical Manichaeans for they finally involve us in idolatry (*shirk*) and dualism."[14]

THE MEANING OF *ISHRĀQ*

The Arabic words *ishrāq* meaning illumination and *mashriq* meaning the east are both derived etymologically from the root *shrq* meaning the rising of the sun. Moreover, the adjective illuminative, *mushriqiyyah*, and Oriental, *mashriqiyyah*, are written in exactly the same way in Arabic. This symbolic identification of the Orient with light which is inherent in the Arabic language and is employed often by the *ishrāqī* sages, has given rise to many difficulties in the interpretations of that wisdom which is both illuminative and Oriental. Already in his *Manṭiq* al-*mashriqiyyīn* most of which is lost, Ibn Sīnā refers to an Oriental wisdom which is superior to the commonly accepted Peripatetic (*mashshā'ī*) philosophy.[15] Due to the fact that the word *mashriqiyyūn* could also be read as *mushriqiyyūn* in Arabic, the latter meaning illuminative, one could interpret the esoteric teachings which Ibn Sīnā proposes as being illuminative as well as Oriental. Since the famous article of Nallino.[16] it has become common opinon that the reading is Oriental and has nothing to do with illumination. Yet, this opinion, however correct it may be linguistically is essentially limited in that it does not take into account the profound symbolism inherent in the language and does not consider the great debt which Suhrawardī and *ishrāqī* wisdom owe to Ibn Sīnā.

Suhrawardī writes that Ibn Sīnā wanted to recapture Oriental philosophy but did not have access to the necessary sources.[17] Yet, if we consider how the sacred geography of the Orient of light and the Occident of darkness in the initiatory trilogy of Ibn Sīnā, *Ḥayy ibn yaqẓān, Risālat al-ṭayr,* and *Salāmān wa Absāl,* is followed by Suhrawardī, how the Shaykh translated several of the treatises of Ibn Sīnā into Persian, and how parts of *Ḥikmat al-ishrāq* resemble closely the commentary of Ibn Sīnā upon the *Theology of Aristotle*, it will become clear how profoundly the roots of *ishrāqī* philosophy lie in certain of the later non-Aristotelian works of Ibn Sīnā and how illumination and the Orient are united in this form of wisdom.

The unification of the meaning of illumination and the Orient in the term *ishrāq* is connected with the symolism to the sun which rises in the Orient and which illuminates all things so that the land of light is identified with that of gnosis and illumination.[18] Inasmuch as the Occident is where the sun sets, where darkness reigns, it is the land of matter, ignorance, or discursive thought, entangled in the mesh of its own logical constructions. The Orient is, on the contrary, the world of light, of being, the land of knowledge, and of illumination which transcends mere discursive thought and rationalism. It is the land of knowledge which liberates man from himself and from the world, knowledge which is combined with purification and sanctity.[19] It is for this reason that Suhrawardī connects *ishrāqī* wisdom with the ancient priest-kings of Persia like Kay Khusraw and with the Greek sages like Asclepius, Pythagoras, and Plato whose wisdom was based on inner purification and intellectual intuition rather than on discursive logic.[20]

In a historical sense, *ishrāqī* wisdom is connected with pre-Aristotelian metaphysics. Jurjānī in his *Ta'rīfāt* calls the *ishrāqīs* "the philosophers whose master is Plato." 'Abd al-Razzāq Kāshānī, the celebrated Sufi, in his commentary upon the *Fuṣūṣ al-ḥikam* of Ibn 'Arabī writes that the *ishrāqīs* derive their chain from Seth, often identified with Agathodemon, from whom craft initiations and Hermetic orders also derive their origin. Ibn Waḥshiyyah in his *Nabataean Agriculture* mentions a class of Egyptian priests who were the children of the sister of Hermes and who were called *ishrāqiyān*.[21] Suhrawardī himself writes in his *Muṭaraḥāt* that the wisdom of *ishrāq* was possessed by the mythological priest-kings of ancient Persia, Kiūmarth, Farīdūn, and Kay Khusraw and then passed on to Pythagoras and Plato, the latter being the last among the Greeks to possess it, and was finally inherited by the Muslim Sufis like Dhu'l-Nūn al-Miṣrī and Bāyazīd Basṭāmī.[22]

Both metaphysically and historically, *ishrāqī* wisdom means the ancient pre-discursive mode of thought which is intuitive (*dhawqī*) rather than discursive (*baḥthī*) and which seeks to reach illumination by asceticism and purification. In the hands of Suhrawardī it becomes a new school of wisdom integrating Platonic and Aristotelian philosophy with Zoroastrian angelology and Hermetic ideas and placing the whole structure within the context of Sufism. In reading the texts of Suhrawardī one is particularly struck by the large number of quotations from the Quran, *Ḥadīth*, and the sayings of earlier Sufis and by the profound transformation into the Islamic mould of all the diverse ideas which Suhrawardī employs. It is by virtue of such integration and transformation that the *ishrāqī* wisdom could come to play such a major role in Shi'ism.

In the introduction to *Ḥikmat al-ishrāq,* Suhrawardī outlines the hierarchy of those who know in a manner which demonstrates how he integrates ancient wisdom into the perspective of Islam. There are, according to this scheme, four major types of "knowers":

1. The *ḥakīm ilāhī*, or *theosophos*, who knows both discursive philosophy, i.e., Aristotelianism, and gnosis (*ta'alluh*). Suhrawardī considers Pythagoras, Plato, and himself among this group.
2. The sage who does not involve himself with discrusive philosophy but remains content with gnosis, like Ḥallāj, Basṭāmī, and Tustarī.
3. The philosopher who is acquainted with discursive philosophy but is a stranger to gnosis like Fārābī or Ibn Sīnā.[23]
4. He who still seeks knowledge (*ṭālib*) but has not yet reached a station of knowledge.

Above all these degrees is that of the Pole (*quṭb*) or Leader (*imām*) who is the head of the spiritual hierarchy and of his representatives (*khulafā'*).[24]

The stations of wisdom are also described in a purely Sufi fashion as degrees of penetration into the Divine Unity expressed by the *shahādah.* In his initiatory treatise, *Ṣafir-i sīmurgh* ("Song of the Griffin"), Suhrawardī enumerates five degress of unity.[25] *la ilāha illa' Llāh,* none is worthy of worship but God, which is the common acceptance of the oneness of God and rejection of any other divinity; *lā huwa illā huwa*, there is no he but He, which is the negation of any otherness than God, i.e., only God can be called "He": *lā anta illā anta,* there is no thou but Thou, which is the negation of all thouness outside of god; *lā anā illā anā*, there is no "I" but the divine "I", which means that only God can say "I"; finally, the highest station of unity which is that of those who say *wa kullu shay' in hālikun illā wajhuhu,* i.e. all things perish except His Face (Essence).[26] The formulations of Sufism become, therefore, the framework of his classification of knowledge into which he tries to place the heritage of universal gnosis and philosophy inherited by Islam.

THE ORIENT AND OCCIDENT IN SACRED GEOGRAPHY

As already mentioned, the term *ishrāq* is closely connected with the symobolism of directions and sacred geography which are essential elements of the traditional sciences. In the trilogy of Ibn Sīnā to which we have already referred, the disciple passes from the Occident which is the world of matter, through intermediate Occidents and Orients which are the heavens and separate substances, to the Orient proper which symbolizes the world of archangels. A similar division of the cosmos occurs in the writings of Suhrawardī. The Occident is the world of matter, the prison into which man's soul has fallen and from which he must escape. The Orient of lights is the world of archangels above the visible cosmos which is the origin of his soul (*rūḥ*). The middle Occident is the heavens which also correspond to the various inner faculties of man. It is important to note that, contrary to Peripatetic philosophy, the *ishrāqīs* hold that the boundary between the Occident and the Orient is set at the *primum mobile;* all that is visible in the cosmos including the celestial spheres is a part of the Occident, because it is still connected with matter, however subtle it may be. The Orient, properly speaking, is above the visible cosmos; it is the world of informal manifestation with its boundary at the heaven of the fixed stars.

In his treatise *al-Qiṣṣat al-ghurbat al-gharbiyyah* ("The Story of the Occidental Exile") in which Suhrawardī seeks to reveal the secrets of the trilogy of Ibn Sīnā, the universe becomes a crypt through which the seeker after truth must journey, beginning with this world of matter and darkness into which he has fallen and ending in the Orient of lights, the original home of the soul, which symbolizes illumination and spiritual realization.[27] The journey begins at the city of Qayrawan in present-day Tunis, located west of the main part of the Islamic world.[28] The disciple and his brother are imprisoned in the city at the bottom of a well which means the depth of matter. They are the sons of Shaykh Hādī ibn al-Khayr al-Yamanī, i.e., from the Yemen, which in Arabic means also the right hand and, therefore, symbolically the Orient, and is connected traditionally with the wisdom of the Prophet Solomon and the ancient sages as the left is connected with matter and darkness.[29] Above the well is a great castle with many towers, i.e., the world of the elements and the heavens or the faculties of the soul. They will be able to escape only at night and not during the day which means that man reaches the intelligible or spiritual world only in death, whether this be natural or initiatory, and in dream which is a second death. In the well there is such darkness that one cannot see even one's own hands, i.e., matter is so opaque that rarely does light shine through it. Occasionally they see the intelligible world during contemplation or in dreams. And so, they set out for their original home.

One clear night an order is brought by the hoopoe from the Governor of the Yemen telling them to begin their journey to their homeland, meaning the reception of a revelation from the intelligible world and the beginning of asceticism. The order also asks them to let go the hem of their dress, i.e., become free from attachment, when they reach the valley of ants, which is the passion of avidity. They are to kill their wives, i.e., passions, and then sit in a ship and begin their journey in the *Name* of God.[30] Having made their preparation they set out for their pilgrimage to Mount Sinai.

A wave comes between the disciple and the son, meaning that the animal soul is sacrificed. Morning is near, that is, the union of the particular soul with the universal soul is approaching. The hero discovers that the world in which evil takes place, meaning this world, will be overturned and rain and stones, i.e., diseases and moral evils, will descend upon it. Upon reaching a stormy sea he throws in his foster-mother and drowns her, meaning that he even sacrifices his natural soul. As he travels on still in a storm, i.e, in the body, he has to cast away his ship in fear of the king above him who collects taxes, meaning death which all mortals must taste. He reaches the Mount of Gog and Magog, i.e., evil thoughts and love of this world enter his imagination. The *jinn*, the powers of imagination and meditation, are also before him as well as a spring of running copper which symbolizes wisdom. The hero asks the *jinn* to blow upon the copper which thus becomes fiery, and from it he builds a dam before Gog and Magog. He takes the carnal soul (*nafs ammārah*) and places it in a cave, or the brain which is the source of this soul. He then cuts the "streams from the liver of the sky", i.e., he stops the power of motion from the brain which is located in the head, the sky of the body. He throws the empyrean heaven so that it covers all the stars, the sun, and the moon, meaning all powers of the soul become of one colour, and passes by fourteen coffins, the fourteen powers of *ishrāqī* psyschology,[31] and ten tombs, the five external and the five internal senses. Having passed through these stages he discovers the path of God and realizes that it is the right path.

The hero passes beyond the world of matter and reaches a light, the Active Intellect which is the governor of this world. He places the light in the mouth of a dragon, the world of the elements, and passes by it to reach the heavens and beyond them to the signs of the Zodiac which mark the limit of the visible cosmos. But his journey is not at an end; he continues even beyond them to the upper heavens. Music is heard from far away, and the initiate emerges from the cavern of limitation to the spring of life[32] flowing from a great mountain which is Mount Sinai. In the spring he sees fish that are his brothers; they are those who have reached the end of the spiritual journey.

He begins to climb the mountain and eventually reaches his father, the archangel of humanity, who shines with a blinding light which nearly burns him. The father congratulates him for having escaped from the prison of Qayrawan, but tells him that he must return because he has not yet cast away all bonds. When he returns a second time, he will be able to stay. The father tells him that above them is his father, the Universal Intellect, and beyond him their relatives going back to the Great Ancestor who is pure light. "All perishes except His essence."[33]

From this brief summary we see how *ishrāqī* wisdom implies essentially a spiritual realization above and beyond discursive thought. The cosmos becomes transparent before the traveller and interiorized within his being. The degrees of realization from the state of the soul of fallen man to the centre of the soul freed from all limitation corresponds "horizontally" to the journey from the Occident of matter to the Orient of lights, and "vertically" to the ascent from the earth to the limits of the visible universe and from there, through the world of formless manifestation, to the Divine Presence.

ḤIKMAT AL-ISHRĀQ

Ishrāqī wisdom is not a "systematic" philosophy so that its exposition in a systematic fashion is hardly possible. What Suhrawardī says in one text seems at first sight to be contradicted in another work, and one has to discover the point of view in each case in order to overcome the external contradictions. In expounding the major points of *ishrāqī* wisdom we will, therefore, follow the outlines of *Ḥikmat al-ishrāq,* the most important text in which this wisdom is expounded, drawing also from the shorter treatises which Suhrawardī wrote as further explanations of his major work.

Ḥikmat al-ishrāq is the fourth of the great doctrinal works of Suhrawardī, the first three dealing with Aristotelian philosophy which is the necessary prerequisite and foundation for illuminative wisdom. It deals with the philsophy of *ishrāq* itself which is written for those who are not satisfied with theoretical philosophy alone but search for the light of gnosis. The book which in the beauty of style is a masterpiece among Arabic philosophical texts was composed during a few months in 582/1186, and, as Suhrawardī himself writes at the end of the book, revealed to him suddenly by the Spirit;[34] he adds that only a person illuminated by the Spirit can hope to understand it.[35] The work consists of a prologue and two sections: the first concerning logic and the criticism of certain points of Peripatetic philosophy, and the second composed of five chapters (*maqālāt*), dealing with light, ontology, angelology, physics, psychology and, finally, eschatology and spiritual union.

In the section on logic he follows mostly the teaching of Aristotle but criticizes the Aristotelian definition. According to the Stagirite, a logical definition consists of genus plus differentia. Suhrawardī remarks, a logical definition consists of genus plus differntia. Suhrawardī remarks that the distinctive attribute of the object which is defined will give us no knowledge of that thing if that attribute can be predicated of any other thing. A definition in *ishrāqī* wisdom is the summation of the qualities in a particular thing which when added together exist only in that thing.

Suhrawardī criticizes the ten categories of Aristotle as being limited and confined only to this universe. Beyond this world there is an indefinite number of other categories which the Aristotelian classification does not include. As for the nine categories of accidents, he reduces them to four by considering relation, time, posture, place, action, and passivity as the one single category of relation (*nisbah*) to which are added the three categories of quality, quantity and motion.

Suhrawardī alters several points of Aristotelian philosophy in order to make it a worthy basis for the doctrine of illumination.[36] A major point of difference between the *ishrāqīs* and the Muslim followers of Aristotle (*mashshā'īs)*, also a central issue of Islamic philosophy, is that of the priority of Being or existence (*wujūd*) to essence (*māhiyyah*).[37] The *mashshā'īs* like the Sufis consider Being to be principial and *māhiyyah* or essence to be accidental with respect to it. Suhrawardī objects to this view and writes that existence does not have any external reality outside the intellect which abstracts it from objects. For example, the existence of iron is precisely its essence and not a separate reality. The *mashshā'īs* consider existence to have an external reality and believe that the intellect abstracts the limitation of a being which then becomes its essence.[38] The argument of Suhrawardī against this view is that existence can be neither substance nor accident and, therefore, has no external reality. For if it is an accident, it needs something to which it is an accident. If this something is other than existence, it proves what we sought, i.e., this something is without existence. If existence is a substance, then it cannot be accident, although we say accidents "are". Therefore, existence is neither substance nor accident and consequently can exist only in the intellect.

The issue involved, which is essential to the understanding of all medieval and ancient philosophy, is the relation between Being and existence, on the one hand, and the archetypes and limitations on the other. The *mashshā'īs* and Sufis consider the universe to consist of degrees of Being and limitations which distinguish various beings from one another. The Sufis, particularly those of the school of Ibn 'Arabī who are concerned essentially with metaphysical doctrines, transpose these limitations into the principial domain and consider them the same as the archetypes or the Platonic ideas. The traditional interpreters of Shaykh al-Ishrāq interpret his doctrine in a way which does not destroy the principiality of being.[39] but rather subsordinates the existence of a thing which is temporary and "accidental" to its archetype which with respect to the terrestrial existence of the thing is principal. In other words, essence (*māhiyyah*) is subordinated to being (*wujūd*), if we understand by this term being *qua* being: but as archetype, it is superior to particular existence which is an "exteriorization" of being. The *ishrāqīs* believe in fact that it is useless to discuss about the principiality of *wujūd* and *māhiyyah,* of being and essence, because the essence or *māhiyyah*, of being. The *ishrāqīs* differ from the *mashshā'īs* in that the former considers the world to be actual in its being and potential in its qualities and attributes, and the latter believes, on the contrary, that the world is potential in its being and actual in its qualities and perfections.[40]

Another important criticism of the Aristotelians by Suhrawardī is that of the doctrine of hylomorphism, of form and matter, which is the foundation of Aristotle's philosophy. As we shall see later, Suhrawardī considers bodies to be darkness and transforms the Aristotelian forms into the guardian lights or angels which govern each being. He defines a body as an external, simple substance (*jawhar basīṭ*) which is capable of accepting conjunction and separation.[41] This substance in itself, in its own essence, is called body *(jism*), but from the aspect of accepting the form of species (*ṣūrah naw'iyyah*) it is called the *materia prima* or *hylé* (*hayūlā*). He also differs from the Aristotelians in defining the place (*makān*) of the body which contains it but as the "abstract" dimension (*bu'd mujarrad*) in which the body is placed. Suhrawardī follows Ibn Sīnā and other *mashshā'īs* in rejectiNg the possibility of a void and an indivisible particle or atom, and an considering the body to be indefinitely divisible even if this division cannot be carried out physicadly.

Other elements of Peripatetic philosophy which Su(rawardī co!Ṅ-í ïB > 0DÍīṛü ts doctrane of te soul and arguments for its subsistence which he believes to be weak and insufficient;[42] its rejection of the Platonic ideas which are the cornerstone of *ishrāqī* wisdom and upon the reality of light which Suhrawardī insists in nearly every doctrinal work; and its theory of vision.

This last criticism is of interest in that Suhrawardī rejects both of the theories of vision commonly held during the Middle Ages. Regarding the Aristotelian theory that forms of objects are imprinted upon the pupil in the eye and then reach the *sensus communis* and finally the soul, Suhrawardī asks how the imprinting of large objects like the sky upon this small pupil in the eye is possible. Since man does not reason at the time of vision which is an immediate act, even if large objects were imprinted in smaller proportions, one could not know of the size of the object from its image. The mathematicians and students of optics usually accepted another theory according to which a conic ray of light leaves the eye with the head of the cone in the eye and the base at the object to be seen. Suhrawardī attacks this view also by saying that this light is either an accident or a substance. If it is an accidant it cannot be transmitted: therefore, it must be a substance. As a substance, its motion is dependent either on our will or it is natural. If dependent on our will, we should be able to gaze at an object and not see it, which is contrary to experience; or if it has natural motion, it should move only in one direction like vapour which moves upward, or stone which moves downward, and we should be able to see only in one direction which is also contrary to experience. Therefore, he rejects both views.

According to Suhrawardī, vision can occur only of a lighted object. When man sees this object, his soul surrounds it and is illuminated by its light. This illumination (*ishrāq*) of the soul (*nafs*) in presence of the object is vision. Therefore, even sensible vision partakes of the illuminative character of all knowledge.

With this criticism of the Aristotelian (*mashshā'ī*) philosophy, Suhrawardī turns to the exposition of the essential elements of *ishrāqī* wisdom itself beginning with a chapter on light, or one might say the theophany of light, which is the most characteristic and essential element of the teachings of this school.[43] Light (*nūr*), the essence of which lies above comprehension, needs no definition because it is the most obvious of all things. Its nature is to manifest itself; it is being, as its absence, darkness (*ẓulmah*), is nothingness. All reality consists of degrees of light and darkness.[44] Suhrawardī calls the absolute Reality the infinite and limitless Divine Essence, the Light of lights (*Nūr al-anwār*).[45] The whole universe, the 18,000 worlds of light and darkness which Suhrawardī mentions in his *Bustān al-qulūb*, are degrees of irradiation and effusion of this Primordial Light which shines everywhere while remaining immutable and for ever the same.[46]

Suhrawardī "divides" reality according to the types of light and darkness. If light is subsistent by itself, it is called substantial light (*nūr jawharī*) or ''abstract'' light (*nūr mujarrad*); if it depends for its subsistence on other than itself, it is called accidental light (*nūr 'araḍī*). Likewise, if darkness is subsistent by itself it is called obscurity (*ghasaq*) and if it depends on other than itself for its subsistence it is called form *(hay'ah)*. This division is also based on the degrees of comprehension.[47] A being is either aware of itself or ignorant of it. If it is aware of itself and subsists by itself, it is incorporeal light, God, the angels, archetypes, and the human soul. If a thing has need of a being other than itself to become aware of itself, it is accidental light like the stars and fire. If it is ignorant of itself but subsists by itself, it is obscurity like all natural bodies, and if it is ignorant by itself and subsists by other than itself, it is form like colours and smells.

All beings are the illumination (*ishrāq*) of the Supreme Light which leaves its vicegerent in each domain, the sun in the heavens, fire among the elements, and the lordly light (*nūr ispahbad*) in the human soul. The soul of man is essentially composed of light; that is why man becomes joyous at the sight of the light of the sun or fire and fears darkness. All the causes of the universe return ultimately to light; all motion in the world, whether it be of the heavens or of the elements, is caused by various regent lights (*nūr mudabbir*) which are ultimately nothing but illuminations of the Light of lights.

Between the Supreme Light and the obscurity of bodies there must be various stages in which the Supreme Light weakens gradually to reach the darkness of this world. These stages are the orders of angels, personal and universal at the same time, who govern all things.[48] In enumerating these angelic orders Suhrawardī relies largely upon Zoroastrian angelology and departs completely from the Aristotelian and Ibn Sīnan schemes which limit the intelligences or angels to ten to correspond to the celestial spheres of Ptolemaic astronomy. Moreover, in the Ibn Sīnan scheme, the angels or intellects are limited to three intelligible "dimensions" which constitute their being, namely, the intellection of their principle, of the necessity of their existence, and of the contingence of their essence (*māhiyyah*).[49] Suhrawardī begins with this scheme as a point of departure but adds many other "dimensions" such as domination (*qahr*) and love (*maḥabbah*), independence and dependence, illumination (*ishrāq*) and contemplation (*shuhūd*) which open a new horizon beyond the Aristotelian universe of the medieval philosophers.

Suhrawardī calls the first effusion of the Light of lights (*nūr al-anwār* or *nūr al-a'ẓam*) the archangel Bahman or the nearest light (*nūr al-aqrab*). This light contemplates the Light of lights and, since no veil exists in between, receives direct illumination from it. Through this illumination, a new triumphal light (*nūr al-qāhir*) comes into being which receives two illuminations, one directly from the Supreme Light and the other from the first light. The process of effusion continues in the same manner with the third light receiving illumination four times, twice from the light preceding it, once from the first light and once from the Supreme Light; and the fourth light eight times, four times from the light preceding it, twice from the second light, once from the first light and once from the Light of lights or Supreme Light.[50] In this manner the order of archangels, which Suhrawardī calls the longitudinal order (*ṭabaqāt al-ṭūl*) or "world of mothers" (*al-ummahāt*) and in which the number of archangels far exceeds the number of intelligences in Aristotelian cosmology, comes into being.[51] Each higher light has domination (*qahr*) over the lower and each lower light, love (*maḥabbah*) for the higher. Moreover, each light is a purgatory or veil (*barzakh*) between the light above and the light below. In this manner the supreme order of angels is illuminated from the Light of lights which has love only for Itself because the beauty and perfection of Its essence are evident to Itself.

The supreme hierarchy of being or the "longitudinal" order gives rise to a new polarization of Being. Its positive or masculine aspect such as dominance, contemplation, and independence gives rise to a new order of angels called the latitudinal order (*ṭabaqāt al-'arḍ*) the members of which are no longer generators of one another; rather, each is integral in itself and is, therefore, called *mutakāfiyah*. Suhrawardī identifies these angels with the Platonic ideas and refers to them as the lords of the species (*arbāb al-anwā'*) or the species of light (*anwā' nūriyyah*). Each species in the world has as its archetype one of these angels, or to express it in another manner, each being in this world is the theurgy (*ṭilism*) of one of these angels which are, therefore, called the lords of theurgy (*arbāb al-ṭilism*). Water is the theurgy of its angel Khurdād, minerals of Shahriwar, vegetables of Murdād, fire of Urdībihisht, etc.[52] Suhrawardī uses the names of the *Amshāspands* (*Amesha Spentās*), the separate powers of Ahurā Mazdā in Zoroastrianism, to designate these archetypes, and in this way unites Zoroastrian angelology with the Platonic ideas. These longitudinal angels are not, however, in any way abstract or mental objects, as sometimes the Platonic ideas are interpreted to be. They are, on the contrary, concrete as angelic hypostases and appear abstract only from man's point of view who, because of his imprisonment in the cage of his senses, considers only the object of the senses to be concrete. These angels are the real governors of this world who guide all of its movements and direct all of its changes. They are at once the intelligences and principles of the being of things.

From the negative and feminine aspect of the logitudinal order of archangels, that is, love, dependence, and reception of illumination, there comes into being the heaven of fixed stars which these angels share in common. The stars are the crystallization into subtle matter of that aspect of the archangels which is "non-Being" or removal from the Light of lights. This "materialization" marks the boundary between the Orient of pure lights or the archangelic world which lies beyond the visible heavens and the Occident which is comprised of increasing condensations of matter from the luminous heavens to the dense earthly bodies.

The latitudinal order of angels or the archetypes gives rise to another order of angels through which they govern the species. Suhrawardī calls this intermediary order the regent lights (al-*anwār al-mudabbirah*) or sometimes *anwār ispahbadī* using a term from ancient Persian chivalry. It is this intermediary order which moves the heavenly spheres the motion of which is by love rather than by nature,[53] and which governs the species as the agent of the archetypes for which the species are theurgies (*ṭilismāt*) or "icons" (*aṣnām*). The *ispahbadī* lights are also the centres of men's souls, each light being the angel of some individual person.[54] As for mankind itself, its angel is Gabriel. Humanity is an image of this archangel who is the mediator between man and the higher world and the focus in which the lights of the Orient are concentrated. It is also the instrument of all knowledge inasmuch as it is the means by which man's soul is illuminated.[55]

This archangel as the Holy Spirit is also the first and supreme intelligence and the first as well as the last prophet, Muḥammad (upon whom be peace), the archetype of man (*rabb al-naw' al-insān*) and the supreme revealer of divine knowledge.

The physics and pschology of *Ḥikmat al-ishrāq* treat of the world of bodies and the world of souls which, along with the world of the intelligences or angels, comprise the totality of this universe.[56] As already mentioned, Suhrawardī does not divide bodies into form and matter. Rather, his division of bodies is based on the degree in which they accept light. All physical bodies are either simple or compound; the simple bodies are divided into three classes: those that prevent light from entering (*ḥājiz*), those which permit the entrance of light (*laṭīf*), and those which permit light to enter in various degrees (*muqtaṣid*) and which are themselves divided into several stages.[57] The heavens are made of the first category in the luminous state. As for the elements below the heavens, they consist earth belonging to the first category, water to the second, and air to the third.[58] Compound bodies belong likewise to one of the above categories, depending on which element predominates in them. All bodies are essentiallya purgatory or isthmus (*barzakh*) between various degrees of light by which they are illuminated and which they in turn reflect.

Suhrawardī rejects the view that the change of bodies is due to particles of one element entering into those of another. As a reason against this view he cites the example of a jug full of water that has been heated, i.e., according to this view particles of fire have entered into it. The volume of the water, however, does not change since it does not spill over; therefore, particles of fire cannot have entered into it. Qualitative change is due rather to the coming into being of a quality which is intermediate between the qualities of the original bodies and which is shared by all the particles of the new compound. For example, when water is heated a new quality between the cold of the water and the heat of the fire is brought into being by the light governing the change.

In the explanation of meteorological phenomena, Suhrawardī follows closely the teachings of Ibn Sīnā and Aristotle in accepting the exhalation and vapour theory. He differs, however, from them in the importance he attaches to light as the cause of all these changes. For example, the heat which is responsible for evaporation is nothing but one of the the effects of reflected light. All changes in fact which one observes in the world are caused by various hierarchies of light.[59] The elements are powerless before the heavens, the heavens are dominated by the souls, the souls by the intelligences, the intelligences by the Universal Intellect, and the Universal Intellect by the Light of lights.

The elements or simple bodies combine to form compounds which comprise the mineral, plant and animal kingdoms, each of which is dominated by a particular light or angel. All that exists in the mineral kingdom is "lighted body" (*barzakh nūriyyah*) the permanence of which is like that of the heavens.[60] Gold and various jewels like rubies make man happy because of the light within them which is akin to the soul of man. This light within the minerals is governed by *Isfandārmudh* which is the master of theurgy for earthy substances.

With greater refinement of the mixture of the elements, plants and animals come into being having their own faculties and powers which are so many "organs" of the light governing them. In higher animals and in man who is the most complete terrestrial being these faculties appear in their perfection. Man as the microcosm contains in himself the complete image of the universe, and his body is the gate of life of all elemental bodies. This body in turn is the theurgy for the *ispahbadī* light which governs each man. All the faculties of the soul are aspects of the light which shines upon all elements of the body and illuminates the power of imagination and memory for which it is the source. This light is connected with the body by means of the animal soul (*rūḥ ḥayawānī*) the seat of which is in the liver and leaves the body for its original home in the angelic world as soon as death destroys the equilibrium of the bodily elements. It is the love (*maḥabbah*) of the light which creates the power of desire as it is its domination (*qahr*) which brings about anger.[61]

Suhrawardī draws heavily upon the psychology of Ibn Sīnā for the enumeration of the faculties of the various souls.[62] It may be said in fact that with a few changes his classification is the same as that of his famous predecessor, despite the different role which the intellect or light plays in governing and illuminating the various faculties in each case. The classification of the various faculties of the soul by Suhrawardi may be outlined as follows:[63]

		attraction (*jādhibah*)
	feeding (ghādhiyyah)	retention (*māsikah*)
Vegetative soul (*al-nafs al-nabātiyyah*)	growth (*nāmiyyah*)	digestion (*hāḍimah*)
	reproduction (*muwallidah*)	repulsion (*dāfi'ah*)
		power of lust (*shahwah*)
Animal soul (*al-nafs al-ḥayawāniyyah*)	power of motion (*muḥarrikah*)	power of anger *ghaḍab*)
	power of desire (*nuzū'iyyah*)	

Man, besides the above faculties and the five external senses, possesses five internal senses which serve as a bridge between the physical and the intelligible worlds and have their counterpart in the macrocosmic order. These senses consist of:

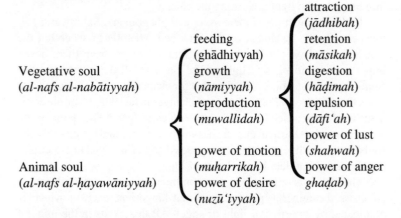

Sensus communis *(ḥiss mushtarik)*	The centre in which all the date of the external senses are collected. It is located in the front of the frontal cavity of the brain.
Fantasy *(khayal)*	The place of storage for the *sensus communis.* It is located in the back of the frontal cavity.
Apprehension *(wahm)*	Governs sensible things by what does not belong to the senses. It is located in the middle cavity.
Imagination	Analyses, synthesizes, and governs forms and

(mutakhayyilah)	is sometimes identified with apprehension. It is located in the middle cavity.
Memory *(ḥāfiẓah)*	The place of storage for apprehension. It is located in the back of the middle eavity.

These faculties are crowned by the intellectual soul (*nafs nāṭiqah*) which belongs to the spiritual world and which, through the network of these faculties, becomes for a period attached to the body and imprisoned in the fortress of nature. Often it is so lost in this new and temporary habitat that it forgets its original home and can be re-awakened only by death or ascetic practices.[64]

The last section of the *Ḥikmat al-ishrāq* concerning eschatology and spiritual union outlines precisely the way by which the spirit returns to its original abode, the way by which the *catharsis* of the intellect is achieved. Every soul, in whatever degree of perfection it might be, seeks the Light of lights, and its joy is in being illuminated by it. Suhrawardī goes so far as to say that he who has not tasted the joy of the illumination of the victorial lights has tasted no joy at all.[65] Every joy in the world is a reflection of the joy of gnosis, and the ultimate felicity of the soul is to reach toward the angelic lights by purification and ascetic practices. After death the soul of those who have reached some measure of purity departs to the world of archetypes above the visible heavens and participates in the sounds, sights, and tastes of that world which are the principles of terrestrial forms. On the contrary, those whose soul has been tarnished by the darkness of evil and ignorance (*aṣḥāb al-shaqāwah*) depart for the world of inverted forms (*ṣuwar mu'allaqah*) which lies in the labyrinth of fantasy, the dark world of the devils and the *jinn*.[66] As for the gnostics or the *theosophos* (*muta'allihīn*) who have already reached the degree of sanctity in this life, their soul departs to a world above the angels.

After leaving the body, the soul may be in several states which Suhrawardī outlines as follows:[67] Either the soul is simple and pure like that of children and fools who are attracted neither to this world nor to the next. Or it is simple but impure and as such is attracted more to this world, so that upon death it suffers greatly by being separated from the object of its desire; gradually, however, it forgets its worldly love and becomes simple as in the first case. Or it is not simple but perfect and pure and upon death joins the intelligible world to which it is similar and has an undescriable joy in the contemplation of God, or it is complete but impure, so that upon death it suffers greatly both for separation from the body and from the first source; gradually, however, the pains caused by alienation from this world cease and the soul enjoys spiritual delights. Or the soul is incomplete but pure, i.e., it has a love for perfection but has not yet realized it; upon death, therefore, it suffers ceaselessly, although the love of this world gradually dies away. Finally, the soul is incomplete and impure, so that it suffers the greatest pain. Man should, therefore, spend the few days he has here on earth to transform the precious jewel of his soul into the image of an angel and not into that of an animal. The highest station to be reached by the soul is that of the prophets (*nafs qudsiyyah*) who perceive the forms of the universals or archetypes natually. They know all things without the assistance of teachers or books. They hear the sounds of the heavens, i.e., the archetypes of earthly sounds, and not just vibrations of the air, and see the intelligible forms. Their souls and those of great saints also reach such degree of purity that they can influence the world of the elements as the ordinary soul influences the body.[68] They can even make the archetypes subsist by will, that is, give them existence.

The knowledge of the prophets is the archetype of all knowledge. In his nocturnal Ascension (*mi'rāj*) the Prophet Muḥammad—upon whom be peace—journeyed through all the states of being beyond the universe to the Divine Presence or microcosmically through his soul and intellect to the Divine Self.[69] This journey through the hierarchy of being symbolizes the degrees of knowledge which the initiate gains as he travels on the Path in imitation of the bringer of revelation who has opened the way for him. A prophet is absolutely necessary as a guide for the gnostic and as a bringer of Law for society. Man needs a society in order to survive and society needs law and order and, therefore, prophets to bring news of the other world and to establish harmony among men. The best man is he who knows, and the best of those who know are the prophets, and the best prophets are those who have brought a revelation (*mursilīn*), and the best of them are the prophets whose revelation has spread over the face of the earth, and the completion and perfection of the prophetic cycle is the Prophet Muḥammad—upon whom be peace—who is the seal of prophethood.[70]

THE INITIATIC NARRATIVES

In a series of treatises written in beautiful Persian prose, Suhrawardī expounds another aspect of *ishrāqī* wisdom which is the complement of the metaphysical doctrine. These works which we have called initiatic narratives are symbolic stories depicting the journey of the soul to God much like certain medieval European romances and poems such as *Parsifal* and the *Divine Comedy* although of shorter length. Unfortunately, in this limited space we cannot deal with all of these narratives each of which treats of a different aspect of the spiritual journey using various traditional symbols such as the cosmic mountain, the griffin, the fountain of life, and the lover and the beloved. Some of the more important of these narratives are the *Risālah fi 'l-mi'rāj* (''The Treatise on the Noctural Journey''), *Risālah fi ḥālat al-ṭufūliyyah* (''Treatise on the State of Childhood''), *Rūzī bā jamā'at-i ṣūfiyān* (''A Day with the Community of Sufis"), *Āwāz-i par-i Jibra'īl* (''The Chant of the Wing of Gabriel''), *'Aql-i surkh* (''The Red Intellect''), *ṣafīr-i sīmurgh* (''The Song of the Griffin''), *Lughat-i mūrān* (''The Language of Termites''), *Risālat al-ṭayr* (''The Treatise on the Birds''), and *Risālah fi ḥaqīqat al-'ishq* (''Treatise on the Reality of Love''). The titles alone indicate some of the rich symbolism which Suhrawardī uses to describe the spiritual journey. Each narrative depicts a certain aspect of the spiritual life as lived and practised by sages and saints. Sometimes theory and spiritual experience are combined as in the *Āwāz-i par-i Jibra'īl*[71] where in the first part of the vision the disciple meets the Active Intellect, the sage who symbolizes the "prophet" within himself who comes from the "land of nowhere" (*nā-kujā-ābād*), and asks certain question, about various aspects of the doctrine. In the second part, however, the tone changes; the hero asks to be taught the Word of God and after being instructed in the esoteric meaning of letters and words, i.e., *jafr*, he learns that God has certain major words like the angels, as well as the supreme Word which is to other words as the sun is to the stars. He learns furthermore that man is himself a Word of God, and it is through his Word that man returns to the Creator. He, like other creatures of this world, is a chant of the wing of Gabriel which spreads from the world of light to that of darkness. This world is a shadow of his left wing as the wrold of light is a reflection of his right wing. It is by the Word, by the sound of the wing of Gabriel, that man has come into existence, and it is by the Word that he can return to the principial state, the Divine Origin, from which he issued forth.

THE ISHRĀQĪ TRADITION

The influence of Suhrawardī has been as great in the Islamic world, particularly in Shi'ism, as it has been small in the West. His works were not translated into Latin so that his name hardly ever appears along with those of Ibn Sīnā and Ibn Rushd as masters of philosophy. But in the East from the moment of his death, his genius in establishing a new school of traditional wisdom was recognized and he was to exercise the greatest influence in Shi'ism. With the weakening of Aristotelianism in the sixth/twelfth century the element that came to replace it and to dominate Islamic intellectual life became a combination of the intellectual Sufism of Ibn 'Arabī and the *ishrāqī* wisdom of Suhrawardī. These two masters who lived within a generation of each other came from the two ends of the Islamic world to Syria, one to die in Damascus and the other in Aleppo, and it was from this central province of Islam that their doctrines were to spread throughout the Muslim East, particularly in Persia. The main link between these two great masters of gnosis was Quṭb al-Dīn Shīrāzī who was, on the one hand, the disciple of Ṣadr al-Dīn Qūnawī, himself a disciple and the main expositor of the teachings of Ibn 'Arabī in the East, and, on the other, the commentator of *Ḥikmat al-ishrāq*.[72]

Throughout the last seven centuries the tradition of *ishrāq* has continued especially in Persia where it played a major role in the revival of Shi'ism during the Safavid period. Among the most important commentaries written on Suhrawardī's works are those of Shams al-Dīn Shahrazūrī and Quṭb al-Dīn Shīrāzī in the seventh/thirteenth century, Wudūd Tabrīzī in the tenth/sixteenth century, and Mullā Ṣadrā in the eleventh/seventeenth century on the *Ḥikmat al-ishrāq,* the commentaries of Shahrazūrī, Ibn Kammūnah, and 'Allāmah Ḥillī in the seventh and eighth/thirteenth and fourteenth centuries on the *Talwīḥāt,* and the commentaries of Jalāl al-Dīn Dawānī in the ninth/fifteenth century and 'Abd al-Razzāq Lāhījī in the eleventh/seventeenth century on the *Hayākil al-nūr.* These commentaries and many others which we have not been able to mention here present a veritable treasure of *ishrāqī* wisdom which has influenced so many philosophers, theologians, and gnostics from Khwājah Naṣīr al-Dīn Ṭūsī and Dawānī to Mīr Dāmād, Mullā Ṣadrā, Shaykh Aḥmad Aḥsā'ī, and Ḥājji Mullā Hādī Sabziwārī. Some of the works of Suhrawardī were also to influence the sages and philosophers in the Mughul Court in India where parts of his writings were even translated into Sanskrit,[73] as they were translated into Hebrew some time earlier. *Ishrāqī* wisdom has, therefore, been one of the universal elements of Eastern intellectuality during the past centuries and, as it is a version of the perennial philosophy, it is touched by the breath of eternity which, as in the case of all expressions of truth, gives it a freshness and actuality that make this wisdom as essential today as it has been through the ages.

NOTES

1. The Arabic word *ḥikmah* is neither philosophy as currently understood in modern European language, i.e., one form or another of rationalism, nor thelogy. It is, properly speaking, theosophy as understood in its original Greek sense and not in any way connected with the pseudo-spiritualistic movements of this century. It is also sapiential inasmuch as the Latin root *sapere,* like the Arabic word *dhawq* by which this wisdom is known, means taste. Moreover, it can be designated as speculative wisdom because *speculum* means mirror and this wisdom seeks to make man's soul a mirror in which divine knowledge is reflected.

2. Shihāb al-Dīn Suhrawardī is often called al-Maqtūl, meaning he who was killed, since he was put to death for certain indiscret formulations. We, however, refer to him as *Shaykh al-Ishrāq* by which name he is universally known among his disciples.
3. The best source for the biography of Shihāb al-Dīn is the *Nuzhat al-arwāḥ wa rawḍat al-ajrāḥ* of his disciple and commentator Shams al-Dīn Shahrazūrī. See also O. Spies and S.K. Khattak. *Three Treatises on Mysticism,* Verlag W. Kohlharmmer, Stuttgart, 1935, pp. 90-101; H. Corbin, *Suhrawardi d'Alep fondateur de la doctrine illuminative (ishrāqī)* G.P. Maisonneuve, Paris, 1939.
4. We are most grateful to Prof. M. Minovi and Mr. M. Dāneshpazhūh of the University of Tehran and to Dr. M. Bayānī, the head of the Tehran National Library, for making these manuscripts available to us.
5. See the introduction in M. Bayānī, *Daw Risāla-yi fārsī-i- Suhrawardī*, Theran, 1925.
6. We follow in part the classification of H. Corbin, however, with some modifications. See Suhrawardī, *Opera Metaphysica et Mystica,* ed. H. Corbin, Vol. I, Ma'ārif Matbaasi, Bibiotheca Islamica, Istanbul, *1945, "Prolégomène,"* pp. xviff.
7. The metaphysical sections of the first three treatises have been published in the first volume of the *Opera* by Corbin and the complete *Ḥikmat al-ishrāq* in the second volume entitled *Oeuvres philosophiques el mystiques (Opera Metaphysica et Mystica, II),* Institut Franco-Iranien, Teheran, and Andrien Maisonneuve, Paris, 1952. Henceforth we shall refer to the two volumes as *Opera,* Volumes I and II.
8. The treatise *Yazdān shinākht* has often been attributed to 'Ayn al-Quḍāt Hamadānī and its authorship remains in any case doubtful. *Bustān al-qutūb* has also appeared under the name *Rawḍat al-qulūb* and has been occasionally attributed to Sayyid Sharīf Jurjānī.
9. A commentary upon the *Fuṣuṣ* of Fārābī of which no trace has as yet been found is also attributed to him.
10. The *ḥakīm muta'allih* which Suhrawardī considers himself and other sages before him to be exactly *theosophos* by which the Greek sages were designated. See the Prologomène by H. Corbin to Suhrawardī'*s Opera,* Vol. II, p. xxiv.
11. Suhrawardī is careful in distinguishing between exoteric Zoroastrians and the sages among Zoroastrians whom he follows. As he writes in *Kalimāt al-taṣawwuf:* "There were among the ancient Persians a community of men who were guides towards the Truth and were guided by Him in the Right Path, ancient sages unlike those who are called the Magi. It is their high and illuminated wisdom, to which the spiritual experiences of Plato and his predecessors are also witness, and which we have brought to life again in our book called *Ḥikmat al-ishrāq.*" MS., Ragip, 1480, fol. 407b, Istanbul, cited in H. Corbin, *Les Motifs zoroastriens dans la philosophie de Sohrawardi,* Editions du Courrier, Tehran, 1946, p. 24. Also Tehran University Library MS. 1979, pp. 34 ff.
12. *Muṭāraḥāt,* Physics, Book VI, cited by H. Corbin in Suhrawardī, *Opera*, Vol. I, p. xli.
13. Originally philosophy like all forms of wisdom consisted of a doctrine, a rite, and a "spiritual alchemy". In Greek civilization the first element gradually separated from the others and became reduced to a theoretical form of knowledge which came to be known as philosophy. In the 55th section of *Talwīḥāt,* Suhrawardī writes how he saw Aristotle, who is most likely Plotinus, the author of the *Theology of Aristotle,* in a dream and asked if the Islamic Peripatetics were the real philosophers. Aristotle answered, "No, not a degree in a thousand." Rather the Sufis, Basṭāmī and Tustarī, are

the real philosophers. Aristotle told Suhrawardī to delve into himself and to pass beyond theoretical knowledge (*'ilm ṣūrī*) to effective realization or the "knowledge by presence" (*'ilm ḥuḍūrī: or shuhūdī*). See the Prolegomène of H. Corbin in Suhrawadī, *Opera*, Vol. I, p. lxx.

14. Suhrawardī, *Opera,* Vol. II, pp. 10-11. Some modern interpreters of Suhrawardī have considered him to be anti-Islamic and of Zoroastrian sympathy. A. von Kremer in his *Geschichte der herrschenden Ideen des Islam,* Leipzig, 1868, pp. 89ff., writes that Suhrawardī was part of the current directed against Islam. On the other hand, the scholarly and sympathetic interpreter of Suhrawardī, H. Corbin, insists on the role of Shayikh al-Ishrāq in reviving the philosophy of Zoroastrian Persia and on his sympathy for Zoroastrian ad Manichean ideas, although he does not consider this revival to be a movement against Islam but rather an integration of ancient Persian myths in "the prism of Islamic spirituality." In any case, all views which consider *ishrāqī* wisdom to be simply a revival of Zoroastrianism or Manichaeism confuse the form with the spirit. There is no doubt that Suhrawardī makes use of Mazdaean symbols especially with regard to angelology, but that is no more reason for calling him Mazdaean than it is to call Jābir ibn Ḥayyān a follower of Egyptian religion, because be used Hermetic symbols. The only criterion of orthodoxy in Islam is the first *shahādah (la ilāha illa' Llāh)* and, according to it, Suhrawardī cannot be said to lie outside the pale of Islam, no matter how strange his formulations may be, Furthermore, the disciples of the *ishrāqī* school consider the Persian sages of whom Suhrawardī speaks to have lived before Plato and Pythagoras and not during the Sassanid period. The genius of Islam to integrate diverse elements into itself is evident here as elsewhere and should not be interpreted as sign of departure from the straight path *(ṣirāṭ al-mustaqīm)* or the universal orthodoxy which embraces all the perspectives within the tradition. The vocation of Islam is the re-establishment of the primordial tradition so that all the streams of the ancient religions and cultures have flowed into it without in any way destroying its purity.

15. Ibn Sīnā, *Manṭiq al-mashriqiyyīn,* Cairo, 1338/1919. pp. 2-4.

16. A. Nallino, "Filosofia 'orientali' od 'illuminativa' d'Avicenna", *Rivista degli studi orientali,* Vol. X, 1925, pp. 433-67. H. Corbin rightly emphasizes the illuminative as well as the Oriental aspect of Ibn Sīnā's Oriental wisdom and its profound connection with the *ishrāqī* school of Suhrawardī. See Corbin, *Avicenne et le récit visionnaire,* Institut Franco-Iranien, Teheran, 1952-54, Vol I, Introduction, p. iii.

17. Suhrawardī, *Opera,* Vol. I, 195.

18. In European languages the word "orient" means both the east and the placing of oneself in the right direction, and refers to the same symbolism.

19. As Corbin states, "*Ishrāq* is a knowledge which is Oriental because it is itself the Orient of knowledge." Suhrawardī, *Opera*, Vol. I, p. xxix.

20. Throughout our writings we use the word "intellect" as the instrument of gnosis, of direct intuitive knowledge where the knower and the known become identical, and distinguish it from reason which is its passive reflection.

21 Ibn Waḥshiyyah, *Ancient Alphabet and Hieroglyphic Characters,* London, 1806, p. 100. These historical connections are discussed by H. Corbin in *Les Motifs zoroastriens dans la philosophie de Sohrawardi,* Editions du Courrier, Teheran, 1325 Solar, p. 18, and the *prolegomène* to Suhrawardī, *Opera*, Vol. I, pp. xxv ff. We are indebted to him for drawing our attention to them,.

22 Suhrawardī, *Opera*, Vol. I, pp. 502-03.

23. Suhrawardī is considering only the Peripatetic aspect of Ibn Sīnā.

24. Suhrawardī, *Opera*, Vol. II, pp. 10-11. Actually, the stations mentioned are more numerous: we have described only the major ones.

25. Suhrawardī, *Risālah ṣafīr-i sīmurgh*, MS. Tehran National Library, 1758, pp. 11-12.

26. In this same treatise Suhrawardī writes that the most noble knowledge is gnosis which lies above human reason. As he says, "To seek the knowledge of God through reason is like seeking the sun with a lamp." *Ibid.*, p. 14.

27. There is a profound correspondence between the microcosm and the macrocosm in all traditional wisdom so that the inward journey of man through the centre of his being corresponds to a journey through the various stages of the universe and finally beyond it. To escape from the prison of the lower soul (*nafs ammārah*) is also to pass beyond the crypt of the cosmos.

28. Suhrawardī, *Opera*, Vol. II, pp. 274ff.

29. It is said that when Christian Rosenkreutz, the founder of the order of the Rosy-Cross, abandoned Europe, he retired to the Yemen.

30. Suhrawardī indicates here the main technique of Sufism which is the invocation (*dhikr*) of one of the Names of God and which Sufi masters call the sacred barque that carries man across the ocean marking the spiritual path to the shore of the spiritual world.

31. These fourteen powers are: Attraction, retention, purgation, repulsion, digestion, growth, sleep, imagination, anger, lust, and the four humours.

32. The inward journey beyond the carnal soul (*nafs*) corresponding externally to the journey beyond the visible universe is described by the *ishrāqīs* symbolically as reaching the fountain of life in which there are found the jewels of the purely spiritual world.

33. Suharwardī, *Opera*, Vol. II. p. 296.

34. The inspiration for the book came to the author on an auspicious day when all the seven planets were in conjunction in the Sign of the Balance.

35. Suharwardī writes that he who wishes to understand the essence of this work should spend forty days in a retreat (*khalwah*) occupying himself only with invocation (*dhikr*) under the direction of the spiritual guide whom he calls in several places *qā'im bi'l-kitāb*.

36. For his criticism, see Suhrawardī. *Opera*, Vol. II, pp. 46ff.

37. The term *māhiyyah* in Arabic is composed of *mā* meaning "what" and *hiyyah* derived from the world *huwa* ("it"). It is the answer given to the question "What is it?". It is used to denote the essence of anything whether the existence of that thing is certain or doubtful, while the word *dhāt* is used to denote the essence of something which possesses some degree of being.

    In Islamic philosophy reality is understood in terms of *wujūd* and *māhiyyah*, the latter meaning the limitation placed upon Being and identified with the Platonic ideas. See S.H. Nasr, "The Polarisation of Being" [*Proceedings of the Sixth*] *Pakistan Philosophical Congress*, Lahore, 1959, pp. 50-55.

38. For a general discussion of this subject in the philosophy of the master of the *mashshā'īs* Ibn Sīnā, see A.M. Goichon, *La Distinction d l'essence et de l'existence d'après Ibn Sīnā (Avicenne),* de Brouwer Descles, Paris, 1937.

39. In fact, as Mullā Ṣadrā asserts, Suhrawardī substitutes light (*nūr*) for Being attributing the former with all the features which the latter term possesses in other schools. We are deeply indebted for the knowledge of this interpretation and many other essential elements of *ishrāqī* doctrines to one of the greatest masters of traditional wisdom in Persia, Sayyid Muḥammad Kāẓim 'Aṣṣār.

40. Although in his *Ḥikmat al-Ishrāq,* Suhrawardī does not speak of the necessary and possible beings, in many of his other treatises like the *Partaw-nāmah, 'Itiqād al-ḥukamā'* and *Yazdān shinākht,* he speaks of the *mashshā'ī* categories of Necessary Being (*wājib al-wujūd*), possible (*mumkin al-wujūd*), and impossible being (*mumtani' al-wujūd*).

41. Suhrawardī defines a substance in *mashshā'ī* fashion as that possible being (*mumkin*) which has no place (*maḥall),* and accident as that possible being which does have a place. He also defines a body as that substance which has height, width and depth, *Partaw-nāmah,* MS., Tehran National Library, 1257, pp. 190ff.

42. In his works Suhrawardī insists on the perishable nature of the body and its being a prison into which the soul has fallen. In the *Bustān al-qulūb*, MS., Tehran Sipahsālār Library, 2911, he gives as argument for the permanence of the soul and its spiritual nature, the fact that the body of man changes its material every few years while man's identity remains unchanged. The *mashshā'ī* doctrine of the soul is essentially one of defining its faculties; the *ishrāqi* view is to find the way by which the soul can escape its bodily prison.

43. Suhrawardī, *Opera*, Vol. II, pp. 106-21.

44. As the quotations we have already cited demonstrate, Suhrawardī insists that he is not dealing with the dualism of the Zoroastrians. Rather, he is explaining the mysterious polarization of reality in this symbolism. The *ishrāqīs* usually interpret light as being and darkness as determination by ideas (*māhiyyah).* They say that all ancient sages taught this same truth but in different languages. Hermes spoke of Osiris and Isis; Osiris or the sun symbolizes being and Isis or the moon, *māhiyyah.* They interpret the pre-Socratic Greek philosophers in the same fashion.

45. Actually this term means both the Divine Essence and its first determination which is the archangel or the Universal Intellect.

46. "The immense panorama of diversity which we call the Universe is, therefore, a vast shadow of the infinite variety in intensity of direct or indirect illuminations of rays of the Primary Light." Iqbāl, *The Development of Metaphysics in Persia,* Luzac & Co., London, 1908. p. 135.

47. In his *Risālah yazdān shinākht,* Maṭba'a-yi 'Ilmī, Tehran, 1316 Solar, pp. 13ff., Suhrawardī divides comprehension (*idrāk*) into four categories:

    (i) Sense of sight which perceives external forms like colours, etc.

    (ii) Imagination (*khayāl*) which perceives images not depending upon external objects.

    (iii) Apprehension (*wahm*) which is stronger than the other two and which perceives the meaning of sensible things, but, like the other two, cannot be separated from the matter of bodies.

(iv) Intellectual apprehension (*'aql*) the seat of which is the heart, the instrument which is a bridge between the human being and the intelligible world, and perceives intelligible realities, the world of angels, and the spirit of prophets and sages.

48. Suhrawardī, *Opera*, Vol. II, pp. 131-32.

49. Ibn Sīnā *Nājat,* M.S. al-Kurdī, Cairo, 1938, pp. 256-57.

50. Suhrawardī, *Opera,* Vol. II, pp. 133ff. also *prolegomène,* II, pp. 42ff. In *ishrāqī* wisdom all of the cosmic hierarchies are understood in terms of a series of illuminations (*ishrāqāt*) and contemplations (*shuhūd*), the first being a descent and the second an ascent.

51. Usually in medieval cosmology the elements, the acceptors of form, are called the "mothers" and the celestial orbits, the givers of form, the "fathers". The term "mothers" used by Suhrawardī to designate the archangelic world should not, therefore, be confused with the elements.

52. Suharwardī, *Opera,* Vol. II, pp. 157ff. Also H. Corbin, *Les Motifs zoroastriens dans la philosophie de Sohrawardi,* Chap. I.

53. The governing light of the heavens moves each heaven by means of the planet attached to it, which is like the organ of the light. Suhrawardī calls this mover *hūrakhsh* which is the Pahlawī name for the sun, the greatest of the heavenly lights. Suhrawardī, *Opera*, Vol. II, p. 149.

    Regarding the motion of each heaven, Suhrawardī writes, "Its illumination is the cause of its motion, and its motion is the cause of another illumination; the persistence of the illuminations is the cause of the persistence of motion, and the persistence of both the cause of the persistence of the events in this world." *Hayākil al-nūr,* MS. Istanbul, Fātiḥ 5426, Part 5.

54. Each being in this world, including man, is connected to the Supreme Light not only through the intermediary angels but also directly. This light which connects each being directly to the Divine Light and places that being in the hierarchy of beings at a place proper to it is called *khurrah.* In ancient Persia it was believed that when a new king was to be chosen, the royal *khurrah* would descend upon him and distinguish him from the other pretenders to the throne.

55 Suhrawardī describes Gabriel as one of the supreme archangels who is the archetype of the "rational species" (*naw' nāṭiq)*, the giver of life, knowledge, and virtue. He is also called the giver of the spirit (*rawān bakhsh*) and the Holy spirit (*rūḥ al-qudus*). Suhrawardī, *Opera,* Vol. II, p. 201.

56 In the *I'tiqād al-ḥukamā'* and the *Partaw-nāmah*, Suhrawardī divides the universe into the world of intelligences (*'ālam al-'uqūl* or *'ālam al-jabarūt)*, the world of souls (*'ālam al-nufūs* or *'ālam al-malakūt)*, and the world of bodies (*'ālam al-ajsām* or *'ālam al-mulūk*). Also ibid., p. 270

57. *Ibid*., p. 187.

58. Suhrawardī considers fire, the fourth of the traditional elements, to be a form of light and the theurgy of *Urdībihisht,* and not one of the terrestrial elements.

59. Suhrawardī gives a different meaning to causality than the Aristotelians whose four causes which he does not accept. For Suhrawardī all these causes are really nothing but light, i.e., everything is made of light and by light, and is given a form by the

archangelic light whom he calls the "giver of forms" (*wāhib al-ṣuwar*) and seeks the Light of lights as its goal and end.

60. Suharwardī, *Opera,* Vol. II, pp. 199-200.

61. *Ibid.,* pp. 204-09.

62. Ibn Sīnā, *Psychologie v. Jehe dile as-Sifā,* ed., J. Bakos, Editions de I'Academice Tehecoslovaque des Sciences, Praque, 1956, Vol. I, pp. 53ff.

63. Suhrawardii, *Partaw-ṇāmah.* pp. 190ff.

64. Suhrawardi, *Hayākil al-nūr,* Sections 6 and 7. In certain other writings Suhrawardī avers that the light of each man is created with his body but survives after it. By creation, however, Suhrawardī means essentially "individualization" and "actualization" rather than creation in the ordinary sense. There is no doubt that his basic teaching is that the spirit or soul comes from the world of light and ultimately returns to it.

65. Suhrawardī, *Opera,* Vol. II, p. 225.

66. This is, properly speaking, the world of the unconscious which has become the subject of study for modern psychologists. It should be clearly distinguished from the world of archetypes which, rather than the "collective unconscious", is the source of symbols.

67. Suhrawardī, *Risālah yazdān shinākht,* pp. 53-63.

68. *Ibid.,* pp. 66ff. Since human souls are brought into being by the celestial souls, they are able to acquire the knowledge which these heavenly souls possess when they are put before them as a mirror. In the dreams of ordinary men this effect occurs occasionally since the external and internal senses which are the veils of the soul are partially lifted. In the case of prophets and saints such effects occur in awakening, i.e., they always reflect the intelligible world in the mirror of their souls so that they have knowledge of the unmanifested world even when awake.

69. The journey to the spring of life which lies at the boundary of the visible heavens symbolizes the journey through the soul (*nafs*), while the journey to the cosmic mountain *Qāf* from which the spring flows and the ascent fo this mountain which lies above the visible heavens symbolize the inner journey to the centre of one's being. In his *Mi'rāj-nāmah,* Suhrawardī describes the symbolic meaning of the nocturnal Ascension of the Prophet which is the model that all Sufis seem to imitate.

70. Suharwardī, *Risālah yazdān shinākht,* pp. 81-82.

71. For the translation into French and analysis of this work, see H. Corbin and P. Kraus, "Le bruissement de l'aile de Gabriel", *Journal Asiatique,* July-Sept. 1935, pp. 1-82.

72. This commentary, finished in 694/1295, appears on the margin of the standard edition of *Ḥikmat al-ishrāq* which is studied in all the thelogical schools in present day Persia. It has been the means by which the doctrines of Suhrawardī have been interpreted through the centuries.

73. Corbin and certain other European scholars have also emphasized the role of *ishrāqī* wisdom in the tenth/sixteenth-century Zoroastrianism and the movement connected with the name of Āzar Kaywān. This curious eclectic movement in which elements of Hinduism, Buddhism, Islam, and Zoroastrianism are combined but which differs greatly from original Zoroastrian doctrines has left behind several works such as the *Dabistān al-madhāhib* and the *Dasātīr* some passages of which seem to be forged.

Such a leading scholar of Zoroastrianism as I. Poure-Davoud considers the whole work to be purposeful falsification. See his article "Dasātīr", *Īrān-i Imrūz,* second year, No. II.

Whatever importance this syncretic movement which is so similar to the religious movements at the Court of Akbar may have had, its followers paid great attention to the writings of Shaykh al-Ishrāq. In fact, one of the disciples of Āzar Kaywān by the name of Farzānih Bahrām ibn Farshād translated several works of Suhrawardī into Persian. For a discussion of the school of Āzar Kaywān. see M. Mu'īn, Āzar Kaywān wa Payruwān-i ū," *Revue de la Faculté des Letters,* Tehran University, Vol. IV, No. 3, 1336/1917. pp. 25-42.

BIBLIOGRAPHY

Subrawardī, *'Aql-i-surkh,* Anjuman-i Dūstdārān-i Kitāb. Teheran, 1332 Solar; "Le bruissement de l'aile de Gabriel *(Risālah āwāz-i par-i Jibra'īl)*" translation and introduction by H. Corbin and P. Kraus. *Journal Asiatique,* July-Sept. 1935, pp. I-82; *Kitāb hayākil al-nūr,* ed. Mohamed Abou Rayan, Grande Librairie Commerciale, Cairo, 1376/1957: *Kitāb ḥikmat al-ishrāq*, Tehran, lithographed edition, 1316/1898, with the commentaries of Quṭb al-Dīn Shīrāzī and Mullā Ṣadrā; *The Lovers' Friend (Risālah mūnis al-'ushshāq). ed.* O. Spies. Jāmi'ah Press. Delhi 1934; *Opera Metaphysica et Mystica,* ed. H. Corbin. vol. I, Ma'arif Matbaasi, Istanbul, 1945, Vo. II, Institut Franco-Iranien, Tehran, 1952; *Risālah yazdān shinākht,* Maṭba'-i 'Ilmi, Tehran, 1316 Solar; *Three Treatises on Mysticism*, ed and tr. O. Spies and S.K. Khattak, Stuttgart, 1935; Jalāl al-Dīn al-Dawānī, *Shawākil al-nūr fī sharḥ-i hayākil al-nūr,* Madras Government Oriental Series, Madras, 1953.

M. Bayānī, *Daw Risāla-yi fārsī-yi Suhrawardī*, Tehran, 1325 Solar; H. Corbin, *Avicenne et le récit visionnaire,* 3 Vols., Institut Franco-Iranien, Tehran, 1952-54: *Les Motifs Zoroatriens dans la philosophie de Sohrawardi,* Editions du Courrier, Tehran, 1325 Solar; *Suhrawardi d'Alep foundateur de la doctrine illuminative (ishrāqī),* G.P. Maisonneuve, Paris, 1939; A. Dānāsirisht, *Afkār-i Suhrawardī wa Mullā Ṣadrā,* Tehran, 1316 Solar; M. Horten, *Die Philosophie der Erleuchtung nach Suhrawardi, Halle a. S., 1912; Die Philosophic des Islam*, Verlag Ernst Rheinhardt, München, 1924; S.M. Iqbāl, *The Development of Metaphysics in Persia,* Luzac & Co., London, 1908: H. Ritter, "Philologika, IX. Die vier Suhrawardī: I. Shihāb al-Dīn...al-Suhrawardī al-Maqtūl", *Der Islam,* 1937. pp. 270-96.

13
The Persian Works of Shaykh al-Ishrāq Shihāb al-Dīn Suhrawardī *

With the life and general philosophical and metaphysical doctrines of Shihāb al-Dīn Suhrawardī, entitled Shaykh al-ishrāq, the master of Illumination, or Shaykh al-Maqtūl or Shaykh al-shahīd, the martyred master, we are not concerned here.[1] They have been amply dealt with elsewhere. Here suffice if to say that in a very short life-span of 38 years, a life that was interrupted so tragically, he founded a new intellectual perspective in Islam, the school of *ishrāq*, and composed over fifty works in Arabic and Persian which are among the most important writings in the annals of Islamic philosophy.[2]

It is with the Persian works of this corpus that we are concerned although the (metaphysical and philosophical message of Suhrawardī does not depend on the language in which he expressed himself but can be seen in both the Arabic and Persian works. The Persian writings, however, contain certain characteristics concerning both the Persian language and the whole cultural world view of Islamic Persia, so that despite belonging to the larger body of Suhrawardī's *opera omnia*, they form a distinguishable group of their own.[3]

The Persian works of Suharwardī that have survived, or at least been discovered until now, and of which I am preparing a complete critical edition,[4] consist of thirteen works, the attribution of two of which to Suharwardī has been doubted by certain scholars. These works include:

I. 1. *Partaw-nāmah* ("Treatise on Illumination")
   2. *Hayākil al-nūr* ("The Temples of Light")
   3. *Alwāḥ-i 'imādī* ("The Tablets dedicated to 'Imād al-Dīn")

II. 4. *Lughat-i mūrān* ("The Language of Termites")
   5. *Risālat al-ṭayr* ("The Treatise of the Bird")
   6. *Ṣafīr-i sīmurgh* ("The Song of the Griffin")

---

* This essay appeared in the *Acta Iranica 1* (January-March 1968) : *12-16 and The Islamic Quarterly* 12 (1968) : 3-8.

7. *Rūzī bā jamā'at-i ṣūfiyān* ("A Day with the Community of Sufis")
8. *Fī ḥālat al-ṭifūlliyyah* ("Treatise on the State of Childhood")
9. *Āwāz-i par-i Jibra'īl* ("The Chant of the Wing of Gabriel")
10. *'Aql-i surkh* ("The Red Archangel")
11. *Fī ḥaqīqat al-'ishq* ("On the Reality of Love") or *Mu'nis al-*'ushshāq ("The Lovers' Friend")

III. 12. *Bustān al-qulūb* ("The Garden of the Heart")
13. *Yazdān shinākht* ("On the Knowledge of God")[5]

The division of these works into three groups is due to the different nature of each. The first group comprises large didactic treatises which resemble, although in more summary fashion, the very large Arabic didactic tetralogy, consisting of *Muqāwamāt, Mutāraḥāt, Talwīḥāt,* and *Ḥikmat al-ishrāq.* The second group consists of the shorter initiatic and mystical romances, the earliest of these kinds of romances in the Persian language, which were mostly written during Suhrawardī's youth.[6] As for the third group, it consists of the two treatises, both fairly long, whose attribution to Suhrawardī some have doubted but which on the basis of evidence drawn both from manuscripts and the content of these works I believe to be by Suhrawardī, especially *Būstān al-qulūb,* which is also mentioned by Shahrazūrī.

These works are among the most lucid and beautiful prose of the Persian language. In the initiatic treatises Suharwardī uses an eminently symbolic language. Each treatise deals with a particular spiritual experience or 'situation' within the spiritual universe. There is no expounding of doctrine explicitly but the depicting of a scene in which all the actors as well as the background symbolize different facets of the journey of the initiate toward spiritual realization and union with the 'Beloved'. The content of these treatises is not the same but the structure and vocabulary as well as the technical terminology are similar in these works. Quite naturally they all have the imprint of the particular genius of their author as well as the characteristic symbolism and language of *ishrāqī* wisdom.

The larger works have a more systematic nature and treat of a more or less complete cycle of doctrine, starting with physics, then leading through psychology to metaphysics. What is of particular interest is that in these treatises the physics resembles that of the Peripatetics and not that of *Ḥikmat al-ishrāq* which is characteristic of the *ishrāqī* school. But the psychology is already very far away from the *De Anima* of Aristotle or even the psychological treatises of Ibn Sīnā. It is fully an *ishrāqī* psychology which considers the soul as a light that must seek, through the dark abysses of the cosmic labyrinth, the primordial, celestial abode from which it originated. The metaphysics is also an illuminationist doctrine much more metaphysical and mystical than rationalistic.

The language of these treatises makes use of the established technical vocabulary of Peripatetic (*mashshā'ī*) philosophy to which certain *ishrāqī* terms are added, these terms being chosen without any artificiality or pedantry. Throughout, many references are made to both Greek and ancient Persian sages and the perennial wisdom which Suharwardī considers to have originated from a divine source and to have been possessed by the elite (*khawāṣṣ*) among both the Greeks and the Persians. Also these works, especially the *Alwāḥ-i 'imādī*, seem to have been written very late in life for in them there are references to his other writings.

A most remarkable feature of these treatises, and one which should dispel once and for all the claim of so many orientalists and a few modern Persian scholars that Suhrawardī represents a national Iranian cultural reaction against Islam or something of the like, is the very large number of Qur'anic verses present in these writings. If we study the history of Islamic philosophy carefully we will discover the strange fact that the first person to have used the Qur'an extensively in philosophical texts is Suhrawardī, who is claimed by so many as leading a movement against Islamic culture. In fact this was the idea furthest from the mind of Suhrawardī. In contrast to al-Fārābī, who never cited Qur'anic verses,[7] and Ibn Sīnā, who in his *al-Shifā'* cited only a single Qur'anic verse, Suhrawardī has filled nearly every chapter of these works with Qur'anic verses. In fact he presents his whole metaphysical and philosophical doctrine as an exegesis upon the Qur'an. At the end of the *Alwāḥ-i 'imādī*, he even interprets the mythical stories of ancient Persian kings and heroes in the light of the Qur'an.

What must be realized is that for Suhrawardī there was no tension between the elements of ancient Persian culture which he adopted in his world view and Islamic wisdom. As Massignon and Corbin have indicated so correctly, Islamic wisdom and gnosis were the mirror in which Suhrawardī, and through him an important element of Persian culture, contemplated its past and once again brought to life its myths and symbols.[8] The relation between ancient Persian wisdom and Islam was, for Suhrawardī, like the relation between the Graeco-Roman heritage and Christianity for the medieval Byzantines and Latins, and not as this situation appeared to the men of the Renaissance. It was a question of harmony and synthesis and not of opposition and antagonism. The case of Suhrawardī is a matter of utmost importance for the modern Persian intellectual for precisely this reason, that he was conscious of the ancient heritage of Persia, wrote in excellent Persian, and yet was a devout Muslim sage. The modern Persian today sometimes feels like the Renaissance European, torn between Islam and the ancient heritage of Persia brought to life for him by modern nationalism. Suhrawardī presents for him the possibility of a synthesis and the solution of the problem of the encounter of Islam and ancient Iran, a problem whose solution can in fact be found only where Suhrawardī sought it, in the world of the immutable archetypes and essences.[9]

The secret of the expansion of Suhrawardī's influence and continuation of his teaching in Islam, and especially in the eastern lands of Islam where the Persian language and culture were dominant, lies in the fact that *ḥikmat al-ishrāq,* the 'Theosophy of the Orient of Light' corresponds to an intellectual possibility within the Islamic framework and fulfilled a deep need of a particular type of Muslim intellectual. It not only drew from ancient Persian sources but was deeply rooted in the Qur'an and for this reason was able to appeal to Arabs, Indians, Turks, and others who were not Persian and displayed no particular interest in ancient Persian history. The spread of Suhrawardī in both Anatolia and the Indian subcontinent cannot simply be brushed aside as unimportant. The spread of Islamic philosophy in India is in fact connected with the school of Suhrawardī. The appearance of the school of *ishrāq* meant both the guarantee of the propagation of Islamic philosophy in a form that was clearer to the heart of Islam than the earlier schools of thought, and the creation of a school that was particularly close to the ethos of Persian Islam and spread wherever Persian Islamic culture was dominant. It also meant the creation of Persian philosophical prose, which with Suhrawardī comes to its own for the first time.

Before Suhrawardī some noteworthy philosophers had written in Persian, chief among them Ibn Sīnā and Nāṣir-i Khusraw. The latter wrote all of his philosophical works in Persian, but, being an Ismaili, expounded a particular form of philosophy which did not accord with the dominant Peripatetic school. Ibn Sīnā for his part wrote the first Peripatetic work in the Persian language, the *Dānish-nāma-yi 'alā'ī.* Yet, although he performed a laudable task, he employed an unknown terminology trying to avoid words of Arabic origin. The result was unsuccessful, as unsuccessful as someone trying to write philosophy in English without using terms of Latin origin. In fact it was so unsuccessful that today a Persian student understands Ghazālī's *Maqāṣid al-falāsifah*, which is almost the Arabic translation of the *Dānish-nāmah*, almost better than Ibn Sīnā's Persian original. This attempt therefore, although heroic, set back the use of Persian as a serious language for philosophy for two centuries. Suhrawardī, in contrast to Ibn Sīnā, did not shy away from the use of words of Arabic origin that had become Persianized, and, although a much greater defender of the wisdom of the ancient Persians, did not grind any axes when it came to the question of language. His philosophical prose is therefore much more natural and easier to understand even for a modern Persian reader than the works of others who wrote philosophy in Persian.

Of this later group two bear comparison with Suhrawardī: one Afḍal al-Dīn Kāshānī and the second Naṣīr al-Dīn Ṭūsī. Kāshānī, the author of a large number of treatises in fine Persian with a heavy Peripatetic leaning,[10] is more difficult to understand than Suhrawardī and in technical vocabulary lies closer to Ibn Sīnā than to Suhrawardī. Ṭūsī, however, the author of the *Nasirean Ethics*, which is among the best-known works of the Persian language, wrote natural and unlaboured, although very refined, prose, but his technical philosophical writings are in Arabic. As for the important figures of the later period, Mīr Dāmād wrote a few philosophical Persian treatises of great difficulty and abstruseness; Ṣadr al-Dīn Shīrazī composed only a single work in Persian prose, his spiritual autobiography and defence, the *Sih aṣl*; and only the *ḥakīms* of the Qajar period like Hājjī Mullā Hādī Sabziwārī and Mullā 'Alī Zunūzī wrote extensive Persian treatises of note.

The Persian philosophical and mystical works of Suhrawardī therefore occupy an almost unique position in Persian literature. They include the first initiatic romances and narratives of Persian and some of the most lucid philosophical prose of the language. Moreover, they contain doctrines and treat problems which bear not only on the intellectual life of the past seven centuries in Persia and other domains of eastern Islam but also concern in a vital fashion those modern Persians who are torn between the pull of modern nationalism and Islamic culture, those who have not as yet become totally deaf to the call of Islam and their spiritual heritage.

NOTES

1. Concerning his life and doctrines see O. Spies, *The Lovers' Friend,* Delhi, 1934; M. Horten, Die Philosophie des Islam, Munich, 1924; the two very significant prolegomena of H. Corbin to Suhrawardī, *Opera Metaphysica et Mystica,* Vol. i, Istanbul, 1945, Vol. ii, Tehran-Paris, 1952, M. Iqbāl, *The Development of Metaphysics in Persia,* London, 1908; S.H. Nasr, *Three Muslim Sages, Cambridge*, 1964; See also M. Abū Rayyān, *Uṣūl al-falsāfat al-ishrāaiyyah,* Cairo, 1959.
2. Concerning the writings of Suhrawardī see the works by H. Corbin and S.H. Nasr cited above. For their classification see L. Massignon, *Recueil de textes concernant*

l'histoire de la mystique en pays d'Islam, Paris, 1939, pp. 111 ff.

The studies of contemporary scholars on the writings of Suhrawardī are based mostly on the list given by Shahrazūrī, the great commentator on Suhrawardī's *Ḥikmat al-ishrāq* in his *Nuzhat al- arwāḥ wa rawḍat al-afrāḥ*. The excellent biography of Suhrawardī and the list of his works contained in this treatise have been published in O. Spies and S.K. Khatak (ed. and trans.) *Three Treatises on Mysticism by Shihabuddin Suhrawardi Maqtul,* Stuttgart, 1935, pp. 90-121 of the Persian and Arabic text.

3. This edition, which is now in press, will be the third volume of the Suhrawardi, *Opera Metaphysicaet Mystica*, and is to appear in the collection of the Institut Franco-Iranien (Tehran-Paris).

4. Shahrazūrī also mentions a commentary upon the *al-Ishārāt wa'l-tanbīhāt* of Ibn Sīnā and a treatise called *al-Mabda' wa'l-ma'ād* in Persian, but neither of these has as yet been discovered. With the large number of words of Suhrawardī manuscripts existing in both Istanbul and the libraries of the Indo-Pakistani sub-continent perhaps one should not give up hope as yet of discovering manuscripts of these works.

5. To this group also belong several Arabic treatises such as *al-Ghurbat al-gharbiyyah* and also *Fī i'Tiqād al-ḥukamā'*, published by Corbin in vol. ii of the *Opera*, and *Risalat al-abraj*, known also as *Kalimat al-dhawqiyyah*, which I plan to include in the edition of Persian works because in structure and thought it belongs to this group. some of these short treatises have been translated into English and French by O. Spies and H. Corbin. The original Persian texts of some have also been published by M. Bayānī, M. Ṣabā, O. Spies, and H. Corbin. See the bibliography in the previous chapter.

6. The reason for this is explained by M. Mahdi in his 'Alfarabi' in L. Strauss and J. Cropsey (eds.), *History of Political Philosophy,* New York 1963, pp. 160-80.

7. See S.H. Nasr, *Three Muslim saqes,* P. 79

8. See S.H. Nasr, 'La cosmographie en Iran pré-islamique et islamique, problème de la continuité dans la civilisation iranienne', Pré-islamique et islamique, le Problème de la continuite' dans la civilisation iraniene', in C.Makdisi (ed.), *Arabic* and *Islamic Studies in Honor of Hamilton Gibb,* Leiden, 1965, pp. 506-24

9. See Afdal al-Din Kāshanī, *Muṣannafāt*, 2 vols., ed. M. Minovi and Y. Mahdavi, Tehran, 1331-7 (A.H. solar).

14

The Spread of the Illuminationist School of Suhrawardī *

After the early period of Islamic history during which the major intellectual and religious perspectives were crystallized and delineated, there is no figure in Islamic intellectual life who has left as much influence upon the later theosophical and philosophical schools of Islam as Suhrawardī, except for Ibn 'Arabī, who was almost his contemporary and whose influence in the eastern lands of Islam was often concurrent with that of Shaykh al-ishrāq (the 'Master of Ishrāq'). Yaḥyā ibn Ḥabash Amīrak Suhrawardī, known in Persia as Shaykh al-ishrāq, lived but thirty-eight years, having been born in Suhraward near Zanjan in 549/1155 and martyred in Aleppo in 587/1191. With the account of this short but meteoric career we are not concerned here[1] nor do we propose to analyse the tenets of the new 'Theosophy of the Orient of Light' *(ḥikmat al-ishrāq)* established by him.[2] Our task is to survey the manner in which his ideas spread and the effect they had upon subsequent phases of intellectual life primarily in the East but also in the West.

Of the immediate students and disciples of Suhrawardī there remains no trace save for reference to the names of one or two men who were his followers.[3] His first real disciple was Shams al-Dīn Muḥammad Shahrazūrī,[4] who lived in the seventh/thirteenth century and wrote commentaries upon his works as well as a moving account of his life in the *Nuzhat al-arwāḥ wa rawḍat al-afrāḥ*.[5] The dates of the life of Shahrazūrī make it most unlikely that he could have been a direct disciple of Suhrawardī, but the intimate manner in which he speaks of *ishrāqī* doctrines and the Shaykh al-ishrāq himself leave no doubt that he

* This essay appeared in the *Islamic Quarterly* 14 (July-September 1970): 111-21 and *Īrān Shināsī* 1 (Summer 1971): 84-102. The French translation of this essay in appeared in Rome: "*La Persia nel Medioevo*" Accademia Nazionale dei Lencei, Rome, 1971 pp. 255-65.

belonged directly to Suhrawardī's school, being perhaps a disciple of one of his disciples. In any case one can state with certainty that he received the oral transmission which in Islamic philosophy is a necessary complement to the written text and a condition *sine qua non* for a full understanding of traditional doctrines. Shahrazūrī was the great propagator and commentator of Suhrawardī's teachings, playing a role that is in many ways analogous to that of Ṣadr al-Dīn al-Qunyawī *vis-à-vis* Ibn 'Arabī. Shahrazūrī wrote a commentary upon the *Talwīḥāt* of Suhrawardi in 680/1281,[6] and the first commentary upon the *Ḥikmat al-ishrāq*, upon which all later commentaries have relied in one way or another.[7]

The seventh/thirteenth century witnessed a wide general interest in the writings of Suhrawardī and in fact it was during this century that *ishrāqī* doctrines penetrated into the intellectual centres of Persia and also Anatolia and Syria. Besides the commentary of Shahrazūrī upon the *Talwīḥāt*, at nearly the same time two other commentaries were also written upon this important work, that of Ibn Kammūnah, written in 667/1269, and that of 'Allāmah Ḥillī, completed some time before 693/1293. Ḥillī's own master, Naṣīr al-Dīn Ṭūsī, although the reviver of Ibn Sīnā's philosophy and known most of all for his contributions to Peripatetic (*mashshā'ī*) philosophy through his *Sharḥ al-ishārāt wa'l-tanbīhāt*, was not only acquainted with Suhrawardī but also influenced by him, especially in the question of God's knowledge of the world. The influence of Suhrawardī upon Naṣīr al-Dīn in fact did not go unnoticed by later Islamic philosophers so that, for example, Mullā Ṣadrā mentions it in his commentary upon Abharī's *al-Hidāyah.*[8] Athīr al-Dīn Abharī himself, although known mostly for his Peripatetic *al-Hidāyah*, was deeply influenced by Suhrawardī and in his *Kashf al-ḥaqā'iq fī taḥrīr al-daqā'iq* follows the Master of Ishrāq completely.[9] Also during the seventh/thirteenth century another of Naṣīr al-Dīn's students, Quṭb al-Dīn Shīrāzī, composed the second major commentary upon the *Ḥikmat al-ishrāq*, which although based on that of Shahrazūrī became much better known than Shahrazūrī work. The first printed lithographed edition of the *Ḥikmat al-ishrāq*, which appeared in Tehran in 1315 (A.H. solar), contains the commentary of Quṭb al-Dīn, and for the past seven centuries nearly all students of *ishrāqī* theosophy have seen Suhrawardī through the eyes of Quṭb al-Dīn.

By the beginning of the eighth/fourteenth century the *ishrāqī* school had become definitely established in Persia and henceforth it remained as an important element of the intellectual life of not only Persia but also the eastern lands of Islam where the Persian Islamic culture has been dominant. In order to study the propagation of Suhrawardī's teachings it would be necessary to follow their spread stage by stage in four different regions: in Persia itself, in the Ottoman world, in the Indo-Pakistani subcontinent and finally in the West where the whole question of whether Suhrawardī was even known or not must be examined.

Let us begin with the Ottoman world. The proximity of Aleppo to Anatolia and the spread of gnostic teachings mostly from Konya in the seventh/thirteenth century in the Turkish-speaking areas of the region made the teachings of the *ishrāqī* school both easily accessible and intellectually attractive in the region that was later to become the heartland of the Ottoman empire. Unfortunately, as far as we have been able to discover, no systematic study of Islamic philosophy in the Turkish-speaking parts of the Ottoman empire has been made save for the domain that touches upon the gnostic school of Ibn 'Arabī. But the large number of manuscripts of Suhrawardī found in Turkish libraries especially in Istanbul, often copied by Turkish scribes, the presence of commentaries and marginal notes upon these works in Arabic and Persian as well as in Turkish by scholars of that region and the presence of many ideas of an '*ishrāqī* colour' in the writings of later Turkish Sufīs of the school of Ibn 'Arabī all indicate the extent to the influence of Suhrawardī in a part of the Islamic world where much remains to be discovered through the study of manuscript material that has not received the attention it deserves until now.

In Persia itself, upon the solid foundations established during the seventh/thirteenth century, a long chain of *ishrāqī ḥakīms* appeared on the scene culminating with the Safavid sages such as Mīr Dāmād and Mullā Ṣadrā, who were deeply impregnated with the teachings of the Master of Ishrāq. Nearly all the Persian philosophers and *ḥakīms* between the seventh/thirteenth and tenth/sixteenth centuries, such as Quṭb al-Dīn Rāzī, Ibn Turkah Iṣfahānī, Jalāl al-Dīn Dawānī, the two Dashtakīs, and Sayyid Sharīf Jurjānī, were influenced by Suhrawardī, and many wrote commentaries upon his works, the writings of Dawānī being particularly important in this respect. Dawānī and Ghiyāth al-Dīn Manṣūr Dashtakī wrote commentaries upon the *Hayākil al-nūr* and Wadūd Tabrīzī on *al-Alwāḥ al-'imādiyyah* as well as glosses upon Quṭb al-Dīn's commentary upon the *Ḥikmat al-ishrāq*.

Meanwhile both the Sufis of the school of Ibn 'Arabī and Shi'ite theologians became interested in and impregnated by Suhrawardī's teachings during this period of general *rapprochement* between the different Islamic intellectual perspectives in Persia.[10] Such masters of gnosis as 'Abd al-Razzāq Kāshānī and Dā'ūd Qayṣarī were well aware of *ishrāqī* teachings while Ibn Turkah sought consciously to combine the teachings of Ibn ʿArabī and Suhrawardī. We must also remember that Quṭb al-Dīn Shīrāzī himself was not only the great expositor of *ishrāqī* teachings but also a Sufi and student of Ṣadr al-Dīn al-Qunyawī. The nature of *ishrāqī* teachings is such as to provide a bridge between philosophy based on ratiocination and pure gnosis. If therefore became inextricably bound up with certain of the later schools of Sufism especially that of Ibn ʿArabī, and the source of *ishrāq* for the *ishrāqī ḥakīms* remained always the light of Islamic esotericism contained usually in Sufism and occasionally in the other forms which Islamic esotericism has taken in Shiʿism.[11]

The integration of *ishrāqī* teachings into Shiʿism was for this and other complex reasons, which we cannot delve into on this occasion, rapid and profound, with the result that during later centuries most of the *ishrāqīs* have been Shiʿite. During the period pre-dating the Safavids, such Shiʿite theologians as Sayyid Ḥaydar Āmulī and especially Ibn Abī Jumhūr, prepared the ground for the integration of *ishrāqī* wisdom into the perspective of Shiʿism. The basic work of Ibn Abī Jumhūr, *Kitāb al-mujlī,* contains major theses of *ishrāqī* theosophy.

The above tendencies culminated in the great renaissance of the Islamic sciences and especially theosophy or *ḥikmat-i ilāhī* during the Safavid period. Nearly all the major figures of this era, such as Mīr Dāmād, Mīr Findiriskī, Mullā Ṣadrā, Sayyid Aḥmad ʿAlawī, Mullā Shamsā Gīlānī, Mullā Muḥsin Fayḍ Kāshānī, ʿAbd al-Razzāq Lāhījī, and Qāḍī Saʿīd Qummī, not to speak of the later traditional philosophers who have carried this tradition to the present day in Persia, were influenced by Suhrawardī. In fact the whole intellectual effort of the Safavid period is unimaginable without the figure of Suhrawardī, even if Mullā Ṣadrā did found a new intellectual perspective based upon the principiality of existence, (*aṣālat al-wujūd*) opposed to Suhrawardī's 'the principiality of quiddity' (*aṣālat al-māhiyyah*). Despite this difference, his vision of the universe remains organically bound to that of Suhrawardī.[12]

The Safavid period, more particularly the eleveth/seventeenth century, witnessed two translations of the *Ḥikmat al-ishrāq* into Persian, one made by Maḥmūd Sharīf ibn Harawī in 1008/1599 and the other by the Zoroastrian Farzānah Bahrām ibn Farshād, a disciple of Ādhar Kaywān who was still alive in 1048/1638. This period was also witness to the commentary of Najm al-Dīn Ḥājjī Maḥmūd Tabrīzī upon the *Ḥikmat al-ishrāq* and the masterful glosses (*Taʿlīqāt*) of Mullā Ṣadrā upon the same work, the latter being one of the most important writings in the tradition of Islamic theosophy and philosophy on eschatology.[13] But more than in these commentaries, the influence of Suhrawardī is seen during this period in the wroks of the *ḥakīms* or the age, whose writings are replete with references to the teachings of Suhrawardī. In fact one of the most outstanding of them, Mīr Dāmād, even chose as his pen-name *Ishrāq* to demonstrate his close association with the spiritual universe of Suhrawardī.

As for the sub-continent, the main thrust of Islamic philosophy into that region can be almost identified with the spread of the *ishrāqī* school in that land. Although from the Ghaznavid period a certain amount of knowledge of Islamic philosophy existed in some of the western regions of the sub-continent, mostly in Ismaili circles, it was with the Tughlugh kings of Delhi such as Sulṭān Muḥammad and Fīrūz Shāh and especially the Mognuls that Islamic philosophy really found a home in the sub-continent and began to gain a notable following. The key figure perhaps in the spread of Islamic philosophy at this time was Fatḥallāh Shīrāzī, himself a student of Ghiyāth al-Dīn Manṣūr Dashtakī,[14] who was thoroughly acquainted with *ishrāqī* theosophy and taught its tenets in the sub-continent. Nearly all later Muslim philosophers of the region, who were in fact closely associated with the 'School of Ispahan' and the writings of Mīr Dāmād and Mullā Ṣadrā, were also closely associated with the universe of discourse of *ishrāqī* theosophy and many of them were *ishrāqīs*. The fame of the *Ḥikmat al-ishrāq* and *Hayākil al-nūr* in Muslim circle of the Sub-continent has been hardly less than in Persia itself. Moreover, it must be remembered that the two translations of the *Ḥikmat al-ishrāq* into Persian, which at that time was the common cultural language of Persia and India, are closely connected with the intellectual world of the subcontinent. Maḥmūd ibn Harawī's translation contains references to Sufism as it developed in the Sub-continent and Bahrām ibn Farshād's translation belongs to an interesting but as yet little-studied aspect of a religious movement that began in Shiraz but played its most important role in Akbar's court. Moreover, the translator was met by the author of *Dabistān al-madhāhib* in Lahore and the translation itself may have been made in the Sub-continent.

Bahrām ibn Farshād belonged to the circle of the Zoroastrian priest, Ādhar Kaywān, who had left Shiraz with his followers to settle in India. Ādhar Kaywān and his disciples were deeply influenced by the teachings of Suhrawardī and considered themselves to be *ishrāqīs*. The *Dabistān al-madhāhib* in fact mentions several figures of this school by name as being *ishrāqīs*.[15] The spread of the teachings of Suhrawardī, which had already integrated the angelology of Zoroastrianism with the gnostic dimension of Islam, into Zoroastrian circles that had lived already for centuries within the bosom of the Islamic world, is yet another startling facet of the remifications of Suhrawardī's doctrines in the later spiritual history of the East. His role in fact in the religious life of Akbar's court and the different attempts to create a bridge between Islam and Hinduism has as yet to be made clear. There is no doubt, however, that through several channels such as Fatḥallāh Shīrāzī, certain currents of Sufism, the school of Dārā Shukūh and the movement of Ādhar Kaywān, his ideas played a major role in the intellectual and spiritual life of the Sub-continent at that time and during subsequent centuries up to the Khayrābādī school and Iqbāl himself. Even Hindu circles were to become acquainted with Suhrawardī and some of his writings came to be known by Hindu scholars and sages.

In glancing over the spread of Suhrawardī's teachings in the East one is startled by the degree to which it influenced even the titles of philosophy and theosophical writings. The earlier works of Islamic philosophy such as those of Ibn Sīnā have names often associated with knowledge or the cure of ignorance such as the *Najāt, Shifā',* and *al-Ishārāt wa'l-tanbīhāt* or simple referring to the contents of the book such as most of the treatises of al-Kindī, Fārābī, and Muḥammad ibn Zakariyyā' Rāzī. Under the influence of *ishrāqī* theosophy many titles began to appear after the seventh/thirteenth century which were in one way or another connected with the symbolism of light. The appearance of such titles is not only contemporary with Suhrawardī and the spread of *ishrāqī* wisdom but definitely caused by this spread. Those who are acquainted with the gnostic, theosophical, and philosophical literature of Persia and the Indian sub-continent during the past seven centuries will readily recall such title as the *Lama'āt* of 'Irāqī, the *Kitāb al-mujlī* of Ibn Abī Jumhūr, the *Ashi''at al-lama'āt* of Jāmī, the *Jadhawāt* of Mīr Dāmād, the *Shawāriq* and the *Mashāriq al-ilhām* of Lāhījī, all written in Persian, and the *al-Shams al-bāziqah* of Mullā Maḥmūd Junpūrī, one of the most famous works of *ḥikmat* in India. Even the Shi'ite theological encyclopaedia of Majlisī, the *Biḥār al-anwār*, has an *ishrāqī* title. The title of the famous *al-Mabāḥith al-mashriqiyyah* of Fakhr al-Dīn Rāzī, the contemporary of Suhrawardī, may also be recalled, but in this case the title is not connected with the *ishrāqī* school. The above-mentioned works and many others of this period which mark a definite departure from the title of works of the earlier period of Islamic history can be partially explained by the influence of the 'Oriental philosophy' (*al-ḥikmat al-mashriqiyyah*) of Ibn Sīnā and the *Mishkāt al-anwār* of Ghazzālī, not to speak of Ibn 'Arabī who already possessed a definite '*ishrāqī* dimension' in addition to his purely gnostic (*'irfānī*) aspect and whose influence is particularly important in the case of 'Irāqī and Jāmī. But the major reason for this change of tone and colour in the later works of *ḥikmat* and the noticeable change in their titles is Suhrawardī and his *ishrāqī* school.

When we turn to the question of the spread of the School of Illumination in the West we must distinguish between the general doctrine of illumination and the doctrines specifically associated with the school of Suhrawardī. Before the Aristotelianization of Christian theology in the thirteenth century the Western theologians shared for the most part the view of St. Augustine that 'the mind knows the truth in the same way that the physical eye sees a body' (*menti hoc est intelligere, quod sensui ridere*).[16] According to St. Augustine the angels are not the instruments of illumination but only prepare the soul for the illumination that comes from God. Herein lies the major difference between the Augustinian theory of knowledge and that of Suhrawardī. Nevertheless, the belief in illumination in Augustinian theology made this theology more akin to the *ishrāqī* doctrines that were to sweep the Islamic world nearly at the same time as Augustinian theology was to be replaced by Thomism in the West. Even an exact contemporary of Suhrawardī, the Cistercian monk Isaac of Stella could write:

> Just as, although the eye of the flesh has from nature the faculty of seeing, and the ear that of hearing, the eye never attains vision through itself, or the ear hearing, without the aid of the outer light or sound; so also the rational spirit, being by the gift of creation capable of knowing the true and loving the good, never attains the actuality of wisdom or charity except when flooded with the radiance and inflamed with the heat of the inner light.[17]

Strangely enough Suhrawardī was never translated directly into Latin and was never able to help fortify and sustain this tradition. His name was never officially known to the West because he appeared on the scene at the very moment when the first major period of translation in Spain was drawing to a close. During this era the earlier Muslim Peripatetics had been translated and these translations were in turn interpreted in such a way as to make the atmosphere in Western intellectual circles ever less conducive to the reception of *ishrāqī* doctrines, even an Ibn Sīnā was only half studied, his 'Oriental Philosophy' having been officially completely neglected.[18] It seems that at this crucial moment of the parting of the ways between Islam and the West, the Islamic world was becoming ever more fully conscious of itself as an 'Orient' (*mashriq*) in both a geographical and symbolical sense, thus turning ever more away from the rationalism of the earlier Peripatetic philosophy to the illumination and ecstasy of *ishrāq* and *'irfān*. The West, which had been in many ways an 'Orient' in the *ishrāqī* sense of the term and had possessed a traditional civilization which more than in any other period of its known history resembled the great Oriental civilizations, was now becoming an Occident, not only geographically but also in the *ishrāqī* sense of concerning itself with the domain of ratiocination that is cut off from the illumination of the Divine Intellect. The migration of Ibn 'Arabī from Andalusia to Syria and the lack of receptivity in the West to the *ishrāqī* doctrines of Suhrawardī are symptoms of this event and in fact symbolic of the parting of ways between two worlds which until now had been treading a similar course. Needless to say, men like Dante and Eckhart were yet to appear but the tendency has already begun in the West in the direction of the 'Occident' or *maghrib* of the intellectual world, in the direction of rationalism which finally, with the razor of Ockham, was to put an end to the life of scholastic theology, at least as the main intellectual force in the West.

On the margin of this main movement, however, the mystical and illuminative tendencies continued to assert themselves and in this domain there may have been contacts with the teachings of Suhrawardī, although this will not be fully known until all the manuscripts are studied. This influence is most likely in the Oxford school of the thirteenth century and such figures as Roger Bacon and even Robert Grossteste. The latter has been credited by Crombie as being the founder of the experimental method,[19] so that some may think of him as standing at the antipodes of illuminative theosophy. But both in Islam and medieval and even Renaissance Europe interest in the observation of nature and experiment often went hand in hand with gnostic and illuminationist tentencies rather than with rationalism, for the mystic and not the rationalist sought after the 'vision' of things in their essential reality and tried to remove the mental image which separates the subject from the object. Many *ishrāqīs* in the East also, foremost among them Quṭb al-Dīn Shīrāzī, were well-known physicists and observers of nature.[20] Be that as it may, we know of the interest of the Oxford school in illumination and that Roger Bacon even wore the dress of the *ishrāqīs* and lectured upon them. Whether this '*ishrāqī*' interest of Bacon refers to the 'Oriental Philosophy' of Ibn Sīnā or to Suhrawardī himself remains to be discovered. No definite conclusion can be reached until many more Latin manuscripts, especially those of this school, are studied.

The possibility of acquaintance with Suharwardī in Spain during the seventh/thirteenth century certainly existed because already Ibn Sab'īn of Andalusia who lived at this time in the Maghrib refers to the *Talwīḥāt* in his *al-Risālat al-faqīriyyah*, and this fact testifies to the widespread acquaintance with Suhrawardī throughout the Islamic world of that time. Whether a man like Roger Bacon, who could read Arabic, could have gained access to one of Suhrawardī's actual works is a question which as mentioned above cannot be answered at the present moment. Also components and elements that format part of the synthesis that Suhrawardī achieved in his *Ḥikmat al-ishrāq*, such as Hermeticism, reached the West independently during the eleventh and twelfth centuries so that some of the alchemical and Hermetical writers bear much resemblance to Suhrawardī in certain aspects of their teachings. The example of Raymond Lull comes particularly to mind in this connection.

Not withstanding these possible lines of contact and influence it can be said that *ishrāqī* theosophy did not penetrate into the main stream of Western intellectual life. Rather, with the triumph of Aristotelianism and the weakening of the more intellectual currents of Christian mysticism illumination become more and more relegated to a marginal place until it became completely divorced from the official theology of the main religious authority in the West, namely the Church. In the general development of European philosophy also, despite the appearance of the Cambridge Platonists and a few less influential German philosophers of the eighteenth and nineteenth centuries like Schelling and Franz van Baader, there was no possibility of an *ishrāqī* type of wisdom, seeing that this philosophy had become divorced from both religion and true mysticism and therefore any possible and legitimate source of illumination. The greatest paradox can be seen in the fact that the age which had completely forgotten illumination in the sense that Suhrawardī gives to it and had moved to the very extremities of the 'Occident' of the *ishrāqī* theosophers is called is some of the Latin languages such as Italian the age of 'illumination' (*illuminismo*).

But inasmuch as the need for true illumination could never be completely suppressed illuminationist teachings appeared from time to time under occultist colours ever more opposed to etablished religious authority, until in the eighteenth century such movements as the 'Illuminated of Bavaria' founded by Adam Weishaupt opposed all established religious authority and hierarchy. The outcome was a far cry from the destiny of *ishrāqī* theosophy in Persia where by the Safavid period the most revered religious authorities were teaching Suhrawardī in corners of mosques to pious students who never missed a canonical prayer and who saw the *ishrāqī* school as a natural growth of one of the branches from the trunk of the tree of Islamic intellectual life.

Although the subject of this paper does not really cover the modern period, we cannot but add a few remarks as a postscript concerning the spread of the teachings of Suhrawardī today in both East and West, for the story of the spread of his influence has not yet come to an end. In Persia Suhrawardī continues as a major intellectual force and it is around him and Mullā Ṣadrā that most of the contemporary students of traditional Islamic philosophy rally.[21] With the coming of modern nationalism, which has resuscitated pre-Islamic sentiments in the minds of certain modernists, the synthesis of Suhrawardī, who integrated the spiritual legacy of ancient Persia into the intellectual world-view of Islam, appears as particularly precious. And his impeceable and beautiful philosophical prose in Persian is without doubt a stimulus for the rejuvenation of Persian as a language of intellectual discourse in contemporary terms.[22] As long as traditional *ḥikmat* and of course the traditional religious teachings and the spiritual discipline which underlie the whole structure of *ishrāqī* theosophy subsist, the influence of Suhrawardī will continue to shine on the intellectual horizon of Persia and much of the rest of the Islamic world.

Even in the West Suhrawardī is now finally becoming known after centuries of neglect, almost completely due to the indefatigable efforts of H. Corbin. In a West where the post-Renaissance development of philosophy has reached a dead end and the purely rationalistic and positivistic schools vie with completely anti-rationalistic philosophies, the synthesis of reason and illumination achieved by Suhrawardī appeals to many minds; not to speak of the vast world of symbols and metaphysical doctrines, which has attracted many who have become acquainted with his writings. Even the young who seek 'illumination' through drugs think that they are interested in Suhrawardī.[23] Acquaintance with his writings is therefore bound to increase in the future.

But it must be stated clearly for the sake of both the serious student and he who is looking for adventure that the *ishrāqī* theosophy of Suhrawardī is a traditional doctrine of a sacred nature that cannot become fully assimilated except by being coupled with the proper spiritual discipline of an orthodox tradition. One can read Suhrawardī and gain an intellectual understanding of him. This is already a great deal and needs an intellectual intuition which is a gift of Heaven and does not come easily. But to become an actual *ishrāqī*, to receive that illumination which transforms one's whole being and results in that ecstasy or *wajd* described by Suhrawardī at the end of his *Ḥikmat al-ishrāq*, one must follow the way of Suhrawardī himself and practice the methods os Sufism or analogous spiritual techniques. The *ishrāqī* theosophy serves most of all the purpose of depicting a universe in which the necessity of such practices becomes a blinding evidence, a universe whose very beauty in fact draws those who possess the necessary qualifications to the doorway of the practical spiritual life, inasmuch as the vision itself is the fruit of having lived such a life. In Persia Suhrawardī's teachings have for centuries performed this important spiritual task. Let us hope that as a living expression of perenial metaphysics it will also perform this task for the few in the West who have detected the real malady of our age and are seeking after the real cures, whose who have come to realize that the reform of the world and of society begins with the reform of oneself.[24]

NOTES

1. Concerning the life of Suhrawardī see H. Corbin's two prolegomena to Suhrawardī, *Opera Metaphysica el. Mystrica,* vol. i. Istanbul, 1945, and vol. ii, Tehran-Paris, 1951; S.H. Nasr, *Three Muslim Sages,* Cambridge (U.S.A.), 1964, chap. ii; S.H. Nasr, ''Shihāb al-Dīn Suhṛawardī in this volume.
2. Concerning the doctrines of Suhrawardī and his school see the above mentioned works as well as Corbin, *Les Motifs zoroastriens dans la philosophie de Suharwardī,* Tehran, 1325 (A.H. solar).
3. In the *Bustān al-jāmi'* (ed. by C. Cahen), *Bulletin d'Etudes Orientales*, vii-viii (Damascus, 1938), 150, the name of one Shams al-Dīn is mentioned as his student but the identity of this figure is not known.
4. Concerning Shahrazūrī see *Kanz al-ḥikmah* by Ḍ Durrī, which is a Persian translation of the *Nuzhat al-arwāḥ*, Tehran, 1316 (A.H. solar), p. 11. Durrī argues from a treatise on the creation of the world (*ḥudūth*) by Mullā Shamsa in which it is stated that Quṭb al-Dīn Shīrāzī has cited Shahrazūrī that Shahrazūrī lived in the seventh/thirteenth century. Other indications substantiate the fact that Shahrazūrī, whose biography is unknown to us, was still alive during the last decades of the seventh/thirteenth century. See also C.E. Sachau, *Chronologie Orientalischer von Albiruni,* Leipzig, 1878 introduction, pp. 1-li.
5. O. Spies has given the Arabic text of this biographical account in his edition of Suhrawardī, *Three Treatises on Mystisicm,* Stuttgart, 1935 pp. 90-121; in our recent edition of Suhrawardī's Persian works, (*Euvres philosophiques et mystiques*, ii (Tehran-Paris, 1970), Persian introduction, pp. 13-30, we have also given a new edited version of Shahrazūrī's biographical account of Suhrawardī as well as its Persian translation by the tenth/seventeenth-century scholar Maqṣūd 'Alī Tabrīzī.
6. See M.T. Danechpazhuh, *Fihrist-i kitābkhāna-yi ihdā'i-yi Āqā-yi Sayyid Muḥammad Mishkāt bi kitāb-khāna-yi Dānishgāh-i Tihrān*, iii, part i (Tehran, 1332), 212.
7. See ibid, p. 455. On the commentaries upon the *Ḥikmat al-ishrāq* see Corbin, prolegomena to vol. ii of Suhrawardī, *Opera Metaphysica et Mystica*, pp. 59-64.
8. See Ṣadr al-Dīn Shīrāzī, *Sharḥ al-hidāyat al-athīriyyah,* Tehran, 1313 (A.H. lunar), pp. 366-7.
9. See Corbin, prolegomena to vol. i of *Opera Metaphysica et Mystica*, p. xxi, note 29.

10. We have dealt with this question in several of our works, including *Three Muslim Sages,* pp. 79-82 and also *Islamic Studies,* Beirut, 1966, pp. 13-14.

11. One must remember that although '*ishrāqī*' usually refers to the school of Suhrawardī, because of the universality of the symbolism of light certain Ṣufis, especially of the Shādhiliyyah Order, have been called *ishrāqī* without this term referring specifically to Suhrawardī and his school. See, for example, the *Illumination in Islamic Mysticism* of 'Abd al-Mawāhib al-Shādhilī, translated by E. Jurji, Princeton, 1938.

12. Ṣadr al-Dīn Shīrāzī, *Le Livre des pénétrations metaphysiques*, Tehran-Paris, 1964, the intorduction of H. Corbin, chaps. iv and v.

13. See H. Corbin, 'La thème de la résurrection chez Mollā Ṣadrā Shīrāzī (1050/1640) commentateur de Sohrawardī (587/1191), *Studies in Mysticism and Religion presented to Gershom g. Scholem,* Jerusalem, 1967, pp. 71-115.

14. See M.A. Alvi and A. Rahman, *Fatḥullah Shīrāzī, A Sixteenth Century Indian Scientist,* New Delhi, 1968.

15. See Corbin, prolegomena to vol. i of Suhrawardī, *Opera Metaphysica et Mystica,* p. lvii.

16. St. Augustine. *De Ordine*, ii 3.10. This view is also confirmed in his *Soliloquies* and explained by E. Gilson in his *The Christian Philosophy of St. Augustine,* trans. by L.E.M. Lynch, New York. 1960, pp. 77-88.

17. Quoted by G.B. Burch in his *Early Medieval Philosophy*, New York. 1951, p.118.

18. This has been fully treated by H. Corbin, *Avicenna and the Visionary Recital*, trans. by W. Trask, New York, 1960, pp. 101-22, and S.H. Nasr, *Three Muslim Sages,* pp. 45-51.

19. See A.C. Crombie, *Robert Grossteste and the Origins of Experimental Science* 1100-1700, Oxford, 1953.

20. This question has been dealt with in our *Science and Civilization in Islam*, Cambridge (U.S.A.), 1968 in several different chapter.

21. See H. Corbin, 'The Force of Traditional Philosophy in Iran Today', *Studies in Comparative Religion,* Winter, 1968, pp. 12-26.

22. On the significance of the Persian works of Suhrawardī see S.H. Nasr, 'The Persian Works of Shaykh al-ishrāq Shihāb al-Dīn Suhrawardī' in this volume.

23. Some time ago the founder of the 'cult of LSD' sent me a message asking for a meeting to be arranged between us, saying that since we were both interested in illumination we had much to talk about.

24. 'The only means of "reforming" a religion is to reform oneself.' F. Schuon, 'No Activity Without Truth', *Studies in Comparative Religion,* Autumn, 1969. p. 199.

The Mission of the [illegible]

[illegible]

11 [illegible]

12 [illegible]

13 [illegible]

14 [illegible] 1966.

15 [illegible]

16 [illegible]

17 [illegible]

18 [illegible]

19 [illegible]

20 [illegible]

21 [illegible]

22 [illegible]

23 [illegible]

24 [illegible]

PART IV

PHILOSOPHERS-POETS-SCIENTISTS

15

'Umar Khayyām: Philosopher-Poet-Scientist*

There is no figure in the history of Persian literature and in fact of Persian and Islamic thought in general who is so famous in the West and yet remains so unknown as far as the totality of his thought is concerned as 'Umar Khayyām. Practically the object of a cult, Khayyām has been seen by many as a hedonist and fatalistic poet since the beautiful but inaccurate rendition of his quatrains by Fitzgerald. Yet, far from being solely the antidote to Victorian moralism, Khayyām was a gnostic and philosopher, a scientist, historian and an expert on calendars and chronology who also wrote poetry of some consequence and beauty in his mother tongue. But he was not Persia's greatest poet whereas he was one of her greatest mathematicians and the foremost philosopher-scientist between Ibn Sīnā and Suhrawardī.

Khayyām wrote little yet what he did write is of great significance. His some dozen surviving treatises include not only the most important work on algebra before the modern period and the famous study of the Euclidean axiom according to which from a single point only one line can be drawn parallel to another line, but also his work on devising the Jalālī calendar which is used in Persia to this day and which is more accurate than the Gregorian calendar. His corpus includes a valuable book on the Persian new year or Naw-rūz as well as important treatises on metaphysics. It also contains not only the well-known quatrains but also the translation into Persian of Ibn Sīnā's sermon *(khutbah)* on unity *(tawḥīd)*.

To understand Khayyām fully, one must read and ponder over all these works in the context of the intellectual tradition from which Khayyām issued and not project the skepticism and sensuality of modern European thought back to a world to which they do not belong. Khayyām

---

This note originally appeared as the preface to *Rubā'yāt of 'Umar Khayyām,* Translated and annotated by Ahmad Saidi, Asian Humanities Press, 1991, pp. xxi-xxiii.

was not a man who lived outside the world of faith and did not live in religious doubt in the manner of many a post-medieval Western philosopher or literary figure. What Khayyām was skeptical about was the absolutization of the relative so characteristic of the everyday human mentality whether it belongs to the traditional world or the anti-traditional modern world. Khayyām never doubted the Absolute but always emphasized the relativity of everything other than the Absolute. He was not against religious certitude but opposed the hypocrisy and fanaticism which lurk always as a danger in a world where faith is strong. He glorified the present moment not to oppose or forget eternity but to emphasize that the present moment *is* our only point of contact with the eternal. The eternal now is the moment in human life when the soul can experience the eternity which characterizes the Divine Presence. While the faithful and the virtuous seek paradise after death, the "friends of God" have always sought Him here and now. The ever recurring assertion of Khayyām that man should "enjoy" the present moment now is another manner of expressing a truth which has been emphasized by Sufis from Rābi'ah to Rūmī, a truth to which in fact allusion is made in many verses of the Quran and in numerous *ḥadīths.* It is only in living in the present now that man can "enter" paradise in this life and experience the Divine Itself to which Sūfis have referred as the Paradise of the Essence *(jannat al-Dhāt).*

Khayyām was also "sensualist" but not in the hedonistic sense in which this term is understood in the context of the mainstream of Christian mysticism especially as it developed in the Latin West. Sensualism is usually opposed to the spiritual in this tradition, whereas in Persian Sufism there is an organic bi-unity between the spiritual and the sensual. In the same way that there is a natural dimension to the supernatural and a supernatural aspect to the natural, there is a spiritualization of the corporeal and a corporealization of the spiritual which is to be seen in many facets of traditional Persian culture ranging from the philosophy of Suhrawardī to the poetry of Ḥāfiẓ, from Persian classical music to everyday religious practices. Khayyām reflects this tradition in his poetry in such a manner that while his imagery is highly sensual, not only is it not opposed to the spiritual but leads to it. The wine of Sufi poetry is not what is found in bottles; rather it is the ecstasy of union which is the fruit of realized knowledge. Khayyām's use of the symbolism of wine can only be fully understood if one remembers Rūmī's assertion that wine has become inebriated from us and not we from the wine.

That is not to say that Khayyām's thought and poetry is simply the same as those of other great Sufi poets of the Persian language, but his imagery and the world view which his language conveys cannot be completely disassociated from the Persian poetic tradition either. Khayyām represents a particular strand of this tradition which emphasizes the transience of the world, the enigmatic character of human existence and the world when seen solely from the human point of view or from the rationalistic perspective, and the combining of sensuality with the most sublime intellectual and metaphysical attitude. Khayyām is the supreme example of many a Persian philosopher, scientist and even religious scholar who, while writing highly technical and rationally ordered works of logic, mathematics or jurisprudence, has also composed some quatrains in the Khayyāmian vein. It happens that Khayyām was the outstanding master of this type of quatrain who brought to perfection, for this kind of philosophical and contemplative poetry, the quatrain form already used as the first vehicle for Sufi poetry in Persian by Abū Sa'īd Abi'l-Khayr and also used for the expression of various forms of philosophical reflection by Ibn Sīnā before him.

After a century during which the name of Khayyām has become a household word thanks to Fitzgerad's translation, or rather adaptation, of the *Rubā'iyyāt,* the time has now arrived for a full re-appraisal of the philosophical works of Khayyām, one of whose major components is the quatrains. The *Rubā'iyyāt* needs to be studied as a profound statement of the views of one of the most remarkable figures of Persian culture and not only as a masterpiece of translation of the Victorian period. To achieve this end, the philosophical and scientific works of Khayyām need to be carefully studied and the *Rubā'iyyāt* made available in a faithful manner while capturing something of its original poetical quality.

16

The World View and Philosophical Perspective of Ḥakīm Niẓāmī Ganjawī *

Wherever intellect brings forth a treasure
Through the Name of God thou wilt make of it a key[1].

Those who have been given the title of *ḥakīm* by the people of Iran have known *ḥikmah* (theosophy)[2] as well as philosophy[3] and it is not a coincidence that such a title has been bestowed upon them. This is the case even if such figures cannot be considered as philosophers or theosophers in the strict sense of these terms. Nowhere is this more true than in the case of Ḥakīm Niẓāmī Ganjawī,[4] the peerless composer of unparalled odes who created some of the most sublime examples of Persian literature. While he did not write philosophical treatises, he not only mastered discursive reasoning and the intellectual sciences of his time, but was also a man of "vision", familiar with "Knowledge by Presence"[5] as well as Sufism and the esoteric tradition which is a major expression of the perennial philosophy.

Niẓāmī appeared at a time when the Islamic sciences had become divided into specific schools of thought. When he began his studies, Mu'tazilite theology (*Kalām)* had passed its zenith and was on the decline. Ash'arite theology, having matured at the hands of such figures as Juwaynī and Ghazzālī, had begun a new stage in its life.

In the Shi'ite tradition, the major works on law and principles of jurisprudence, that is the four books of twelve-Imam Shi'ism had laid the foundation for future intellectual activities.[6] Ismā'īlī theology and philosophy had also reached their climax with the rise of such figures as Abū Ḥātam Rāzī, Ḥamīd al-Dīn Kirmānī and Nāṣir-i Khusraw.

---

* This essay was originally written in Persian and appeared in *Ā'īna-yi jahān-i ghayb,* Bank Melli Press, 1974, pp. 17-26. The essay was translated into English by Mehdi Aminrazavi and published in *The Muslim World* 82 (July-October 1992) 191-200.

In philosophy, following the initial endeavors of al-Kindī, Īrānshahrī and a few others, the Peripatetic school had gained the upper hand over other existing schools. The Peripatetic tradition which was perfected at the hands of such giants as al-Fārābī, Abu'l-Ḥasan 'Āmirī, Ibn Sīnā and their commentators, had dominated even such schools as the Hermetic and Neo-Pythagoreans.

Religious sciences such as Quranic exegesis *(tafsīr)* and prophetic tradition *(Ḥadīth),* both in the Shi'ah and Sunni branches had gone through prolific periods of activity. In the 6th/12th century, serious scholarship was prevalent in all the branches of the religious sciences in particular hermeneutics which in addition to philosophical and theological interpretations, produced extensive gnostic interpretations and exegeses.[7]

In mathematics and the natural sciences, a period of intense activity had passed and the works of such masters as Ibn Sīnā and Bīrūnī had become available for the seekers of knowledge. The serious students of intellectual sciences in the centers of learning were able to avail themselves of astronomical and mathematical achievements which had reached their climax in the 5th/11th century.[8]

When Niẓāmī, who was an unusually gifted child, began his formal education, he encountered a vast ocean of Islamic sciences. He studied the religious sciences as his works reflect and mastered the art of Quranic interpretation and *Ḥadīth* which are the fundamental and foundational bases of the Islamic sciences. He was well versed in philosophy and theology and was familiar with the existing diversity of intellectual ideas and philosophical schools. He had also spent a number of years studying mathematics and took special interest in astronomy which is rare amongst the great poets of the Persian language. In such disciplines as grammar, genealogy and history, in particular that of ancient Persia, he attained the competence suited for a master of his stature.

In the years when Niẓāmī lived and composed his everlasting poems, the Peripatetic philosophy in the Eastern lands of Islam was on the decline while the philosophical theology of Juwaynī and Ghazzālī was flourishing. One of the most outstanding members of this school, Imam Fakhr al-Dīn Rāzī, was a contemporary of Niẓāmī. On the contrary in the Western part of the Islamic world Peripatetic philosophy was very much alive and such figures as Ibn Ṭufayl and Ibn Rushd were adding a new branch to the rich tree of philosophical tradition in Islam, a branch from which the West benefitted and which became a source of inspiration for many of the intellectual figures of that land.

In Persia itself at the time the most important philosophical activity was the establishment of a new philosophical and theosophical school by the "Master of Illumination", Shihāb al-Dīn Suhrawardī. These two figures were contemporary and a work such as *Makhzan al-asrār* of Niẓāmī was perhaps written at the same time as the Persian mystical narratives of Suhrawardī while Niẓāmī's later works were written simultaneously with *Ḥikmat al-ishrāq* "The Theosophy of the Orient of Light" and some of the later works of Suhrawardī. These two giants, however, did not know each other but what is significant is that while Ḥakim Niẓāmī was portraying the Persian-Islamic world view through his poetical genius, another *ḥakīm,* Suhrawardī, was charting a new course toward Ultimate Reality using philosophical discourse and intellectual intuition. The presence of these two great thinkers is an indication of the richness of the intellectual milieu of the 6th/12th century and provides a response to those who claim that the tradition of intellectual activity ceased following the attacks of Ghazzālī against the Peripatetics.

Despite Niẓāmī's thorough familiarity with almost all aspects of the Islamic sciences from the transmited to the intellectual such as theology, philosophy, cosmology and astronomy not to mention gnosis and the history of philosophy and religion, we cannot consider him to have been a follower of a particular philosophical or theological school, such as being a *mashshā'ī* or Ash'arite. Perhaps it can be said that he followed the *ḥikmah* based on faith, the type of wisdom which is deeply ingrained in the Quran, while remaining fully aware of the philosophy and theology of the *mashshā'īs*, Ash'arites and Mu'tazilites.

On such topics as God's Essence, Attributes and Qualities, and the origin of man Niẓāmī speaks as an accomplished master who has traveled far on the spiritual path and has been able to witness the incorporeal world with his inner eye. To describe the pure and transcendental Essence of God and His manifestations in all aspects and levels of existence, in his poetry he uses a language similar to that of the texts written by the great masters of gnosis. In the introduction to his *Makhzan al-asrār* "The Treasure of Secrets"[9] which is his most important philosophical and gnostic work, he states:

Existent before all creation, more eternal than all eternities,
Ancient Lord of the eternal universe, Decorator of the neck of the Pen with a necklace.
Revealer of the secrets of the mysterious heaven,
Secret Goals of those who know the divine mysteries.
Source of every spring of liberty, Author of all existence.[10]

God is not only the creator of the world in the theological and literary understanding of this term, but also the originator of existence and source of all theophanies as the gnostics have asserted. In this world as well as in all other realms of existence, whatever has benefitted from the emanation of existence is none other than the theophany of His Names and Qualities.

If it is the head of the spinning wheel, it is filled with His ring,
If it is the heart of matter, it is filled with ecstasy for Him.

What can be found amongst the exalted and imaginative poetical metaphors of Niẓāmī concerning metaphysical or theological discussions are none other than the perennial truths of which Muslim gnostics and *ḥakīms* have spoke. In fact before Niẓāmī some of those who possessed *ma'rifah* (gnosis) such as Aḥmad and Muḥammad Ghazzālī and 'Ayn al-Quḍāt Hamadānī had elaborated extensively on the same themes.

Having praised Almighty God and commenting on the Origin and Its manifestations, Niẓāmī in most of his works, in particular *Makhzan al-asrār,* offers an extensive discussion of the inward and outward states of the Prophet of Islam. Niẓāmī identifies the inner reality of the Prophet as the most sublime example of creation which Ibn 'Arabī later identifies as the "perfect man". Niẓāmī demonstrates his vast knowledge of Quranic exegesis and *Ḥadīth* in dealing with the characteristics of the Prophet.

There are few Persian poets who have commented on the spiritual character of the Prophet of Islam from a gnostic *('irfānī)* point of view as much as Niẓāmī. In the *Makhzan al-asrār* alone, he gives a description of the Prophet's nocturnal ascent *(mi'rāj)* in four sections, each of which depicts a profound portrayal of the Prophet's status and is amongst the masterpieces of Persian literature. In some of his other works such as *Sharaf-nāmah* ("Treatise on Virtue"),[11] *Iqbāl-nāmah* ("Treatise on Fortune"),[12] *Khūsraw wa Shīrīn,*[13] and *Laylī wa Majnūn,*[14] Niẓāmī composed majestic poems of great beauty in which he described the ascent of the Prophet to heaven. Perhaps it is not a coincidence that the most exquisite miniature depicting the Prophet's ascent belongs to the *Khamsah* of Niẓāmī now preserved in the British Museum.

The nocturnal ascent was not only the profoundest experience in the life of the Prophet, but it is also the supreme archetype of the spiritual journey for those in Islam who walk upon the path towards Ultimate Reality. The spiritual anthropology of Islam also depends on this event since the depth and breadth of human existence comes to light through the state which the Prophet experienced through his Nocturnal Ascent.

Following his gnostic interpretation of the reality of the *mi'rāj,* Niẓāmī speaks of human nature from a gnostic point of view, using

Quranic concepts. In a beautiful set of poems he calls man the vice-gerent of God but his superiority over other creatures especially animals who are closer to him in the existential hierarchy than others is not because of his intelligence but as a result of his ability to master his own ego. In the *Makhzan al-asrār* he alludes to this point and states:

Once thy ego is obedient to thee,
The coin of purity shall be cast in thy name.
To disobey the ego, is a sign of mastery,
To abandon the ego, is a power of prophecy.

Niẓāmī's emphasis on the necessity of attaining virtue and beautifying the inner self has presented an image of Niẓāmī as an ethical thinker and social reformer. Those who have not paid attention to his gnostic views have always noted the significance of his ethical teachings and have considered his moral character to have been the reason for calling him *ḥakīm*.

Niẓāmī had not only mastered the intellectual aspects of gnosis, but also followed the spiritual practices of the gnostic path. It is for this reason that he remains within the mainstream of the Islamic tradition of *ḥikmah,* a tradition that regards the highest form of philosophy to be the fruit of the purification of one's ego and in fact considers this to be the necessary condition for the true learning of philosophy and gnosis *(ma'rifah).*

The gnostic view of the world, which sees the corporeal world as temporal and yet the theophany of the incorporeal world, is apparent throughout the works of Niẓāmī. He sees the signs of Divine Power and Wisdom everywhere and criticizes those who deny the Divine Presence. In some of his poems, Niẓāmī even prays to God to dismantle the order of the universe and reveal His power throughout existence. He states:

Cast aside the design and bring forth the outward,
The rotation of the wheel, in motion and motionlessness.
Obliterate this sign from the body of the crescent,
Open this veil from a bundle of imaginings.
To confess to Thy divinity is,
To confess to one's own non-existence.

Niẓāmī does more than merely propagate a gnostic view of the universe. He praises Sufism and the truth that lies at the heart of it. In a poem which also inspired Ḥāfiz he states:

This order is based upon farsightedness,
Mastership is slavehood to the dervishes.

In his poems, Niẓāmī makes frequent references to ascetic practices and contemplation by those on the path. In a chapter entitled "The Virtues of Spiritual Retreat" in the *Makhzan al-asrār,* Niẓāmī portrays a profound picture of his inner visions and expresses them in a beautiful poem.

I have no knowledge of that fruit of which I partook on that night.
How could I have known that the new moon, whose gridle is light, would keep away from her lovers?
She was in love with her own lover; her desire was a hundred times greater than mine
The heart in its desire says: "What harm could have come to our day, had it not burnt the veil of our night
"And had it made the night safe, that it might have endured to the day of resurrection?"
I search everywhere for the light of that night
which was like the sun, and do not find it even in my dreams.[15]

It is this introspection and inner journey that finally allows the truth to shine forth within the heart of the seeker. Niẓāmī insists that those who have journeyed on the path will witness the Divine Reality and he then criticizes those who reject the vision of God.

Witnessing Him is without accident and substance,
For He is beyond accident and substance.
Since it is suitable for the absolute,
God has been seen and is "visible".
Seeing Him should not be hidden from the eye,
Blind is he who claims that He cannot be seen.

It is this inner vision of the incorporeal world which reveals the unstable and temporal nature of the corporeal world and brings to light its essence which, contrary to common belief, is not an independent reality but is a mirror reflecting the realities of the archetypal world.

Stand up and rend asunder the heavens,
There is no loyalty in this game of backgammon.
Do not seek the image of the Beloved by the gate of union with it,
Do not seek the virtue of fairness from its Attribute.

Niẓāmī's poems are commentaries upon various facets of Sufi and gnostic doctrines in Islam. He should be regarded in a sense as a Sūfi poet whose inner detachment from the world enabled him to portray the corporeal manifestations of the archetypes. From a philosophical point of view what is noteworthy in his works is his command and masterly use of philosophical terminology. In his poems he has repeatedly discussed the logical structure of the Peripatetics. His acute knowledge of the Peripatetic philosophy is noticeable through his exposition of such concepts as substance and accidents, and necessity and contingency in their precise definitions drawn from Peripatetic philosophers.

Niẓāmī also paid special attention to Pythagorean philosophy and its symbolic significance. In his poems he refers often to the symbolic significance of numbers. For example concerning the annihilation of the world he says:

Five hundred and fifty is sufficient to be asleep,
The day is long, hurry to the gathering.

He attaches great importance to the numbers seven and twelve which are of special symbolic significance. Through these numbers, which are keys to the understanding of the inner harmony of various levels of existence, he seeks to discover and in fact discovers the inner relations between different creatures. He compares the seven parts of the body to seven caliphs and the seven tales of Isfandiyār and his seven ordeals which have a cosmological significance.

Seven Caliphs are at one house,
Seven tales are contained in one story.

Such attention to the symbolism of the number seven reaches its climax in the tale *Haft paykar* ("Seven Bodies").[16] It is in this symbolic story that Niẓāmī alludes to the number seven as the key to understanding the cosmos and reveals the relationship between the seven heavens, seven colors and seven climes in a a lyrical and dramatic manner. This is similar to the Ikhwān al-Ṣafā' who, while they paid attention to the Peripatetic view of natural philosophy, were faithful commentators of Pythagorean philosophy. While Niẓāmī had penetrated into the world of philosophy and theology in the tradition of Ibn Sīnā and other *mashshā'īs,* he was particularly interested in the Pythagorean philosophy and applied numbers in their symbolic and esoteric meaning and the very structure of some of his poems.

In addition to various philosophical traditions, Niẓāmī had mastered different branches of the sciences in particular astronomy, astrology, natural history and anatomy. It can be said that without his familiarity with the fundamentals of these sciences, understanding of his poetry in its entirety is not possible. Niẓāmī's use of traditional astronomy in describing the tempraments in the *Makhzan al-asrār* or his references to the principles of astronomy throughout his *Khamsah* ("Quintet") are rather unique among the poets of the Persian language.

Although Niẓāmī had mastered the intellectual sciences, every fiber of his being was yearning towards the abode of love. He had a profound understanding of love from its human and external stages to Divine Love. While his works reveal facets of human love and the heroines in his poems possess in particular an astonishing this worldly reality, he does not see love only in its limited sense. Love for him is love in humility and eventually annihilation in Divine Love. Majnūn does not only seek union with a beautiful woman and his inner yearning is not limited to human feelings. Nor is Laylī only a corporeal being whose beauty vanishes gradually. Majnūn seeks eternal beauty and Laylī is that beauty which symbolizes the Divine Mysteries. She is the light which illuminates the night, the light whose corporeal manifestation is Laylī. In his love stories such as *Khūsraw wa Shīrīn* and *Laylī wa Majnūn*, one sees some of the profoundest masterpieces of Persian literature regarding the philosophy of love. Niẓāmī has created a bridge between the world of the spirit and beautiful forms of the world below, the world which is itself a ladder to the other world.

In addition to his mastery of gnosis, philosophy and the other sciences, Niẓāmī was well acquainted with the history of philosophy. He had benefitted from the rich heritage of such Muslim scholars as Abū Sūlaymān Sijistānī, Abu'l- Ḥasan 'Āmirī, Ibn Hindū and Ibn Fatak who had compiled the history and sayings of the ancient philosophers. His familiarity with the history of philosophy is apparent in a number of his works such as the *Iskandar-nāmah* ("Treatise Dedicated to Alexander").[17] His description of the sages of ancient Greece and India is an indication of the extent of his mastery of the history of ideas. For example, in his *Iskandar-nāmah*, in describing creation he says in the name of Hermes:

I wonder of this dome, the glory of the sea,
It is in suspense like smoke on top of a mountain.
Above this fearsome smoke,
There is a luminous light, pure and clear.
Before light, this dark cloud is a veil,
Openings have become far from openings.
Wherever the smoky cloud was pierced,
A beam of light burst through.
The heavens from the moon to the sun,
Are but rays of light that shine through the veil.
The coming to be of creation, I know truly,
How the world was created in the beginning, I know not.

At the same time as Niẓāmī, the Master of Illumination, Suhrawardī also regarded the stars not as luminous bodies in the sky, but as the glowing of the luminous world through the openings which exist in the sky. Suhrawardī also attributes this view to the illuminationists of ancient Persia and Hermes and the Greek Hermeticist.[18] Niẓāmī's poetic description of Hermes's view is a repetition of Suhrawardī's view and indicates a common source. In the *Iskandar-nāmah,* in a section entitled "The End of Aristotle" coming at the time of his death he writes:

He cleansed the oil from the oil lantern,
And ordered an apple to be brought from the garden.
The player put the apple in his hand,
With one smell he gave up his ghost, the patient one.

According to this story which was well known to the ancients, Aristotle in the last hours of his life answered the questions of his students as he held an apple in his hand. His conversations are gathered in a treatise entitled *The Treatise of the Apple* ("Kitāb al-Tuffāhah"). The Persian translator of this Neoplatonic treatise which has been attributed to Aristotle is Bābā Afḍal Kāshānī who has referred to the same story. These two cases are clear indications of Niẓāmī's familiarity with the history of philosophy not only as a historian but also as a *ḥakīm* who was well aware of the philosophies of his predecessors and used their ideas for his own philosophical ends.

In this regard for example, the *Iskandar-nāmah,* if interpreted at its profoundest level, concerns the inner journey of man through different worlds and his becoming embellished by gaining perennial wisdom which is represented by various *ḥakīms* from different civilizations. Iskandar (Alexander), according to this interpetation, is the same as the heart-intellect of man and the center of knowledge which, once exposed to the teaching of the sages, attains perennial wisdom. Finally, he drinks from the fountain of life and becomes a prophet since whenever the intellect is able to free itself from the bondage of the world, it becomes illuminated and the means for union of man with the world of the Spirit. It then becomes like an inner prophet which confirms within the being of man the revelations brought by the prophets.

Niẓāmī's interest in the perennial wisdom (or *philosophia perennis)* which is a single truth but manifested in various forms in different historical periods, and within various historical traditions makes him study and respect other religions. He makes frequent references to other religions beside Islam which is an indication of his knowledge of the history of other religions and his respect for them. In some instances he addresses a Muslim, Zoroastrian and a Christian the same way and warns them of their deeds.

Once his vision benefitted from Divine Grace,
He came to know himself and thus to know God.
Oh thou who art neither a Muslim nor a Zoroastrian,
Thou art a water spring without a drop of cloud.

Niẓāmī was not a philosopher like Fārābī, Ibn Sīnā and Suhrawardī or an expositor of theoretical Sufism like Ibn 'Arabī and 'Abd al-Razzāq Kāshānī. However, he should be regarded as a philosopher and a gnostic who had mastered various fields of Islamic thought which he synthesized in a way that brings to mind the tradition of the *hakīms* who were to come after him such as Quṭb al-Dīn Shīrāzī and Bābā Afḍal Kāshānī, who, while being masters of various schools of knowledge, attempted to synthesize different traditions of philosophy, gnosis and theology.

Niẓāmī is not only one of the greatest poets of the Persian language, but is an interpretor of the spiritual world, learned in the Islamic sciences, a poet whose works are worthy of being studied from a philosophical and gnostic as well as a literary point of view. This great thinker was a unique artist who to a large extent provided the formal structure for that vast and limitless ocean which is the *Mathnawī* of Rūmī. Furthermore, Niẓāmī himself succeeded at the same time in reflecting in the mirror of Persian poetry the highest gnostic and philosophical truths and to make manifest the mysteries of the hidden world in the dress of the world of manifestation in the form of poems of great beauty.

NOTES

1. This article, written originally in Persian, was an introduction by the author to the Persian translation of Peter J. Chelkowski's, *Mirror of the Invisible World,* New York, Metropolitan Museum of Art, 1975, entitled, *Ā'īna-yi jahān-i ghayb,* Tehran, Bank-i Melli Iran Press. 2535 (1976).

2. S.H. Nasr translates *ḥikmah* as "theosophy". This should be understood from its etymological roots to mean "Divine Wisdom" and not the 19th century movement in England with a similar name.

3. Philosophy in this context is in reference to the rationalistic philosophy of the Peripatetics. Rationalism in its pure sense is considered to be inconsistent with *ḥikmah* which advocates a synthesis of reason *('aql)* and intellectual intuition *(dhawq).*

4. His full name is Abū Muḥammad Ilyās, the son of Yūsuf, known as Niẓāmī. He was born in Ganjah, a city in today's Republic of Azarbaijan in 539 A.H. and died in 614. For more information on his life see the Introduction to *Dāstān-i Khusraw wa Shīrīn,* ed. by A. Āyatī, Tehran, Amīrkabīr Press, 1974.

5. "Knowledge by Presence" *(al-'ilm al-ḥuḍūrī)* is an epistemological theory which was first formulated in a coherent philosophical manner by Suhrawardī in the 6th/12th century A. H. According to it, man knows himself directly and without mediation. The essential components of this theory are knowledge and asceticism. For more information on this see, Ha'iri, Mehdi, *Epistemology in Islamic Philosophy—Knowledge by Presence,* Albany, SUNY Press, 1991.

6. These texts which provide a complete source of Shi'ite *ḥadīth* are: al-Kulaynī, *Ḥadīth uṣūl al-kāfī;* Shaykh Qummī, *Man lā yaḥḍaruha'l faqīh;* and al-Ṭūsī, *al-Istibṣār* and *Tahdhīb al-aḥkām.*

7. This type of spiritual interpretation known as *ta'wīl,* means literally to take something back to its origin and is one that Niẓāmī uses extensively to offer an esoteric interpretation of Quranic verses.

8. For more information see, Nasr, *Science and Civilization in Islam,* Cambridge, Islamic Text Society, 1987.

9. *Makhzan al-asrār* is a mystical and gnostic text which also deals with moral issues. It contains over 3250 verses which have been dedicated to the king of Arzanjan, Malik Bahrām Shāh ibn Dāwūd. This work which contains 20 sections has influenced a number of poets some of whom are: Jāmī in his *Tuḥfat al-aḥrār,* Amīr Khuwsraw in his *Maṭla' al-anwār* and Khājū in his *Rawḍat al-anwār.*

10. This is a translation by Darab, G.H., *The Treasury of Mystries,* London, Arthur Probsthain 1945, p. 89.

11. *Sharaf-nāmah,* also known as *Muqbil-nāmah* is the first part of *Iskandar-nāmah* and contains 6800 verses. Niẓāmī completed this work in 597 A.H.

12. The *Iqbāl-nāmah* which has also been called *Khirad-nāmah* is the second part of his major and last work *Iskandar-nāmah.* The *Iqbāl-nāmah* which contains over 3800 verses was completed in 603 A.H. when Niẓāmī was 74 years old.

13. *Khusraw wa Shīrīn* is one of the most sublime examples of Persian poetry containing over 6500 verses. Written in 580 A.H., he dedicated this work to Sulṭān Tughrul ibn Arsalān, hoping to receive his patronage. This work is a depiction of both human and gnostic love which Niẓāmī illustrates in the form of human love.

14. *Laylī and Manjūn* was composed after *Khusraw wa Shīrīn* in 584 A.H. and contains 4700 verses. It took Niẓāmī only four months to complete the work. It was Shīrwān Shāh who asked Niẓāmī to write this work on the basis of its original Arabic version and he reluctantly accepted. The reason for this reluctance was that since the original story had taken place in Arabia, Niẓāmī found the physical surrounding in which the story had taken place not to be too poetic for him. However, Niẓāmī created the necessary ambience by Persianizing the story. For more information see 'Abd al-Muḥammad Āyatī's introduction to *Dāstan-i Khusraw wa Shīrīn,* p. 15-16.

15. Dārāb's translation in *The Treasury of Mystics,* p. 145.

16. This work has also been called *Bahrām-nāmah* and *Haft-gunbad* which contains over 5000 verses of poetry and was dedicated to 'Alā' al-Dīn Kirap Arsālan, the governor of Maraghah. Niẓāmī using the traditional symbolism of the beloved, the number seven and astronomical symbolism, offers a symbolic allegorical presentation of the legendary love affairs of Bahrām Gūr, one of the Sassanid kings.

17. *Iskandar-nāmah* is the last work of Niẓāmī which has a distinct order in which every poem has a prefix. Some have argued that the book consists of three sections. In the first section, *Sharaf-nāmah,* Alexander is viewed as a conqueror; in the second section, *Khirad-nāmah,* he is a virtuous man; and in the third section *Iqbāl-nāmah,* Alexander is a prophet-like figure. In the beginning of the *Sharaf-nāmah* Niẓāmī tells us that he has been inspired in his dream to compose such a book.

18. For more information on this issue see S. H. Nasr, *Three Muslim Sages,* Delmar, N. Y., Caravan Book, 1975, p. 69.

17

Afḍal al-Dīn Kāshānī and the Philosophical World of Khwājah Naṣīr al-Dīn Ṭūsī *

If the supreme heaven exclaims
"The learned among the learned, the most learned of all,"
From each angel, in place of praise
There shall arise the chant "Afḍal, Afḍal".
(Naṣīr al-Dīn Ṭūsī)

THE PHILOSOPHICAL CIRCLE OF NAṢĪR AL-DĪN

Scholarly research of the past few decades has gradually revealed the great importance of the circle of Khwājah Naṣīr al-Dīn Ṭūsī in post-Mongol Persia for the revival of the Islamic sciences especially in the fields of mathematics and astronomy[1] although much remains to be discovered in this fecund but until recently neglected period in the history of the Islamic sciences. Strangely enough, however, much less attention has been paid to the remarkable philosophical revival in the 7th/13th century in whose bosom various forms of scientific activity took place. The *Akhlāq-i nāṣirī* of Naṣīr al-Dīn himself is well-known in the West[2] as are some of his Ismā'īlī tratises[3] and a few articles and essays have been devoted to his various philosophical views[4], while his theological and religious importance has at least been recognized.[5] But even this colossal figure of Islamic thought and one of the greatest of Islamic philosophers has hardly been studied thoroughly as far as his numerous works of an intellectual character, which range from logic to pure metaphysics, are concerned. This neglect is to be seen even more in the case of other important intellectual figures who were his contemporaries such as his

* This essay originally appeared in *Islamic Theology and Philosophy: Studies in Honor of George F. Hourani,* ed. by Michael E. Marmura, State University of New York Press, 1984, pp. 249-264.

associate, Quṭb al-Dīn Shīrāzī, himself one of the foremost among Muslim philosopher-scientists, who has received little attention among Western scholars as far as his monumental philosophical works like the *Durrat al-tāj* are concerned.

The 7th/13th century was, however, a very significant one from the point of view of the later intellectual history of Islam, especially in Persia and the adjacent areas, for it marked the revival of Ibn Sīnā's philosophy, the elaboration of Suhrawardī's *ishrāqī* doctrines and the establishment of the more systematic expressions of Sufi metaphysics, thereby laying the ground for what was to follow during the next three centuries leading finally to the grand syntheses of the Safavid period especially in the works of Ṣadr al-Dīn Shīrāzī.[6] The intellectual world in which Naṣīr al-Dīn breathed was witness to a number of important Islamic philosophers and metaphysicians some of whom were directly related to the circle of Naṣīr al-Dīn and others played a more indirect role in the creation of the intellectual world to which he belonged.

An important philosopher, who was the link between Naṣīr al-Dīn and Ibn Sīnā, is Farīd al-Dīn Dāmād, from Nayshapur. The student of Ṣadr al-Dīn Sarakhsī[7] and also Fakhr al-Dīn Rāzī, Farīd al-Dīn was at once philosopher and gnostic and highly revered by philosophers of this period in Khorasan. A contemporary of Farīd al-Dīn, named Kamāl al-Dīn ibn Yūnus al-Mawṣilī, was not only a peerless musician and mathematician but a philosopher with special interest in all the Abrahamic religions and great knowledge of the Bible to the extent that he is said to have taught the Torah to the Jews and the Gospels to the Christians. Another contemporary, Abu'l- Ma'ālī Ṣadr al-Dīn Qunyawī, was the great expositor of the teachings of Ibn 'Arabī, while another figure of the same period, Jamāl al-Dīn Baḥrānī, was known as an outstanding commentator of Ibn Sīnā, having written commentaries upon the *Risālat al-ṭayr, al-Qaṣīdat al-'ayniyyah* and *al-Ishārāt wa'l- tanbīhāt* of the master of Islamic Peripatetic philosophy. There were also other noteworthy figures of this epoch such as Shams al-Dīn Kīshī, the teacher of Qūṭb al-Dīn Shīrāzī, Shams al-Dīn Khusrawshāhī who taught Ibn Sīnā's works, especially the *'Uyūn al-ḥikmah*, Najm al-Dīn Dabīrān Kātibī, author of *Ḥikmat al-'ayn* and a popular treatise on logic entitled *al-Risālat al-shamsiyyah* and also teacher of Qūṭb al-Dīn Shīrāzī, Athīr al-Dīn Abharī, author of the popular *Kitāb al-hidāyah,* upon which Mullā Ṣadrā wrote his well-known commentary, and also author of a work entitled *Ishārāt* echoing the title of the work of Ibn Sīnā whom Abharī followed in his philosophical perspective.[8]

THE LIFE OF AFḌAL AL-DĪN KĀSHĀNĪ

In this constellation of notable intellectual figures, one of the most remarkable, and probably after Naṣīr al-Dīn and Quṭb al-Dīn the most significant of that period in Persia, was Afḍal al-Dīn Muḥammad Kāshānī known in Persia as Bābā Afḍal, who lived in the early part of the 7th/13th century and who died probably around the middle of that century. Little is known of his life despite his great fame as both a saint and a poet. Although some of the earlier sources had stated the date of his death as late as 707/1307-08, recent research has revealed that he probably died at least fifty or sixty years earlier, possibly as early as around 610/1213-14, since he was already known to Naṣīr al-Dīn when the latter composed his *Sharḥ al-ishārāt* in which Afḍal al-Dīn is quoted.[9] What is known with certainty about him is that he lived most of his life in Kashan, that he spent some time in prison accused of being a magician,[10] and that he was buried nearby in the town of Maraq where to this day his mausoleum is a center of pilgrimage. He is in fact considered as one of the great saints in the central region of Persia. In his mausoleum is to be found one other tomb which is purported to be that of the king of Zanzibar. In any case it is known that his fame had spread far even in his own lifetime and that he was held in the highest esteem by Naṣīr al-Dīn as the quatrain at the beginning of this essay bears out. The claim made in some of the early histories that he was an uncle of Naṣīr al-Dīn cannot, however, be substantiated.

Afḍal al-Dīn or Bābā Afḍal was at once poet, philosopher and Sufi saint. A practicing Sufi of the highest station, hence the title of Bābā which was given at this time to some of the outstanding masters of *taṣawwuf,* he lived a simple personal life while composing some of the most beautiful quatrains of the Persian language, writing many philosophical treatises, teaching disciples and receiving visitors from different walks of life in his native Kashan. His life was devoted to the practice of Sufism, to contemplation, meditation and invocation, but he was also a most creative philosopher in the traditional sense and an outstanding artist who combined the beauty of expression with subtlety of thought and who wrote works ranging from the intricacies of logic to the ecstasy of Divine Union.

WORKS

The writings of Bābā Afḍal, almost all of which are in Persian, stand out as among the greatest prose works of the Persian language and unparalleled in Persian philosophical prose. They are to the various branches of traditional philosophy what the *Gulistān* of Sa'dī is to ethics.[11] Their literary quality has caused many authorities of Persian literature to consider them as almost a "miracle" *(i'jāz)* in the way in which they are able to express the most difficult questions of traditional philosophy in the simplest and also most flowing Persian language whose beauty is matched in the annals of Persian philosophic prose only by the Persian treatises of Suhrawardī.[12]

The works of Bābā Afḍal which we have been able to locate or to which we have seen reference in dependable sources are as follows:[13]

1. *'Araḍ-nāmah* ("Treatise on Accidents") - (Persian)—Critical edition in Minovi and Mahdavi (ed.), *Muṣannafāt,*[14] vol. I, pp. 147-153. This is one of Afḍal al-Dīn's most extensive and comprehensive treatises dealing with cosmology, epistemology, logic and to a certain extent ontology with special emphasis upon types of knowers and modes, stations and degrees of knowledge. An appendix contains a summary treatment of astronomy and physics.
2. *Ash'ār* ("Poems") - (P)—As yet there is no complete edition of all the poems of Afḍal al-Dīn although most of the quatrains have been collected by Naficy in his *Rubā'iyyāt* (483 have been included). Seven *ghazals* have also been included by Naficy in his introduction (pp. 46-50). A number of *ghazals* and *rubā'īs* have also been included in M., vol. II, pp. 731-736.
3. *Āyāt al-ṣan'ah fi'l-kashf 'an maṭālib ilāhiyyah sab'ah* ("Portents of Divine Workmanship concerning the Unveiling of Seven Divine Propositions") - (A)—Published quite uncritically in *Jāmi' al-badā'i',* ed. Muḥyī al-Dīn al-Kurdī, Cairo, 1919, pp. 201-204. Contains a brief discussion of the Absolute for which Kāshānī uses the term *huwiyyah,* as well as a brief reference to the intellect, the soul and the body which he defines in an Illuminationist and Platonic rather than Aristotelian manner.
4. *Chahār 'inwān* ("Four Titles") - (P)—An opus comprised of selections of Ghazzalī's *Kīmiyā-yi sa'ādat* on Sufism, printed in a lithograph edition in Tehran in 1303 (A.H. lunar).
5. *Imanī az buṭlān-i nafs dar panāh-i khirad* ("Protection from the Vanity of the Carnal Soul through Refuge in Wisdom") (P)—Edited in M. Vol. II, pp 601-607. A discussion of the value of knowledge as determining the worth of the soul, the importance of seeking that knowledge which is the source of all knowledge, this principal knowledge being Self-knowledge. There is also a brief discussion of the independence of knowledge of both body and soul (understood

as the psyche) and finally the means whereby man can take refuge in true knowledge or wisdom.

6. *Jāwīdān-nāmah* ("Treatise on Eternity") - (P)—Edited in M., vol. I, pp. 259-323. Edited also by S. N. Taqawī, Tehran, 1312 (A.H. solar). One of the major works of Afḍal al-Dīn, which commences with a classification of the sciences on the basis of speech, action and thought, then proceeds to a long discussion of the "science of the self" wherein he deals with theology and theodicy as well as the reason for the existence of diversity of religious forms. The third chapter entitled "On the Origin" deals with why man seeks an origin for things, then space, time, the genesis of man, and the function of angels and demons in the cosmic economy. Chapter four deals with the end and treats questions of eschatology, the development of the soul while attached to the body and its posthumous becoming. In an appendix Afḍal al-Dīn deals with the traditional science of numbers *(al-jafr)* as the keys for the understanding of both the cosmic book and the Book of God, considering the fact than man can read and write as a proof of the attribute of speech and "writing" *(kitābah)* of the Sacred Scriptures which belongs to God.
7. *Mabādī-yi mawjūdāt-i nafsānī* ("On the Origin of Psychic Beings") *(P)*—Edited in M., vol. II, pp. 585-597; —also edited in *Jilwah,* vol. I, 1324 (A.H. solar), pp. 121-128. A summary treatment of the classification of beings, substance and accidents, and universals through which all particulars are known.
8. *Madārij al-kamāl* ("Degrees of Perfection") also known as *Gushāyish-nāmah* (The Treatise of Opening) - (A and P)—Written first in Arabic by Afḍal al-Dīn and then rendered into Persian by himself, only the Persian text has been printed so far in M., vol. I, pp. 3-49. This is a treatise concerned mostly with ethics which in seven chapters deals with perfection, its grades, what distinguishes various degrees of perfection, how one can achieve ethical and spiritual perfection and the central role that knowledge plays in the attainment of the highest degree of perfection.
9. *Makātīb* ("Letters") - (P)—Seven letters which are mostly answers to questions posed to him by friends and disciples mostly on metaphysical, ethical and religious matters edited in M., vol. II, pp. 681-728.
10. *Al-Minhāj al-mubīn* ("The Evident Way")—Also known as *Risālah dar 'ilm wa manṭiq* ("Treatise on Science and Logic") - (P with an

appendix in A)—Edited in M. vol. II, pp. 477-582. The most thorough work of Afḍal al-Dīn on logic dealing with both concepts and judgments and giving an extensive discussion of the various forms of syllogism. In its lucidity of expression this opus is unique among works on logic in the Persian language. Some scholars claim that *al-'Ilm wa'l-manṭiq* is by Ibn Sīnā and that *al-Minhāj al-mubīn* is not a direct Persian translation but closely based upon it.

11. *al-Mufīd li'l-mustafīd* ("A Work Profitable to those Anxious to Learn") Printed in Tehran in 1310 (A.H. solar) by S. N. Taqawī, this work is a synopsis of the teachings of Afḍal al-Dīn based again on the primacy of knowledge and written from a sapiential point of view. Some manuscripts have attributed it to Ghazzālī.
12. *Mukhtaṣarī dar ḥāl-i nafs* ("An Epitome on the Soul") - (P)—Edited in M., vol. II, pp. 461-66. This is a translation into Persian by Afḍal al-Dīn from an Arabic epitome of the *De Anima* of Aristotle, the translation being attributed by some to Ḥunayn ibn Isḥāq.[15] Actually the Arabic text, probably translated from Syriac, is based more on commentaries upon the *De Anima* than the text itself.
13. *Rah anjām-nāmah* ("Treatise on the Path to the Final Goal") -(P)—Edited in M., vol. I, pp. 55-80; also edited by S. M. Mishkāt in *Silsila-yi intishārāt-i Dānishkada-yi Ma'qūl wa Manqūl,* vol. 5, 1315 (A.H. solar), pp. 26-57. In three chapters the author deals with ontology and epistemology beginning with the discussion of self-knowledge which leads to the knowledge of Being and the hierarchy of existence and concluding with the final and formal cause of the soul which is again none other than knowledge.
14. *Risāla-yi 'ilm-i wājib* ("Treatise on the Knowledge of the Necessary Being") - (P)—An as yet unpublished treatise dealing with God's knowledge of all things based on the principles of self-awareness and the awareness by the cause of the effect. The manuscript of this work has been mentioned by Danechepazhuh *(op. cit.,* p. 436).
15. *Risāla-yi nafs-i Arisṭū* ("The Treatise De Anima of Aristotle") - (P)—Edited in M., vol. II, pp. 389-458; also edited by Malik al-Shu'arā' Bahār, Tehran (1316 and 1333) and Isfahan (1333 A.H. solar). The translation from the Arabic of three chapters of Aristotle's *De Anima* with a brief summary of the views of Aristotle concerning the nature of the soul.[16]
16. *Risāla-yi tuffāḥah* or *Sīb-nāmah* ("Book of the Apple") - (P)—Edited in M. vol. I, pp. 113-144; also published in Tehran in 1311 (A.H.

solar) by H. Iṣfahānī (Mubaṣṣir al-salṭanah) as *Tuffāḥiyyah* and by D.S. Margaliouth with an English translation.[17] Translation from Arabic of what came to be known in the Latin West as *Liber de pomo* which Muslims believed to have been dictated by Aristotle on his death-bed while he was holding an apple in his hand. The work is of Neoplatonic and possibly Hermetic inspiration. [18]

17. *Sāz wa pirāya-yi shāhān-i purmāyah* ("Accoutrements and Ornaments of Worthy Kings") - (P)—Edited in M., vol. I, pp. 83-110; also published in Tehran in 1311 (A.H. solar) by H. Iṣfahānī. This is the most important work in political philosophy and the study of society by Afḍal al-Dīn in which he speaks of the relation between political power, religion and virtue on the basis of the aristocratic principle as understood in the traditional sense of being related to inner virtue rather than any external conditions and determinations. Afḍal al-Dīn relates the hierarchy existing in human society to knowledge and considers as viable and praiseworthy that social system which reflects the hierarchy of knowledge among its members. In this unique work he speaks of the meaning of *adab* and *farhang* or culture in its traditional sense—in their relation to the *Sharī'ah* and *siyāsah* and the importance for the king to possess *adab* and *farhang* and inculcate them in society.
18. *Sharḥ fuṣūṣ al-ḥikam* ("Commentary upon the Bezels of Wisdom") - (P) —S. Naficy in the introduction to his edition of the *Rubā'iyyāt* (pp. 78-9) reports from his teacher that the latter had seen a commentary by Afḍal al-Dīn upon Ibn 'Arabī's celebrated *Fuṣūṣ al-ḥikam* but the manuscript has not been found by later scholars and the work has never seen the light of day. Certain scholars such as Danechepazhah *(op. cit.,* p. 499) believe that this work may have been mistaken for the well-known commentary of 'Abd al-Razzāq Kāshānī.
19. *Sharḥ Ḥayy ibn Yaqẓān* ("Commentary upon the Living Son of the Awake") - (P)—In this introduction to the *Risāla-yi tuffāḥah* (p. 6), Ḥ. Iṣfahānī states that after residing for seven years in Kashan in search of works by Afḍal al-Dīn, he found a manuscript in which was contained Afḍal al-Dīn's Persian commentary upon Ibn Sīnā's well-known visionary recital, *Ḥayy ibn Yaqẓān*. Copies of this manuscript exist but it has never been printed.
20. *Taqrīrāt wa fuṣūl-i muqṭa'ah* ("Discourses and Short Chapters") - (P) —Edited in M. vol. II, pp. 611-672. Some thirty six short pieces

covering a vast array of subjects ranging from metaphysics and episteomology to music, ethics and eschatology and including also a few supplications and prayers which are among the most beautiful in the Persian language.

21. *Yanbūʻ al-ḥayāt* ("The Spring of Life") known also as *Zajr al-nafs* ("The Reprimand of the Soul") - (P)—Edited in M. vol. I, pp. 331-385. This translation from the Arabic text known as the *Naṣā'iḥ* of Hermes[19] consists of thirteen chapters in the form of supplications following the style of the *Munājāt* of Khwājah 'Abdallāh Anṣārī of Herat. As is the case of other Muslim philosophers, Afḍal al-Dīn considers Hirmis to be Idrīs al-nabī or the Prophet Idrīs and believes the text which he has rendered into a Persian of inspirational quality to be of prophetic origin.

SOURCES OF AFḌAL AL-DĪN AND HIS INTELLECTUAL PERSPECTIVE

To speak of the sources of Afḍal al-Dīn's doctrines, one must mention first of all that "vertical" source of his inspiration, the Self of whose realization he speaks at every turn. Being the great saint that he was, his world view was obviously not based on historical sources alone. Even his use of earlier sources was conditional and molded by his vision of Reality which determined his intellectual perspective from on high. But to the extent that one finds elements of various schools that preceded him in his writings, one can speak of historical sources which played a role as "horizontal" causes in the formation of his doctrines.

Afḍal al-Dīn was first and foremost a devout Muslim and in fact a Muslim saint and drew move than anything else from the Quran and *Ḥadīth*, from the Islamic tradition by virtue of which and in whose bosom he was able to gain access to the direct vision of the empyrean of Divine Wisdom. He was also well versed in the works of the Sufis who preceded him especially the early masters of *al-ma'rifah* and also Ghazzālī, and in his poetry followed upon the foundations of earlier Persian Sufi poetry. Afḍal al-Dīn was also fully versed in the various schools of Islamic philosophy as they had developed before him especially in Persia. He knew the formal logic of Fārābī and Ibn Sīnā and was especially familiar with the latter's teachings not only in logic but in all branches of philosophy. It is unfortunate that Afḍal al-Dīn's commentary upon the *Ḥayy ibn Yaqẓān* has not been printed and studied, for his teachings reflect some relation with Ibn Sīnā's "Oriental Philosophy" *(al-ḥikmat al-*

mashriqiyyah), a relationship which this commentary would naturally clarify more than any of Afḍal al-Dīn's existing works.

The attraction of Bābā Afḍal to the study of the soul is reflected in the translations made into Persian of Greek philosophical texts. All four are concerned with the soul, two by Aristotle being directly related to the study of the soul and its faculties while the *Liber de pomo* and *De Castigatione animae* are also concerned with the nature and entelechy of the soul. It is characteristic of Afḍal al-Dīn that he cuts across the classical schools of philosophy to include texts of not only Aristotelian and Neoplatonic but also Hermetic origin. In this concern he follows to some extent certain earlier Ismā'īlī philosophers and also Suhrawardī whom he resembles in more than one way but whose characteristic teachings he does not echo except perhaps in his definition of space and bodies.

Afḍal al-Dīn's teachings mark in fact the beginning of an important transformation which takes place in Islamic philosophy from the 7th/13th century onward. Beginning with the consolidation of various Islamic schools of thought and until that time, the different intellectual perspectives such as Peripatetic philosophy, Ismā'īlī philosophy, different schools of *Kalām,* Sufism, and in the 6th/12th century the *ishrāqī* school were cultivated and developed distinctly even if there were interactions as between Peripatetic philosophy and *Kalām.*[20] Even figures such as Fārābī and Naṣīr al-Dīn Ṭūsī, who were masters of different schools of thought wrote works on each school without bringing in the perspective of other schools in which they were also masters. In his *Sharḥ al-ishārāt,* Naṣīr al-Dīn is an Ibn Sīnan *mashshā'ī* philosopher, except in the one case of the question of God's knowledge of the world where he mentions Suhrawardī's teachings. Likewise, in the *Taṣawwurāt,* Naṣīr al-Dīn speaks as an Ismā'īlī philosopher and his *Tajrīd* is the foundation for Twelve-Imām Shi'ite *Kalām.* To this day, in traditional circles where Islamic philosophy is taught, the student is taught to master first each school of thought separately and not to confuse or cause arguments from different schools to interpenetrate *(khalṭ al-mabḥath).* It is in fact only after mastering each perspective separately that the later schools in which a synthesis is made are studied.

Afḍal al-Dīn stands at the beginning of this process of the gradual synthesis of the different sapiential and philosophical schools in Islam which was to culminate with the monumental work of Ṣadr al-Dīn Shīrāzī in the 11th/17th century. Afḍal al-Dīn was at once a Sufi, a poet, a theologian and philosospher. He dealt at the same time with logic, cosmology, epistemology, metaphysics and gnosis. He sought to present the diverse elements of the traditional sciences but unified by the light of gnosis or that knowledge which ultimately unites the knower with the known and which issues ultimately from the very substance of intelligence.[21] In his world there is a complete wedding between all branches of knowledge and the sacred upon the basis of the positive appreciation of the intellect as that ray which issues from the Divine Self and which finally enables man to know not only himself but the Self of every self. In his works the various branches of traditional knowledge become so many means of access to the Supreme Science which for him is Autology.[22]

CHARACTERISTICS OF AFḌAL AL-DĪN'S TEACHINGS

To give a full account of the gnostic and philosophical teachings of Bābā Afḍal would require a book length work, for when one studies all of his works, one realizes that although he did not write as much as Kindī, Fārābī or Ibn Sīnā, he is a major intellectual figure whose metaphysical penetration, power of synthesis and gift for expression rank him among the foremost of Islamic metaphysicians and philosophers. Just in logic to which little attention has been paid, he is worthy of special consideration on two accounts: Firstly, for being able to mold a whole vocabulary of logical terms in Persian which are of much significance from a linguistic and philosophical point of view and which are more in conformity with the genius of the Persian language than the terminology devised by Ibn Sīnā in his *Dānish-nāmah* from which to be sure, Afḍal al-Dīn must have benefitted. Secondly, there are certain new features in Afḍal al-Dīn's logic of which the most famous is his view concerning *qiyās-i khulf* or the syllogism *per impossibile*. This view being quoted by Naṣīr al-Dīn in his *Sharḥ al-ishārāt,* then by Quṭb al-Dīn in his *Sharḥ ḥikmat al-ishrāq* and finally by Mullā Ṣadrā in his *Ḥashiyah ("Glosses")* upon Quṭb al-Dīn's commentary.[23]

Like most Islamic philosophers, Afḍal al-Dīn was also interested in the classification of the sciences which, however, he based on a foundation that differs from the well-known classifications of Fārābī and Ibn Sīnā while incorporating both the intellectual *('aqlī)* and transmitted *(naqlī)* sciences.[24] Afḍal al-Dīn begins with the basic Quranic distinction between *al-dunyā* and *al-ākhirah*, or this world and the hereafter, and makes this at once ontological and eschatological distinction the basis for his classification of the branches of knowledge.[25]

According to Afḍal al-Dīn, there are three types of knowledge *('ilm):* that of this world *(dunyā)*, that of the other world *(ākhirah)* and the world of thought *(andīshah)* which is intermediate between the two. These three branches of knowledge are in turn divided as follows:

- Knowledge of this World
  - knowledge of words
    - general level embracing common use of language
    - level of the elite
      - music
      - logic
      - grammar
  - knowledge of actions
    - science dealing with the crafts
    - science of scribes, the occult sciences and alchemy
    - science of private and public life of man *(Sharī'at)* ethics

---

- Knowledge of the World of Thought
  - logical definition and demonstration
  - arithmetic
  - geometry and astronomy
  - natural philosophy and medicine
- Knowledge of the other world
  - the Science of Unity *(tawḥīd)*
  - the Science of the End of Things

Afḍal al-Dīn bases the sciences dealing with this world upon the two primary functions of the human being, namely the production of words and actions issuing from various parts of his body which connect him to this world. The world of thought is the intermediary between this world and the next and the means with the aid of which man is able to reach the spiritual world. Afḍal al-Dīn emphasizes especially the importance of logic in this intermediate domain. Finally, the knowledge of the other world, which he calls also the science of "the horizons and the souls" *(āfāq* and *anfus)* using the well-known Quranic terminology,[26] can be gained in this world but has its effect upon the soul in such a way that the effect remains beyond the barrier of death.

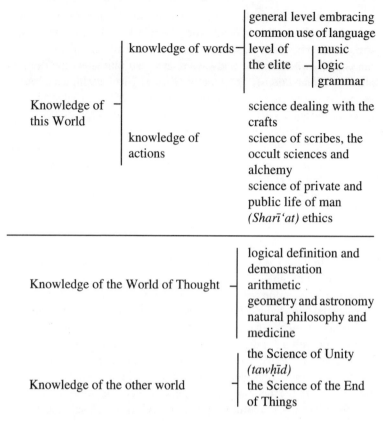

In metaphysics although Afḍal al-Dīn does deal briefly with ontology, using the famous distinction of Ibn Sīnā between the Necessary, contingent and impossible being, and giving a division of existants according to the principle of the great chain of being,[27] Afḍal al-Dīn's metaphysics is based most of all upon principial knowledge which relates to the Supreme Self as the source of all that is and all that knows. For him ontology *(wujūd-shināsī)* is always related and ultimately the same as autology *(khud-shināsī)*. For Afḍal al-Dīn the light of intelligence *(khirad or 'aql)* is ultimately a reflection of Divine Light. All knowledge partakes of the sacred quality of this Light because knowledge *is* light and therefore like light partakes of levels of gradations.[28] The categories of logic are themselves reflections of the Divine Intellect upon the human mind and enable man to gain certitude on their own level precisely because they are related to the supra-human Intellect.

It is within this completely sapiential perspective in which principial knowledge predominates over everything, that Afḍal al-Dīn develops the doctrine of the unity of the intellect and the intelligible *(ittiḥād al-'āqil wa'l-ma'qūl),* a doctrine which became famous in the teachings of Mullā Ṣadrā.[29] In the act of knowing, the intellect and the intelligible become unified and through this union the very being of the person who performs the act of intellection *(al-'āqil)* is affected. Man's being is transformed by essential knowledge. Hence to know God is to be transformed into His Image upon which man was originally made. It is to become oneself while to know oneself is for the same reason the key to ultimate knowledge, in both cases knowledge being of course of a realized order and requiring all the moral conditions and spiritual virtues which alone would enable man to realize his theomorphic nature, or to become himself.[30]

In one of his beautiful supplications Afḍal al-Dīn summarizes his intellectual and spiritual perspective in these words:

> "O God, Thy grandeur is an obstacle to knowledge of Thee. Whoever gains access to Thy Presence through the ray of Thy Light, that is the intellect, and becomes free from the darkness of fantasy, imagination, sense, body and nature through that Light, with every breath his desire for the love of Thy Presence increases. Unless he loses the light of his existence in the Sun of the Universal Spring and becomes completely drowned in It so that all duality disappears, he will not know the Truth."[31]

Afḍal al-Dīn's emphasis upon knowledge causes him to turn over and over again to the science of the soul, to that pneumatology which many call psychology but which in any case should not be confused with modern disciplines using the same name. Afḍal al-Dīn does deal with faculties of the soul in the Peripatetic sense but this type of concern is always combined with his interest in pointing to the necessity of the soul to perfect itself to the stage whereby it can experience the stations of annihilation *(fanā')* and subsistence *(baqā')* and gain that supreme knowledge which is at once that of the Transcendent Principle and Immanent Self.[32]

There is also some discussion of cosmology in Afḍal al-Dīn's writings. He is an avid defender of the archetypal world in favor of the Platonic school and in opposition to the Peripatetics. He in fact distinguishes between three worlds: the world of Lordship *(rubūbiyyah)*, the intermediate world which he calls *malakūt* and the world of nature, all of whose forms are reflections of the realities contained in the higher realms of universal existence.[33] He also considers the hierarchy of existence in relation to time rather than "space" and distinguishes between *zamān, dahr, wujūd* and *huwiyyat,* the latter term meaning the supra-ontological principle of all reality.[34] Moreover, he shows interest in the question of motion which was the heart of Peripatetic physics and discusses the various types of motion including violent motion, that Achilles heel of Peripatetic physics. In this question he follows the teachings of Ibn Sīnā and Abu'l-Barakāt Baghdādī.[35]

Afḍal al-Dīn was also interested in the religious and social life of man which he again treated from the perspective of the primacy of knowledge. In the *Jāwīdān-nāmah* he discusses the various kinds of difference between religions and schools within a single religion on the basis of whether the differences are in the knowledge of the principle of Unity, on the founder of the religion, on points of interpretation of various schools concerning as to who is the *imām,* and finally on the views of various groups within a single school.[36] Moreover, he relates the finality of Islam in the prophetic cycle to the perfection of knowledge which, once having attained complete universality and totality with Islam, no longer requires the descent of a new revelation.

The study of human society is also based by Afḍal al-Dīn on the ultimate goal of human existence which is the attainment of knowledge. All social and political institutions are therefore judged according to their role in preparing man for this end and their success is dependent on the degree to which they are able to aid man in gaining both knowledge and the virtues which make the attainment and realization of knowledge possible. Moreover, the hierarchy within human society and among human beings is based upon the knowledge and virtue which they possess rather than on any external social or economic factors.[37]

POETRY

Afḍal al-Dīn is without doubt the greatest poet among the outstanding philosophers of Islam. In the Persian world, known for a gallaxy of poets of outstanding brilliance, Afḍal al-Dīn stands out on his own. His quatrains especially have become part and parcel of classical Persian literature and many authorities consider him as the greatest master of the *rubāʿī* form in Persian after Abū Saʿīd and Khayyām. But whereas Khayyām's perpsective is based on the relativization of all existence in the light of the Absolute, a perspective which has been misunderstood as skepticism in the modern world, Bābā Afḍal's poetry speaks always from the perspective of the certitude which issues from unitive knowledge.

For example, there is mentioned in the *Ātishkada-yi ādhar* a quatrain of Bābā Afḍal, written supposedly as answer to a quatrain by Naṣīr al-Dīn. Although historically this exchange seems unlikely, the poem demonstrates clearly the spirit of the delicate and metaphysically penetrating poetry of Bābā Afḍal.[38] According to this source, Naṣīr al-Dīn sent the following quatrain to Bābā Afḍal :

A cup whose parts have been molded together,
Even a drunkard would not consider it right to break.
These lovely hands, feet and wrists
Why were they created and why destroyed?

To this quatrain Bābā Afḍal gives the response:

When the pearl of the soul became united with the body of the shell
Through the water of life it gained human form.
When the pearl became formed, it broke the shell
And came to embellish the corner of the headware of the king.

For Afḍal al-Dīn there is a wisdom in every act of creation even if this be hidden to the undiscerning eye. If God causes the human body to die, it is because like the sea shell which serves its function to nurture the pearl after which it is opened and cast away, the body dies after having served its function to enable the soul to perfect itself through this short journey of terrestrial life which man is destined to undergo in order to reach the Abode of Permanence.

AFḌAL AL-DĪN IN THE ISLAMIC PHILOSOPHICAL TRADITION AND SUFISM

In many ways this remarkable sage from Kashan occupies a unique position in the Islamic intellectual tradition in that among the Islamic philosophers he is without doubt the most universally recognized Sufi saint revered by the learned and the populace alike while among the Sufis he is the person most devoted to philosophy. In this last respect Suhrawardī, who lived shortly before him, can be compared to him as can in a sense ʻAyn al-Quḍāt Hamadānī, although the latter was strictly speaking more of an *ʻārif* than *ḥakīm*. But neither figure possessed at once and to the same degree both the dimensions of philosophical prominence and sanctity in the classical Sufi sense as did Afḍal al-Dīn. This sage was a *wali* and in fact Sufi master who at the same time wrote remarkable treatises on metaphysics, logic and epistemology in an incredible literary style. His metaphysical expositions are in fact more flowing and continuous than those of an Ibn ʻArabī who can be characterized by discontinous flashes of inspiration.

During fourteen centuries of Islamic history, Sufism which issues from the very essence of the Islamic revelation has manifested itself in several different climates. Sometimes it has become wed to the world uniquely dominated by the Quran and *Ḥadīth* as in the early centuries. Sometimes it has intermingled with the world of poetry and expressed itself mostly in the language of love. And yet at other times it has worn the dress of Ashʻarite *Kalām* and harmonized itself with this form of theology where this school has become dominant. Occasionally also it has wed itself to traditional Islamic philosophy or *falsafah* and made of the categories of philosophy so many stages for the realization of *sophia*. Thanks to the esoteric teachings of Islam, this type of Sufism was able to bestow upon philosophy its original meaning once again before it had become reduced to rationalism.

Afḍal al-Dīn Kāshānī stands as a major representative of this last type of Sufism. His spiritual message is purely sapiential and completely rooted in Quranic spirituality and Muḥammadan poverty. At the same time he is a most important figure in the development of later Islamic philosophy. For this reason, he is especially significant today in an Islamic world where a type of fideist interpretation of Islam has made confrontation with the intellectual and philosophical challenges of the modern world to result in catastrophes which threaten the Islamic tradition itself. Afḍal al-Dīn represents to an eminent degree a marriage between intelligence and piety, between submission to the Divine Will and knowledge ranging from the logical to the unitive. It is such a wedding within a unified vision that is so clearly needed for the Islamic world and it is the study of such a harmonious perspective within the Islamic tradition that can aid Western students of Islam most in gaining a better understanding of this tradition in its inward and integrating aspect. For these reasons as well as the innate value of Afḍal al-Dīn's writings as a lucid and eloquent expression of wisdom in its Islamic form, one hopes that more attention will be paid to this until now more or less neglected figure of both Sufism and Islamic philosophy.

NOTES

1. The discoveries concerning this period are based mostly on the pioneering work of E. S. Kennedy. For his summary of the scientific achievements of Naṣīr al-Dīn and his school see his, "The Exact Sciences in Iran under the Saljuqs and Mongols," in J. A. Boyle (ed.), *The Cambridge History of Iran,* vol. 5, Cambridge, 1968, pp. 659ff. Since the publication of this article research on the astronomical school at Maraghah and the achievement of Naṣīr al-Dīn and scientists associated with him have been further expanded by Kennedy himself as well as J. Saliba, W. Hartner and others.
2. Thanks mostly to the translations of G. Wickens as *The Nasirean Ethics,* London, 1964.
3. See especially his *Rawḍat al-taslīm* or *Taṣawwurāt,* trans. W. Ivanow, Bombay, 1950; and *Maṭlūb al-mu'minīn,* ed. with notes by W. Ivanow, Bombay, 1933.
4. See W. Chittick, "Mysticism vs. Philosophy in Earlier Islamic History: the al-Ṭūsī, al-Qūnawī Correspondence," *Religious Studies,* vol. XVII, 1981, pp. 87-104: M. Horten, *Die philosophischan Ansichten von Rāzī und Ṭūsī (1209 und 1273),* Bonn, 1910; and *idem., Die spekulative und positive Theologie des Islam. Nach Razi (1209 gestorben) und ihre Kritik durch Ṭūsī (1273 gestorben),* Leipzig, 1912.

   On Naṣīr al-Dīn in general see S. H. Nasr, "al-Ṭūsī," the next chapter in this book; and several studies by E. Wiedemann on Naṣīr al-Dīn in his *Anfsätze zur arabischen Wissenschaftsgeschichte,* New York, 1970: and B. H. Siddiqui, "Naṣīr al-Dīn Ṭūsī," in M.M. Sharif (ed.), *A History of Muslim Philosophy,* vol. I, Wiesbaden, 1963, pp. 564-580.
5. See R. Strothmann, *Die Zwölfer-Schi'a: zwei religions-geschichtliche Charakterbilder aus der Mongolenzeit,* Leipzig, 1926. Even in this work, however, very little attention has been paid to the *Kitāb al-tajrīd,* the basic text of Twelve- Imam Shi'ite *Kalām* which has never been satisfactorily translated or exhaustively studied in English.

   The already cited studies made by Horten on Ṭūsī concern partly his theological views but they are devoted most of all to his philosophical criticism of Ash'arite theology.
6. See S. H. Nasr, *Islamic Life and Thought,* Albany (N. Y.), 1981, chapter 14; Nasr, *Ṣadr al-Dīn Shīrāzī and his Transcendent Theosophy,* Boulder (Colorado), 1978, chapter 4; and H. Corbin, *En Islam iranien,* vol. IV, Paris, 1971, pp. 54-122.
7. Ṣadr al-Dīn himself was the student of Afḍal al-Dīn Jīlānī who was a student of Abu'l-'Abbās Lūkarī, the celebrated disciple of Bahmanyār who in turn was one of Ibn Sīnā's foremost disciples. This chain is emphasized in traditional circles of Islamic philosophy because the oral transmission from master to student plays such a central role in the continuity of the tradition of Islamic philosophy.
8. On these and other figures who were contemporaries of Naṣīr al-Dīn see M. T. Mudarris Raḍawī, *Aḥwal wa āthār-i ustād-i bashar wa 'aql-i hādī-'ashar Muḥammad al-Ṭūsī mulaqqab bi Khwājah Naṣīr al-Dīn,* Tehran, 1334 (A. H. solar); also M. Madarris Zanjānī, *Sarguzasht wa 'aqā'id-i falsafī-yi Khwājah Naṣīr al-Dīn Ṭūsī,* Tehran, 1335 (A. H. solar), especially pp. 1-90.
9. The most extensive biographical study of Bābā Afḍal is still to be found in the introduction of Sa'īd Naficy to his edition of the *Rubā'iyyāt* of Afḍal al-Dīn Kāshānī, Tehran, 1311 (A.H. solar), pp. 1-33. On Bābā Afḍal see also the introduction of M. Minovi and Y. Mahdavi to their critical edition of his works, the *Muṣannafāt,* vol. I,

Tehran, 1331 (A.H. solar), vol. II, Tehran, 1337 (A.H. solar); S. Naficy, "Afḍal al-Dīn Kāshānī," *Wafā*, vol. 2, 1303 (A.H. solar), pp. 10-16 and 118-123; M. Muḥīṭ Tabāṭabā'ī, "Bābā Afḍal Zindānī," *Muḥīṭ*, vol. I, no. 1, 1321 (A.H. solar), pp. 433-436 and 499-502; Muḥammad al-Khuḍayrī, "Afḍal al-Dīn al-Kāshānī, faylsūfun maghmūrun," *Da'wat al-taqrīb min khilāl Risālāt al-islām,* ed. M. al-Madanī, Cairo, 1966, pp. 183-190; A. 'A. Ḥalabī, *Tārīkh-i falāsafa-yi īrānī,* Tehran, 1351 (A.H. solar), pp. 611-623.

As for Western sources, there is practically no literature available on him save for references in the standard histories of Persian literature such as those of H. Ethé, E. H. Whinfield, E. G. Browne and J. Rypka. See for example Rypka, *Iranische Literaturgeschichte,* Leipzig, 1959, p. 219.

10. Afḍal al-Dīn was apparently imprisoned by a local governor of his home city who disliked the sage and who sent him to prison on the pretext of being a magician *(sāḥir).* Some of the later hagiographers have mistaken this governor whose name was Ayāz with the Ayāz of Maḥmūd of Ghaznah's court and confused the two periods of history. A recently discovered *qaṣīdah* of Afḍal al-Dīn referring to his imprisonment makes it clear that he served the prison term in Kashan and that there was a stranger who served with him and who might have been a king of Zanzibar who was his disciple and who according to tradition is buried next to him. See P. Bayḍā'ī, "Ḥabsiyya-yi Ḥakīm Afḍal al-Dīn Kāshanī," *Yaghmā,* vol. IV, 1330 (A.H. solar), pp. 414-417. The text of the *qaṣīdah* in question is published in this essay for the first time.

11. On Persian philosophical works see S. H. Nasr, "The Significance of Persian Philosophical Works in the Tradition of Islamic Philosophy," in this volume.

12. Suhrawardī, *Oeuvres philosophiques et mystiques vol. II, Oeuvres en persan (Opera Metaphysica et Mystica III),* ed. S.H. Nasr, Tehran, 1977, the Persian introduction where we have dealt with the literary features and qualities of those remarkable treatises.

13. A less complete bibliography of Afḍal al-Dīn is given by Naficy in the introduction of his edition of the *Rubā'iyyāt,* pp, 54-79; see also M. T. Danechepazhah, "Niwishtahā-yi Bābā Afḍal," *Mihr,* vol. VIII, no. 7, 1331 (A.H. solar), pp. 433-436; no.8, pp. 499-502.

14. In this bibliography henceforth P shall denote Persian, A Arabic and M the *Muṣannafāt.* All works which appear in M. have been edited critically. These are the only prose works of Afḍal al-Dīn that have had a critical edition.

15. The Arabic text from which Afḍal al-Dīn had made his translation has been published by A. Fu'ād al-Ahwānī as an appendix to his edition of *Talkhīs kitāb al-nafs li Abi'l-Walīd ibn Rushd,* Cairo, 1950.

16. In the introduction to his edition of Afḍal al-Dīn's rendition of this work, M. Bahār, Iran's foremost twentieth century poet, has spoken extensively of the literary qualities of this and other Persian writings of Bābā Afḍal.

The *De Anima* was translated into Arabic by Isḥāq ibn Ḥunayn and edited by A. Badawī, *Islamica,* vol. 16, Cairo, 1954, pp. 1-88.

17. See D. S. Margoliouth, "The Book of the Apple, ascribed to Aristotle," *Journal of the Royal Asiatic Society,* April, 1892, pp. 187-252.

18. On this work, which was well-known by the intermediary of a Hebrew translation in the Latin West as *Liber de pomo et morte incliti principis philosophorum Aristotelis,* see J. Kraemer, "Das arabische Originales 'Liber de pomo'," in *Studi Orientali in onore di G. Levi della Vida,* Rome, vol. 1, 1956, pp. 484ff. This study contains the text of the Arabic original from which Afḍal al-Dīn made his translation.

19. This is based on an Arabic text which has been published among others by P. Philémon, Beirut, 1903; and A. Badawī in his *al-Aflāṭūniyyāt al-muḥdathah 'ind al-'arab,* Cairo, 1955, pp. 51-116.

    See also L. Massignon, "Inventaire de la littérature hermétique arabe," in A.D. Nock and A. J. Festugiére *La Révélation d'Hermès Trismégiste*, 4 vols., Paris, 1949-1954, Appendix III.

20. See Nasr, *Islamic Life and Thought,* chapter 6; and Nasr, *Three Muslim Sages,* Albany (N. Y.), 1975, pp. 79-82.

21. We have dealt with this theme extensively in our *Knowledge and the Sacred,* New York, 1981, especially chapter 4.

22. The term "autology" is used here in the sense given to it by A. K. Coomaraswamy in his *Hinduism and Buddhism,* New York, 1943, pp. 10ff.

23. See Ṭūsī, *Sharḥ al-ishārāt,* Tehran, 1305 (A. H. lunar), p. 86; Quṭb al-Dīn, *Sharḥ ḥikmat al-ishrāq,* Tehran, 1315 (A.H.), p. 117; and Mullā Ṣadrā, *ibid.* The reference of Mullā Ṣadrā to Afḍal al-Dīn which is more or less a repetition of Naṣīr al-Dīn's is as follows:

    Mullā Ṣadrā adds that only a philosopher with great mastery of logic could make such a subtle discovery.

24. On the signification of the classification of the sciences in Islam see Nasr, *Science and Civilization in Islam,* Cambridge (U.S.A.), 1968, chapter two.

25. See his *Jāwīdān-nāmah* in M., vol. I, pp. 260-262, where he gives an account of his classification of the sciences again on the basis of the primacy of knowledge.

26. On the meaning of these terms in the Islamic cosmological and philosophical tradition see Nasr, *An Introduction to Islamic Cosmological Doctrines,* p. 6.

27. See especially his *Rah anjām-nāmah,* M. vol. I, pp. 56ff.

28. This aspect of Afḍal al-Dīn's teachings along with his whole psychology is close to the perspective of Suhrawardī without being *ishrāqī* in the specific sense of the term in its association with the school founded by Suhrawardī.

29. Mullā Ṣadrā even wrote a treatise by this name. See Nasr, *Ṣadr al-Dīn Shīrāzī and His Transcendent Theosophy,* p. 42.

30. See F. Schuon, *Understanding Islam,* trans. D.M. Matheson, London, 1976, chapter 1; and his *From the Divine to the Human,* trans. G. Polit and D. Lambert, Bloomington (Ind.), 1982.

31. M. vol. II, p. 652.

32. See for example his *Madārij al-kamāl* which deals extensively with the exposition of the science of the soul. On the importance of self-knowledge see M., vol. I, p.. 150.

33. See M., vol. I, pp. 151-152.

34. *Ibid.,* p. 166.

35. *Ibid.,* pp. 166-168.

36. *Ibid.,* pp. 262-263.

37. The *Sāz wa pīrāya-yi shāhān* which contains most of Afḍal al-Dīn's social and political teachings is an important document of classical Islamic political thought but it has never been studied seriously in any Western sources.

38. Quoted in Naficy, *op. cit.,* p. 21.

18

Muḥammad ibn Muḥammad Naṣīr al-Dīn Ṭūsī *

LIFE

Naṣīr al-Dīn, known to his compatriots as Muḥaqqiq-i Ṭūsī, Khwāja-yi Ṭūsī, or Khwājah Naṣīr, (1201-1274) is one of the best-known and most influential figures in Islamic intellectual history. He studied the religious sciences and elements of the "intellectual sciences" with his father, a jurisprudent of the Twelve Imam school of Shi'ism at Ṭūsī He also very likely studied logic, natural philosophy, and metaphysics with his maternal uncle in the same city. During this period he also received instruction in algebra and geometry. Afterward he set out for Naishapur, then still a major center of learning, to complete his formal advanced education; and it was in this city that he gained a reputation as an outstanding scholar. His most famous teachers were Farīd al-Dīn al-Dāmād, who through four intermediaries was linked to Ibn Sīnā and his school and with whom Ṭūsī studied philosophy; Quṭb al-Dīn al-Miṣrī, who was himself the best known student of Fakhr al-Dīn al-Rāzī (1148-1209), with whom Ṭūsī studied medicine, concentrating mostly on the text of Ibn Sīnā's *Canon;* and Kamāl al-Dīn ibn Yūnus (1156-1242), with whom he studied mostly mathematics.

This period was one of the most tumultuous in Islamic history: Mongols were advancing toward Khurasan from Central Asia. Therefore, although already a famous scholar, Ṭūsī could not find a suitable position and the tranquillity necessary for a scholarly life. The only islands of peace at this time in Khurasan were the Ismaīlī forts and mountain strongholds, and he was invited to avail himself of their security by the Ismā'īlī ruler, Naṣīr al-Dīn Muḥtashim. Ṭūsī accepted the invitation and went to Quhistan, where he was received with great honor and was held

* This essay originally appeared in the *Dictionary of Scientific Bibliography,* Vol. XIII (ed.) by C. Gillespie., New York : Charles Scribner's Sons, 1976, pp. 508-514.

in high esteem at the Ismāʻīlī court, although most likely he was not free to leave had he wanted to. The date of his entrance into the service of the Ismāʻīlī rulers is not known exactly but was certainly sometime before 1232, for it was during that year that he wrote his famous *Akhlāq-i nāṣirī* for the Ismāʻīlī ruler. During his stay at the various Ismāʻīlī strongholds, including Alamut, Ṭūsī wrote a number of his important ethical, logical, philosophical, and mathematical works, including *Asās al-iqtibās* (on logic) and *Risāla-yi muʻīniyyah* (on astronomy). His fame as a scholar reached as far as China.

Hulāgū ended the rule of the Ismāʻīlī in northern Persia in 1256. His interest in astrology, and therefore his respect for astronomers, combined with Ṭūsī's fame in this field, made Hulāgū especially respectful toward him after he had captured Alamut and "freed" Ṭūsī from the fort. Henceforth Ṭūsī remained in the service of Hulāgū as his scientific adviser and was given charge of religious endowments *(awqāf)* and religious affairs. He accompanied Hulāgū on the expedition that led to the conquest of Baghdad in 1258 and later visited the Shiʻite centers of Iraq, such as Hillah.

Having gained the full confidence of Hulāgū, and benefiting from his interest in astrology, Ṭūsī was able to gain his approval to construct a major observatory at Maraghah. Construction began in 1259, and the Īlkhānī astronomical tables were completed in 1272 under Abāqā, after the death of Hulāgū. In 1274, while at Baghdad, al-Ṭūsī fell ill and died a month later. He was buried near the mausoleum of the seventh Shiʻite Imam, Mūsā al-Kāẓim, a few miles from Baghdad.

WORKS

Nearly 150 treatises and letters by Naṣīr al-Dīn al-Ṭūsī are known, of which twenty-five are in Persian and the rest in Arabic. There is even a treatise on geomancy that Ṭūsī wrote in Arabic, Persian, and Turkish, demonstrating his mastery of all three languages. It is said that he also knew Greek. His writings concern nearly every branch of the Islamic sciences, from astronomy to philosophy and from the occult sciences to theology. Of the two, Ibn Sīnā was the better physician and Ṭūsī the greater mathematician and more competent writer in Persian. But otherwise their breadth of knowledge and influence can be compared very favorably. Moreover, the writings of Tūsī are distinguished by the fact that so many became authoritative works in the Islamic world.

Ṭūsī composed five works in logic, of which *Asās al-iqtibās* ("Foundations of Inference"), written in Persian, is the most important. In fact, it is one of the most extensive of its kind ever written, surpassed only by the section on logic of Ibn Sīnā's *al-Shifā'*. In mathematics Ṭūsī composed a series of recensions *(taḥrīr)* upon the works of Autolycus, Aristarchus, Euclid, Apollonius, Archimedes, Hypsicles, Theodosius, Menelaus, and Ptolemy. The texts studied by students of mathematics between Euclid's *Elements* and Ptolemy's *Almagest* were known as the "intermediate works" (*mutawassiṭāt*); and the collection of Ṭūsī's works concerning this "intermediate" body of texts became standard in the teaching of mathematics, along with his recensions of Euclid and Ptolemy. He also wrote many original treatises on arithmetic, geometry, and trigonometry, of which the most important are *Jawāmi' al-ḥisāb bi'l-takht wa'l-turāb* ("The Comprehensive Work on Computation with Board and Dust"), *al-Risālat al-shāfi'iyyah* ("The Satisfying Treatise"), and *Kashf al-qinā fī asrār shakl al-qitā'* known as the *Book of the Principle of Transversal,* which was translated into Latin and influenced Regiomontanus. The best-known of Ṭūsī's numerous astronomical works is *Zīj-īlkhānī* ("The Īlkhānī Tables"), written in Persian and later translated into Arabic and also partially into Latin, by John Greaves, as *Astronomia quaedam ex traditione Shah Cholgii Persae una cum hypothesibus planetarum* (London, 1650). Other major astronomical works are *Tadhkirah* ("Treasury of Astronomy") and his treatises on particular astronomical subjects, such as that on the astrolabe. He also translated the *Ṣuwar al-kawākib* ("Figures of the Fixed Stars") of 'Abd al-Raḥmān al-Ṣūfī from Arabic into Persian. In the other sciences al-Ṭūsī produced many works, of which *Tanksūkh-nāmah* ("The Book of Precious Materials") is particularly noteworthy. He also wrote on astrology.

In philosophy, ethics, and theology Tūsī composed a commentary on *al-Ishārāt wa'l-tanbīhāt* ("The Book of Directives and Remarks") of Ibn Sīnā; the *Akhlāq-i nāṣirī (Naṣīrean Ethics),* the best-known ethical work in the Persian language, and the *Tajrīd* ("Catharsis"), the main source book of Shi'ite theology, upon which over 400 commentaries and glosses have been composed. Ṭūsī wrote outstanding expositions of Ismaili doctrine, chief among them the *Taṣawwurāt* ("Notions"), and composed mystical treatises, such as *Awṣāf al-ashrāf* ("Qualifications of the Noble").

Ṭūsī also composed lucid and delicate poetry, mostly in Persian.

SCIENTIFIC ACHIEVEMENTS

In logic Ṭūsī followed the teachings of Ibn Sīnā but took a new step in studying the relation between logic and mathematics. He also elucidated the conditional conjunctive *(iqtirānī)* syllogism better than his predecessor. He converted logical terms into mathematical signs and clarified the mathematical signs employed by Abu'l-Barakāt in his *Kitāb al-mu'tabar* ("The Esteemed Book"). Ṭūsī also distinguished between the meaning of "substance" in the philosophical sense and its use as a scientific term, and clarified the relation of the categories with respect to metaphysics and logic.

In mathematics al-Ṭūsī's contributions were mainly in arithmetic, geometry, and trigonometry. He continued the work of Khayyām in extending the meaning of number to include irrationals. In his *Shakl al-qitā'* he showed the commutative property of multiplicatiton between pairs of ratios (which are real numbers) and stated that every ratio is a number, *Jawāmi' al-ḥisāb,* which marks an important stage in the development of the Indian numerals, contains a reference to Pascal's triangle and the earliest extant method of extracting fourth and higher roots of numbers. In collaboration with his colleagues at Maraghah, Ṭūsī also began to develop computational mathematics, which was pursued later by al-Kāshī and other mathematicians of the Timurid period.

In geometry Ṭūsī also followed the work of Khayyām and in his *al-Risālah al-shāfi'iyyah* he examined Euclid's fifth postulate. His attempt to prove it through Euclidean geometry was unsuccessful. He demonstrated that in the quadrilateral *ABCD,* which *AB* and *DC* are equal and both perpendicular to *BC,* and the angles *A* and *D* are equal, if angles *A* and *D* are acute, the sum of the angles of a triangle will be less than 180°.[1] This is characteristic of the geometry of Lobachevski and shows that al-Ṭūsī, like Khayyām, had demonstrated some of the properties of the then unknown non-Euclidean geometry. The quadrilateral associated with Saccheri was employed centuries before him by Thābit ibn Qurrah, al-Ṭūsī, and Khayyām.

Probably Ṭūsī's most outstanding contribution to mathematics was in trigonometry. In *Shakl al-qitā',* which follows the earlier work of Abu'l-Wafā', Manṣūr ibn 'Irāq, and Bīrūnī, Ṭūsī for the first time, as far as modern research has been able to show, developed trigonometry without using Menelaus' theorem or astronomy. This work is really the first in history on trigonometry as an independent branch of pure mathematics and the first in which all six cases for a right-angled spherical triangle are set forth. If *c* =the hypotenuse of a spherical triangle, then:

$$\cos c = \cos a \cos b \qquad \cot A = \tan b \cot c$$
$$\cos c = \cot A \cot B \qquad \sin b = \sin c \sin B$$
$$\cos A = \cos a \sin B \qquad \sin b = \tan a \cot A.$$

He also presents the theorem of sines:

$$\frac{a}{\text{Sin } A} = \frac{b}{\text{Sin } B} = \frac{c}{\text{Sin } C}$$

It is described clearly for the first time in this book, a landmark in the history of mathematics.

Ṭūsī is best-known as an astronomer. With Hulāgū's support he gained the the necessary financial assistance and supervised the construction of the first observatory in the modern sense. Its financial support, based upon endowment funds; its life span, which exceeded that of its founder; its use as a center of instruction in science and philosophy; and the collaboration of many scientists in its activities mark this observatory as a major scientific institution in the history of science. The observatory was staffed by Quṭb al-Dīn al-Shīrāzī, Muḥyī al-Dīn al-Maghribī, Fakhr al-Dīn al-Marāghī, Mu'ayyad al-Dīn al-'Urḍī, 'Ali ibn 'Umar al-Qazwīnī, Najm al-Dīn Dabīrān al-Kātibī al-Qazwīnī, Athīr al-Dīn al-Abharī, Ṭūsī's sons Aṣīl al-Dīn and Ṣadr al-Dīn, the Chinese scholar Fao Mun-ji, and the librarian Kamāl al-Dīn al-Aykī. It had excellent instruments made by Mu'ayyad al-Dīn al-'Urḍī in 1261-1262, including a giant mural quadrant, an armillary sphere with five rings and an alidade, a solstitial armill, an azimuth ring with two quadrants, and a paralactic ruler. It was also equipped with a fine library with books on all the sciences. Twelve years of observation and calculation led to the completion of the *Zīj-i īlkhānī* in 1271, to which Muḥyī 'al-Dīn al-Maghribī later wrote a supplement. The work of the observatory was not confined to astronomy, however; it played a major role in the revival of all the sciences and philosophy.

Ṭūsī's contributions to astronomy, besides the *Zīj* and the recension of the *Almagest,* consist of a criticism of Ptolemaic astronomy in his *Tadhkirah,* which is perhaps the most thorough exposition of the short-comings of Ptolemaic astronomy in medieval times, and the proposal of a new theory of planetary motion. The only new mathematical model to appear in medieval astronomy, this theory influenced not only Quṭb al-Dīn Shīrāzī and Ibn al-Shāṭir but also most likely Copernicus, who followed closely the planetary models of Naṣīr al-Dīn's students. In chapter 13 of the second treatise of the *Tadhkirah,* Ṭūsī proves that "if one circle rolls inside the periphery of a stationary circle, the radius of the first being half the second, then any point on the first describes a straight line, a diameter of the second."[2] E. S. Kennedy, who first discovered this late medieval planetary theory issuing from Maraghah, interprets it as "a linkage of two equal length vectors, the second rotating with constant velocity twice that of the first and in a direction opposite the first."[3] He has called this the "Ṭūsī-couple" and has demonstrated (see Figures 1 and 2) its application by Ṭūsī, Quṭb al-Dīn, and Ibn al-Shāṭir to planetary motion and its comparison with the Ptolemaic model.[4]

This innovation, which originated with Ṭūsī, is without doubt the most important departure from Ptolemaic astronomy before modern times. Except for the heliocentric thesis, the "novelty" of Copernicus' astronomy is already found in the works of Ṭūsī and his followers, which probably reached Copernicus through Byzantine intermediaries.

The most important mineralogical work by Ṭūsī is *Tanksūkh-nāmah,* written in Persian and based on many of the earlier Muslim sources, such as the works of Jābir ibn Ḥayyān, al-Kindī, Muḥammad ibn Zakariyyā' al-Rāzī, 'Uṭārid ibn Muḥammad, and especially Bīrūnī, whose *Kitāb al-jamāhir fī ma'rifat al-jawāhir* ("The Book of Multitudes Concerning the Knowledge of Precious Stones") is the main source of Ṭūsī's work. In fact the *Tanksūkh-nāmah,* which derives its name from the Turco-Mongolian word meaning "something precious," probably is second in importance in the annals of Muslim mineralogy only to Bīrūnī's masterpiece.

Ṭūsī's work comprises four chapters. In the first he discusses the nature of compounds; the four elements, their mixture, and the coming into being of a 'fifth quality" called temperament *(mizāj),* which can accept the forms of different species; and the role of vapors and the rays of the sun in their formation, in all of this following closely the theories of Ibn Sīnā's *De Mineralibus.* An interesting section is devoted to colors, which Ṭūsī believes result from the mixture of white and black. In jewels, colors are due to the mixture of earthy and watery elements contained in the substance of the jewel.

The second chapter is devoted exclusively to jewels, their qualities, and their properties. Special attention is paid to rubies, the medical and occult properties of which are discussed extensively. In the third chapter Ṭūsī turns to metals and gives an alchemical theory of metallic formation, calling sulfur the father and mercury the mother of metals. He also enumerates the seven traditional metals, including *khārṣīnī.* Like so many Muslim philosopher-scientists, al-Ṭūsī accepts the cosmological and mineralogical theories of alchemy concerning the formation of metals without belonging to the alchemical tradition or even discussing the transmutation of base metal into gold. A section on perfumes ends the book, which is one of the major sources of Muslim mineralogy and is valuable as a source of Persian scientific vocabulary in this field.

Of all the major fields of science, Ṭūsī was least interested in medicine, which he nevertheless studied, generally following the teachings of Ibn Sīnā. He also composed a few works on medicine including *Qawānīn al-ṭibb* ("Principles of Medicine") and a commentary on Ibn Sīnā's *Canon,* and exchanged letters with various medical authorities on such subjects as breathing and temperament. He expressed certain differences of opinion with Ibn Sīnā concerning the temperament of each organ of the body but otherwise followed his teachings. Ṭūsī's view of medicine was mainly philosophical; and perhaps his greatest contribution was in psychosomatic medicine, which he discusses, among other places, in his ethical writings, especially *Akhlāq-i naṣīrī (Naṣīrean Ethics).*

Ṭūsī was one of the foremost philosophers of Islam, reviving the Peripatetic *(mashshā'ī)* teachings of Ibn Sīnā after they had been eclipsed

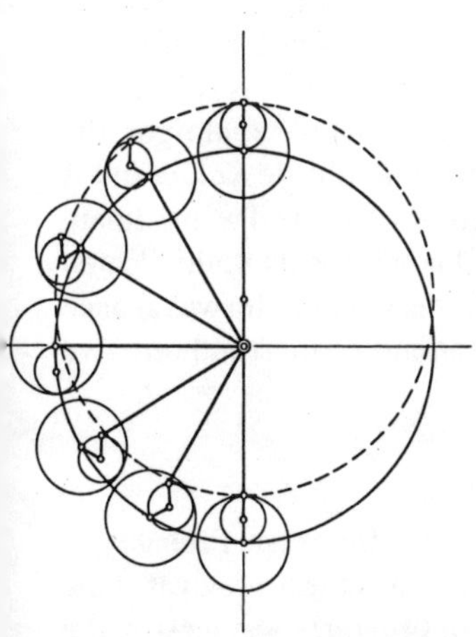

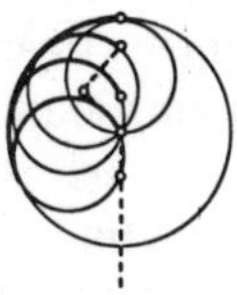

FIGURE I

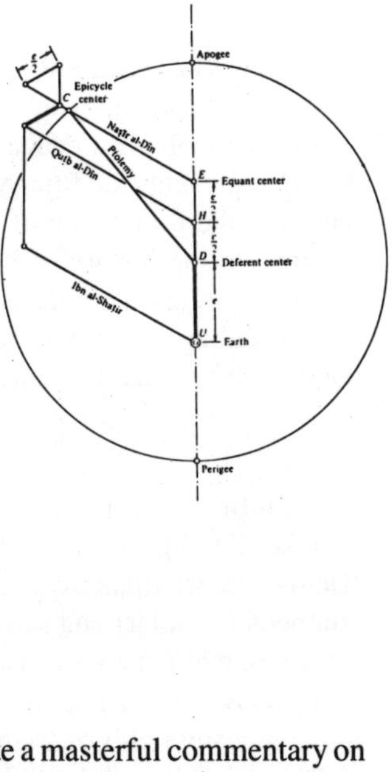

for nearly two centuries by *Kalām.* He wrote a masterful commentary on the *Ishārāt wa'l-tanbīhāt* of Ibn Sīnā, which Fakhr al-Dīn al-Rāzī had attacked severely during the previous century. In this work, which is unusual among Muslim philosophical works for its almost mathematical precision, al-Ṭūsī succeeded in rekindling the light of philosophy in Islam. But while claiming in this work to be a mere follower of Ibn Sīnā, in several places questions of God's knowledge of particulars, the nature of space, and the createdness of the physical world clearly shows his debt to Shihāb al-Dīn Suhrawardī and some of the Muslim theologians. Al-Ṭūsī in fact marks the first stage in the gradual synthesis of the Peripatetic and Illuminationist *(ishrāqī)* schools, a tendency that became clearer in the writings of his foremost student, Quṭb al-Dīn Shirāzī. He also wrote many philosophical treatises in Persian, so that his prose in this field must be considered, a long with the writings of Naṣīr-i Khusraw, Suhrawardī, and Afḍal Al-Dīn Kāshānī, as the most important in the Persian language.

In ethics Ṭūsī composed two major works, both in Persian: the *Akhlāq-i muḥtashimī* ("The Muḥtashimī Ethics") and the much better-known *Naṣīrean Ethics,* his most famous opus. Based upon the *Tahdhīb al-akhlāq* ("The Refinement of Character") of Muskūyah (Miskawayh), the *Naṣīrean Ethics* expounds a philosophical system combining Islamic teachings with the ethical theories of the Aristotelian and, to a certain extent, the Platonic traditions. The work also contains an elaborate discussion of psychology and psychic healing. For centuries it has been the most popular ethical work among the Muslims of India and Persia.

In Twelve Imam Shi'ism, Ṭūsī is considered as much a theologian as a scientist and philosopher because of his *Tajrīd,* which is still central to Shi'ite theological education. A work of great intellectual rigor, the *Tajrīd* represents the first systematic treatment of Shi'ite *Kalām* and is therefore the foundation of systematic theology for the Twelve Imam Shi'ites. In the history of Islam, which is known for its multitalented figures of genius, it is not possible to find another person who was at once an outstanding astronomer and mathematician and the most authoritative theologian of a major branch of Islam.

INFLUENCE

Tūsī's influence, especially in eastern Islam, was immense. Probably, if we take all fields into account, he was more responsible for revival of the Islamic sciences than any other individual. His bringing together so many competent scholars and scientists at Maraghah resulted not only in the revival of mathematics and astronomy but also in the renewal of Islamic philosophy and even theology. Ṭūsī's works were for centuries authoritative in many fields of Islamic learning; and his students, such as Quṭb al-Dīn and 'Allāmah Ḥillī, became outstanding scholars and scientists. His astronomical activities influenced the observatories at Samarkand and Istanbul and in the West to a much greater extent than was thought to be the case until recently; and his mathematical studies affected all later Islamic mathematics. In fact, the work of Ṭūsī and his colloborators at Maraghah moved eastward to influence Chinese science, which, as a result of the Mongol invasion, had a much closer relationship with Islam.

The school of Ṭūsī also influenced later Indian science as cultivated under the Moguls and even as late as the eighteenth century, as can be seen in the observatory constructed by Jai Singh II, which indirectly reflects the observatory of Maraghah.

In the West Ṭūsī is known almost entirely as an astronomer and mathematician whose significance, at least in these fields, is becoming increasingly evident. In the Muslim East he has always been considered as a foremost example of the "wise man" *(ḥakīm)*, one who, while possessing an acute analytical mind, which he devoted to mathematical, astronomical, and logical studies, extended the horizon of his thought to embrace philosophy and theology and even journeyed beyond the limited horizon of all mental activity to seek ultimate knowledge in the ecstasy provided by gnosis *('irfān)* and Sufism.

NOTES

1. E. S. Kennedy, "The Exact Sciences in Iran Under the Seljuqs and Mongols," in *Cambridge History of Iran,* V (Cambridge, 1968), 659-679.
2. E. S. Kennedy, "Late Medieval Planetary Theory," in *Isis,* 57, (1966), 365-378.
3. *Ibid.*
4. *Ibid.*, 369, 367.

BIBLIOGRAPHY

Ṭūsī's major published work is *The Naṣīrean Ethics,* translated by G. M. Wickens (London, 1964).

Secondary literature includes A. Carathéodory Pasha, *Traité de quadrilatère* (Constantinople, 1891); B. Carra de Vaux, "Les sphères célestes selon Naṣīr-Eddīn Attūsī," in P. Tannery, ed., *Recherches sur l'histoire de l'astronomie ancienne* (Paris, 1893), app. 4, 337-361; A. P. Youschkevitch, and B. A. Rosenfeld, *Die Mathematik der Lander des Ostens in Mittelalter* (Berlin, 1960), 277-288, 304-308; E. S. Kennedy, "Late Medieval Planetary Theory," in *Isis,* 57 (1966), 365-378; and "The Exact Sciences in Iran Under the Seljuqs and Mongols," in *Cambridge History of Iran,* V (Cambridge, 1968), 659-679; M. Mudarris Raḍawī, *Aḥwal wa āthār-i ustād al-bashar .... Khwājah Naṣīr al-Dīn* (Tehran, A.H. 1334, 1955 A.D.); S. H. Nasr, *Three Muslim Sages* (Cambridge, Mass., 1968; New York, 1970); G. Sarton, *Introduction to the History of Science,* II, pt. 2 (Baltimore, 1931), 1001-1013; A. Sayili, *The Observatory in Islam* (Ankara, 1960); B. H. Siddiqui, "Naṣīr al-Dīn Ṭūsī," in M. M. Sharif, ed., *A History of Muslim Philosophy,* I (Wiesbaden, 1963), 564-580; A. S. Saidan, "The Comprehensive Work on Computation With Board and Dust by Naṣīr al-Dīn al-Ṭūsī," in *al-Abḥāth,* 20, no. 2 (June 1967), 91-163, and no. 3 (Sept. 1967), 213-293, in Arabic; and *Yādnāma yi Khwājah Naṣīr al-Dīn Ṭūsī,* I (Tehran, A. H. 1336, 1957 A.D.), in Persian.

19

Quṭb al-Dīn Shīrāzī *

Quṭb al-Dīn Maḥmūd (1236-1311) was born into a well-known family of physicians and Sufis. His father, Ḍiā' al-Dīn Mas'ūd, was both a Sufi master attached to Shihāb al-Dīn Suhrawardī and a famous physician; and under his guidance Quṭb al-Dīn received his early training in both medicine and Sufism. At the time of his father's death Quṭb al-Dīn was but fourteen years old, yet he was entrusted with his father's duties as physician and ophthalmologist at the Muẓaffarī hospital in Shiraz, where he remained for ten years.

At the age of twenty-four his love of learning led Quṭb al-Dīn to leave his position at the hospital in order to devote himself fully to his studies, especially in medicine. He studied Ibn Sīnā's *Canon* with several of the best-known masters of his day, but he could not find a teacher who satisfied him completely. He therefore traveled from city to city, seeking masters who could instruct him in both the medicine and the philosophy of Ibn Sīnā, a figure who attracted him greatly. In his journeys Quṭb al-Dīn met many Sufi masters, whose gatherings he frequented. He traveled in Khorasan, Iraq, and Anatolia, meeting most of the medical authorities of the day. Also during these journeys he was initiated formally into Sufism at the age of thirty by Muḥyī al-Dīn Aḥmad ibn 'Alī, a disciple of Najm al-Dīn Kubrā.

Around 1262 Quṭb al-Dīn became associated with his most famous teacher, Naṣīr al-Dīn al-Ṭūsī, at Marāghah; his superior intelligence soon made him Ṭūsī's foremost student. With Ṭūsī he studied both astronomy and the philosophy of Ibn Sīnā, particularly *Al-Ishārat wa'l-tanbīhāt* ("Book of Directives and Remarks"). After a long period during which he was closely conncected with the circle of Naṣīr al-Dīn, Quṭb al-Dīn left

* This essay originally appeared in the *Dictionary of Scientific Biography*, Vol. XI, (ed.) by C. Gillespie, New York: Charles Scribner's Sons, 1976, pp. 247-53.

Maraghah for Khurasan to study with another well-known philosopher, Najm al-Dīn Dabīrān Kātibī al-Qazwīnī. His studies later took him to Qazvin and Baghdad, where he stayed at the Niẓāmiyyah school. From there he set out for Qonya and became a follower of the celebrated Sufi and disciple of Ibn 'Arabī, Ṣadr al-Dīn al-Qunyawī, with whom he studied the religious sciences such as Quranic commentary and *Ḥadīth*. After the death of Ṣadr al-Dīn, Quṭb al-Dīn left Qonya to become judge in Sivas and Malatya, starting the period during which some of his major works appeared.

When he later moved to Tabriz, Quṭb al-Dīn attracted the attention of the son of Hulāgū Khan, Aḥmad Takūdār, who was then ruling Persia. The latter sent him as ambassador to the court of the Mamluk ruler of Egypt, Sayf al-Dīn Qalā'ūn. This journey was of major scientific importance for him, for during this period he gained access to some of the important commentaries upon Ibn Sīnā's *Canon* which he had long sought and which were to serve him in the preparation of his major commentary upon this work. In 1283 he finally began to write this commentary, which occupied him for most of the rest of his life.

From Egypt, Quṭb al-Dīn returned to Tabriz, where he met the important scholarly figures of his day, such as the learned vizier and historian Rashīd al-Dīn Faḍlallāh. It was in this capital of the IlKhanids that he died, after nearly fourteen years spent mostly in seclusion and devoted to writing. His love of learning became proverbial in Persia; he was given the honorific title 'Allāmah, rare in medieval times, and the historian Abu'l-Fidā' gave him the title al-Mutafannin, "master in many sciences." He was also called "the scholar of the Persians." He was known as a master chess player and an excellent player of the lute, and he spent much of his time on these two pastimes.

Although Quṭb al-Dīn was among the foremost thinkers and scholars of Islam, only two of his works have been printed: the *Durrat al-tāj* and the *Sharḥ ḥikmat al-ishrāq,* the latter only in a lithographed edition. The rest of his writings remain in manuscript. The entire body of his thought cannot be known until these works are edited and made accessible for study.

Quṭb al-Dīn's geometrical works are the following:

1. The Persian translation of Naṣīr al-Dīn al-Ṭūsī's *Taḥrīr uṣūl uqlīdus* ("Recension of the *Elements* of Euclid").
2. *Risālah fī ḥarakat al-daḥrajah wa'l-nisbah bayn al-mustawī wa'l-munḥanī* ("Treatise on the Motion of Rolling and the Relation Between the Straight and the Curved").[1]

Those on astronomy and geography are the following:

3. *Nihāyat al-idrāk fī dirāyat al-aflāk* ("The Limit of Understanding of the Knowledge of the Heavens"). Quṭb al-Dīn's major astronomical work, it consists of four books: introduction, the heavens, the earth, and the "quantity" of the heavens. There are sections on cosmography, geography, geodesy, meteorology, mechanics, and optics, reflecting both the older scientific views of Ibn al-Haytham and Bīrūnī and new scientific theories in optics and planetary motion. This work was completed around 1281 and has been commented upon by Sīnān Pāshā.
4. *Ikhtiyārāt-i muẓaffarī* ("Muẓaffarī Selections"). This work, one of Quṭb al-Dīn's masterpieces, contains his own views on astronomy and is perhaps the best work on astronomy in Persian. It is a synopsis of the *Nihāyah*; is composed, like that work, of four sections; and was written sometime before 1304.
5. *Al-Tuḥfat al-shāhiyyah fi'l-hay'ah* ("The Royal Gift on Astronomy." Composed shortly after the *Nihāyah* (in 1284), to solve more completely problems begun in the earlier work, it constitutes, along with the *Nihāyah* Quṭb al-Dīn's masterpiece in mathematical astronomy. About these two works Wiedemann wrote, "Kuṭb al-Dīn has in my opinion given the best Arabic account of astronomy (cosmography) with mathematical aids."[2] This work, like the *Nihāyah,* was cele-brated in later Islamic history and has been commented upon by Sayyid Sharīf and 'Alī Qūshchī.
6. *Kitāb fa'altu fa-lā ta'lum fi'l-hay'ah* ("A Book I Have Composed, But Do Not Blame [Me for It], on Astronomy").
7. *Kitāb al-tabṣirah fi'l-hay'ah* ("The *Tabṣirah* on Astronomy").
8. *Sharḥ al-tadhkirat al-naṣīriyyah* ("Commentary Upon the *Tadhkirah* of Naṣīr -Dīn"). Commentary upon the famous *Tadhkirah* of Naṣīr al-Dīn Ṭūsī and also on the *Bayān maqāṣid al-tadhkirah* of Muḥammad ibn 'Alī al-Himādhī.
9. *Kharidā al-'ajā'ib* ("The Wonderful Pearl").
10. *Khulāṣat iṣlāḥ al-majisṭī li-Jābir ibn Aflaḥ* ("Extracts of *Correction of the Almagest* of Jābir ibn Aflaḥ").
11. *Ḥall mushkilāt al-majisṭī* ("Solution of the Difficulties of the Almagest"). A work that is apparently lost.
12. *Taḥrīr al-zīj al-jadīd al-riḍwānī* ("Recension of the New Riḍwānī Astronomical Tables").
13. *al-Zīj al-sulṭānī* ("The Sulṭānī Astronomical Tables"). These tables have been attributed to both Quṭb al-Dīn and Muḥammad ibn Mubārak Shams al-Dīn Mīrak al-Bukhārī.

Medical works by Quṭb al-Dīn include the following:

14. *Kitāb nuzhat al-ḥukamā' wa rawḍat al-aṭibbā'* ("Delight of the Wise and Garden of the Physicians"), also known as *al-Tuḥfat al-sa'diyyah* ("The Presentation to Sa'd") and *Sharḥ kullīyyāt al-qānūn* ("Commentary Upon the Principles of the *Canon* of Ibn Sīnā"). This is the largest work by Quṭb al-Dīn, in five volumes. He worked on it throughout his life and dedicated it to Muḥammad Sa'd al-Dīn, the vizier of Arghūn and the IlKhanid ruler of Persia.
15. *Risālah fi'l-baraṣ* ("Treatise on Leprosy").
16. *Sharḥ al-urjūzah* ("Commentary Upon Ibn Sīnā's *Canticum*").
17. *Risālah fi bayān al-ḥājah ila'l-ṭibb wa ādāb al-aṭibbā' wa-waṣāyāhum* ("Treatise on the Explanation of the Necessity of Medicine and of the Manners and Duties of Physicians").

Teosophical, philosophical, and encyclopedic works are the following:

18. *Durrant al-tāj li- ghurrat al-dībāj fi'l-ḥikmah* ("Pearls of the Crown, the Best Introduction to Wisdom"). This encyclopedic philosophical and scientific work in Persian comprises an introduction on knowledge and the classification of the sciences; five books *(jumlah)* dealing with logic, metaphysics, natural philosophy, mathematics, and theodicy; and a four-part conclusion on religion and mysticism. The introduction, and the books on logic, metaphysics, and theodicy, were published by S. M. Mishkāt (Tehran, 1938-1941), and book 4 on mathematics, excluding certain portions on geometry, by S. H. Ṭabasī (Tehran, 1938-1944).

The philosophical sections of *Durrat al-tāj* were greatly influenced by the writings of Ibn Sīnā and Suhrawardī; the geometry is mostly a Persian translation of Euclid's *Elements* with the paraphrases and commentaries of al-Ḥajjāj and Thābit ibn Qurrah. The astronomy is a translation of the *Summary of the Almagest* of 'Abd al-Malik ibn Muḥammad al-Shīrāzī, and the music is taken from al-Fārābī, Ibn Sīnā, and 'Abd al-Mu'min. In the sections on religion and ethics, Quṭb al-Dīn made use of the writings of Ibn Sīnā and Fakhr al-Dīn al-Rāzī; and in Sufism or mysticism, of the *Manāhij al-'ibād ila'l-ma'ād* of Sa'd al-Dīn al-Farghānī, a disciple of Mawlānā Jalāl al-Dīn Rūmī and Ṣadr al-Dīn al-Qunyawī.

19. *Sharḥ Ḥikmat al-ishrāq* ("Commentary Upon the Theosophy of the Orient of Light"). The best known commentary upon Suhrawardī's *Ḥikmat al-ishrāq,* it was published in a lithographed edition (Tehran, 1897).
20. *Sharḥ kitāb rawḍat al-nāẓir* ("Commentary upon the *Rawḍat al-*

nāẓir"). A commentary upon Naṣīr al-Dīn al-Ṭūsī's *Rawḍat al-nāẓir* on questions of ontology.

21. *Sharḥ al-najāt* ("Commentary upon the *Najāt*"). Commentary upon Ibn Sīnā's *Kitāb al-najāt.*
22. *Al-Sharḥ wa'l-ḥāshiyah 'ala'l-ishārāt wa'l-tanbīhāt* ("Commentary and Glosses Upon the *Ishārāt"*). Commentary upon Ibn Sīnā's last philosophical masterpiece, the *Ishārāt.*
23. *Ḥāshiyah 'alā ḥikmat al-'ayn* ("Glosses Upon the *Ḥikmat al-'ayn").* The first commentary upon Najm al-Dīn Dabīrān al-Kātibī's well-known *Ḥikmat al-'ayn,* upon which many commentaries appeared later.
24. *Unmūzaj al-'ulūm* ("A Compendium of the Sciences").
25. *Wajīzah fi'l-taṣawwur wa'l-taṣdīq* ("A Short Treatise on Concept and Judgment").
26. *Risālah dar 'ilm-i akhlāq* ("Treatise on Ethics"). A treatise in Persian which is apparently lost.

The rest of the works by Quṭb al-Dīn treat the sciences of language and strictly religious questions, and there is no need to deal with them here. He also left a few poems of some literary quality.

PHILOSOPHY AND THEOLOGY

Quṭb al-Dīn belonged to that group of Muslim philosophers between Suhrawardī and Mullā Ṣadrā who revived the philosophy of Ibn Sīnā after the attacks of al-Ghazzālī, giving it at the same time an illuminationist quality drawn from the teaching of Suhrawardī. After his teacher Naṣīr al-Dīn Ṭūsī, Quṭb al-Dīn must be considered the foremost philosophical figure during the four centuries which separated Suhrawardī from Mullā Ṣadrā. Quṭb al-Dīn was also a leading example of the Muslim sage or *ḥakīm*, who was the master of many disciplines and wrote definitive works in each of them. His *Durrat al-tāj* is the outstanding Persian encyclopedia of Peripatetic philosophy. Written on the model of Ibn Sīnā's *al-Shifā',* it has additional sections devoted to Sufism and strictly religious matters not found in earlier Peripatetic works. His commentary upon the *Ḥikmat al-ishrāq,* although based mostly upon that of Shahrazūrī, rapidly replaced the latter as the most famous such work. Later generations saw Suhrawardī mostly through the eyes of Quṭb al-Dīn. His theological and religious writings also commanded great respect. The thirteenth and fourteenth centuries were marked in Persia by the gradual rapprochement of the four intellectual schools of theology *(Kalām),* Peripatetic philosophy *(mashshā'ī)*, illuminationist theosophy *(ishrāq),* and gnosis *('irfān)*. Quṭb al-Dīn was one of the key figures who brought this about and prepared the way for the synthesis of the Safavid period. He was at once a fervent disciple of Ibn Sīnā, the master of Peripatetics; a commentator on Suhrawardī, the founder of the *ishrāqī* school; and a student of Ṣadr al-Dīn al-Qunyawī, the closest disciple of the greatest expositor of the gnostic teachings of Islam, Ibn 'Arabī. Furthermore he was a theologian and religious scholar of note. To all of these he added his remarkable acumen in mathematics, astronomy, physics, and medicine, for which he has become known as such as a scientist as a philosopher.

MATHEMATICS

Quṭb al-Dīn attached a metaphysical significance to the study of mathematics, which he viewed more in the Pythagorean than in the Aristotelian manner. He saw it as the means to discipline the soul for the study of metaphysics and theosophy. His greatest contributions came in astronomy and optics, which were then part of the mathematical sciences, rather than pure mathematics in the modern sense.

OPTICS

After Ibn al-Haytham there was a relative lack of interest in optics among Muslims; the optical writings even of Naṣīr al-Dīn al-Ṭūsī show a definite decline in comparison. Probably mostly because of the spread of Suhrawardī's newly founded school of illumination, which made light synonymous with being and the basis of all reality, a definite renewal of interest in optics occurred in the thirteenth century, for which Quṭb al-Dīn was largely responsible. Although he did not write separate treatises on optics, his *Nihāyat al-idrāk* contains sections devoted to the subject. He was especially interested in the phenomena of the rainbow and must be considered the first to have explained it correctly. He concluded that the rainbow was the result of the passage of light through a transparent sphere (the raindrop). The ray of light is refracted twice and reflected once to cause the observable colors of the primary bow. The special attention paid by Quṭb al-Dīn and his students was in fact responsible for the creation in Islam of a separate science of the rainbow *(qaws qazaḥ)*, which first appeared in the classification of the sciences at this time. The significance of Quṭb al-Dīn in optics also lies in his transmission of the optical teachings of Ibn al-Haytham to al-Fārisī, who then composed the most important commentary upon Ibn al-Haytham's *Optics,* the *Tanqīḥ al-manāẓir.*

Also of interest in this field is Quṭb al-Dīn's theory of vision in his *Sharḥ ḥikmat al-ishrāq,* in which he rejected both the Euclidean and the Aristotelian theories and confirmed the *ishrāqī* theory, according to which vision occurs when there is no obstacle between the eye and the object. When the obstacle is removed, the soul of the observer receives an illumination through which the whole of the object is perceived as a single reality.

ASTRONOMY

Quṭb al-Dīn wrote at the beginning of his *Ikhtiyārāt* that the principles of astronomy fall under three headings: religion, natural philosophy, and geometry. Those who study this science become dear to God, and the student of astronomy becomes prepared for the understanding of the divine sciences because his mind is trained to study immaterial objects. Moreover, through the study of astronomy the soul gains such virtues as perseverance and temperance, and aspires to resemble the heavenly spheres. He definitely believed that the study of astronomy possessed a religious value and he himself studied it religiously and with reverence.

Quṭb al-Dīn played a major role in the observations made at Maraghah which led to the composition of the *Īl-khānī zīj,* although his name is not mentioned in its introduction. In his *Nihāyah* he suggested that the values listed in the *Īlkhānī zīj* for the motion of the apogee were not based on calculation from the successive equinoxes but were dependent upon repeated observations. He asserted that the shift in the solar apogee could be confirmed by comparing the values found in Ptolemy and the later astronomical tables preceding the *Īlkhānī zīj,* which implies recourse to frequent observations. Quṭb al-Dīn was keenly interested in scientific observation, but this in no way reduced his viewpoint to empiricism or detracted from his theoretical interests or philosophical vision.

Quṭb al-Dīn emphasized the relation between the movement of the sun and the planets in the way that is found later in the writings of Regiomontanus, and which prepared the way for Copernicus. In fact, through the research of E.S. Kennedy and his associates, it has been discovered that new planetary models came out of Maraghah which represent the most important departure from the Ptolemaic model in medieval times and are essentially the same as those of Copernicus, provided one ignores the heliostatic hypothesis.

The Maraghah school sought to remove a basic flaw from the Ptolemaic model for planetary motion, namely, the failure of certain

Ptolemaic configurations to conform to the principle that celestial motion must be uniform and circular. To remedy this situation Naṣīr al-Dīn Ṭūsī proposed in his *Tadhkirah* a rolling device consisting of two vectors (to use the modern terminology) of equal length, the second moving with a constant velocity twice that of the first but in the opposite direction. This device Kennedy has named the "Ṭūsī couple."

Quṭb al-Dīn in his *Nihāyah* and *al-Tuḥfat al-shāhiyyah,* both of which, like the *Tadhkirah,* are divided into four parts, sought to work out this model for the different planets but apparently never did so to his full satisfaction, for he kept modifying it. In fact, he produced the two above-mentioned works within four years, in an attempt to achieve the final answer. In the several manuscripts of each, the two works contain successive endeavors to reach a completely satisfactory solution to what is definitely Quṭb al-Dīn's most important achievement in astronomy.

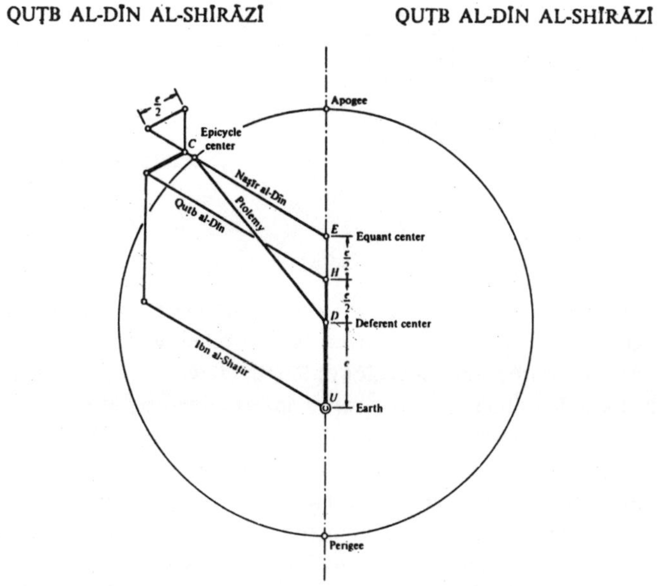

FIGURE 1

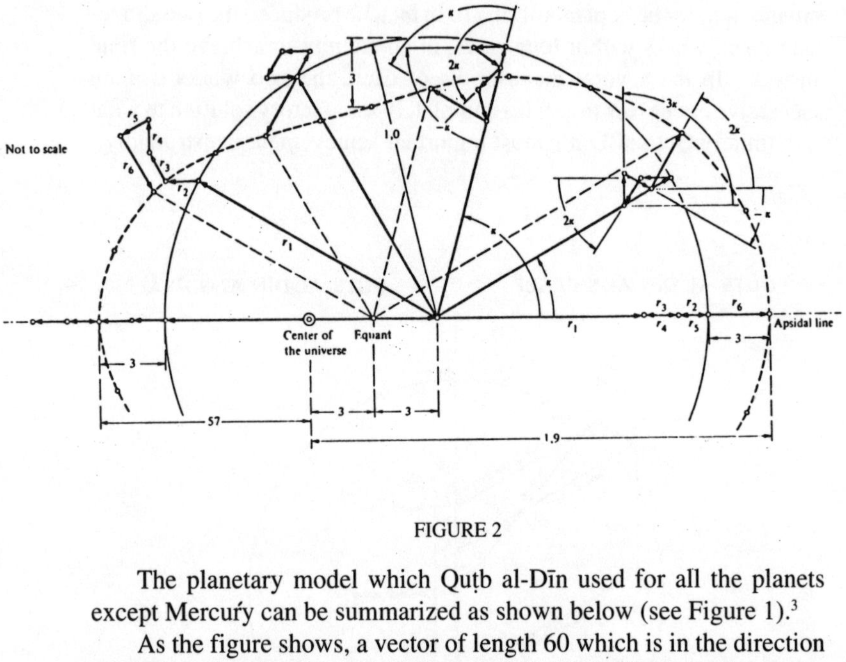

FIGURE 2

The planetary model which Quṭb al-Dīn used for all the planets except Mercury can be summarized as shown below (see Figure 1).[3]

As the figure shows, a vector of length 60 which is in the direction of the mean longitude is drawn from a point midway between the equant center and the deferent center. Another vector, with a length equal to half the eccentricity, rotates at the end of this vector.

Because of the great eccentricity of Mercury, its model requires special conditions. Figure 2 demonstrates how Quṭb al-Dīn was finally able to create a model which fulfilled the conditions for this planet.

As E. S. Kennedy—to whom we owe this analysis and figure—states: The first vector *ri* is of length 60, it issues from the deferent center, and it has at all times the direction of the mean planet. The next four vectors, each of length $c/2$ [where $c = 3$, because the eccentricity of Mercury is 6], make up two Ṭūsī couples. The last vector *rb* has length *c*. The initial positions and rates of rotation of all the vectors are as shown on the drawing, where *k* is the mean longitude measured from apogee.[4]

This model represents the height of the techniques developed at Maraghah to solve the problems of planetary motion. Quṭb al-Dīn also applied these techniques to the solution of the problem of the moon, trying to remove some of the obvious flaws in the Ptolemaic model. But in this matter another Muslim astronomer who adopted these techniques, Ibn al-Shāṭir, was more successful. He produced a model that was greatly superior to that of Ptolemy, the same that was produced later by Copernicus.

GEOGRAPHY

The interest of Quṭb al-Dīn in observation is also evident in geography. Not only did he write on geography in his *Nihāyah,* drawing from earlier Muslim geographers, especially Bīrūnī, but he traveled throughout Asia Minor, examining the route to be followed by the Genoese ambassador of the Mongol ruler Arghūn to the Pope, Buscarello di Ghizalfi. In 1290 he presented a map of the Mediterranean to Arghūn based on observations made of the coastal areas of Asia Minor.

PHYSICS

In his Peripatetic works Quṭb al-Dīn generally followed the physics of Ibn Sīnā, but in the *Sharḥ ḥikmat al-ishrāq* he developed a physics of light which is of particular interest. In it he considered light as the source of all motion, both sublunar and celestial. In the case of the heavenly spheres, motion is a result of the illumination of the souls of the spheres by Divine Light. He divided bodies into simple and compound, and these in turn into transparent and opaque, so that light and darkness, rather than the Aristotelian hylomorphism, dominate his physics. He also reinterpreted meteorological phenomena in terms of light and light phenomena.

MEDICINE

Quṭb al-Dīn's major contribution to medicine was his commentary upon Ibn Sīnā's *Canon,* which was celebrated in later centuries in the Islamic world but has not been analyzed thoroughly in modern times. This work seeks to explain all the difficulties in the *Canon* relating to general principles of medicine. Quṭb al-Dīn based it not only on his own lifelong study of the text and what he had learned from his masters in Shiraz, Maraghah, and other cities, but also on all the important commentaries he found in Egypt, especially the *Mūjiz al-qānūn* of Ibn al-Nafīs, the *Sharḥ al-kulliyyāt min kitāb al-qānūn* of Muwaffaq al-Dīn Ya'qūb al-Sāmarrī, and the *Kitāb al-shāfī fi'l-ṭibb* of Abu'l-Faraj ibn al-Quff. In medicine, as in philosophy, Quṭb al-Dīn did much to revive the teachings of Ibn Sīnā and had an important role in the propagation of Avicennan medicine, especially from the fifteenth century onward in the Indian subcontinent.

INFLUENCE

The most famous students of Quṭb al-Dīn were al-Fārisī, the outstanding commentator on Ibn al-Haytham; Quṭb al-Dīn Rāzī, the author of many famous works, including the *Muḥākamāt,* a "trial" of the relative merits of the commentaries of Naṣīr al-Dīn Ṭūsī and Fakhr al-Dīn Rāzī upon the *Ishārāt* of Ibn Sīnā; and Niẓām al-Dīn al-Nayshāpūrī the author of *Tafsīr al-taḥrīr,* on Naṣīr al-Dīn Ṭūsī's *Recension of the Almagest.* Quṭb al-Dīn's influence continued through these and other students, and also through his writings, especially the *al-Tuḥfat al-sa'diyyah* in medicine, *Nihāyat al-idrāk* in astronomy, and *Sharḥ ḥikmat al-ishrāq* in philosophy, the last having become a standard text of Islamic philosophy in the traditional schools of Persia. His writings were also one of the influential intellectual elements that made possible the Safavid renaissance in philosophy and the sciences in Persia, and his name continued to be respected and his works studied in the Ottoman and the Mogul empires.

NOTES

1. One of the few treatises of Quṭb al-Dīn analyzed thoroughly in a European language, is E. Wiedemann, "Ueber eine Schrift ueber die Bewegung des Rollens und die Beziehung zwischen dem Geraden und dem Gekruemmten von Quṭb al Dīn Maḥmud b. Mas'ūd al Schīrāzī," in *Sitzungsberichte der physikalisch-medizinischen Sozietät in Erlangen,* 58-59 (1926-1927), 219-224.
2. Article on Kuṭb al-Dīn al-Shīrāzī, in *Encyclopaedia of Islam,* 1st ed., 11, 1167.
3. E. S. Kennedy, "Late Medieval Planetary Theory," in *Isis,* 57, pt. 3 (1966), 367, 373.
4. *Ibid.,* 373-374.

BIBLIOGRAPHY

I. ORIGINAL WORKS. Quṭb al-Dīn's published works are *Durrat al-tāj,* pt. I, 5 vols., S. M. Mishkāt, ed. (Tehran, 1938-1941); pt. II, 5 vols. S. H. Ṭabasī, ed. (Tehran, 1938-1944); and *Sharḥ ḥikmat al-ishrāq* (Tehran, 1897).

II. *SECONDARY LITERATURE.* See E. S. Kennedy, "Late Medieval Planetary Theory," in *Isis,* 57, no. 3 (1966), 365-378; M. Krause, "Stambuler

Handschriften islamischer Mathematiker," in *Quellen und Studien zur Geschichte der Mathematik, Astronomie und Physik,* Abt. B, Studien, 3 (1936), 437-532; M. Minovi, "Mullā Quṭb Shīrāzī," in *Yād-nāma-yī īrānī-yī Minorsky* (Tehran, 1969), 165-205; M. T. Mīr, *Pizishkān-i nāmī-yī pārs* (Shiraz, 1969), 110-117; S. H. Nasr, *Science and Civilization in Islam* (Cambridge, Mass., 1968), 56 and *passim;* G. Sarton, *An Introduction to the History of Science,* II (Baltimore, 1941), 1017-1020; A. Sayili, *The Observatory in Islam* (Ankara, 1960), *passim;* H. Suter, "Die Mathematiker und Astronomen der Araber," in *Abhandlungen zur Geschichte der mathematischen Wissenschaften* (1990), 158; Qadrī Ḥāfiẓ Tuqān, *Turāth al-'arab al-'ilmī fi'l-riyāḍiyyāt wa'l-falak* (Cairo, 1963), 425-427; and E. Wiedemann, "Zu den optischen Kenntnissen von Quṭb al Dīn al Schîrâzî," in *Archiv für die Geschichte der Natur wissenschaften und der Technik,* 3 (1912), 187-193; "Üeer die Gestalt, Lage und Bewegung der Erde sowie philosophisch-astronomische Betrachtungen von Quṭb al Dīn al Schīrāzī," *ibid.,* 395-422; and "Über eine Schrift über die Bewegung des Rollens und die Beziehung zwischen dem Geraden und den Gekruemmten, von Quṭb al Dīn Maḥmūd b. Mas'ūd al Schīrāzī," in *Sitzungserichte der Physikalisch-medizinischen Sozietät in Erlangen,* 58-59 (1926-1927). 219-224.

20

The Status of Rashīd al-Dīn Faḍlallāh in the History of Islamic Philosophy and Science*

Rashīd al-Dīn Faḍlallāh is a renowned *ḥakīm,* physician, historian and political philosopher of the Mongol period. In later historical accounts of Rashīd al-Dīn, he is described as the powerful minister of Maḥmūd Ghāzān whose fame is considered to be due to the historical role which he played. Despite his significance, many of his works in science and philosophy are forgotten and, therefore, a thorough investigation of his place amongst the Islamic scientists remains a difficult task. Rashīd al-Dīn lived in an era whose intellectual life and vitality has remained obscure and much research remains to be done to shed light on it. His intellectual merit has been further obscured by centuries of Western scholarship which has regarded the intellectual aspects of Islamic culture and civilization to be merely a chapter of Western intellectual thought.

The events following the 6th/12th and 7th/13th century which mark a turning point between the Christian and the Islamic civilizations have not, until recently, attracted the attention of Western scholars of Islamic culture. Even that part of the eastern scholarly community which follows Western patterns of scholarship has not paid sufficient attention to this era.[1] It is not until recent times that gradually the significance of the astronomical and mathematical activities of this period, as well as the philosophical and gnostic *('irfānī)* schools of thought are beginning to be known.

The Mongol invasion damaged enormously the social and economical structures of many Islamic countries in the east, in particular Persia. However, despite what has been stated in many of the texts dealing with

---

* This essay was originally written in Persian and appeared in *Irānshināsī,* 2 (1349 A.H.s) : 1-22. It has been translated by Mehdi Aminrazavi into English and has been published as "The Status of Rashid al-Dīn Faḍlallah in the History of Islamic Philosophy and Science", *Islamic Culture,* Vol 68, No. 1, Jan 1994, pp. 1-10.

this period, the Mongol invasion was not responsible for the vanishing of intellectual activities in the Islamic world. It is only after reviewing thousands of manuscripts in the field of science and philosophy belonging to this period that the scientific and philosophical status of the years following the Mongol invasion can be precisely determined.

From what has been learned so far, it can be concluded that due to the special interest of the Mongols in astronomy, the mathematical sciences were revived. The rise of mathematical science, which began a new intellectual life in this era, brought with itself a revival of philosophical activities. Therefore, the 7th/13th century witnessed the emergence of numerous scientists and Peripatetic philosophers such as Khāwjah Naṣīr al-Dīn Ṭūsī, Quṭb al-Dīn Shīrāzī, Dabīrān-i Kātibī, Muḥyī al-Dīn Maghribī and 'Allāmah Ḥillī who were outstanding figures in science and philosophy.

Scientific activities in this era were not, however, carried out continuously and did not have a social foundation. They were primarily supported by the patronage of powerful individuals, such as Faḍlallāh himself. With the diminishing of the Islamic educational curriculum in the traditional schools *(madrasahs)* and the reconstruction of new *madrasah's* in the following century, most of the religious and intellectual sciences found a home in the Sufi centers *(khānaqāhs)*. The Sufis of this era were the true saviors of the Islamic sciences.

The 7th/13th century witnessed a profound change in the Islamic intellectual life especially in Iran which gradually led to the emergence of the great centers of learning during the Safavid period. From the 7th/13th century onward, the philosophy of illumination (*ḥikmat al-ishrāq*) began to spread in Persia in a systematic manner and gnosis *('irfān)* which in the beginning of this century, was developed on a grand scale by Muḥyī al-Dīn ibn 'Arabī, quickly found such important proponents as Quṭb al-Dīn Shīrāzī, Fakhr al-Dīn 'Irāqī and Sa'd al-Dīn Ḥamūyah, leaving a profound mark upon the gnostic and philosophical views of many Persians.[2]

Also, it was in this century that a rapprochement between the schools of Peripatetics *(mashsha'īs)*, the illuminationists *(ishrāqīs)*, theology *(Kalām)* and gnosis *('irfān)* began to take place and gradually gave rise to such figures as Quṭb al-Dīn Shīrāzī, Ibn Turkah Iṣfahānī and Sayyid Ḥaydar Āmulī. These masters who came from different schools of thought attempted to synthesize various theological and philosophical perspectives and thereby laid the groundwork for the emergence of such philosophers as Mīr Dāmād and Mullā Ṣadrā.[3]

Rashīd al-Dīn Faḍlallāh came on the scene at a time when the movement to synthesize various schools of thought in Islam had already begun. In fact, one of his closest friends, Ṣadr al-Dīn Muḥammad Turkah, who composed *al-Ḥikmat al-rashīdiyyah,* a treatise dedicated to Faḍlallāh, belongs to a family, one of whose notable members a century later composed the first treatise on the rapprochement of philosophy and gnosis entitled *Tamḥīd al-qawā'id.* It appears that Faḍlallāh was familiar with various philosophical and scientific schools in Islam and the intellectual path which he pursued was similar to Qūṭb al-Dīn Shīrāzī and some of the other scholars of his time.

* * *

Let us now discuss briefly Rashīd al-Dīn's interest in Sufism. Rashīd al-Dīn had great respect for Sufism and in many instances in his *Maktūbāt* he mentions the importance of Sufism to one of his children and states: "So, the delight of the eye and fruit of the heart, may God aid you with His grace, know that you have been created to accomplish a great task and in your nature lies the divine secret and the light of vicegerency, a precious gift that has been given to you. Behold, so that Divine Light and secrets [bestowed upon you] are not to vanish if you follow your desires."[4] In another place he states: "Beautify yourself with the jewel of the path and the cloak of truth which is the state of 'poverty' for the spiritual elites. Know that poverty in which the Prophet has taken pride [when he said] "poverty is my pride", consists of six states: repentance, submission, purity, acceptance, ṣatisfaction in heart, isolation."[5]

Rashīd al-Dīn and his statements about the principles and stages of poverty clearly demonstrate his familiarity with Sufism. Sufism for him is not only a dimension of Islam but is the very heart of the Quran and the inner message of the Islamic faith. It is for this reason that in advising his son to follow the path of Sufism, he states: "Hold a firm grip on the Quran in that from the deep trap of the world one cannot reach the angelic world and see the incorporeal world except by divine grace. Behold onto the divine rope o you faithful, with that you shall succeed. From the darkness of [worldly] desires, except through following the path of prophet Muḥammad one cannot be saved."[6]

Rashīd al-Dīn's firm belief in the necessity of having a spiritual master was like other Sufis of his era who considered Sufism not to be only mental and abstract phenomenon but believed in guidance under the direction of a spiritual master. "The first item that is necessary and the first duty of a *sālik* is to seek a perfect master and a learned guide to direct him toward inner purification."[7]

It is not easy to decipher if Rashīd al-Dīn had an interest in a particular type of Sufism or if he was affiliated with a Sufism order. In some of his works, however, he uses certain expressions of Ibn 'Arabī such as *insān-i kāmil* (the perfect or universal man). From the manner of his elucidation, however, it is possible to conclude that he may have belonged to the Suhrawardiyyah Sufi order which was founded in the 6th/12th century.

From a theological point of view, we can say that Rashīd al-Dīn Faḍlallāh belonged to the school of Ash'arite *Kalām* (theology) which after Imam Fakhr al-Dīn Rāzī gained a philosophical dimension. In fact, Faḍlallāh in his works repeatedly refers to Imam Fakhr and has designated the fourteenth treatise of *al-Tawḍīḥāt al-rashīdiyyah* as a defense of the theologians *(mutakallimīn)* whom he calls *"ḥukamā-yi islām"* (the sages of Islam).[8] In the second treatise of the *al-Tawḍīḥāt al-rashīdiyyah* entitled "On the Classification of Beings" he elucidates the difference between the views of theologians and the *ḥukamā'* on the nature of substance and seems to prefer the path of the theologians to that of the philosophers.[9] Despite this, he relies on a philosophical language and in some cases such as the theory of emanation and the incorporeal world, he sides with the philosophers and supports their views.

Faḍlallāh also had precise knowledge of the Peripatetics' philosophical definitions. For example, with regard to substance he say: "With regard to the definition of substance, it stands by itself and is in need of His existence only and nothing else." Rashīd al-Dīn's tendency in *Kalām* is the continuation of the school of Imam Fakhr Rāzī and those who in the 7th/13th and 8th/14th centuries practiced philosophical theology. Although theologians knew the opinion of the philosophers, they followed the Ash'arite *Kalām* except that they had philosophized it. Philosophical theology which cannot be found in the works of the theologians prior to Imam al-Ḥaramayn Juwaynī, therefore, was a new chapter in Islamic intellectual thought.

Rashīd al-Dīn cannot be regarded as a philosopher like Ibn Sīnā or Khwājah Naṣīr al-Dīn Ṭūsī, however, although he undoubtedly knew a great deal of philosophy. Although his treatises are more theological than philosophical, there are many chapters which show his thorough knowledge of philosophy and his familiarity with the works of his predecessors, in particular Ibn Sīnā. For example, in his treatise *On the Classification of Beings,* he classifies all beings into necessary and contingent, and contingent being into substance and accident and substance into sensible and non-sensible substance, etc.....[10] He also knew a great deal of natural science, not only as a physician but also as a philosopher interested in the natural sciences. In a number of his writings written in the form of questions and answers, he made direct references to the natural sciences and issues related to the elements and their composition.

At the time of Rashīd al-Dīn *ishrāqī,* (illuminationist) philosophy was gradually spreading in Iran and the important commentary of Quṭb al-Dīn Shīrāzī to Suhrawardī's masterpiece, *Ḥikmat al-ishrāq* is an example of that. Despite this, it is not clear to what extent Rashīd al-Dīn was influenced by it. The texts and treatises of Rashīd al-Dīn, which we have reviewed, do not contain an elaborate discussion of *ishrāqī* philosophy. In the fourteenth treatise of *al-Tawḍīḥāt al-rashīdiyyah* entitled *"Fī jawāb 'an mu'āriḍī Ḥujjat al-islām"* (''On Answering those Who Object to the Ḥujjat al-Islām'') he defends Ghazzālī's interpretation of the Quranic verses on light, especially those in the *Mishkāt al-anwār* which are very similar to some of the fundamental beliefs of the *ishrāqīs.* It is not unlikely that Rashīd al-Dīn's closeness to the school of Khwājah Naṣīr al-Dīn Ṭūsī and his familiarity with Quṭb al-Dīn Shīrāzī's commentary [upon the *Ḥikmat al-ishrāq*] may have also familiarized him with Suhrawardī's *Ḥikmat al-ishrāq.*

What is certain, however, is that Rashīd al-Dīn attempts in his philosophical treatises to bring about a rapprochement between philosophy and theology *(Kalām).* While in some instances he criticized rationalistic philosophy from the *Sharī'ite* point of view, he remained a proponent of philosophical thinking. To this end he wrote a treatise on the defense of the intellect[11] in which he tried to demonstrate that the views of theologians and philosophers are ultimately compatible. He also attempted to reconcile the intellectual and transmitted knowledge as well as reason and faith.[12]

From our survey of Rashīd al-Dīn's unpublished works, it has become certain that his works represent another attempt to wed a variety of Islamic intellectual schools which is characteristic of the 7th/13th and 8th/14th centuries.

* * *

The aspect of Rashīd al-Dīn's thought that has not received the attention it deserves by Iranian scholars, are his views on the history of religious and scientific thought. Rashīd al-Dīn has written the best description of Buddhism in the history of Islamic thought[13] and after Bīrūnī he should be regarded as the most important Muslim scholar of Hinduism outside of India. Also, his elaborations of Chinese sciences are unique in their own right.

Altogether, perhaps the greatest service of Rashīd al-Dīn to Islamic sciences has been to expand the frontier of the branches of knowledge, such that it became inclusive of Chinese, Indian and even Byzantine cultures. In this respect, he did even more toward the universalization of knowledge than the founders of the Islamic sciences. Rashīd al-Dīn was on the one hand interested in Chinese and Indian sciences and on the other hand paid special attention to Christian philosophy and theology. In the eighth section of *As'ilah wa ajwibah* (''Questions and Answers'') he answers the questions of a foreign philosopher and in a lengthy response to the seventh question he engages in comparative theological speculation and responds in an amazingly clear manner. Zeki Validi Togan indicates that the philosopher to whom Rashīd al-Dīn responded to may have been George Chioniades of Tirabizond.[14]

In reference to the Arabic version of the same book, which is more extensive than the Persian version, Tūqān tells us that Rashīd al-Dīn discusses the relationship between the intellect and faith from Jewish, Christian and Buddhist points of view and thereby demonstrates his interest in ecumenical studies. Considering the great interest in the field of comparative religion and ecumenical studies in today's world and the lack of sufficient research by Muslim scholars on world religions, Rashīd al-Din can serve as an important source for future studies in this field.[15]

* * *

From a scientific point of view, Rashīd al-Dīn has made three contributions; establishment of scientific foundations, writing of texts on science and medicine and finally, his role in spreading the Chinese sciences among Muslims. With regard to the establishment of scientific foundations, Rashīd al-Dīn can be regarded as the direct heir to Khāwjah Naṣīr al-Dīn and, in fact, his *Jāmi' al-tawārīkh* holds a very important position in the school of Naṣīr al-Dīn.

Rashīd al-Dīn was very much interested in non-Islamic nations and had invited Indian, Chinese and Byzantinian scientists to the "Rashīdī Quarters" [in Tabriz] in order to convene international scientific meetings. Since in addition to Persian and Arabic, he knew Mongolian, Chinese and Hebrew, his scholarship was further enriched by refering to other sources besides Islamic texts.

Although, after the Mongol invasion, the vast network of scientific centers that depended on his patronage had collapsed, their activities and his attempts to harmonize the activities of different scientists was of great importance for the history of Islamic science.[16]

Rashīd al-Dīn's interest in medicine was such that he would offer substantial rewards to researchers. Perhaps it was for this reason that from the farthest regions of the Islamic countries, such as Morocco, books were written and sent to him in Tabriz. Even after becoming minister, he continued to build hospitals and wrote commentaries on Ibn Sīna's medicine. His patronizing the writing of medical books and the establishment of medical centers was an important element in the revival of medical science in the 8th/14th century.

Perhaps the most important contribution of Rashīd al-Dīn to the sciences in general and medicine in particular, was the introduction of Chinese science to the Muslims and, in particular, Persians. *Jāmī' al-tawārīkh* not only contains useful information concerning the scientific exchanges between the scientists of Persia, Central Asia and China, but also shows the status of science in Persia and China at that time.[17] This book also alludes to Rashīd al-Dīn's patronage of new books written on Indian, Chinese and Mongolian medicine. In Chinese and Mongolian medicine, a four-volume book was composed. The first volume is in Persian and was discovered a few years ago by Zeki Velidi-in a library at Ayasophia entitled *Tanksūkh-nāma-yi ilkhānī dar funūn wa 'ūlūm-i khatā'ī.*[18] The information contained therein must have been gathered by the famous Chinese physician Wang-Shuho since this volume bears his name.

The value of the *Tanksūkh-nāmah* in introducing Chinese science to Persians is that it familiarized them with the Chinese sciences at the time and increased the influence of Chinese and Mongolian sciences, especially on astronomy and medicine, to Persia. Introducing the Chinese sciences to Persia became a means through which the West came to know of Chinese medical science. Recent research[19] indicates that the anatomical pictures in *Tanksūkh-nāmah* have been adopted from the famous Chinese text *Ts'un hsin huan Chung t'u.* These pictures and their illustrations in all likelihood influenced the new school of anatomy in 8th/14th century Italy whose founder, Mundinus de Bologna was familiar with Islamic sources on medical science.

This is an aspect of Rashīd al-Dīn's scientific significance which has not received the attention it deserves. In addition to the influence of Islamic science on the West in the 6th/12th century through Andalusia and Sicily, the West came in contact with later developments in Islamic science, especially astronomy, and the school of Khāwjah Naṣīr al-Dīn Ṭūsī and his followers such as Qūṭb al-Dīn Shīrazī.[20] How the West came to know of this phase of Islamic science is not as yet clear but it may have been through Byzantinum. Considering the activities of Rashīd al-Dīn in gathering the Byzantinian scientists in Tabriz and his correspondence with them which shows they knew of his works, perhaps it was through this channel that not only Chinese science but also later developments of Islamic science such as what occurred in Maraghah came to be known in the West. Rashīd al-Dīn with his universal love of knowledge became the means through which later Islamic science influenced the West.

While many of Rashīd al-Dīn's works are still in their unedited form and not available to scholars, it is only through further research and a more thorough look at the Greek and Byzantine sources that the precise role of Rashīd al-Dīn in this second and unknown wave of the resurgence of Islamic science and its influence upon the West can be determined.

The result of future research cannot but be to show further the significance of this unique historian, *ḥakīm* and statesman.

NOTES

1. See S. H. Nasr *Ma'āri-fi islāmī dar jahān-i mū'aṣīr,* Tehran, 1348 A.H.S., and also S.H. Nasr, *Science and Civilization in Islam,* Introduction.
2. For more information see chapter 3 of S.H. Nasr *Three Muslim Sages,* Delmar, New York, Caravan Press, 1975; also S.H. Nasr, "Suhrawardī" in this volume; and S.H. Nasr, "Seventh Century Sufism and the School of Ibn 'Arabi', *Journal of the Regional Cultural Institute* (RCD), Vol. 1, Sprin 1967, pp. 45-50
3. For more information on this subject see numerous works of Sayyīd Jalāl al-Dīn Āshtīyānī on Mullā Ṣadrā, in particular his introduction to *al-Shawāhid al-rubūbiyyah,* Mashhad, 1368 A.H. and *Sharḥ al-mashā'ir,* Mashhad, 1384 A.H.; also the introduction by S.H. Nasr to Mullā Ṣadrā's *Risālah-yi si aṣl,* Tehran, 1345 A.H.S.
4. *Rashīdī Correspondence,* (ed.) by Muḥammad Shafī' Lahor 1367 A.H., p. 294.
5. Ibid., p. 102.
6. Ibid., p. 206.
7. Ibid., p. 289.
8. Ibid., see *On the Division of Beings,* the second treatise of *al-Tawḍīḥāt al-rashīdayyah.*
9. "So that I brought the classification of beings in accordance with the opinion of the theologians, who are among the *ḥakīms* in Islam and the ancient sages (Greeks) and recent sages, preferring the path of theologians over the path of the *hukama'* in that its aspects belong to the heart and are closer to the understanding of most of the seekers..." in *al-Tawḍīḥāt al-rashīdiyyah*, Qūlīch 'Alī Pāshā edition, No. 854, third treatise "On the elucidation of beings", p. 1.
10. *al-Tawḍīḥāt al-rashīdiyyah*, second treatise "on classification of beings", p. 2.
11. See the fifteenth treatise in *al-Tawḍīḥāt al-rashīdiyyah* entitled "Fī bayān faḍīlat al-'aql wa'l-'ilm."
12. For example, on the unity of the Origin and His Attribute he states: "For all the *ḥakīms* and non-theologians it is determined and obvious that God is a unity who is the first of first causes and the last of last causes. [He is] the first emanator of all emanations and what is issued forth from Him is transcendent and sacred. The totality of His Attributes are perfection and infinitude and His completeness is devoid of any deficiency and inadequacy. Whatever emanates from Him is from wisdom such that

no one can object to it. Otherwise perfection and justice would remain unmanifested." Zeki Velidi Togan, "A Document Concerning Cultural Relations Between the Ilkhanids and Byzantines" *Islam Tetkleri Enstitüsü Dergisi,* Cild III, CUs 3-4, 195901960 (Istanbul, 1965). Page 32 of the text is a photocopy of *al-As'ilah wa'-ajwibah*" from the edition No. 2180, Aya Sophia.

13. K. Jahn, "On the Mythology and Religion of Indians in the Medieval Moslem Tradition," *Mélanges d'Orientalisme offerts ā Henri Massé,* Tehran, 1963, pp. 18-97.

14. Zeki Velidi Togan, "A Document Concerning Cultural Relations Between the Ikhanids and Byzantines," see p.15 of the English text.

15. For more information see, S.H. Nasr, "Islam and the Encounter of Religions," *Islamic Quarterly,* Vol. X, No. 3 and 4, 1966, pp. 47-68; and also, *The Role of Historical Scholarship in Changing the Relation Among Religions,* Leiden, 1968, pp. 23-47.

16. For further information about the status of Rashīd al-Dīn in the history of science, see G. Sarton, *An Introduction to the History of Islam,* Vol. III, Part 1, Balitmore 1947, pp. 969-976.

17. For instance in describing the biography of Hulāgū, he refers to a chemistry laboratory, and it is also the first source which discusses the printing industry of China.

18. Refer to M. Minovi, "Translation of Chinese Sciences into Persian in the 8th Century, A.H.", *Journal of the Faculty of Letters,* Tehran, No.1, Year 3, Mehr, 1334 A.H.S. p.1-26 and also Süheil Ünver (ed.), *Tanksūk nāmei ilḥān derfünūn ūlūmu hatāī mukaddimesi* with an introduction by A. Gül Pinarli, Istanbul 1939, also, Abdulhak Adnan, "Sur le Tanksukname," *Isis,* Vol. 32, 1941, pp. 44-47, also, Zeki Velidi Togan, *Türk Yürdü,* Vol. XXVI, pp. 45-48; A. Dragunov, "A Persian Transcription of Ancient Mandarin," *Bulletin de l' Academie des Sciences de l' Urss, Classe des Sciences Sociales,* 1931, pp. 354-375.

19. For more information see: S. Miyasita, "A Link in the Westward Transmission of Chinese Anatomy in the Later Middle Ages," *Isis,* Vol.58, 4, No.194, 1967, pp. 486-490.

20. For example, recent studies by E.S. Kennedy and associates indicate how the astronomical theories of Quṭb al-Dīn and Khwajah Naṣīr have influenced Copernicus and other Western astronomers of the Renaissance era. For more information, see: E.S. Kennedy, "Late Medieval Planetary Theory," *Isis,* Vol.57, 3, No.189, 1966, pp. 365-378; V. Roberts, "The Planetary Theory of Ibn al-Shaṭīr," *Isis,* Vol. 57,2, No.188, 1966, pp. 208-219.

PART V

LATER ISLAMIC PHILOSOPHY

21

The School of Isfahan*

INTRODUCTION

One of the most curious aspects of the Western study of Muslim intellectual life is that with one or two exceptions practically no serious research has ever been made into the spiritual and intellectual treasures of Twelve Imam Shi'ism in any of the European languages.[1] As a result, not only Westerners but even the Muslims whose contact with the Shi'ah world is mainly through Western sources have remained totally ignorant of the remarkable intellectual life which has persisted to this very day in centres of Shi'ism, especially in Persia. Inasmuch as it was especially but not exclusively Shi'ah world that much of the intellectual life of Islam, especially in the sciences and traditional wisdom (*ḥikmat*),[2] took refuge after the seventh/thirteenth century, this ignorance has helped to strength the totally erroneous notion that Islam fell into complete intellectual decadence after the Mongol invasion. Just as a closer study of the Muslim world at large will show that in art, government, Sufism, and many other aspects of Islamic life there was anything but decadence until fairly recently, a study of the Shi'ah world will reveal that even in the sciences, philosophy, and *ḥikmat* the Muslims have, with one gap of a century and a half, continued to flourish up to the present century. It will reveal that just as Safavid art is one of the high points of Islamic art, so is the intellectual life of Shī'ism in this period one of the apogees of Muslim history, producing sages like Ṣadr al-Dīn Shīrāzī, usually known as Mullā Ṣadrā. Perhaps one day histories of philosophy will not have chapters on Islam which end abruptly with Ibn Rushd or possibly Ibn Khaldūn but will trace the chain to the present century and end once and for all the dangerous illusion that the present-day Muslims are separated from their own tradition by centuries of intellectual "vacuum". Our aim in this chapter is hardly one of filling this lacuna; rather it is to give some of the

* This essay originally appeared in the *A History of Muslim Philosophy,* Edited by M. M. Sharif, Vol. 2, Wiesbaden: O. Harrassowitz, 1966. pp. 904-932.

background and intellectual perspectives of Safavid Persia, where Twelve-Imam Shi'ism became for the first time a completely independent political and cultural entity, an entity which has dominated every phase of life in Persia ever since.

The coming to power of the Safawids in Persia is one of the most fascinating chapters of Muslim history and marks one of the instances in which the influence of Sufism upon the social and political life of Islam is felt directly. Beginning as a Sufi brotherhood which traced its lineage as well as its name to the great saint Shaykh Ṣafī al-Dīn Ardibīlī,[3] the Safavids soon developed into a well-organized political force which was to conquer the whole of Persia and to transform it into a political force which was to conquer the whole of Persia and to weld it into a political unity for the first time since the fall of the Sassanid Empire. The Sufi order continued under the spiritual direction of a series of descendants of Shaykh Ṣafī, and its members in the ninth/fifteenth century adopted a twelve-sided red hat for which they became known as the *qizil-bāsh* (red heads). The order grew in power in the politically disorganized Persia of the ninth/fifteenth century and under Ismā'īl (892/1487-930/1523-24) succeeded in defeating the local rulers and unifying the whole of Persia.

Shāh Ismā'īl was crowned in Tabriz in 905/1499 marking the beginning of the reign of the Safavids which was to last over two centuries until in 1133/1720 the Afghans conquered Persia, sacked the Safavid capital at Ispahan, and killed Shāh Sulṭān Ḥusayn, the last of the Safavid rulers. During this period Persia, which until now had been partly Shi'ah and partly Sunni, wavering between these two orthodox perspectives of the Islamic revelation, became completely Twelve-Imam Shi'ah, and Shi'ism, which had until now remained a minority creed, found itself as the official religion of an empire and had to face political and social issues it had never been forced to face before.[4]

No longer molested by an external force and faced with a large number of practical social problems, Shi'ah theology, *Kalām*, which had always served as the walls of the citadel of the faith,[5] lost much of its earlier vigour while jurisprudence, *fiqh*, having to face new situations, became highly developed. More important for our purpose is the fact that the predominantly Shi'ah culture of Persia prepared the background for the flourishing of the doctrines of *ishrāqī* gnosis (illuminationistic wisdom),[6] philosophy, and the sciences. The efforts of the chain of sages after Khwājah Naṣīr al-Dīn Ṭūsī, who had kept the study of these subjects alive, suddenly found the necessary environment for the development of this form of wisdom.[7] We have connected this wisdom symbolically with the school of Ispahan, which spread throughout Safavid Persia as well as in Iraq, Syria, and India with which the Persians had very close contacts. The centres of its life were not only Ispahan, the Safavid capital, but also other cities like Shiraz, Kashan, Qazwin, and Tabriz. Furthermore, some of the most important figures like Shaykh Bahā' al-Dīn 'Āmilī, and Sayyid Ni'matallāh Jazā'irī, who played a vital role in the establishment of Shi'sm in Persia, were 'Arabs from 'Amil near Damascus and Bahrain, two centres which had been preserving the Shi'ah tradition for centuries.[8]

The Shi'ahs have developed the Ja'farī school of Law named after the sixth Imam, Imam Ja'far al-Ṣādiq, as well as theology (*Kalām*) and other traditional studies, namely, language, history, *Ḥadīth* and commentary upon the Quran, jurisprudence (*fiqh*), principles of jurisprudence (*uṣūl*),[9] theology,[10] and *ḥikmat*, this last being a combination of gnosis, theosophy, and philosophy which forms the main subject of our present study.

ḤIKMAT

The form of wisdom which has survived until today in the Shi'ah world as *ḥikmat* can neither be wholly identified with philosophy as currently understood in the West, nor with theosophy which has unfortunately become identified in the English-speaking world with pseudo-spiritualist movements, nor with theology.[11] As developed in the Safavid period and continued to the present day, *Ḥikmat* consists of several threads knit together by the matrix of Shi'ism. The most important of these elements are the esoteric teachings of the Imams, especially as contained in the *Nahj al-balāghah* by the first Imam 'Alī, the *ishrāqī* wisdom of Suhrawardī which contains in itself aspects of ancient Persian and Hermetic doctrines, the teachings of the earlier Sufis, especially the gnostic doctrines of Ibn 'Arabī, and the heritage of the Greek philosophers. It is, therefore, not too surprising if many of the treatises on *ḥikmat* begin with logic and end with ecstasy experienced in the catharsis (*tajrīd*) and illumination of the intellect. They contain as a necessary basis some preparation in logic which they share with the Peripatetics (*mashshā'ūn*), but instead of remaining bound to the plane of reason they use this logic as a springboard for their flight into the heaven of gnosis.

The group of sages who between the death of Ibn Rushd, the so-called terminating point of Islamic philosophy, and the Safavids prepared the ground for the intellectual revival of the school of Ispahan are usually not much better known outside Persia than the Safavid sages themselves. They include a series of philosophers and scientists like Khwājah Naṣīr al-Dīn Ṭūsī, better known in the Western world as a scientist then a philosopher and theologian, Quṭb al-Dīn Rāzī, Mīr Sayyid Sharīf Jurjānī, Jalāl al-Dīn Dawānī, and Ibn Turkah Iṣpahānī,[12] all of whom sought to reconstruct Muslim intellectual life through a gnostic interpretation of the writings of Ibn Sīnā, Suhrawardī, and the Sufis, and who carried further the attempt already begun by al-Fārābī, extended by Ibn Sīnā in his Quranic commentaries, and carried a step further by Suhrawardī, to correlate faith (*īmān*) with philosophy.[13] The precursors of the Safavid sages include also a series of pure gnostics, both Shi'ah and Sunnī, although this distinction is not essential in Sufism, who spread the doctrines of Ibn 'Arabī, the Andalusian sage and the formulator of gnostic doctrines in Islam in the Eastern lands of Islam.[14] These Sufis include Ṣadr al-Dīn Qunawī, Fakhr al-Dīn 'Irāqī, 'Abd al-Razzāq Kāshānī, 'Alā' al-Dawlah Simnānī,[15] 'Abd al-Raḥmān Jāmī,[16] and two others who are especially important in introducing the gnostic doctrines of ibn 'Arabī into the Shi'ah world, Ibn Abī Jumhūr and Mullā Ḥaydar 'Alī Āmulī.[17] One must also mention another great spiritual leader, Mawlānā Jalāl al-Dīn Rūmī, whose influence has extended throughout Persia during the past seven centuries.

MAJOR FIGURES OF THE SCHOOL OF ISPAHAN

To write down even the mere names and works of all the important authors of the Safavid period would in itself require a book because in nearly every field of religious science many notable figures arose during this period of great intellectual activity. In theology, jurisprudence, and related sciences it is enough to mention only a few names like that of Zayn al-Dīn ibn 'Alī ibn Aḥmad Jabā'ī (911/1505-966/1558), commonly known as the second martyr (*shahīd-i thānī*) because of his having been put to death by the Ottomans, the author of numerous treatises which still form a part of Shi'ah religious education, 'Alī ibn 'Abd al-'Alī 'Āmilī known as Muḥaqqiq-i Karakī (d. 945/1538), the author of *al-Najmiyyah* in theology and many other treatises and commentaries, the two Majlisīs, Muḥammad Taqī (1003/1594-1070/1659), the author of *Rawḍat al-Muttaqīn*, and his son Muḥammad Bāqir (1037/1628-1110/1699), the greatest of the Safavid theologians and scholars to whom we shall turn later.[18]

As for the *ḥukamā'*, those who cultivated this particular form of wisdom which they called *ḥikmat*, they include Ṣadr al-Dīn Shīrāzī, better known as Mullā Ṣadrā, to whom a separate chapter has been devoted in the present work, Sayyid Aḥmad 'Alawī, Mīr Dāmād's son-in-law and the commentator of Ibn Sīnā's *Shifā'*, Mulla Muḥmmad Bāqir Sabziwārī (d. 1090/1669), the commentator of the *Ishārāt* and the metaphysics of the *Shifā'*, and of the *Dhakhiral al-ma'āfī,* Rajab 'Alī Tabrīzī (d. 1080 ?/ 1670), a thinker with nominalist tendencies and the author of *Risāla-yi ithbāt-i wujūd,* 'Abd al-Razzāq Lāhījī (d.1071/1661), a student of Mullā Ṣadrā and author of some of the most important books of *ḥikmat* in Persian like the *Gawhar murād, Sarmāy-i īmān*, and the *Mashāriq al-ilhām,* glosses upon the commentary of Khwājah Naṣīr al-Dīn Ṭūsī upon the *Ishārāt*, and a commentary upon Suhrawardī's *Hayākil al-nūr*, and Qāḍī Sa'īd Qummī (1049/1640-1103 ?/1692), a gnostic and theologian, the author of the *Arba'īnāt, Kilīd-i bihisht*, and a commentary upon the *Athulujiyyā* attributed to Aristotle but now known to be a paraphrasis of the *Enneads* of Plotinus.

In addition to these authors, there are a few other major figures about whom we have chosen to speak somewhat more fully hoping that in this way we can depict the various aspects of the intellectual life of the Safavid period. These figures include Shaykh Bahā' al-Dīn 'Āmilī, Mīr Dāmād,[19] perhaps the central figures in the School of Ispahan, Mīr Abu'l-Qāsim Findiriskī, Mullā Muḥsin Fayḍ Kāshī, and the second Majlisī whom we have already mentioned.

If space had allowed, we would have also considered the purely Sufi writings such as the commentary upon the *Gulshan-i rāz* by Muḥammad Lāhījī, which is one of the best books on Sufism in Persian, and the works by the masters of other Sufi orders such as the *Tuḥfā-yi 'abbāsī* by the *dhahabī* Shaykh, Shaykh Mu'adhdhin Khurāsānī.

Shaīkh Bahā' al-Dīn 'Āmilī.—The most colourful figure of the Safavid period was without doubt Bahā' al-Dīn 'Āmilī, better known as Shaykh-i Bahā'ī.[20] His father was the leader of the Shi'ah community of 'Āmil and a student of Shahīd-i Thānī. After his teacher's death in 966/ 1559, he set out with his son towards Persia. Bahā' al-Dīn, who was born in Baalbek in 953/1546, was then only thirteen years old and well qualified to master the Persian language. In Persia he continued his studies in the religious sciences, poetry, and *ḥikmat* and soon became the leading scholar of his day and the *Shaykh al-Islām* of Ispahan. Despite his nearness to the court and necessary participation in worldly life he was a gnostic and spent many of the last years of his life travelling with the dervishes and visiting various Sufi masters. He finally passed away in 1030/1622 while returning from the *ḥajj.*[21]

Shaykh Bahā' al-Dīn was the leading theologian and jurist of his time and the leader of the *'ulamā'* of Ispahan. He was at the same time an outstanding Sufi, one of the best of the Safawid poets who revived the

'Irāqī style and wrote poetry in the tradition of Rūmī and Ḥāfiẓ, the leading architect of the Safavid period, whose masterpieces such as the Shāh mosque of Ispahan still stand among the summits of Muslim architecture,[22] and the greatest mathematician and astronomer of his period.

In an age when the theologians, jurists, *ḥakīms,* natural historians, sophists, logicians, and Sufis were well-marked groups, sometimes in external conflict with one another, Shaykh-i Bahā'ī was respected by all these groups, from the wandering dervishes, the *qalandars,* to the court *'ulamā'* each of which considered the Shaykh its own. His genius lay precisely in showing the nothingness of all sciences before divine gnosis, while at the same time having a mastery of each science. Yet each of Shaykh-i Bahā'ī's writings has become a standard source of reference in its own field. Some of his important works include *Jāmi'-i 'abbāsī* on jurisprudence in Persian; *Fawā'id al-ṣamadiyyah* on Arabic grammar which is still in wide use; a treatise on algebra, the *Khulāsah fi'l-ḥisāb*;[23] several treatises on astronomy including the *Tashrīḥ al-aflāk*; a treatise on the astrolabe, *'Urwat al-wuthqā*; general Quranic commentaries; many works on various aspects of the *Sharī'ah*; the *Kashkūl,* a collection of Arabic and Persian writings which ranks among the most famous Sufi works; and a series of *mathnawīs* such as *Bread and Sweet, Cat and Mouse, Milk and Sugar,* and the *Ṭūṭī-nāmah.*[24]

It is especially in the didactic poems, the *mathnawīs,* that the particular genius of Shaykh-i Bahā'ī for expressing sublime truths in simple language and in witty anecotes becomes manifest. In these poems his spirit is very similar to that of Mawlānā Jalāl al-Dīn Rūmī whom he follows in spirit as well as in form. In the long poem the *Cat and the Mouse* in which the cat symbolizes exoteric and formal knowledge and the mouse esotericism, the theme is the danger of hypocrisy which the exoteric view always faces and the necessity in the religious and social structure for esoteric knowledge. Shaykh-i Bahā'ī also emphasizes throughout the work the supremacy of intellectual intuition over discursive knowledge. As an example we mention below the story of a Mu'tazilite and a Sufi who appears in the guise of a madman named Buhlūl.

During the reign of one of the caliphs, a Mu'tazilite was chosen as the imam of a mosque. One day Buhlūl entered the mosque with a brick hidden under his dress and joined the congregation after the prayers to listen to the imam's sermon. The imam in the Mu'tazilite fashion mentioned that Satan is not harmed in hell because he is made of fire and since a thing cannot harm its own kind, the fire of hell cannot harm him.

Upon hearing this, Buhlūl became infuriated but held back his anger. The imam continued his sermon by saying that both good and evil are by divine consent. Again Buhlūl became angry but once again succeeded in remaining quiet. The imam added that on the Day of Judgment man would be actually able to see God. Upon hearing this, Buhlūl took out the brick from under his dress, threw it at the imam breaking his head and ran away. The caliph raging with fury was about to call for Buhlūl when Buhlūl himself walked into the palace and without any greetings sat at the head of the court. The caliph asked him with great anger as to why he has attacked the imam. Buhlūl answered by pleading to the caliph to give him permission to explain how by his act he had done nothing discourteous, and when given the permission addressed the bleeding imam and said that since according to his own words a thing cannot harm its own kind, a brick cannot harm the imam's head since both are made of clay. Futhermore, he asked the imam if he had felt any pain upon being hit on the head and if he could see the pain. Upon getting the reply that the imam did not see the pain, Buhlūl asked how could a man unable to see pain, a creation of God, see the Creator. Finally, Buhlūl added that since all acts are done through divine consent, God must have given consent to his throwing the brick and so the imam should not complain of an act to which God has consented. Upon hearing this, the imam, the symbol of rationalism, had to remain silent before Buhlūl, the symbol of intellectual intuition.[25]

The writings of Shaykh-i Bahā'i are also replete with passages about the nothingness of all human knowledge as against divine gnosis. For example, in the poem *Nān wa ḥalwā* (Bread and Sweet) he says:

Formal science is nothing but altercation;
It results in neither intoxication[26] nor contemplation.
It continually brings congelation to man's nature;
What's more, Mawlawī[27] does not believe in it.
If someone tells thee that of thy life,
There remains with certainty but a week,
Thou in this one week will busy thyself
With which science, O accomplished man!
There is no science but the science of love,[28]
The rest is the deception of the wretched Satan.
There is no science but the Quranic commentary and *Ḥadīth,*
The rest is the deception of the perverse Satan.
The mysteries will never become known to thee,
If thou hast for student a hundred Fakhr-i Rāzī's.[29]
All who do not love the face of the Beautiful
The saddle and the rein are appropriate for them.[30]

That is, he who does not have love for the Friend,
Bring for him the saddle and the headstall.[31]
He who has not fallen in love with his beautiful Face,
Erase his name from the tablet of humanity.
A breast that is empty of the love of the Beautiful,
Is an old leather bag full of bones.
A breast if devoid of the Beloved,
Is not a breast but an old chest.
A heart which is empty of the love of that Beauty,
Count it as a stone with which the Devil cleans himself.
These sciences, these forms and imaginings,
Are the excrements of Satan upon that stone.
If thou allowest other than the science of love in thy heart,
Thou wilt be giving Satan the stone to clean himself.
Be ashamed of thyself, O villain!
That thou carriest the Devil's cleaning stone in thy pocket.
Wash the tablet of the heart from the Devil's excrement;
O teacher!, give also the lesson of love.
How long wilt thou teach the wisdom of the Greeks?
Learn also the wisdom of those who have faith.[32]
How long with this jurisprudence and baseless theology,
Wilt thou empty thy brain? O exuberant one!,
Thy life is spent in discussing conjugation and syntax,
Learn also a few words about the principles of love.
Illuminate thy heart with resplendent lights,
How long wilt thou lick the bowl of Avicenna?
The Lord of the universe, the King of this world and the next[33]
Called the left-over of Aristotle and Avicenna,
When has the illuminated Prophet called it a remedy?
Go rip thy breast in a hundred places,
And clear thy heart of all these stains.[34]

Not only does Shaykh-i Bahā'ī suggest that man should not busy himself solely with formal science and that he should seek to reach the divine gnosis hidden in the revelation, but he also reminds man that he should not become so accustomed to this world as to forget his original home. It has been a constant theme of the gnostics throughout the ages that the spiritual man being a stranger in this world must take the perilous journey to return to his original abode.[35] In the same *Nān wa ḥalwā,* while commenting upon the Prophet's saying: "The love of the country comes from faith", he writes:[36]

"This country is not Egypt, Iraq, or Syria,
Ir is a city which has no name.
Since all these countries belong to this world,
The noble man will never praise them.
The love of this world is the source of all evil,
And from evil comes the loss of faith.
Happy is the person who, through divine guidance,
Is led in the direction of that nameless city.
O son thou art a stranger in these countries;
How wretched art thou to have become accustomed to it!
Thou hast remained so long in the city of the body,
That thou hast completely forgotten thy own country.
Turn away from the body and gladden thy soul,
And remember thy original home.
How long wilt thou, O victorious falcon!
Remain away from the sphere of the spirit?
It is a shame for thee, O artful one!
To shed thy feathers in this ruin.
How long, O hoopoe of the city of Saba![37]
Wilt thou remain in estrangement with feet tied?
Seek to untie the cords from they feet,
And fly where 'there is no space.' "[38]

Shaykh-i Bahā'ī was one of those rare falcons who, while outwardly in the midst of this world, had flown to the "land of nowhere." He did not write in the technical sense so much about *ḥikmat* as Mīr Dāmād or Mullā Muḥsin Fayḍ did, but he reached such a degree of spiritual realization above and beyond theoretical formulations that all of his writings are spiritually precious. Even his compositions in the various religious and natural sciences bear the perfume of his spirituality. His writings present a balance between the exoteric and the esoteric, the metaphysical and the cosmological, which serves as an example of what the relation between the various aspects of a tradition might be and could be when the principial integrating influence of gnosis is present.

Mīr Dāmād.—One of the most influential figures of the Safavid school was Muḥammad Bāqir Dāmād, better known as Mīr Dāmād. He and his pupil, Mullā Ṣadrā, must be considered to be the greatest *ḥakīms* of the period. Being the grandson of Muḥaqqiq-i Karakī and descendant of a distinguished Shi'ah family, Mīr Dāmād received the best education possible in all branches of religious learning. His most famous teacher was Shaykh Ḥusayn ibn 'Abd al-Ṣamad 'Āmilī, the father of Shaykh-i Bahā'ī, who later on became his most intimate friend and companion at the Safavid Court.[39] Mīr Dāmād soon became a leading authority on *Kalām, ḥikmat, fiqh* and even in the occult and natural sciences.[40] In Ispahan he attracted numerous students to himself. His most famous disciples were Mullā Ṣadrā, Sayyid Aḥmad 'Alawī, the commentator of the *Shifā',* Mullā Khalīl Qazwīnī whose commentary upon the *Uṣūl al-kāfi* is very well known in Persia, and Quṭb al-Dīn Ashkiwarī, the author of a universal sacred history and several philosophical and gnostic treatises.[41] Mīr Dāmād more than anyone else was responsible for the revivification of Ibn Sīnā's philosophy and *ishrāqī* wisdom within the context of Shi'ism and for laying the ground for the monumental work of Mullā Ṣadrā. Mīr Dāmād did much to revive what he referred to as the Yamanī wisdom (*falsafa-yi yamanī*), the wisdom of the prophets, in contrast to the more rationalistic philosophy of the Greeks.[42] He has been entitled the Third Teacher (*Mu'allim-i thālith)* after Aristotle and Fārābī.

The writings of Mīr Dāmād, both in Arabic and Persian, many of which are incomplete, are written in a very obstruse style which adds to the difficulty of understanding their contents. These writings include several treatises on *Kalām*; works on *fiqh* such as *Shāri' al-najāt; al-Ufuq al-mubīn* on Being, time, and eternity; *al-Ṣirāṭ al-mustaqīm* on the relation between the created and the eternal; *Taqwīm al-īmān* on Being, creation, and God's knowledge; several other major treatises on *ḥikmat* including the *Qabasāt,*[43] *Taqdīsāt, Jadhawāt,* and *Sidrat al-muntahā*;[44] several Quranic commentaries such as *Amānat-i ilāhī*; commentaries upon the *Istibṣār* of Khwājah Naṣīr al-Dīn Ṭūsī and the metaphysics of the *Shifā*'; the *Khalsat al-malakūt* on gnosis;[45] and a collection of poems in Persian and Arabic including the *Mashāriq al-anwār*, written under the pen name, *Ishrāq*. After a life-time spent in writing, teaching, and reading the Quran to which he was much devoted, and having prepared the ground for the whole group of sages, especially Mullā Ṣadrā who were to carry his ideas to their ultimate perfection, Mīr Dāmād died on the way between Najaf and Karbalā' in Iraq in 1041/1631.

The thought of Mīr Dāmād is marked by two features which distinguish him from the other *ḥakīms* of the period, the first the organization of his treatises and the second the notion of eternal creation, *ḥudūth-i dahrī*, which is the central and ever-recurring theme in his writings. As for the organization of his works, such as the *Qabasāt* and *Taqdīsāt*, it differs for the most part from that of the traditional Muslim books on philosophy and *ḥikmat* which usually begin with logic and then proceed to natural philosophy (*ṭabī'iyyāt*), mathematics (*riyāḍiyyāt*), and theology (*ilāhiyyāt*).[46] For example, in the *Qabasāt* the ten chapters of the book concern the various meanings of creation and the divisions of being, kinds of anteriority, multiplicity, appeal to the Quran and the *Ḥadīth*, nature, time, and motion, criticism of logic, divine omnipotence, intellectual substances, chain of Being, and finally predestination.[47]

The second marked feature of Mīr Dāmād's exposition of *ḥikmat* concerns the notion of time. It is well known that the question whether the world is created (*ḥādith*) or eternal (*qadīm*) has been one of the major points of dispute between the philosophers and theologians in both Islam and Christianity as well as among the Greeks.[48] Mīr Dāmād seeks a solution to this question by dividing reality into three categories: *zamān* or time, *dahr* and *sarmad;* the latter two are kinds of eternity. This division is ontological and not just logical or theoretical.[49]

The Divine Essence or ipseity (*Dhāt*) is above all distinctions and qualities; yet it is also the source of the Divine Names and Attributes which are both one with the Essence and yet distinct from It. This immutable relation between the Essence and the Attributes, which cannot be changed from either side, the Attributes being a necessary determination (*ta'ayyun*) of the Essence to Itself by Itself, Mīr Dāmād called *sarmad*. It is an eternity in the absolute sense, above all contingencies. The Names and Attributes, which are the principles of the archetypes, Platonic ideas, or the lords of the species (*rabb al-naw'*) as the *ishrāqīs* call them, in turn generate the world of change. They are the immutable intelligences of this world, and each species in this world is a theurgy (*ṭilism*) for its archetype. The relation between the immutable archetypes and the world of change is like the reflection of the moon in a stream of water in which the image of the moon remains unchanged while the substance in which it is reflected, i.e. water, flows on continually. This relation between the immutable and the changing, Mīr Dāmād calls *dahr*. Finally, the relation between one change and another is called time (*zamān*), in the sense of quantity and measure of change as Aristotle had already described it.[50]

Since this world was brought into being through the intermediate world of the archetypes, its creation is *dahrī* not *zamānī*, i.e. the world was not created in a time which existed before the world came into being but with respect to a *dahr* which stands above the world.[51] The creation of this world is, therefore, *ḥudūth-i dahrī, ibdā'*, and *ikhtirā'* and not *ḥudūth-i'zamānī, waḍ'*, and *takwīn* Time has a reality in its own plane of being, but in the world of *dahr*, the world of the archetypes, time does not even exist. Moreover, the changing physical world (*'ālam-i jismānī)* depends for its existence upon non-existence (*'adam*) in the world of the archetypes. While it exists in time (*zamān*), it is non-existent in *dahr* and has no share in the angelic mode of being, proper to the world of *dahr*, of which it is not more than a coagulation. Likewise, the world of *dahr,* of the archetypes, is non-existent in the Divine Essence, in the world of *sarmad* (the eternal world). In the Divine Essence (*Dhāt*) there is neither *dahr* nor *zamān*, neither archetype nor body; God is lone in His majesty.[52] Yet, *dahr* exists on its own level and *zamān* on its own. *Sarmad* is the cause of *dahr* and *dahr* the cause of *zamān*,[53] so that ultimately the Divine Essence is the cause of all things, while in its essence nothing may even be said to exist.

The *Jadhawāt,* the contents of which we will now briefly survey, is one of the works in which Mīr Dāmād presents the complete cycle of his metaphysical ideas combined as usual with the Quranic text, the *Ḥadīth*, and his own verse.[54] In the first *jadhwah* or particle of fire, of which the word *jadhawāt* is the plural, Mīr Dāmād divides the "book of Divine existence", of the chain of Being, into two parts, one in which there is an effusion or theophany (*tajallī*) away from the Divine Essence and the other in which there is a return to the Origin: the first extending from the Divine Essence to prime matter of *hylé* and the other from the *hylé* back to the origin of all existence. Moreover, each chain is divided into a longitudinal (*ṭūlī*) order and a latitudinal (*'arḍī*) order.[55] The longitudinal order of the chain of effusion includes five essential degrees:

1. The degree of pure intelligences, the victorial lights (*anwār-i qāhirah*) the first member of which is the Universal Intellect (*'aql-i kull*), i.e. the first light to issue forth from the Light of lights (*nūr al-anwār*).
2. The degree of heavenly souls (*nufūs-i falakiyyah*), the governing lights (*anwār-i mudabbirah*), the first member of which governing the first heaven is called the universal soul (*nafs-i kull*).
3. The degree of the natural souls (*nufūs-i munṭabi'ah*) and the archetypes of the heavens, the planets, the four natures, the elements, and compounds.[56]
4. The degree of bodily form (*ṣūrat-i jismiyyah*), i.e. the Aristotelian form, which is an extended substance and is of one species.
5. The degree of *hylé*, from the matter of the highest heaven to that of the world of generation and corruption.[57]

   As for the longitudinal order of the chain of return to the Divine Essence, it too includes five stages:

1. The degree of the absolute body (*jism-i muṭlaq*) and bodies comprising the elements and the heavens.
2. The degree of composed bodies which come into being from the combination of the elements and have a species of their own, e.g. minerals.

3. The degree of plants possessing the vegetative soul.
4. The degree of animal possessing the animal soul.[58]
5. The degree of men possessing the rational soul which is of the same substance as the intelligences of the descending chain, above both of which there is nothing but the Truth (*Ḥaqq*) Itself.[59]

Each of these degrees, both in the descending and the ascending chains, have their several members that constitute the latitudinal extension of each degree.

The world of the intelligences (*mujarradāt*) is called the world of the invisible (*ghayb*), or command (*amr*), or *malakūt*, or intellect (*'aql*), or life (*ḥayāt*), or light (*nūr*), while the world of bodies is called the world of creation (*khalq*), visible (*shahādat),* or dominion *(mulk),* or darkness (*ẓulamāt*). Man's nature is composed of these two worlds in such a way that he contains the whole world in himself; he is the micrososm as the world is the macrocosm. His intellect is like the sun, his soul like the moon, and his body like the earth; and as is the case with the heavens, man can also have an inner eclipse, i.e., the earth of his body can prevent the light of the sun of the intellect from shining upon the moon of the soul. The purpose of the two chains of descent and ascent is to bring into being man, who contains both chains within himself and who can, therefore, ascend to heaven as well as descend to the lowest depths of existence.

The macrocosm is a conscious being whose head is the highest heaven, whose heart is the sun, and whose other organs correspond with those of man. It is compared symbolically to a man whose head is pointed towards the North Pole, the right side towards the west, the face towards heaven, the feet towards the south, and the left side towards the east.

The totality of these degrees, the macrocosm and the microcosm together, is the Book of God, in which each being is a word or rather a letter.[60] These words and letters are written by the Divine Pen (*Qalam*) which symbolizes the Intellect. The Pen writes the truth of things upon the human soul which is called the *ispahbadi* light (*nūr-i ispahbadī*). More specifically, the Pen writes the truth of things upon the soul of the Prophet who in turn "writes" the knowledge of things upons the soul of man and, through the intelligences, upon the pages of creation and existence. The intelligences are not limited to the nine heavens, but as the *ishrāqīs* have asserted, in number they equal the fixed stars in addition to the heavens and extend all the way down to the heaven of the moon. The intelligence of this heaven is called "the giver of forms" (*wāhib al-ṣuwar*) or the Active Intellect (*'aql-i fa''āl*) which gives being as well as form to the sublunary region.[61]

The heaven of the fixed stars is the meeting place of the corporeal and intellectual lights, the boundary between formal and formless manifestation. This heaven has its own soul and intelligence but, in addition, each star in it is also a possessor of an intelligence and a soul proper to itself. As to the other heavens, they also have their general intelligence and soul as well as particular intelligences and souls all of which cast their illuminations upon the sublunary region. The intelligence of the heaven of the sun is Gabriel whose grace is spread throughout the heavens and the earth.

Having considered the chain of Being, Mīr Dāmād turns to a discussion of unity (*tawḥīd*) starting from "there is no divinity but God" (*la ilāha illa'Llāh)* to "there is no being but He and no truth but He" (*lāmawjūdun illā Huwa wa la ḥaqqun illā Huwa*).[62] For the real gnostic every being is nothing but Being. Mīr Dāmād compares the relation of Being to existence with that of the number one to other numbers, which runs through all numbers without entering into them, which relation neither the soul not the intellect can understand, yet its effect is felt everywhere.[63] The Divine Being by His essential unity encompasses all things; His unity is before, with, and after both *dahr* and *zamān*. His unity before *dahr* is the unity of His command; with *dahr*, the unity of the Universal Intellect; after *dahr*, the unity of the Universal Soul, unity with time (*zamān*), and unity of the elements and compounds.

As for the generation of multiplicity from unity, Mīr Dāmād rejects the Peripatetic view of authors such as Ibn Sīnā who consider that the First Intellect brings multiplicity into being by the three relationships possible for it: necessity by something other than itself, the intellection of the Divine Essence, and the intellection of its own essence. For Mīr Dāmād just as the number of intelligences is unlimited so are their possible relationships beyond the number determined by the Peripatetics.[64] Likewise, the intelligences have a great many illuminations and effusions beyond the categories set forth by the Aristotelians, one intelligence being victorial (*qāhir*) and the other passive and receptive (*maqhūr*). Each heaven as well as each body, simple or composed, has its archetype (*rabb al-naw'*) in the world of Divine Command (*'ālam-i amr*) which is changeless and is to its species what the soul of man is to his body.

Between the world of intelligences and the physical world there is an intermediary world, the so-called eighth climate which Mīr Dāmād, following the ancient *ishrāqī* sages calls *hūrqalyā*,[65] the world of separated imagination (*khayāl-i munfaṣil*), or the purgatory (*barzakh*). Human imagination is itself regarded as a gulf extending from this vast cosmic ocean. This world contains the forms of Platonic ideas of all physical bodies without being in a specific place. The mythical cities of Jābulqā and Jābursā[66] are located in it, and bodily resurrection on the Last Day, miracles, and the passage of great distances in a short time, all take place in this intermediary world which is a bridge to be crossed before reaching the purely spiritual world.

In order to cross this bridge and make the return journey through the ascending chain, man must become familiar with the Divine Names, especially the Great Name (*ism-i a'ẓam*) which contains all the others. All the prophets and saints derive their being from these Names, and the creatures are their effects. The spiritual world is called the world of invocation (*'ālam-i tasbīḥ*) because the realities of that world are immersed in the Divine Names. Man, therefore, can regain that world only by invoking the Names and becoming unified with them.[67] The gnostic who has achieved this end sees the whole world through the intelligible world; in fact, he sees nothing outside the Divine. As long as man lives in this world, no matter how much he has separated his soul from his body and achieved *catharsis (tajrīd)*, he is still in time and space. It is only when he dies and leaves the world of darkness for that of light that he becomes completely free from the condition of terrestrial existence, of *zamān*, and it is only then that he enters into sempiternity (*dahr*).

The inner constitution of man forms a bridge between the worlds of time and eternity, the sensible and the intelligible. Man possesses four degrees of perception: sensation (*iḥsās*), imagination (*takhayyul*), apprehension (*tawahhum*), and intellection (*ta'aqqul*), the degrees which stretch between the visible world and the invisible world. The soul (*nafs*) is the link between these two worlds; on the one hand, it abstracts perceptions from the sensible world and, on the other, receives the illumination of the intelligible world which it clothes in the forms of the sensible, i.e., words and names which are the external dress of truths.[68]

Mīr Dāmād echoes earlier Sufi and Pythagorean doctrines in assigning a particular significance to the numerical symbolism of letters. He writes: "The world of letters corresponds to the world of numbers, and the world of numbers to the world of Being, and the proportion of the world of letters to the proportion of the world of numbers and the proportion of the world of numbers to the combinations and mixtures of the world of Being."[69] He calls the science of the properties of letters and their combination divine medicine and says that letters have come into being from the conjunction of planets with the signs of the Zodiac, for example *alif* has come into being by Mars crossing the first degree of Aries. He establishes correspondence between the twenty-eight letters of the

Arabic alphabet and the equal number of the stations of the moon and works out this correspondence in great detail.[70]

In establishing a relation between numbers, letters of the alphabet, and the heavens, Mīr Dāmād, like many sages before him, seeks to point out the common ground between the book of revelation and the book of nature, as well as the relation between the sensible world and the intelligible world. In his writings it is quite clear that both metaphysics and cosmology are to be found in the esoteric (*bāṭinī*) meanings of the Quran and that through the understanding of the symbolism of letters and numbers and the sapiential exegeses of sacred books one can come to know not only the Quran which corresponds to the world of creation, the *Qur'ān-i tadwīnī*, but also the Quran which is the archetype of all manifestation, the *Qur'ān-i takwīnī*, i.e. the *logos* or the Reality of Muḥammad (al-*ḥaqīqat al-Muḥammadiyyah*).

Mīr Abu'l-Qāsim Findiriskī—The third of the famous triumvirate of sages from Ispahan,[71] Mīr Findiriskī, spent much of his life travelling outside Persia, especially in India where he was highly respected by most of the princes and where he made the acquaintance of many Hindu sages. He became well acquainted with Hinduism and even wrote a commentary upon the Persian translation of the *Yoga Vasiṣtha* by Niẓām al-Dīn Pānīpatī, which is one of the major works on Hinduism in Persian. In the Muslim sciences he was a master in philosophy (*ḥikmat*), mathematics, and medicine, and taught the *Shifā'* and the *Qānūn* of Ibn Sīnā in Ispahan where he dies in 1050/1640.

The most interesting aspect of Mīr Findiriskī's life is his complete detachment, even externally, from the world. As a Sufi, in spite of his having advanced very far upon the Path and having reached the state of pure contemplation and illumination, he mingled with the common people and wore the coarsest wool, and yet he was one of the most respected men in the Safavid Court.[72] His manner resembled that of the Hindu yogis with whom he had had so much contact. He was a real man among men and one of the most striking Sufis of his time. While completely detached from the world and even from purely formal learning, he composed several impotant treatises including one on motion (*al-ḥa rakah*), another on the arts and sciences in society (*ṣanā'iyyah*), the book on Yoga already mentioned, *Uṣūl al-fuṣūl* on Hindu wisdom, and a history of the Safavids. Moreover, he, like Mīr Dāmād and Shaykh-i Bahā'ī, was an accomplished poet showing the development in him of the gnostic element which is the only possible common ground between traditional philosophy and poetry. The most famous of his poems is a *qaṣīdah*, based upon that of Nāṣir ibn Khūsraw Dihlawī, which is one of the best known poems on *ḥikmat* in Persian. It has been taught and commented upon many times since its composition, the more famous commentaries on it being those of Muḥammad Ṣāliḥ Khalkhālī and Ḥakīm 'Abbās Dārābī. Because of the importance of this poem in summarizing some of the basic elements of *ḥikmat* as it was revived during the Safavid period, the English translation of some of the verses is given below.

Heaven with these stars is clear, pleasing and beautiful;
Whatever is there above it a form.[73]
The form below, if by the ladder of gnosis
Is trodden upward, becomes the same as its principle.
No outward apprehension can understand this saying,
Whether it be that of an Abū Naṣr or of an Abū 'Alī Sīnā.[74]
If life were not an accident under this ancient heaven,
These bodies would be forever alive and erect.
But whatever is an accident must first have a substance;
The intellect is our loquacious witness to this claim.
If one can obtain these qualities[75] from the sun,
The sun is itself light and shine upon all things while keeping its unity.
The intellectual form which is endless and immortal
With or without all things is a totality and unity.
Of the life of the universe, I say that if thou knowest the relation of the soul and the body,
In the heart of every particle, then life becomes both evident and hidden.
God has placed seven heavens above us,
And seven others on the other side of the world in the life to come.
Thou canst reach heaven by their means,
Be true and walk the straight path for there is no falsehood there.
He who worships the world, the door of heaven will never open to him,
The doors will not open even if he stands before them.
He who is annihilated in Him finds eternal life;
He who is busy with himself, his affair is doubtless a failure.
The jewel is hidden in the mysteries of the ancient sages,
Only he who is wise can discover the meaning of these mysteries.
Pass beyond these words for they are forsaken by the people of the world;
Find the Truth and tread its path, if thou art righteous.
Whatever is outside thy essence will do thee no good,

Make thyself harmonious whether it be today or tomorrow.
The Being that is pure has no limit or description;
It is neither outside of us, nor with us, nor without us.
A beautiful thought is only beneficial when combined with virtuous deeds;
A thought with virtuous action is efficient and beautiful.
To talk of goodness is not like doing good,
The name of sweetmeat on the tongue is not like sweetmeat itself....
In this world and the next, with the world and without it,
We can say all these of Him, yet He is above all that.
The intellect is a ship, passion a whirlpool, and knowledge the mast,
God is the shore and the whole cosmos the sea.
The shore is reached with certainty; the sea of the possible has become the necessary....[76]
How good it would be if the sages before us had said everything completely,
So that the opposition of those who are not complete[77] would be removed.
Desire keeps the soul in bondage in this world;
While thou hast desire, thy feet are tied.
Each wish in this world is followed by another wish;
The wish must be sought beyond which there is none other."

Mīr Findiriskī occupied himself not only with metaphysics and the theoretical sciences but also with the sciences of society, of traditional society in which the social structure itself has a directly based on metaphysical principles. In his treatise on arts and sciences (*ṣanā'iyyah*),[78] he distinguishes between twelve vocations or arts and sciences in society depending upon the subject with which each one deals. The subjects of the arts and sciences he enumerates are as follows: (i) The subject is universal and the discussion concerns knowledge as well as action from both of which there comes only good; (ii) the subject is universal and the discussion concerns both knowledge and action from both of which there comes evil; (iii) the subject is universal and the discussion concerns knowledge from which there comes only good; (iv) the subject is universal and the discussion concerns knowledge from which there comes only evil; (v) the subject is universal and the discussion concerns action from which there comes only good; and (vi) the subject is universal and the discussion concerns action from which there comes only evil. To this list Mīr Findiriskī adds a series of arts and sciences the subject of which is no longer universal. These include (vii) those arts and sciences the subject of which is particular and the discussion concerns knowledge and action from which there comes only good; (viii) the subject is particular and the discussion concerns knowledge and action from which there comes evil; (ix) the subject is particular and the discussion concerns only knowledge from which there comes only good; (x) the subject is particular and the discussion concerns only knowledge from which there comes evil; (xi) the subject is particular and the discussion concerns only action from which there comes only good; and, finally, (xii) the subject is particular and the discussion concerns only action from which there comes evil.[79]

The first of the twelve categories listed above concerns the prophets, saints, and sages, the most exalted of men, who maintain the order of the universe, there being a prophet for each cycle of history and each people. The second concerns those who oppose the prophets and sages, those who are the deniers of truth, and the sophists and agnostics who are the lowest of men. The third class consists of those who support Gnosis and *ḥikmaṭ* The fourth class is the opposite of the third, i.e., that of the enemies of *ḥikmat* and theology, consistingof those who, seeking differences in the expressions of the various sages, have denied the one truth which lies behind this diversity.[80] The fifth category is that of the jurists (*fuqahā'*) who cultivate the practical sciences, and the sixth is that of their opposites like Mazdak,[81] who concern themselves only with their bodies and remain oblivious of the order of both this world and the next.

The last six categories concern particular arts and sciences. The first of them, or the seventh in our list, is that of professionals in particular arts, like physicians, engineers, and astronomers; and the eighth is that of their opposites, i.e., those who misuse each of these arts. The ninth category is like the particular sense of an organ of the body and concerns people who have only a theoretical knowledge of various arts and sciences, like music, medicine, or the principles of jurisprudence. The tenth is its opposite and in it are included those who make a false claim to know these sciences theoretically. The eleventh category concerns arts and sciences which are limited to a particular subject, and the twelfth its opposite which concerns the rejection of these same arts and sciences.

In this classification we can already see the hierarchic structure of society at the top of which stand the prophets and saints in whom knowledge and action are combined, below them the *ḥukamā'* and the theologians, them those concerned with practical arts and the particular sciences. The nobility of a vocation in each case depends upon the nobility of the subject-matter treated. Likewise, the degree of degradation of a person or group depends upon the truth that has been denied; the higher the degree of a truth, the baser is he who denies it. The categories outlined by Mīr Findiriskī reflect the hierarchy within *ḥikmat* itself. In both cases the religious sciences like theology are considered to stand above the natural sciences, *ḥikmat* above theology, and the wisdom of the prophets and saints above all the other categories.

Mullā Muḥsin Fayḍ Kāshānī.—Muḥammad ibn Shāh Murtaḍa ibn Shāh Maḥmūd, better known as Mullā Muḥsin or Fayḍ-i Kāshānī, is after Mullā Ṣadrā, the most famous of the sages of the generation following that of Mīr Dāmād, Shaykh-i Bahā'ī, and Mīr Findiriskī. Born in Kashan in 1007/1600, he spent some years at Qum and then came to Shiraz to complete his studies with Mullā Ṣadrā whose daughter he later married. He also studied with Mīr Dāmād and Shaykh-i Bahā'ī but was more closely associated with Mullā Ṣadrā. Just as Mīr Dāmād produced a series of outstanding students, the best known of whom was Mullā Ṣadrā—the greatest of the Safavid *ḥakīms* to whom we shall turn in the next chapter—Mullā Ṣadrā in turn produced a galaxy of famous students among whom Fayḍ-i Kāshānī and Mullā 'Abd al-Razzāq Lāhījī, both his sons-in-law, are the most important.[82]

The genius of Mullā Ṣadrā consisted largely in unifying the three perspectives of formal revelation or *shar'*, purification of the soul leading to illumination (*kashf*), and rational demonstration (*falsafah*) into a single universal vision in which all these paths lead to the same truth. All of his followers sought to preserve the unity established by their master, each emphasizing some one aspect of it. For example, later sages like Qāḍī Sa'īd Qummī, Mullā 'Alī Nūrī, and Āqā 'Alī Zunūzī sought to correlate revelation and reason, and Āqā Muḥammad Bīdābādī and Āqā Muḥammad Riḍā' Qumsha'ī reason and gnosis. Others continued the path trodden by Mullā Ṣadrā himself and emphasized the harmony of all the three paths mentioned above. Mullā Muḥsin Fayḍ and Ḥājjī Mullā Hādī Sabziwārī, a the most famous Persian thinker of the last century, belong to this last group. Mullā Muḥsin's writings display a harmonious integration of reason, revelation, and gnosis with lesser emphasis upon reason. He succeeded perhaps more than anyone else in the Shi'ah world to bring about a complete harmony between Law and spiritual life, *Sharī'ah* and *Ṭarīqah.*

In many ways Mullā Muḥsin may be considered to be a Shi'ah Ghazzālī, not only because of his preoccupation with harmonizing the exoteric and the esoteric views, but also for his treatment of a spiritualized ethics which forms the requirement for following the Path. He even rewrote the well-known *Iḥyā' 'ulūm al-dīn* of Ghazzālī under the name of *al-Maḥajjat al-bayḍā' fī iḥyā' al-iḥyā'*, substituting traditions (*aḥādīth*) from the Shi'ite sources for those from the Sunni ones given by Ghazzālī.[83]

The writings of Mullā Muḥsin both in Arabic and Persian are too numerous to mention here.[84] Among the more famous, one may name *Ḥaqq al-yaqīn; 'Ayn al-yaqīn* and *'Ilm al-yaqīn* on *ḥikmat; al-Ṣāfī, al-Wāfī*, and *al-Shāfī* on Quranic commentary and *Ḥadīth*; *Mafātiḥ al-sharāyi'* on jurisprudence, *al-Taṭhīr* on ethics; *Jalā' al-'uyūn, Zād al-sālik*, and *Kalimāt-i maknūnah* on Sufism, *Uṣūl al-ma'ārif* on *ḥikmat;* numerous treatises on the esoteric meaning of acts of worship, on various invocations, on particular sciences including astronomy; selections from and commentaries on the *Rasā'il* of the Ikhwān al-Ṣafā', the *Futūḥāt al-makkiyyah* of Ibn 'Arabī, and the *Mathnawī* of Jalāl al-Dīn Rūmī; and a large collection of poems consisting mostly of verses of Sufi inspiration. His works both in poetry and prose have remained very popular in Persia and his ethical and social teachings have attracted particular attention in the past decades.

Mullā Muḥsin's thought marks the final integration of *ḥikmat* into Shi'ism. *Ḥikmat* in Persia had been moving in this direction for many centuries from the time of al-Fārābī and Ibn Sīnā. Suhrawardī Maqtūl took the decisive step in regarding knowledge as personal illumination by the heavenly guide or "guardian angel. Mullā Ṣadrā following him made the Universal Intellect the instrument of knowledge. Mullā Muḥsin took a further step in this direction in identifying this intellect with the Shi'ah Imams, in whom the light of Muḥammad (*al-nūr al-muḥammadī*) is manifested and who are called the innocent (*ma'ṣūm*) intellects.[85] Only by union with them, with the pure intellects, can one gain ultimate knowledge.

One of the important treatises of Mullā Muḥsin, in which gnosis, *ḥikmat,* and *shar'* are blended in characteristic fashion, is the *Kalimāt-i maknūnah* written in a mixture of Arabic and Persian.[86] It treats of a complete cycle of theoretical gnosis so that its discussion gives a fair example of the totality of Mullā Muḥsin's general perspective.

The work begins by assuring the reader that there is no way of reaching the essence of the Truth because the Truth encompasses all things. Everything is Its manifestation, but only the *élite (khawāṣṣ)* know what they see. Being is like light, but since its opposite does not exist in this world as in the case of physical light which stands opposed to darkness, one cannot come to know it so easily. God is hidden because of the excess of His light; no veil can cover Him because veil is a limitation and God is above all limitations.[87] Being *is* the Truth which subsists by Itself, while everything else subsists by It. Being is not just a mental concept, the meaning of Being in the mind consisting only of a reflection of Being Itself.

The Divine Attributes and Names are identical with the Divine Essence, while in themselves they are distinct. Likewise the forms of all beings in the Divine Intellect, i.e., the quiddities or essences, the *māhiyyāt* or *al-a'yān al-thābitah,*[88] are in one respect identical with and in another distinct from the Esence. Each being subsists by one of the Divine Names and its very existence consists in the invocation of that Name. The archetypes, *al-a'yān al-thābitah,* have two aspects; on the one hand, they are the mirrors in which Truth is reflected, in which case they are hidden and Truth is manifest; and, on the other hand, Truth is the mirror in which they are reflected, in which case truth is hidden and they are manifest. These two aspects correspond also to two states of contemplation: one of the Truth (*ḥaqq*) and the other of creation (*khalq*). The perfect gnostic contemplates both mirrors; he sees the cosmos as a mirror in which the Truth is reflected, and his own essence as a mirror in which both the cosmos and theTruth are reflected. Mullā Muḥsin advises the sage to take a further step in eliminating himself also so that there remains nothing but the Truth.[89]

Mullā Muḥsin follows certain earlier Sufis in considering the world to be re-created at every instant,[90] so that its continuity is only appareant. The real continuity is "vertical", i.e., between the Truth and its manifestations, not "horizontal" and "substantial", i.e., between the parts and instances of the created world. The world is like a flowing stream which, although apparently a continuous and subsistent body, changes at every instant, each particle of it perishing at every instant and a new particle coming to take its place.

The creation of the world or the effusion of unity into multiplicity does not take place immediately but through the Divine Names, each creature being the theophany (*tajallī*) of a particular Name. The Name Allah is the supreme master (*rabb al-arbāb*) of all the names, the theophany of which is the Universal Man (*al-insān al- kāmil*). Although the stages in which creation comes into being are numerous, Mullā Muḥsin names five degrees which mark the main steps. In the first degree is the Divine Essence which is above all distinctions and determinations; in the second are the Names which are the manifestations of the Truth in the world of Divinity, *ulūhiyyah*; in the third are the Divine Acts and world of spirits which are the manifestations of the Truth in the world of Lordship, *rubūbiyyah*; in the fourth is the world of the "ideas" and imagination (*khayāl*)[91] which is the manifestation of the Truth in the world of varying forms; and in the fifth is the world of the senses which is the manifestation of the Truth in determined forms.[92] Everything in the physical world has its archetype in the world of imagination, while everything in the world of imagination has its archetype in the world of Lordship, and everything in the world of Lordship is a form of one of the Divine Names, each Name an aspect of the Divine Essence.

Man alone among creatures is able to cast aside these veils and reach the Divine Origin of things. He has a particular soul brought into being with his body, which soul is independent of matter, and also a universal soul which exists before the body and is manifested only in the spiritual *élite*. Moreover, man has a vegetative soul consisting of the faculties of attraction, repulsion, digestion, growth, and retention originating in the liver; and animal soul consisting of the faculties of the five senses originating in the heart; a sacred rational soul (*nafs-i nāṭiqa-yi qudsiyyah*) with the faculties of meditation (*fikr*) and invocation (*dhikr*); and the universal Divine Soul (*nafs-i kulliyya-yi ilāhiyyah*), not possessed by all men, with the faculty of reaching the station of annihilation (*fanā'*) in the Divine.[93]

The goal of each man should be to awaken the potential faculties within him until all the accidential obstacles are removed and he becomes identified with the Universal Man, the theophany of the supreme Name. Then he will be able to contemplate Absolute Being and thereby fulfil the purpose of all creation and sustain the whole universe.

The Universal Man is either a prophet or a saint. Absolute prophethood (*nubuwwat-i muṭlaq*) is the supreme station, the perfect "form" of unity, the first Pen, and the Pole of Poles, *quṭb al-aqṭāb*, upon which all the prophets and saints depend. The inner (*bāṭin*) dimension of this prophecy is absolute sainthood (*wilāyat-i muṭlaq*). Mullā Muḥsin identifies absolute prophethood with the Light of Muḥammad, and absolute sainthood with the light of 'Alī. The prophethood of all prophets depends upon absolute prophecy as the sainthood of all saints depends upon absolute sainthood. Prophethood began with Adam and found its completion in the Prophet Muḥammad. Sainthood will reach its completion gradually until it culminates in the twelfth Imam, the Mahdī. Absolute prophethood is the treasure of all possible perfections and the whole cosmos is the expansion and manifestation of its inner qualities.[94]

Gnosis and illumination are themselves the fruit of the tree of prophethood. Mullā Muḥsin insists that the source of *ḥikmat* was originally the sacred spirit of the prophets; this wisdom, however, was misunderstood and misinterpreted by men of the later period, i.e., the

Peripatetics and other later schools of Greek philosophy, and was revived only in the light of the revelation of the Prophet of Islam and his family. He who wishes to be initiated into it must, therefore, seek the aid of the prophets and saints and this can be achieved only by invocation and meditation and the purification of the heart. Only he who has trodden this path and become a true *ḥakīm* can be considered the real heir to the saints and the prophets.[95]

Mullā Muḥammad Bāqir Majlisī.—One cannot terminate a study of the intellectual life of the Safavid period without mentioning the two Majlisīs, father and son, especially the son Muḥammad Bāqir who stands as one of the outstanding figures of the period. The first Majlisī, Muḥammad Taqī (1003/1594-1070/1659), was one of the students of Shaykh-i Bahā'ī and an outstanding theologian and Sufi of his time.[96] His son, the second Majlisī (1037/1628-1110/1699), however, surpassed his father in fame and power and became the most dominant figure of Shi'ism. Having studied with his own father, Mulla Khalīl Qazwīnī, and Mullā Muḥsin Fayḍ, he in turn became the master of over a thousand disciples including Sayyid Ni'matallāh Jazā'irī, well known for his many writings, especially the account of his own life as a student.

The second Majlisī is especially famous for revivifying the various branches of the 'Shi'ite sciences and for assembling the writings of the earlier doctors of Shi'ism and prophetic *ḥadīths* into encyclopedias which have henceforth become the main reference for all who undertake religious education in the Shi'ah *madrasahs*. The most important and famous of these is the *Biḥār al-anwār* summarized in the *Safīnat al-biḥār* of Shaykh 'Abbās Qummī, the lithographed edition of which occupies twenty-four volumes; *Ḥaqq al-yaqīn* in *uṣūl; Ḥayāt al-qulūb*, a commentary upon the *Tadhhīb al-aḥkām* of Khwājah Naṣīr al-Dīn Ṭūsī; and the *Mir'āt al-'uqūl*, a twelve-volume commentary upon the *Uṣūl al-kāfī* of Kulaynī in which Majlisī for the only time in his writing career enters into purely intellectual (*'aqlī*) questions and treats of many essential religious subjects, especially eschatology and the conditions before the appearance of the Mahdī, from an intellectual rather than a purely "confessional" point of view.[97]

Of special interest in the religious life of Persia is Majlisī's opposition to Sufism and even the denial that his own father, the first Majlisī, was a Sufi.[98] Furthermore, supported by the court and many of the theologians and doctors, he opposed the intellectual method of the *ḥakīms* and philosophers with the result that both the Sufis and the ḥakīms fell into disgrace and had much difficulty in official religious circles. The dynasty which had begun as the extension of a Sufi order ended by opposing all Sufism and gnosis itself. It was not long after the death of the second Majlisī in fact that the Safavid dynasty itself fell before the onslaught of the Afghāns, and Ispahan, the historic as well as the symbolic centre of this period of great intellectual activity, was sacked and its libraries burnt.

CONCLUSION

This form of wisdom or *ḥikmat,* some features of which we have sought to outline here, did not die with the termination of the Safavid dynasty. In the thirteenth/eighteenth century Sufism was revived in Persia by Ma'ṣūm 'Alī Shāh and Shāh Ṭāhir Dakanī, two Ni'matallāhī masters sent by Riḍā' 'Alī Shāh from Deccan to Persia. It was persecuted for a period but began to expand with the establishment of the Qajars. Likewise, the school of *ḥikmat* continued through the students of Mullā Ṣadrā and others from one generation to another and it produced indirectly such figures as Shaykh Aḥmad Aḥsā'ī, the founder of the Shaykhī movement,[99] who was opposed to Mullā Sadrā but also Ḥājji Mullā Hādī Sabizwārī, and several other outstanding figures in the Qajar period, the light of whose teachings has not yet disappeared from the horizon of Persia. One can hardly understand the intellectual life of Islam in its totality without taking into account this last major period of Muslim philosophical activity, lasting from the Safavid period to the present, to the understanding of which we hope this chapter will serve as an introduction and as an inventive for further exploration.

NOTES

1. A few authors like Gobineau, Donaldson, and E. G. Browne have touched upon certain aspects of Shi'ism in their writings; the only European author, however, who has delved with serious intention into the Shi'ah intellectual world, is Henry Corbin, who during the past twenty years has done much to introduce the rich heritage of Shi'ism, especially as it has developed in Persia, to the Western world.
2. For the meaning of this word which denotes wisdom, refer to the chapter on Shihāb al-Dīn Suhrawardī in this volume.
3. Shaykh Ṣafī (647/1249-735/1334), one of the most impotant of Shi'ah Sufi saints, is still greatly respected by the Sufis; his tomb in Ardibil has remained until today an important place of pilgrimage. Being the disciple of Shaykh Zāhid Gīlānī, he was already a significant figure in his own day as testified by the biographical works like the *Ṣafwat al-ṣafā'* by Ibn Bazzāz, and Rashīd al-Dīn Faḍlallāh's letters to the saint and to the governor of Ardibil in his *Munsha'āt-i rashīdī.* See also, E.G. Browne, *A Literary History of Persia,* Vol. IV, Cambridge University Press, Cambridge, 1924, Chap. II.

4. For a history of the Safavid period, see E.G. Browne, *op. cit.,* Vol. IV; L. Lockhart, *The Fall of the Ṣafavid Dynasty and the Afghān Occupation of Persia,* Cambridge University Press, Cambridge, 1958, and the traditional Persian sources of which some of the more important include the *Ṣafawat al-ṣafā'* by Ibn Bazzāz, *Aḥsan al-tawārīkh* by Ḥasan Bayk Rumlū, *Zubdat al-tawārīkh* by Muḥammad Muḥsin ibn 'Abd al-Karīm, and the universal history *Nāsikh al-tawārīkh* by Mirzā Taqī Sipihr.
5. The purpose of theology is to protect the truths of a revelation against false reasoning; its role is, therefore, defensive. It is the shell which protects the inner spiritual life, not that life itself. If there were no danger of rationalism and false reasoning, there would be no need for theology. We, therefore, see theology coming into being with rationalistic philosophy, and where there is no tendency toward rationalism, there is no need for theology as this word is currently understood.
6. For a discussion of the meaning of *ishrāqi* wisdom, refer to the chapters on Suhrawardī.
7. The reason why the pre-Safavid sages of Persia like 'Alī ibn Turkah Iṣpahānī and Ibn Abī Jumhūr as well as the Safavid authors themselves have been neglected in the Western world, is that the quality of their wisdom is primarily gnostic (*'irfānī*) like that of Shaykh al-Akbar Muḥyī al-Dīn ibn 'Arabī by those doctrines they were all influenced; that like him they can be understood neither by the rationalistic philosophers nor by the mystics as they have come to be understood since the Renaissance.
8. For the name of some of these Arab Shi'ah scholars, see E. B. Browne, *op. cit.,* Vol. IV, Chap. VIII.
9. The science of *uṣūl* as an independent science has grown into monumental proportions only in the past few centuries reaching its height in the hands of Shaykh Murtaḍā Anṣārī, the famous doctor of the Qajar period, who only a century ago made *uṣūl* into a science matching *Kalām* in its logical subtleties.
10. Shi'ah theology reached its height in the seventh/thirteenth century in the hands of men like Khwājah Naṣīr al-Dīn Ṭūsī and 'Allāma-yi Ḥillī.
11. See the chapter on Suhrawardī. Generally, *ḥikmah* in Arabic or *ḥikmat* in Persian means phisosophical and theresophical wisdom in addition to the particular sense given to it as a divine science.
12. For the series of commentators and expositors of *ishrāqī* wisdom, see the section on Suhrawardī in this volume.
13. It is unfortunate that in books treating the relation between faith and reason in Islam like A. J. Arberry's *Revelation and Reason in Islam,* London, 1957, most of these authors are not taken into serious consideration.
14. For an account of the doctrines of Ibn 'Arabī, see T. Burcekardt (Tr.), *La Sagesse des prophètes,* Paris, 1955; also *idem, Introduction to Sufi Doctrine,* tr. M. Matheson, Sh. Muḥammad Ashraf, Lahore, 1959, which is an excellent general introduction to Ibn 'Arabī's school of Sufism. See also Corbin, *L'Imagination creatrice dans la soufisme d'Ibn 'Arabi,* Flammarion, Paris, 1958, which contains some useful chapters on his ideas and their spread in the East.
15. See S. M. Ṣadr, *Shaykh 'Alā' al-Dawlah Simnānī,* Dānish Press, Tehran, 1334/1915.
16. This great Persian Sufi poet and sage has written several well-known summaries of Ibn 'Arabī's doctrine including the *Lawā'iḥ* translated by Whinfeld and Qazwīnī, Luzac & Co., London, 1928; the *Ashī'at al-lama'āt,* and the *Naqd al-nuṣūṣ.*

17. The *Kitāb al-mujlī* of Ibn Abī Jumhūr and *Jāmi' al-asrār* and *Jāmi' al-ḥaqā'iq* of Mullā Ḥaydar 'Alī Āmulī are among the most important sources of Shi'ah gnostic doctrines.

18. The best traditional sources for these earlier Shi'ah authors are the *Rawḍat al-jannāt* of Muḥammad Bāqir Khunsārī, lithographed edition, Tehran, 1306/1888; *al-Dharī'ah* of Āghā Buzurg Tīhrān, al-Gharrā, Press, Najaf, 1355/1936 on; the *Tārīkh-i 'alam arā-yi 'abbāsī* of Iskandar Bayg Munshī, Tehran, 1334/1954; and of more recent composition the *Rayḥānat al-adab* of Muḥammad 'Alī Tabrīzī, Sa'dī Press, Tehran, 1331-33A.H. Solar; the *Qiṣaṣ al-'ulamā'* of Mīrzā Muḥammad Tunikābunī, Islāmiyyah Press, Tehran, 1313A.H. Solar; *Fihrist-i kutub-i ihdā'i-i Āqā-yi Mishkāt* by M. B. Dānish-pazhūh, University Press, Tehran, 1335/1956; see also H. Corbin, "Confession extatiques de Mīr Dāmād" in the *Mèlanges Louis Massignon,* Institut Français de Damas, Damas, 1956 pp. 331-78.

19. See Corbin, *op. cit.,* pp. 333ff.

20. His name should not in any way be connected with the heterodox Bahā'ī movement of the thirteenth/nineteenth century.

21. For an account of the life and works of Shaykh-i Bahā'ī, see *Tārikh-i 'ālam ārā-yi 'abbāsī,* pp. 155-57; also Naficy, *Aḥwāl wa ash'ār-i fārsī-i Shaykh-i Bahā'ī,* Iqbāl Press, Tehran, 1316/1937.

22. Shaykh-i Bahā'ī is said to have built a bath-house named *Gulkhan* which had always hot water without any fuel being used in it. When it was pulled down, people discovered a single candle burning under the water tank.

23. This book on mathematics which helped greatly in reviving the study of the mathematical sciences in Persia was a standard text-book for centuries and has been commented upon several times and translated into Persian by Muḥammad Amīn Najafi Ḥijāzī Qummī and into German by G. H. F. Nesselmann who published the text and the translation in Berlin in 1843. Shaykh-i Bahā'ī revived the study of mathematics and astronomy in Persia after one hundred years of neglect, having himself learnt these sciences in Herat.

24. For a list of the nearly ninety works attributed to him, see his *Kulliyyāt-i 'ash'ār-i fārsī,* ed. M. Tawhīdīpūr, Maḥmūdī Press, Tehran, 1336/1957, pp. 42-45.

25. *Ibid.*, pp. 164-66.

26. Intoxication symbolizes ecstasy and spiritual union.

27. Maulānā Jalāl al-Dīn Rūmī is commonly referred to as Mawlawī in Persian. This verse refers to Mawlawī's well-known rejection of rationalism in favour of gnosis (The leg of the rationalist is a wooden leg.....).

28. Love symbolizes gnosis or the science which comes through contemplation and illumination rather than analysis and discursive thought.

29. Reference is to the famous theologian Imam Fakhr al-Dīn Rāzī.

30. This verse is in Arabic and is repeated immediately with only a little change in Persian.

31. That is, he is like a beast of burden.

32. Reference is to the wisdom of the Sufis as contrasted with that of the Greeks, the *ḥikmat-i īmānī* and the *ḥikmat-i yūnānī.*

33. The Prophet Muḥammad (upon whom be peace).

34. Shaykh-i Bahā'ī, *Kulliyyāt....*, pp. 18-19.

35. This theme appears in certain Hermetic writings, the *Acts of Thomas,* the Grail story, as well as in Islam in the visionary narratives of Ibn Sīnā and many of Suhrawardī's gnostic tracts such as *Qiṣṣat ghurbat al-gharbiyyah;* see H. Corbin, *Avicenne et le récit visionnaire,* Institut Franco-Iranien, Tehran, and A. Maisonneuve, Paris, 1952-54, Vol. I, Chap. 3, and Suhrawardī, *Oeuvres philosophiques et mystiques,* Vol. II, Institut Franco-Iranien, Tehran, and A. Maisonneuve, Paris, 1954, Prolégomène by H. Corbin.

36. Shaykh-i Bahā'ī, *Kulliyyāt* ..., p. 23.

37. A city in the south of Arabia with which the name of the Queen of Sheba is associated.

38. *Lā makān,* meaning beyond the world of cosmic manifestation. Suhrawardī refers to this point which is the top of the cosmic mountain *Qāf,* as *nā kujā ābād*; see Suhrawardī, "Le bruissement de l'aile de Gabriel," tr. H. Corbin and P. Kraus, *Journal Asiatique,* Juillet-Sept., 1935, pp. 41-42.

39. For an account of the life and writings of Mīr Dāmād, see M. Tunikābunī, *Qiṣaṣ al-'ulamā,* pp. 333-35; *Rayḥānat al-adab,* Vol. IV, pp. 117-21; *Rawḍat al-jannāt,* pp. 114-16; *Tārīkh-i 'ālam ārā-yi 'abbāsī,* pp. 146-47; Danishpazhuh, *Fihrist....*, Vol. III, 1, p. 152 and the good Introduction to his life and thought by H. Corbin, "Confessions extatiques de Mīr Dāmād," pp. 340 ff.

40. It is said that he had much interest in the life of the bees and had accumulated a good deal of observational data about them.

41. For an account of these and other students of Mīr Dāmād, see H. Corbin, *op. cit.,* pp. 345-46.

42. The "Yamanī philosophy" means the wisdom revealed by God to man through the prophets and through illumination; Yaman (Yemen) symbolizes the right or oriental *(mashriqī)* side of the valley in which Moses heard the message of God. It is, therefore, the source of divine illumination in contrast to the Occident, the source of Peripatetic philosophy, the Occident symbolizing darkness and analytical reason on the plane of philosophy, i.e., rationalism. See H. Corbin, "Le récit d'initiation et l'hermétisme en Iran," *Eranos Jahrbuch,* Vol. XVII, 1949, pp. 136-37. For the symbols of the Orient and Occident in *ishrāqī* wisdom see the chapter on Suhrawardī in this volume.

43. This major work has been commented upon several times. One of its most curious commentaries is that of Muḥammad ibn 'Alī Riḍā ibn Āqājānī, one of the students of Mullā Ṣadrā; it runs over a thousand pages.

44. These last two works are among the important books on *ḥikmat* in Persian, the others being in Arabic. Some manuscripts attribute *Sidrat al-muntahā* to Mīr Dāmād's student, Sayyid Aḥmad 'Alawī, although in the *Jadhawāt* Mīr Dāmād refers to this work as being his own. In any case it is a product of his school.

45. For a translation and discussion of this work, see H. Corbin, *op. cit.,* pp. 350ff.

46. See for example the *Shifā'* or *Najāt* of Ibn Sīnā and the *Kitāb al-mu'tabar* of Abu'l-Barakāt al-Baghdādī. In some cases as in the *Dānish-nāma-yi 'Ala'ī* of Ibn Sīnā and many later *ishrāqī* writings, the book begins with metaphysics and then proceeds to natural philosophy in the manner of Plato rather than Artistotle.

47. See Mīr Dāmād, *Qabasāt,* Shaykh Maḥmūd Burūjirdī, Shiraz, 1315/1897.

48. For a general discussion of this question, see L. Gardet, *La Pensée religieuse d'-Avicenne,* J. Vrin, Paris, 1951, pp. 38 ff., and A. K. Coomaraswamy, *Time and Eternity,* Artibus Asiae, Ascona, 1947, Chap. IV.

49. Mīr Dāmād, *Qabasāt,* pp. 1-10.

50. *Ibid.*, p. 7.

51. Mīr Dāmād argues that time itself is the measure of the movement of the heavens and a condition for the existence of this world so that one cannot speak of a time before the creation of the world; *Qabasāt,* p. 20.

52. For a comparison and affinity of these ideas with those of Ibn 'Arabī, see *La Sagesse des prophètes,* Chapters I and II.

53. In presenting this view of creation, Mīr Dāmād draws heavily on earlier writings from Plato's *Timaeus* and the so-called *Theology of Aristotle* to the *Shifā'* of Ibn Sīnā and the *Kitāb al-mu'tabar* of Abu'l-Barakāt. In each case he also criticizes the view of the previous writers who considered the world either to be eternal in itself or created in time from outside. Mīr Dāmād's *Risālah fī madhhab Arisṭaṭālis* is devoted to a discussion of the difference between the views of Plato and Aristotle on the question of time and eternity drawing on Fārābī's *Kitāb jam' bayn al-ra'yayn.* Mīr Dāmād's treatise is published on the margin of the *Qabasāt,* pp. 140-57.

54. The *Jadhawāt* (Bombay, lithographed edition, 1302/1884, pp. 203) begins with a poem in praise of 'Ali ibn Abī Ṭālib the first lines of which are as follows:

> O herald of the nation and the soul of the Prophet,
>
> The ring of thy knowledge surrounds the ears of the intelligences.
>
> O thou in whom the book of existence terminates,
>
> To whom the account or creation refers
>
> The glorified treasure of the revelation,
>
> Thou art the holy interpreter of its secrets.

55. Suhrawardī also divides the angelic world into the longitudinal and the latitudinal orders, a division the influence of which upon Mīr Dāmād is easy to discern. On the question of angelology the Safavid sages remained faithful to the *ishrāqī* scheme combined with that of Ibn Sīnā. See the chapter on Suhrawardī.

56. The natures refer to the warm and cold, wet and dry, and the elements to the four traditional ones, fire, air, water, and earth.

57. Mīr Dāmād and Mullā Ṣadrā, unlike Aristotle and his followers, posit some form of matter in every degree of formal manifestation.

58. Mīr Dāmād mentions that there are 1,400 species of animals, 800 belonging to sea and 600 to land.

59. *Jadhawāt,* pp. 2-13.

60. *Ibid.*, pp. 13-18.

61. *Ibid.*, pp. 18-28.

62. *Ibid.*, pp. 28 ff.

63. In discussing *tawḥīd,* Mīr Dāmād draws not only on Ibn Sīnā and Suhrawardī but even on the *Nahj al-balāghah* of the first Shi'ite Imām, the *Ṣaḥīfa-yi sajjādīyyah* of the fourth Imam, and other Shi'ah sources. He regards Pythagoras as the Imam of the Semitic sages *(ḥukamā'-i sāmī)* and one who received his wisdom through revelation. This view going back to Philo is held among the great majority of the Muslim sages and historians of philosophy.

64. *Jadhawāt,* pp. 38ff.

65. This intermediary region plays an important role in the thought of Mullā Ṣadrā and even more in the writings of Shaykh Aḥmad Aḥsā'ī, the founder of the Shaykhīs who still survive in Kerman.

66. These are two famous mythical cities through which initiates pass in their journeys and they appear often in initiatic narratives in Persian.

67. *Jadhawāt,* pp. 54-63.

68. *Ibid.*, p. 100.

69. *Ibid.*, p. 103. In the same work, p. 92, the last part of which is wholly devoted to the important traditional Muslim science of *jafr,* he considers numbers to be the principles of beings, the illumination from the intelligible world, the "Michael of the degree of existence" and adds that if a person acquires all the knowledge of numbers he will gain complete knowledge of the physical world. This view is very close to that of Pythagoras and his school. See Aristotle, *Metaphysica,* Book V. In both cases number is not just the quantity of modern mathematics, but a "personality," an entity which possesses a definite qualitative aspect. For the notion of the Pythagoreans, see H. Keyser, *Akróasis,* Verlag Gert Hatje, Stuttgart, 1947.

70. For a profound study of this subject as developed before Mīr Dāmād, see S. T. Burckhardt, *La Clé spirituelles de l'astrologie musulmane d'après Ibn 'Arabī,* Editions Traditionelles, Paris, 1950.

71. The other two are Shaykh-i Bahā'ī and Mīr Dāmād who were close friends of Mīr Findiriskī and shared with him the respect and honour of the Safavid Court. For an account of the life of Mīr Findiriskī whose complete name is Mīr Abu'l-Qāsim ibn Mīrzā Bayg Ḥusayn Findiriskī, see *Rayḥānat al-adab,* vol. III, pp. 231-32.

72. The story is told of him in most biographies that one day Shāh 'Abbās, trying to admonish him for mixing with the common people, said, "I hear some of the leading scholars and sages have been attending cock-fights in the bazaar." Mīr Findiriskī, knowing that the remark was meant for him, replied, "Your majesty, rest assured, I was present but I saw none of the *'ulamā'* there." See *Riyāḍ al-'arifin,* p. 276.

73. The text of this *qaṣīdah* and the commentary by Khalkhālī have been published in Tehran, lithographed edition, 1325/1907. This verse refers to the celestial archetypes of Platonic ideas and their earthly reflections or shadows.

74. Reference is to Fārābī and Ibn Sīnā, the two early masters of *mashshā'ī* philosophy in Islam.

75. "Qualities" means multiplicity of forms which become evident only when light shines upon them.

76. The later Muslim authors following Ibn Sīnā divide reality into the Necessary Being *(wājib al-wujūd),* the possible being *(mumkin al-wujūd)* and the being that is impossible *(mumtani' al-wujūd).*

77. All arguments begin because each side considers only one aspect of the Truth. But those who are "complete," that is, have a vision of the totality of the Truth, never enter into arguments.

78. Mīr Findiriskī, *Risāla-yi ṣanā'iyyah,* Sa'ādat Press, Tehran, 1317 Solar.

79. *Ibid.,* pp. 13-54.

80. Mīr Findiriski adds that all the Greek philosophers before Aristotle were saying the same thing in different languages and that if one is instructed in the secrets *(rumūz)* of *ḥikmat,* Hindu wisdom, and the *Theology of Aristotle* (i.e., the *Enneads* of Plotinus), all the different expressions will have the same meaning for him.

81. Mīr Findiriskī mentions Mazdak as the person who by a false interpretation of the Avesta preached the communization of women and property. He also mentions the Carmathians *(Qarāmiṭah)* as belonging to this group.

82. Mullā-yi Lāhījī known as Fayyāḍ, author of several important treatises on *ḥikmat* in Persian and Arabic mentioned already, deserves a separate study as one of the major figures of this period. There are brief accounts of him in E. G. Browne, *op. cit.,* Vol. IV, pp. 408-09, 435. See also the introduction by Sayyid Muḥammad Mishkāt to the new edition of *al-Maḥajjat al-bayḍā',* Vol. I, Islāmiyyah Press, Teheran, 1380 Solar, in which the significance of Fayḍ's doctrines and in particular the present work on ethics is discussed.

83. See Mullā Muḥsin Fayḍ-i Kāshānī, a*l-Maḥajjat al-bayḍā' fī iḥyā' al-iḥyā',* 4 Vols., Islāmiyyah Press, Tehran, 1380-81A.H. Solar, in which in ten sections he deals with Sufi ethics based on Shi'ah sources but following closely the model of the *Iḥyā'*.

84. The *Rayḥānat al-adab,* Vol. III, pp. 242-44, mentions 120 works by him. For the account of Mullā Muḥsin's life and writings, consult also *Qiṣaṣ al-'ulamā',* pp. 322-33, and *Riyāḍ al-'ārifīn,* pp. 388-89.

85. Mullā Muḥsin Fayḍ, *Ā'īna-yi shāhī,* Mūsawī Press, Shiraz, 1320/1902, p. 5.

86. *Kalimāt-i maknūnah,* Tehran, lithographed edition, 1316/1898. Henceforth our reference to this work will be to this edition.

87. *Ibid.*, p. 15.

88. For an explanation of these terms see Seyyed Hossein Nasr, "Being and Its Polarisation," *Pakistan Philosophical Journal,* Vol. III, No. 2, October 1959, pp. 8-13. In the general discussion among the ḥakīms as to whether these essences (or being) are principial, Mullā Muḥsin sides with the school of *aṣālat-i wujūd,* the principiality of being, and considers the *māhiyyāt* to be the accidents of Being. This question has been dealt with in the chapter on Suhrawardi.

89. *Kalimāt-i maknūnah,* pp. 31ff. Mullā Muḥsin describes these stages also as the *'ilm al-yaqīn,* in which one "sees" nothing but the Divine Essence, Names, and Acts; the *'ayn al-yaqīn,* in which one "sees" nothing but the Essence and Names, and the *ḥaqq al-yaqīn* in which there remains only the Divine Ipseity.

90. See T. Burckhardt, *Introduction to Sufi Doctrine,* pp. 64ff.

91. This term should be taken here in its negative connotation; but it has a positive meaning in Sufi cosmology and marks an intermediate stage between the sensible world and the spiritual world. See H. Corbin, *Imagination créatrice....,* Chap. II.

92. *Kalimāt-i maknūnah,* p. 61.

93. *Ibid.,* pp. 74-75.

94. *Ibid.,* pp. 167ff.

95. *Ibid.,* pp. 214-19.

96. *Rayḥānat al-adab,* Vol. III, pp. 46-62. The *Mir'āt al-aḥwāl-i jahān namā* by Aḥmad ibn Muḥammad Bāqir Iṣpahānī Bihbahānī is devoted to his life and works.

97. For the writings and life of the second Majlisī, see *Rayḥānat al-adab,* Vol. III, pp. 455-60; Danishpazhuh, *Fihrist....,* Vol. V., p. 1137. The *Fayḍ-i qudsī* by Mīrzā Ḥusayn Nūrī is devoted completely to his life and writings. Majlisi wrote thirteen Arabic and fifty-five Persian books which altogether occupy nearly a million and a half lines.

98. He devoted a treatise, the *I'tiqādāt,* to rejecting Sufism.

99. Shaykh Aḥmad is responsible for the last important religious movement within Shi'ism and should be studied separately as a founder of a particular sect. The leaders of this sect called the Shaykhīs claim to have knowledge of all things, and so each of them from the time of Shaykh Aḥmad to the present has composed a large number of treatises on all the sciences. For a list of the works of Shaykh Aḥmad and the other leaders of the Shaykhīs, see Abu'l-Qāsim ibn Zayn al-'Ābidīn ibn Karīm, *Fihrist-i kutub-i marḥūm-i Aḥsā'ī wa sā'ir-i mashāyikh-i 'iẓām,* 2 Vols., Sa'ādat Press, Kerman, 1337 A.H. Solar.

BIBLIOGRAPHY

Abu'l -Qāsim ibn Zayn al-'Ābidīn ibn Karīm, *Fihrist-i kutub-i marḥūm-i Aḥsā'ī wa Sā'ir-i mashāyikh-i 'iẓām,* Sa'ādat Press, Kerman, 1337 A.H. Solar; Āghā Buzurg al-Tihrāni, *al-Dharī'ah,* al-Gharrā' Press, Najaf, 1355/1936 on; Bahā' al-Dīn 'Āmilī, *Kulliyāt-i ash'ār-i fārsī,* ed. M. Tawḥīpūr, Maḥmūdī Press, Tehran, 1336 A.H. Solar; E.G. Browne, *A Literary History of Persia,* Cambridge University Press, Cambridge, 1924, Vol. IV; H. Corbin, "Confessions extatiques de Mīr Dāmād," *Mélanges Louis Massignon,* Institut Français de Damas, Damas, 1956; M. B. Danishpazhuh, *Fihrist-i kitāb khāna-yi ihdā'i-i āqā-yi Sayyid Muḥammad-i Mishkāt,* University Press, Tehran, 1332-35 A.H. Solar; C. Gobineau, *Religions et philosophies dans l'Asie centrale,* Gallimard, Paris, 1933; R. Q. Hidāyat, *Riyāḍ al-'ārifīn,* Āftāb Press, Tehran, 1316 A. H. Solar; Iskandar Bayg Munshī, *Tārīkh-i 'ālam arā-yi 'abbāsi,* Mūsawī Press, Tehran, 1334 Solar; Muḥammad Bāqir Khunsārī, *Rawḍat al-jannāt,* Teheran, lithographed edition, 1306/1888; M.B. Mīr Dāmād, *Jadhawāt,* Bombay, lithographed edition, 1304/1886; *Qabasāt,* Shaykh Maḥmūd Burūjirdī, Shiraz, 1315/1897; A. Mīr Findiriskī, *Risāla-yi, Ṣanā'iyyah,* ed.by A. A. Shihābī, Sa'ādat Press, Tehran, 1317A. H. Solar; Mullā Muḥsin Faīyḍ-i Kāshānī, *Kalimāt-i maknūnah,* Tehran, lithographed edition, 1316/1898; *al-Maḥajjat al-bayḍā' fī iḥyā' al-iḥyā',* 4 Vols., Islāmiyyah Press, Tehran, 1380-81; Nūrallāh Shūshtarī, *Majālis al-mu'minīn,* Islāmiyyah Press, Tehran, 1334/1955; Shibāb al-Dīn Suhrawardī, *Opera Metaphysica et Mystica,* Vol. I, Ma'ārif Mathaasi (Bibliotheca Islamica, 16), Istanbul, 1945, and *Oeuvres philosophiques et mystiques,* Vol. II, Institut Franco-Iranien, Andrien Maisonneuve, Paris, 1952; H. Corbin, "Prolegomènes"; Muḥammad 'Alī Tabrīzī, *Rayḥānat al-adab,* Sa'dī Press, Tehran, 1331-33A.H. Solar; T. Tunikābunī *Qiṣaṣ al-'ulamā',* 'Ilmiyyah Press, Teheran, 1313 A.H. Solar.

22

Ṣadr al-Dīn Shīrāzī (Mullā Ṣadrā)*

LIFE AND WORKS

The intellectual activity revived in Persia during the Safavid period, some features of which we have discussed in the previous chapter, "The School of Ispahan", found its culmination in Ṣadr al-Dīn Shīrāzī known to his compatriots as Ākhūnd Mulla Ṣadrā and to his disciples as simply Ākhūnd or as Ṣadr al-Muta'allihīn, i.e., the foremost among the theosophers. This figure, about whom nearly by the whole intellectual life of Persia has revolved in the past three centuries and a half and who is one of the major expositors of Islamic intellectual doctrines in the Shi'ah world, has remained until today almost completely unknwon outside Persia, even in other Muslim countries. Many have heard of his name, and nearly all travellers to Persia since the Safavid period, who have been interested in the intellectual life of the country, have recognized his importance and have been impressed by his fame;[2] yet no one outside a group of his disciples in Persia, who have kept his school alive until today, has done justice to his doctrines in presenting them to the world at large.

Mullā Ṣadrā, whose complete name is Ṣadr al-Dīn Muḥammad, was born in Shiraz in about 979/1571,[3] the only son of Ibrāhīm Shīrāzī. A member of the famous Qawām family of Shiraz, Ibrāhīm held the post of a vizier and was a powerful political and social figure in his native city. The young Ṣadr al-Dīn exhibited his exceptional intelligence from childhood and was given the best possible education in Shiraz.

Having completed his early studies, he became intensely interested in the intellectual sciences (*al-'ulūm al-'aqliyyah*), especially metaphysics, and, therefore, left Shiraz for Ispahan which was at that time the capital and major seat of learning in Persia. In Ispahan he studied first with

* This essay originally appeared in the *A History of Muslim Philosophy*, Edited by M.M. Sharif, Vol. 2, 1966, pp. 932-961.

Bahā' al-Dīn 'Āmilī, learning the transmitted sciences (*al-'ulūm al-naqliyyah*) from him and later with Mīr Dāmād who was his most famous master in the intellectual sciences.[4] Within a few years he became himself a recognized master in all the branches of formal learning especially in *ḥikmat*[5] in which he soon surpassed his own teachers.

Not satisfied simply with formal learning, Mullā Ṣadrā left worldly life in general and retired to a small village named Kahak near Qūm where he spent fiften years in asceticism and purification of his soul until, as he claims in his introduction to the *Asfār*, he became endowed with the direct vision of the intelligible world. He now came to "see" through illumination (*ishrāq*) what he had previously learnt theoretically from books.

Having reached both formal and spiritual perfection, Mullā Ṣadrā returned once again to the world. Meanwhile Allāhwirdī Khān, the Governor of Shiraz, had built a large *madrasah* and invited Mullā Ṣadrā to return to Shiraz as the head of the new school. Ākhūnd accepted the offer and returned to his native city, making the school of Khān the major centre of intellectual sciences in Persia.[6] He remained there until the end of his life spending the last period of his terrestrial existence entirely in teaching and writing.

Despite his extreme piety which is shown by the fact that he made the pilgrimage to Mecca seven times on foot—he died in Basrah in 1050/1640 during the seventh journey—Mullā Ṣadrā was often molested by some of the exoteric '*ulamā'* who could not accept his gnostic interpretation of the doctrines of the faith and who denounced him publicly on more than one occasion. It was only the influence of his powerful family that made it possible for him to continue his teaching activities.

Mullā Ṣadrā's life, then, can be divied into three distinct periods: the period of childhood and schooling in Shiraz and Ispahan, the period of asceticism near Qum at the end of which the composition of the *Asfār* was begun, and the period of teaching and writing which represents the result and fruition of the other two periods. His life is itself testimony to one of the main aspects of his wisdom, that in order to be effective theoretical knowledge must be combined with spiritual realization.

The writings of Mullā Ṣadrā, nearly all of which were composed in the last period of his life, are almost without exception of great merit and have been among the main sources from which the later generations of theologians, philosophers, and gnostics have drawn their inspiration. All his writings concern either religious sciences or metaphysics, theodicy or *ḥikmat,*[7] and are in a very clear and fluent style making them more easily understandable to the reader than the writings of his predecessors like Mīr

Dāmād.[8] Since Mullā Ṣadrā's writings are nearly completely unknown outside Persia, we take this opportunity to list the works which, according to the leading living authorities and the best historical evidence, were written by him.[9] The works dealing with metaphysics and intellectual sciences include: *al-Asfār al-arba'ah; al-Mabda' wa'l-ma'ād; Sirr al-nuqṭah* (possibly not authentic); *al-Shawāhid al-rubūbiyyah,* his most lucid and synoptic work; *al-Ḥikmat al-'arshiyyah,* glosses upon the *Ḥikmat al-ishrāq* of Suhrawardī Maqtūl; commentary (*sharḥ*) upon the *Hidāyah* of Abharī;[10] glosses upon the metaphysical parts of Ibn Sīnā's *Shifā'*; *Fī ittiḥād al-'āqil wa'l-ma'qūl; Fī ittiṣāf al-māhiyyah bi'l-wujūd; Fī bad' wujūd al-insān; Fi'l-taṣawwur wa'l-taṣdīq; Fī'l-jabr wa'l-tafwīḍ; Fī ḥudūth al-'ālam; Fī ḥashr; Fī sarayān al-wujūd; Fī'l-qaḍā' wa'l-qadar; Fī tashakhkhuṣ; al-Masā'il al-qudsiyyah; Iksīr al-'ārifīn; al-Wāridāt al-qalbiyyah; al-Qawā'id al-malakūtiyyah; Ḥall al-mushkilāt al-falakiyyah;* introduction to *'Arsh al-taqdīs* of Mīr Dāmād; *al-Maẓāhir;* glosses upon *Rawāshiḥ al-samāwiyyah* of Mīr Dāmād, *Khalq al-a'māl; Kasr al-aṣnām al-jāhilīyyah; al-Mizāj; al-Ma'ād al-jismānī; al-Tanqīyah* in logic; *dīwān* of poems in Persian; and answers to various questions on philosophy.

The works that are primarily concerned with the religious sciences include the Quranic commentary; *Mafātīḥ al-ghayb, Asrār al-āyāt;* commentary upon a large number of the verses of the Qur an; commentary upon a few prophetic *aḥādīth* on *Imāmah;* glosses upon the Quranic commentary of Bayḍāwī; glosses upon the *Tajrīd* of Khwājah Naṣīr al-Dīn Ṭūsī, and upon Qūshjī's commentary upon the *Tajrīd* (of doubtful authenticity); glosses upon the commentary upon the *Lum'ah,* commentary upon the *Uṣūl al-kāfi* of Kulaynī, one of the four major sources of Shi'ah Law;[11] *Mutashābih al-qur'ān;* and a Persian treatise called *Sih aṣl* on the soul and its destiny.[12]

Mullā Ṣadrā composed also several quatrains in Persian, a few of which are mentioned in the traditional sources and some appear in his own handwriting on the first page of his commentary upon the *Hidāyah.*[13] They deal mostly with the Sufi doctrine of the unity of Being (*waḥdat al-wujūd*), which may be considered to be the central theme of Mulla Ṣadrā's doctrinal formulations. For example, in one of the quatrains he says:

The Truth is the spirit of the universe and the universe the body,
And the orders of the angels are the sense of this body;
The heavens, elements, and compounds are its organs;
Lo! unity is this, and the rest nothing but rhetoric.

In dividing the writings of Mullā Ṣadrā into the intellectual and the religious ones, we do not in any way wish to imply that these two categories are completely separated in his view. On the contrary, one of the major achievements of Mullā Ṣadrā consisted in uniting and harmonizing religion and the intellectual sciences. All of his works, even in philosophy, are replete with the Qur anic verses in support of his conclusions; and all of his religious works, even the Qur anic commentaries, are full of gnostic and intellectual interpretations. One can only say that some of Ākhūnd writings are concerned more with religious questions and other more with intellectual ones.

Likewise, among the above-mentioned works some are more gnostic in character and others are presented in a more discursive language, although they all bear the fragrance of gnostic doctrines. Among writings which are of a more gnostic vein one may mention *al-Shawāhid al-rubūbiyyah, al 'Arshīyyah, Asrār al-āyāt*, and *al-Wāridāt al-qalbiyyah*, and among those which are presented in a more discursive language are the *Sharḥ al-hidāyah* and the commentary upon the *Shifā'*.

Without doubt the most important work of Mullā Ṣadrā is the *Asfār al-arba'ah*. It is comparable in dimension and scope to the *Shifā'* and the *Futūḥāt al-makkiyyah* and in a way stands midway between the Peripatetic encyclopedia of Ibn Sīnā and the compendium of esoteric sciences of Ibn 'Arabī. The title of *Asfār* itself has been the cause of much difficulty to the few Orientalists who are acquainted with the book. The word *asfār* is the broken plural for *safar* meaning journey as well as *sifr* meaning "book" related to the Hebrew *sefer*. So it was that Gobineau considered the work to be a series of books on travel and E.G. Browne believed that the title meant simply "the four books."[14]

Both views are, however, erroneous. Actually, *asfār* means journeys but not the account of travels in the ordinary sense of the word as Gobineau understood it to be. As Mullā Ṣadrā himself mentions in his introduction to the book, the *Asfār* consists of the following four stages or journeys of initiatic realization (*sulūk*); (i) the journey of the creature or creation (*khalq*) towards the Creator or the Truth (*Ḥaqq*), (ii) the journey in the Truth with the Truth, (iii) the jouney from the Truth to creation with the Truth, and (iv) the journey with the Truth in the creation. This monumental work is, therefore, an account of the stages of the journey of the gnostic, systematized in a logical dress.

In content, the first book of the *Asfār* deals with Being and its various manifestation; the second with the simple substances, i.e., the intelligences, souls, and bodies and their accidents including, therefore, natural philosophy; the third with the Divine Names and Qualities; and the fourth with the soul, its origin, becoming, and end. All these topics are treated in detail taking into account the views of previous sages and philosophers so that the work as a whole is quite voluminous.[15] In a sense this vast *opus* is the culmination of a thousand years of contemplation and thought by Muslim sages as well as the foundation of a new and original intellectual perspective which issues forth from within the Islamic of the Islamic tradition.

SOURCES OF MULLĀ ṢADRĀ'S DOCTRINES

According to Mullā Ṣadrā, there are two forms of knowledge: that derived from formal instruction *(al-'ilm al-ṣūrī)* and that which comes from intellectual intuition *(al-'ilm al-ladunī)*. The first is acquired in school with the aid of a teacher, and the second, based upon a greater degree of certainty than the first, is the science possessed by the prophets and saints and arrived at through the purification of the soul and the catharsis *(tajrīd)* of the intellect.[16] There are then, according to this view, two sources for Mullā Ṣadrā's ideas, one formal and in a sense historical, i.e., manifested in history before him, and the other spiritual and invisible. Regarding this second source, which may be called his "guardian angel" or "hidden Imam," the source of all inner illumination, we have little to say except to emphasize its importance in Mullā Ṣadrā's view.

It is with the first category that we are primarily concerned here. There are five principal elements which are clearly detectable in the new synthesis brought about by Mullā Ṣadrā; they are also found, though less explicitly, in the doctrines of the Safavid sages before him. These elements include the philosophy of Aristotle and his followers, the doctrines of the Neoplatonic sages, especially Plotinus whose *Enneads* the Muslims considered to be a work of Aristotle, the teachings of Ibn Sīnā, the gnostic doctrines of Ibn 'Arabī, and the principles of the Islamic revelation, especially the more esoteric teachings of the Prophet and the Shi'ah Imams.[17] Among these sources the last two are of particular importance. Mullā Ṣadrā created a new school of *ḥikmat,* on the one ḥand, by putting the intuitions of the gnostics and especially of Ibn 'Arabī and his followers into a logical dress and, on the other hand, by drawing out the philosophical and metaphysical implications of the teachings of the Imams especially as contained in the *Nahj al-balāghah,* creating thereby what may be called a distinctly and purely Islamic school of *ḥikmat* based especially upon the Quran, the Hadith and the inspired doctrines which form the very basis of Shi'ism.

Mullā Ṣadrā, like Suhrawardī, held in great esteem the pre-Socratic philosophers and sages of Greece, both historical and mythological, and regarded Thales, Anaximander, Agathedemon, Empedocles, Pythagoras, Socrates, Plato, and Aristotle as the last group of sages in the ancient world to have possessed wisdom in its entirety. He, like many other Muslim *ḥakims*, considered Greek philosophy not to have started with Aristotle but to have ended with him and believed all the later Greek sages to have been masters of various arts and sciences other than metaphysics.[18] For Mullā Ṣadrā, therefore, Greek philosophy was essentially the wisdom of the Hebrew prophets inherited, systematized, and later in part forgotten by the Greeks, a wisdom which was integrated into the Muslim intellectual perspective and brought to full fruition in the light of the Islamic revelation. That is why when Mullā Ṣadrā wishes to reject some aspects of the teachings of either the Peripatetics or the Illuminationists he appeals so often first to the Quran and the *Ḥadīth* and then to those fragmentary sayings of the pre-Socratic philosophers with which the Muslims were acquainted.

MULLĀ ṢADRĀ'S METHOD AND THE CHARACTERISTICS OF HIS SCHOOL

The particular genius of Mullā Ṣadrā was to synthesize and unify the three paths which lead to the Truth, viz., revelation, rational demonstration, and purification of the soul, which last in turn leads to illumination. For him gnosis, philosophy, and revealed religion were elements of a harmonious ensemble, the harmony of which he sought to reveal in his own life as well as in his writings. He formulated a perspective in which rational demonstration or philosophy, although not necessarily limited to that of the Greeks, became closely tied to the Quran and the sayings of the Prophet and the Imams, and these in turn became unified with the gnostic doctrines which result from the illuminations received by a purified soul.[19] That is why Mullā Ṣadrā's writings are a combination of logical statements, gnostic intuitions, traditions of the Prophet, and the Quranic verses. Through the symbolic interpretation of the sacred text he demonstrated the gnostic quality of the esoteric meaning of revelation and through intellectual intuition he made rational and discursive thought subservient to the universal truths of gnosis. In this fashion he achieved that synthesis of science and revelation in the light of gnosis and in the general perspective of Islam towards which Fārābī and Ibn Sīnā—the latter particularly in his Quranic commentaries—had aimed and which Ghazzālī, Suhrawardī, and the whole chain of sages extending from the Seljuq to the Safavid period had sought to achieve from various points of view.[20]

In metaphysics or, more generally speaking, *ḥikmat* itself, Mullā Ṣadrā is credited with founding the third major school of Muslim "philosophy", the first two being the Peripatetic school, the greatest exponent of which in the Islamic world was Ibn Sīnā, and the Illuminationistic or *ishrāqī* school founded by Suhrawardī.[21] Mullā Ṣadrā adopted certain principles from each school as, for example, the hylomorphism from the Peripatetics and the gradation of Being and the celestial archetypes from the Illuminationists. Moreover, he added certain principles drawn from the teachings of the Sufis like Ibn 'Arabī such as the continual becoming of the substance of the world and unity of Being which had never appeared as principles of any school of *ḥikmat* and were never systematized in the logical language of the *ḥakīms* before Ākhūnd's time. That is why Mullā Ṣadrā is often credited with founding a new and original form of wisdom in the Muslim world which is usually called *al-ḥikmat al-muta'āliyah* as distinguished from *al-ḥikmat al-mashshā'iyyah* (Peripatetic philosophy) and *al-ḥikmat al-ishrāqiyyah* (Illuminationist theosophy).[22]

DIVISION OF THE SCIENCES

Before discussing the basic features of Mullā Ṣadrā's doctrines it is useful to consider his conception of the relation of the sciences to one another and especially the meaning and significance accorded to *ḥikmat.* In the introductory chapter of the *Asfār,* he divides the sciences, following the Peripatetics, into theoretical wisdom consisting of logic, mathema-tics, natural philosophy, and metaphysics, and practical wisdom consisting of ethics, economics, and politics.[23]

In the treatise *Iksīr al-'ārifīn,* he outlines a somewhat more complete and in a way more original division of the sciences.[24] According to this scheme, the sciences *('ulūm)* are either of this world *(dunyawī)* or of the other *(ukhrawī)*; the first is divided into three categories: the science of words *('ilm al-aqwāl)*, the science of acts *('ilm al-af'āl)*, and the science of states of contemplation or thought *('ilm al-aḥwāl* or *afkār).*

The science of words comprises the sciences of the alphabet, word-construction, syntax, prosody, poetics, and the meanings of terms in logic. The science of acts consists of what belongs to various material objects from which the arts of weaving, agriculture, and architecture come into being; what is of a higher degree such as the art of writing, the science of mechanics, alchemy, etc.; what belongs to providing a living for the individual and the society from which the sciences of family, law, politics, and the *Sharī'ah* are created; and, finally, what belongs to the acquisition of spiritual and moral virtues and the casting away of evil from which the "science of the path" (*'ilm al-ṭarīqah*), i.e., Sufism, comes into being. As for the science of states of thought, it consists of the sciences of logical demonstration, the science of arithmetic, the science of geometry including astronomy and astrology, and the sciences of nature including medicine and the various sciences dealing with minerals, plants, and animals.

The sciences of the other world which are not accessible to the ordinary intelligence of men and are not destroyed with the death of the body include the knowledge of angels and intellectual substances, the knowledge of the Preserved Tablet (*al-lawḥ al-maḥfūẓ*), and the knowledge of the Exalted Pen (*al-qalam al-a'lā*), i.e., of the Divine Decree and of the first determination of the Divine Essence which Mullā Ṣadrā, following the earlier Sufis, calls also by the name of the Reality of Muḥammad (*al-ḥaqīqat al-muḥammadiyyah*). These sciences also include the knowledge of death, resurrection, and all that pertains to life hereafter.[25]

Among all the pursuits with which man can occupy himself in this life, none stands in as exalted a position as *ḥikmat* the divisions of which we have outlined above. And among its branches none is as imporant and principial as metaphysics or the science of the principle of things, so that this branch of knowledge alone is often considered worthy of being called *ḥikmat*. Mullā Ṣadrā defines this science as "coming to know the state of the essence of beings as they are, to the extent of human capacity" or "a man's becoming an intellectual world (microcosm) corresponding to the objective world (macrocosm)," or, to quote still another definition, "the comprehension of universals and catharsis from the world of matter."[26]

The above definitions imply that *ḥikmat* is a purely intellectual form of knowledge in which the knower himself undergoes a certain transformation in the process of knowing and his soul becomes a mirror in which the cosmic hierarchy and metacosmic realities are reflected. With such a conception then it is no wonder that Mullā Ṣadrā spent so much of his life in teaching and writing about *ḥikmat* only and regarded all the other sciences as its subsidiaries.

PRINCIPLES OF MULLĀ ṢADRĀ'S DOCTRINES

In discussing the basic principles of *ḥikmat* as understood and expounded by Mullā Ṣadrā, we have chosen to mention those major principles of his thought which distinguish him from his predecessors and which are the characteristic elements of his metaphysics. The doctrines of the Peripatetic and Illuminationistic schools as well as the ideas of Ibn 'Arabī and his followers form the common background for the metaphysics of Mullā Ṣadrā.

There are four topics in each of which Mullā Ṣadrā has departed from earlier philosophical perspectives and which form the principles of his whole intellectual vision. These four subjects concern (1) Being an its various polarizations, (2) substantial motion or the becoming and change of the substance of the world, (3) knowledge and the relation between the knower and the known, and (4) the soul, its faculties, generation, perfection, and final resurrection. We shall consider these questions in the above-mentioned order, emphasizing in each case the particular complexion given to these subjects by Mullā Ṣadrā.

1. *Unity and Gradation of Being.* The cornerstone of Mullā Ṣadrā's doctrines is the principiality and the unity and gradation of Being. As we have already mentioned,[27] one of the major points of contention among Muslim philosophers and theologians concerned the question whether existence or the quiddities *(māhiyyāt)* of things are principial. We saw that the Muslim Peripatetics like the Sufis believed in the principiality of Being, i.e., the objective reality of Being independent of mental abstractions, and considered the quiddities to be nothing but accidents, while the Illuminationists beginning with Suhrawardī and followed by Mullā Ṣadrā's own teacher, Mīr Dāmād, developed a "metaphysics of essences" and held the opposite view that existence is an accident and that the essences are principial. In this debate Mullā Ṣadrā sided definitely with the Peripatetics and Sufis in accepting the principiality of Being, and opposed the Illuminationists.

On the question of the unity and gradation of Being, however, Mullā Ṣadrā departed from Peripatetic teachings completely. In the view of the Muslim Peripatetics the being of each thing is in essence different and distinct from other beings while it is principial with respect to its own quiddity. According to Ākhūnd, however, Being is the same reality in all realms of existence; it is a single reality but with gradations and degrees of intensity. Just as we say the light of the sun, the light of a lamp, or the light of a glowworm, and mean the same subject, i.e., light, but with different predicates, i.e., under different conditions of manifestation, so in the case of Being, the being of God, of a man, of a tree, or of a heap of earth are all one Being or one reality but in various degrees of intensity of manifestation.[28] Moreover, Being, no matter where it manifests itself, appears always with its attributes or armies *('asākir),* as they are traditionally called, such as knowledge, will, power, etc.[29] A stone, because it exists, is a manifestation of Being and, therefore, has knowledge, will, power, and intelligence like men or angels. However, since at the level of a stone the manifestation of Being is very weak, these attributes are hidden and not perceptible.[30]

The various beings in the world of manifestation are all limitations of the one reality or Being. These limitations are abstracted by the mind and become the forms of quiddities *(māhiyyāt)* of things, and when transposed into the principial domain, they become the Platonic ideas or archetypes. Unlike Being which is objectively real and in fact *is* the reality of the cosmos, the *māhiyyāt* are accidents of Being abstracted by the mind without having a reality independent of Being. Even the archetypes *(al-a'yān al-thābitah)* possess a "form" of Being which in this case is God's knowledge of them.

What distinguishes the earthly manifestation of things from their celestial archetypes is not a gradation of the *māhiyyāt* from more subtle to more gross modes of existence, as certain followers of the Illuminationist school believe. Rather, it is the intensity of Being which determines the level of existence of each creature. If the light of Being shines upon the form or quiddity of a man with a greater intensity than now, he will become the man of the intermediate world *(barzakh)* and if the intensity is greater still he will become the celestial man identified with his heavenly archetype.

Absolute Being itself, which is the proper subject for metaphysics, is above all limitations and, therefore, above all forms or *māhiyyāt,* above all substances and accidents. It is the "Form of forms" and the Agent of all acts. By manifesting Itself longitudinally *(ṭūlī).* It brings into being the various orders of Being from the archangels to terrestrial creatures and by manifesting Itself latitudinally *('arḍī)* It creates the various members of each order of Being.[31] Being is the reality of all things so that the knowledge of anything is ultimately the knowledge of Its being and, therefore, of Being Itself. Likewise, the archetypes exist eternally through God's knowledge of them; their being is in fact this very knowledge without which they would have no share whatsoever in Being.

Since Being is unity in multiplicity and multiplicity in unity,[32] it partakes of logical distinctions and divisions while remaining in essence indivisible and above all polarizations. Mullā Ṣadrā goes into great detail about the various divisions and categories of Being and in fact most of the first book of the *Asfār* is concerned with them. We mention here a few of the divisions which Ākhūnd discusses with great rigour in his various writings, especially in the monumental *Asfār.*

One division of Being is into connective being *(al-wujūd al-irtibāṭī)* and self-subsistent being *(al-wujūd al-nafsī).* Connective being is that which connects a subject with a predicate as in the statement: " Man *is* a rational animal." Self-subsistent being is one which stands independently by itself and is not simply the means of connecting two terms. This category of being which exists in itself is in turn divided into three kinds: that which in objective existence is not the quality of something else and is called substance *(jawhar),* that which is the quality of something else and is called accident *('araḍ),* and, finally, that which has need of no cause outside of itself, i.e., the Being of God. From another point of view Mullā Ṣadrā considers the being of all things other than God to be the connective being *(wujūd al-rābiṭ)* and only the Being of God to be Being *per se.*[33]

Another division of Being adopted by Mullā Ṣadrā is that of the necessary *(wājib),* possible *(mumkin),* and impossible *(mumtani')* beings which nearly all the Muslim philosophers and many theologians coming after Ibn Sīnā and, following his example, have accepted.[34] If the intellect considers a being and finds that the meaning of being is essential to it, i.e., lies in its essence, and that there are no causes outside it which have brought it into being, that being is called the Necessary Being. If it has need of a cause outside itself it is called possible being. Moreover, the attribute of possibility pertains to its quiddity as well as to its being. The possibility of its being concerns its relation to its particular being, and the possibility of its being concerns its relation to the Necessary Being. The being or existence of each object, therefore, depends upon the being of God and the knowledge of anything upon the knowledge of the root or principle of its own being. Since the root or basis of the Necessary Being is unknowable, the knowledge of the being of things remains also unknowable to us and it is only the quiddities or *māhiyyāt* which we can know.

These quiddities, as already mentioned, are the limitations placed upon being and abstracted by the mind. The intellect in perceiving any object immediately analyses it into being and quiddity, the latter consisting of the limit or determination of the former. It is only in the case of the Divine Being that such an analysis cannot be made because Absolute Being has no *māhiyyah.* One can say that It is without *māhiyyah* or that Its Being and *māhiyyah* are identical.

The quiddities in themselves are only mental concepts without a separate objective existence so that the effects produced by things come from their being and not from their quiddity. Likewise, cause and effect are categories of being which in one case becomes the cause and in the other the effect of things.

The *māhiyyāt* are either particular or universal; the latter either exist before particulars or are abstracted by the intellect from particulars.[35] The universals which exist independently of all particulars are the archetypes of Platonic ideas upon the reality of which Suhrawardī had insisted against the view of the Peripatetics. Mullā Ṣadrā likewise criticizes

Aristotle and Ibn Sīnā for considering the Platonic ideas to be nothing but the forms of things impinged upon the Divine Intellect. He insists upon the reality of the archetypes in a spiritual world that is completely independent of the world of particulars as well as of all mental images formed in the human mind.[36] Ākhūnd praises Suhrawardī and accepts fully the reasons he had given for the existence of the Platonic ideas or "masters of the species" *(arbāb al-anwāʻ)*. There is a spiritual man in the spiritual world who is the real cause for the activities and ontological qualities of the terrestrial man; likewise in the case of other species each has an intelligible idea or archteype which governs all the activities and life of that species on earth.

The archetype is in essence one with its particulars but differs from them in characteristics which arise from the substance or "matter" of the particulars. The archetype appears different in each stage *(ṭawr)* of manifestation while in the realm of reality it is one and the same truth. The beings of this world are the reflections and shadows of the archetypes so that they are like them and share in their reality and at the same time are different from them in being less real and farther removed form the source of Being.

One of the principles for which Ākhūnd is famous is called *imkān al-ashraf* or "the possibility of that which is superior." According to this principle, just as each being in treading the path of perfection passes through various stages from the lowest to the highest, so it is necessary that for each imperfect being in this world there be degrees of being in the higher stages of the cosmic hierarchy, since each being has descended from the Divine Principle through intermediate stages of being. For example, the being of man on earth in his present state of imperfection necessitates the being of man in the intermediary world of souls, and the latter the being of the spiritual man in the intelligible world. According to this principle, therefore, the very existence of quiddities in their earthly state of being necessitates the existence of these forms in the intermediate world of souls or the world of inverted or reflected forms *(al-amthāl al-muʻallaqah)* and these in turn necessitate their existence in the spiritual world of simple intellectual substances.

After showing that the *māhiyyāt* are in reality limitations of being, Mullā Ṣadrā goes on to assert that the logical distinction made by Aristotle and all the later philosophers between substance and the accidents which together form the ten categories concerns only the *māhiyyāt*; Being, properly speaking, is neither substance nor accident but above both. When we say of a thing that it is such and such a substance or that its particular quality and quantity are its accidents, we refer only to its *māhiyyah* and not to its being.

The relation of cause and effect, however, contrary to that of substance and accidents, concerns only the being of things.[37] All things in the universe have a cause and an effect and since everything is a manifestation of Being, every effect is but an aspect of its cause and cannot in essence differ from it. That is why the well-known principle that from unity only unity can issue forth, *ex uno non fit nisi unum,* must be true. From the Divine Essence which is simple and one, only a simple being can issue forth. Mullā Ṣadrā calls this first manifestation of the Divine Essence Extended Being *(al-wujūd al-munbasiṭ)*, the first intellect, the sacred effusion *(al-fayḍ al-muqaddas)* or the Truth of truths *(ḥaqīqat al-ḥaqā'iq)* which he considers to be one in essence but partaking of degrees and stages of manifestation.[38]

He divides reality into three categories: of the Divine Essence, of "Absolute Being" which he identifies with Extended Being, and of relative being which is that of the creatures.[39] The cause of all things, therefore, is Extended Being which in turn is the first determination of the Divine Essence. God is, thus, the Cause of causes and the Ultimate Source of all effects to be seen in the universe, because all causes and effects arise from the beings of things and all beings are in reality the stages of the One Being.

To terminate our discussion of the manifestations of Being in cosmic existence we must also consider the question of form and matter. On this question Mullā Ṣadrā sides with the Peripatetics and is against the Illuminationists in accepting the theory of hylomorphism. In his view, howeve, matter is not limited to the corporeal domain. Rather, it is the aspect of potentiality which manifests itself in all the realms of existence according to the conditions of that particular realm. Bodies have a matter belonging to the corporeal world, and souls *(anfās)*, a matter conformable to the subtle world of the psyche; moreover, in each world matter is a lower degree of being of the form with which it is united and for that reason accompanies it in all realms of existence until the highest realm which is the world of pure intelligences *(mujarradāt)*. That is why, as Ākhūnd expresses it, matter has love for form which forever compels it to seek union with it (form). Only in the intelligible world, which is also called the *'ālam al-jabarūt,* are the spiritual realities completely separated from and free of all species of matter, even the most subtle.

2. *Substantial Motion.* The question of potentiality leads to that of motion because motion, as Aristotle said, is becoming actual of that

which is potential. Mullā Ṣadrā rejects the possibility of sudden change from one substance to another which the Peripatetics accepted along with gradual change. Rather, he considers all change to be a form of motion and introduces the idea of substantial motion *(al-ḥarakat al-jawhariyyah)*,[40] which is another of the well-known principles associated with his name, as a basis of his whole outlook from which he goes on to prove the creation of the world in time, bodily resurrection, and many other doctrines that will be discussed in the course of this chapter.

It is well known that the Muslim Peripatetics, following Aristotle, limited motion to only four of the ten categories, i.e., quantity *(kamm)*, quality *(kayf)*, place *(makān)*, and substance,[41] the last understood only in the sense of generation and corruption. Ibn Sīnā rejected completely substantial motion in any sense other than instantaneous coming into being and passing away and argued that since the essence of a thing depends upon its substance, if that substance were to change, its essence would also change and lose its identity.[42]

Following the Sufis, Mullā Ṣadrā considered the world to be like a stream of water which is flowing continually and believes motion to be nothing but the continuous regeneration and re-creation of the world at every instance.[43] According to him, it is not only the accidents but the substance of the universe itself that partakes of motion and becoming, i.e., continuous re-creation and rebirth.[44] In order to prove this assertion, Ākhūnd makes use of several arguments. For example, he writes that it is an accepted fact that accidents have need of a substance upon which they depend for their being and properties. Their subsistence depends upon its creation and regeneration. Therefore, every change which takes place in the accidents of a body must be accompanied by a corresponding change in the substance; otherwise the being of the former would not follow the being of the latter. Or, in other words, since the effect must be the same as its cause, the cause or substance of a changing accident must itself be changing.

In addition, it is known that all beings in the universe are seeking perfection and are in the porcess of becoming and change in order to overcome their imperfections. Since divine manifestation never repeats itself, God creates new theophanies at every moment in order to remove imperfections and bring new perfections to things. The matter of each being, therefore, is continuously in the process of wearing a new dress, i.e., being wed to a new form, without, however, casting away its older dress. It is only the rapidity of this change that makes it imperceptible and guarantees the continuity and identification of a particular being through the stages of substantial motion.

According to Mullā Ṣadrā each body consists of matter and two forms: one, the form of the body which gives matter dimensions and the possibility of accepting other forms, and the other the form of the species *(Ṣuwar naw'iyyah)* which determines the species and identity of the body. Each of these two forms is at every instant changing, and matter is taking on new forms at every moment. Moreover, at each stage of substantial change the totality of a being which itself consists of form and matter may be considered to be the matter of the aspect of potentiality for the next stage the actualized aspect of which then becomes the form.

The power or force which motivates this change is nature which is a force hidden within the cosmic substance. In fact, since Being comes before nothingness, motion in this world comes before rest through the force immanent in the cosmos. Needless to say, this motion is limited to the degrees of cosmic existence in which matter is present, i.e., to corporeal and subtle manifestation, and does not extend to the world of pure intelligences or archteypes which are beyond all change.

Substantial motion itself has also the two aspects of change and permanence. Each form has two faces, one in the world of archetypes and the other in nature, the first permanent and the second in continuous renewal. The substance of the world itself is, therefore, the intermediary between permanence and change; it possesses two aspects, one which is continuously in motion and the other, which Mullā Ṣadrā identifies with the intelligences, above all change.

Time, for Ākhūnd as for Aristotle, is the quantity of motion, which, in a world of continuous substantial motion, becomes an inherent feature of cosmic existence.[45] It is, more specifically, the measure of the substantial motion of the heavens but not the measure of their rotation as held by the Peripatetics. The heavens, according to Mullā Ṣadrā, are in continuous contemplation of the perfection of their beloveds, i.e., the universal intellects which at every instant cause a new form to be projected upon the essence of the universal souls. The cause of celestial motion is, therefore, the desire to reach perfection, a goal which, because of its limitlessness, makes celestial motion endless. The heavens are in continuous creative worship, their motion being a sign of their contemplation of the Divine by means of the intelligences, and their causing generation and growth in nature through their illumination being a sign of their act of creation. The whole world, therefore, both in its gross and subtle domains, partakes of substantial motion, and time is the measure of this motion as it occurs in the heavens where it is most regular as well as regulatory.[46]

Mullā Ṣadrā makes use of the principle of substantial motion to explain many of the most intricate problems of metaphysics and physics including the relation between permanence and change which we have already mentioned, the creation of the world, the creation of the soul, and various eschatological questions. This principle can, therefore, be regarded as one of the distinguishing features of his doctrinal formulation.

As to the question of creation Ākhūnd opposes the simple creation *ex-nihilo* of the theologians who believe the world to have been brought into being in time from utter nothingness. Likewise, he rejects the view of the Peripatetics who believe the world to have been created only in essence or *in principio* but not in time and the view of Mīr Dāmād about *al-ḥudūth al-dahrī.*[47] Mullā Ṣadrā believes that creation is in time *(al-ḥudūth al-zamānī)* because through substantial motion the being of the universe is renewed at every moment or, more explicitly, that the world is created at every instant, so that one can say that the being of the world depends upon its non-being at a previous moment. Where he differs from the theologians is that his conception of creation *ex-nihilo* is complementary to the view that the archetypes of the world of creation exist changelessly in the intelligible world and that the world is connected with its Divine Origin through a permanent hierarchy.

This hierarchy begins with the first determination of the Essence which Ākhūnd, following the Sufis, calls the Reality of Muḥammad.[48] This is followed by the pure intelligences which are completely separated from matter and potentiality, the last of which is the giver of forms to the universe and the governor of the world of generation and corruption.[49] This last intellect is like a mill that grinds out new forms at every moment to feed the *hylé* of the world. It governs the world according to Divine Decree and gives revelation to prophets and inspiration to saints. Following the intelligible hierarchy there is the world of cosmic imagination or inverted or reflected forms or the purgatory between the intelligible and the material domains and, finally, the visible universe. The world is, therefore, created in time in the sense that its being is renewed after a moment in which it "was not"; at the same time it is the terminal state of an immutable hierarchy which through the subtle and angelic realms of being relates the visible cosmos to its Divine Source.

3. *Divine and Human Knowledge.* From what we have already said, it is clear that for Mullā Ṣadrā knowledge forms the very substance of cosmic manifestation itself and is moreover the gate to and means of salvation for the soul. Like all other gnostics Ākhūnd considers knowledge and being, or from another point of view, the knower and the known,[50] to be essentially the same and identifies the being of things with God's knowledge of them.[51] God knows His own Essence and His

Essence is none other than His Being, and since His Being and Essence are the same, He is at once the knower, knowledge, and the known.

In the case of the pure intellects or forms that are completely divorced from matter also, the intellect and the intelligible are the same, the difference in the two instances being that, although knowledge of the intellects is identical with their being, it is not identical with their quiddities, since their being surpasses their quiddities, whereas in the cases of God knowledge is identical both with Being and quiddity, since God's quiddity is the same as His Being.[52]

Mullā Ṣadrā rejects the Peripatetic notion that God's knowledge of things is the projection of their forms upon His Essence as well as the idea followed by many Illuminationists that God's knowledge is the presence of the very forms of things in His Essence. Rather, he uses the gnostic symbol of a mirror and considers the Divine Essence a mirror in which God sees the forms or essences of all things and in fact, through the contemplation of these forms or archetypes in the mirror of His own Essence, He brings all things into being. Moreover, since the forms of all creatures, universal as well as particular, are reflected in His Essence, God has knowledge of every particle of the universe.[53]

Mullā Ṣadrā divides knowledge *('ilm)* into acquired *(ḥuṣūlī)* knowledge and innate or presential *(ḥuḍūrī)* knowledge and, like the Illuminationists, divides the latter category into the knowledge of a thing of itself, of a cause of its effect, and of an effect of its cause. Perception is for him a movement from potentiality to actuality and an elevation in the degree of being in which the perceiver or knower rises from his own level of existence to the level of existence of the inulligahle form of the intelligible form of that which is perceived through the union between the knower and the known which characterizes all intellection.

As for acquired knowledge or the knowledge of the human soul of things other than itself, it is not a reflection of the forms of things upon the soul and the soul does not have a passive role in the act of knowing. Rather, since man is a microcosm composed of all degrees of existence, his knowledge of things comes from the contemplation of these forms in the mirror of his own being much like Divine Knowledge with the difference that God's knowledge leads to objective existence *(al-wujūd al-'aynī)* of forms, while man's knowledge leads only to their mental existence *(al-wujūd al-dhihnī)* . Otherwise, man's soul has a creative power similar to that of God; its knowledge implies the creation of forms in the soul—forms the subsistence of which depends upon the soul as the subsistence of the objective universe depends upon God.[54]

According to Mullā Ṣadrā, mental existence or the presence in the mind of forms that yield knowledge of things as well as knowledge of itself is above the categories of substance and accidents and is ultimately identical with Being Itself. The knowledge that the soul has of things is just like the illumination of the light of Being. This knowledge establishes the form of that which is perceived in the mind, as Being establishes and manifests the forms and quiddities of things externally. Moreover, it repeats in an inverted order the degrees of cosmic manifestation. Just as cosmic existence originates from the Divine Essence through the world of the intelligences and consists of the degrees of cosmic souls, bodies, forms, and matter, so knowledge begins from the senses, then rises to the level of the imagination, apprehension, and finally intellection ascending the scale of Being to the summit from which the whole of universal manifestation has descended.

4. *The Soul, Its Origin, Becoming, and Entelechy.* Another of the important changes which Mullā Ṣadrā brought about in the formulation of *ḥikmat* was the emphasis he laid upon the importance of psychology or the science of the soul (*'ilm al-nafs*) above and beyond what Peripatetic philosophy had accorded to it. Moreover, he removed the discussion of psychology from physics or natural philosophy and made it a branch of metaphysics and a study that is complementary to the science of the origin of things.[55]

The soul *(nafs)*, according to Mullā Ṣadrā, is a single reality which first appears as the body *(jism)* and then through substantial motion and an inner transformation becomes the vegetative soul, then the animal soul, and finally the human soul. This development occurs from within the substance of the original body without there being any effusion from the heavenly souls or the Active Intellect.[56] The substance of the human sperm is at first potentially a plant; then as it grows in the womb it becomes actually a plant and potentially an animal. Shortly before birth, it is actually an animal and potentially human. Then it is born as human and finally at the age of adolescence it become fully human and potentially either an angel or a disciple of the devil.[57] All of these stages lie hidden within the first substance or germ which through substantial motion traverses the degrees of being until it becomes completely divorced from all matter and potentiality and enjoys immortality in the world of pure intelligences.[58] The soul is, therefore, brought into being with the body but it has spiritual subsistence independent of the body.[59] Or, to be more precise, the soul at the beginning "is" the body which through inner transformation passes through various stages until it becomes absolutely free from matter and change.

The soul in each stage of its journey acquires a new faculty or set of faculties. As a mineral it has the faculty of preserving its form and as a plant, the faculties of feeding, growth, and the transformation of foreign substanaces into its own form. As an animal the faculties of motion and various forms of desire are acquired, and as a higher animal it develops in addition to the external senses the inner faculties of memory and imagination.[60] Finally, in man the five inner faculties: *sensus communis (ḥiss al-mushtarik)* which perceives forms, apprehension *(wahm)* which perceives meanings, fantasy *(khayāl)* which preserves forms, memory *(dhākirah)* which preserves meanings and the double faculty of imagination *(mutakhayyilah)*, and thought *(mutafakkirah)* which in the first case governs the sensible and in the second the intelligible domains, are also acquired.[61] Throughout its development it is the same single soul which in one case appears as sight, in another as memory, and in yet another as desire. The faculties are not something added to the soul but it is the soul itself or, in a more esoteric sense, Being itself which appears in various forms in each case.[62] The soul passes through this stream of becoming—the world—and the various parts of its course are marked by the archetypes or Platonic ideas that distinguish one species from another. It wears a new dress and a new guise at each point of the stream but the traveller is throughout one and the same.[63]

Although the enumeration of the inner faculties by Mullā Ṣadrā is essentially the same as that made by previous Muslim authors borrowing it from Aristotle, there is one point in which Mullā Ṣadrā departs from the Peripatetics completely. It is well known that Aristotle considered only the universal intellect to be immortal and the Muslim Peripatetics such as Ibn Sīnā accorded immortality only to the intellectual part of the human soul. Mullā Ṣadrā, following certain Sufi and Hermetic teachings, asserts that the faculty of imagination enjoys also a form of immortality or at least existence independent of the body. He considers the universe to consist of three domains: the intelligible world, the sensible world, and an intermediate world *(barzakh)* of imagination which is macrocosmic as well as microcosmic. The faculty of imagination in man as well as in some of the higher animals is, according to Ākhūnd, a microcosmic counterpart of the cosmic imagination and has the power of creating forms. Upon the death of the body, this faculty, like the intellectual part of the soul, enjoys a form of life of its own and may in fact lead the soul to the intermediate world if it is the dominant element in the soul.

Mullā Ṣadrā, like other Sūfis, compares the soul to the cosmos on the one hand and to the Quran on the other, identifying the higher states of being of the soul with the esoteric meanings of the Quran.[64] There are seven degrees of existence for the soul as there are seven heavens and seven levels of interpretation of the Quran. These degrees he enumerates as nature *(ṭabī'ah),* soul *(nafs)*, intellect *('aql),* spirit *(rūḥ)*, secret *(sirr)*, hidden secret *(khafī),* and the most hidden state *(akhfā)* which is that of perfect union with God.[65] Each corresponds to a state of being, the totality extending from the life of nature or the senses to the divine life of union with God.

According Mullā Ṣadrā from another point of view the soul has two faculties the practical *('amalī)* and the theoretical *('ilmī* or *naẓarī)*, which latter at first is dependent upon the former but later becomes completely independent. The practical faculty consists of four stages: making use of the Law *(Sharī'ah)* of various religions sent to guide mankind, purifying the soul from evil qualities, illuminating the soul with spiritual virtues and the sciences, and finally annihilating the soul in God, beginning with the journey to God and then in God and finally with God.[66]

As for the theoretical faculty it too is divided into four stages: the *potential* or *material* intellect *(al-'aql al-hayūlānī)* which has only the capability of accepting forms, *habitual* intellect, *(al-'aql bi'l-malakah)* which knows only simple and preliminary truths such as the truth that the whole is greater than its parts, the *active* intellect *(al-'aql bi'l-fi'l)* which no longer has need of matter and concerns itself solely with intellectual demonstrations and is either acquired or bestowed as a divine gift and finally the acquired intellect *(al-'aql al-mustafād)* which is the Active Intellect that has been united with the divine origin of all existence. These stages are also road-marks upon the path trodden by the soul without implying any form of multiplicity; the soul remains the one traveller traversing all these stages on the road to perfection, the fruit and end of which is union with God.

Mullā Ṣadrā deals with eschatology in great detail in many of his works and departs completely from the usual philosophical language in the treatment of this subject. His language is primarily that of the Qur an and the *Ḥadīth* and of the gnostics. According to Ākhūnd, the relation of this world to the next is like that of the mother's womb to this world. While the child is in his mother's womb he is actually in this world as well, but being separated from this world does not know of its existence. Likewise, man, while in this world is also in the next but the majority of men are unaware of the invisible world. Only the gnostics "see" the other world while they are here on earth and that is because for them terrestrial existence has become transparent.

Ākhūnd divides cosmic beings into five classes each of which has a destiny and an end proper to its nature:[67] the pure intelligences separated from all potentiality; the intelligences which govern the heavens; the various psychic entities belonging to the world of the imagination such as the *jinn* and certain parts of the human soul, animal and vegetable souls; and, finally, minerals and elements. The separated intelligences subsist forever in the Divine Essence and are never separated from it. As for the rational soul *(al-nafs al-nāṭiqah)*, it is either perfect, as the souls of the heavens and of some men, and, in both cases, returns to God, or else it is imperfect. In the latter case it is either devoid of all desire for perfection as in the animals and those human beings who have committed much evil in this life, or it is desirous of perfection like many persons who, having chosen the wrong path, realize their mistake and wish to be guided towards the Truth. In the former case the soul, like other psychic entities belonging to the intermediary world, after separation from the body becomes united with the forms of the intermediary world of imagination *(ʻālam al-mithāl)*;[68] in the latter case the soul suffers after its separation from the body until it is finally purified and united with God.

Plants are either used as food by men and animals and, therefore, share in their destinies, or have an independent existence, in which case, after the end of their terrestrial existence, they join their archetypes in the world of pure forms. Likewise with minerals and the elements; they too become united with their intelligible counterparts after their terrestrial existence terminates. In fact, these terrestrial beings are united with their archetypes even while they are on earth, but only the gnostics are aware of this reality.

As for man's bodily resurrection on the Last Day, Mullā Ṣadrā considers it to be one of the great mysteries of metaphysics revealed only those who have reached the highest stage.[69] He accepts bodily resurrection which he interprets in a particular fashion. It is known that man's individuality and distinguishing characteristics come from his soul and not from his body because the substance of the body changes every few years without in any way destroying the unity of the human being. Of the faculties of the soul, however, intellection and imagination are innate to it, while the vegetative and animal faculties such as the external senses and passions are received by it through the body. According to Ākhūnd, in the next world all souls will receive the power to create external forms as prophets and saints do here in this world. For example, each soul can create the pleasure received through sight from within itself without the need of what appears to us here as an external organ. In other words, the organs of the body which appear as "external" to the soul are created from within the soul in the next world so that the resurrection of the soul is really complete with the body according to all the meanings we can give to the word "body."

The difference between paradise and hell lies in that the souls in paradise have the power to bring into being all the forms that are beautiful and pleasant, all the flowers and *houris* of paradise, while the impure souls in hell have only the power to bring into being ugly and tormenting forms and are in fact forced to suffer by the very forms they will have created. Mullā Ṣādrā adds, however, that ultimately the pains suffered in the inferno will come to an end and, as Ibn 'Arabī had said, the fires of hell will freeze and all will return to the Divine origin of things.[70]

THE SIGNIFICANCE OF MULLĀ ṢADRĀ AND HIS INFLUENCE

As mentioned in the introduction to this chapter, the importance of Mullā Ṣadrā lies not only in rekindling the lamp of learning and reviving the intellectual sciences fully for the first time in the Muslim world after the Mongol invasion, but also for uniting and harmonizing revelation, gnosis, and philosophy together. Some authors have criticized Mullā Ṣadrā for taking certain principles from Ibn 'Arabī, Fārābī, and Suhrawardī and have, therefore, refused to accept his "originality." But as Aristotle has said so justifiably, there is nothing new under the sun. One cannot create a metaphysics of one's own as if metaphysics were a mechanical invention. The principles have always been and will always be the same. What determines the originality of an author in a traditional civilization like that of Islam is his ability to reinterpret and reformulate the eternal verieties in a new light and thereby create a new intellectual perspective.

Regarded in this way, Mullā Ṣadrā must certainly be considered to be one of the most significant figures in the intellectual life of Islam. Coming at a moment when the intellectual sciences had become weakened, he succeeded in reviving them by co-ordinating philosophy as inherited from the Greeks and interpreted by the Peripatetics and Illuminationists before him with the teachings of Islam in its exoteric and esoteric aspects. He succeeded in putting the gnostic doctrines of Ibn 'Arabī in a logical dress. He made purification of the soul a necessary basis and complement of the study of *ḥikmat,* thereby bestowing upon philosophy the practice of ritual and spiritual virtues which it had lost in the period of decadence of classical civilization. Finally, he succeeded in correlating the wisdom of the ancient Greek and Muslim sages and philosophers as interpreted esoterically with the inner meaning of the Qur-an. In all these matters he represents the final stage of effort by several generations of Muslim sages and may be considered to be the person in whom the streams, which had been approaching one another for some centuries before, finally united.[71]

More specifically, Mullā Ṣadrā was able to harmonize his doctrinal formulation with the teachings of Islam in such a way as to overcome all the major difficulties which the Peripatetic philosophers met in the face of the teachings of the Quran and for which al-Ghazzālī criticized them so severely.[72] Of particular significance was his divorcing metaphysics to a large extent both from Ptolemaic astronomy and Aristotelian physics. While in Europe Galileo, Kepler, and Newton were destroying the homogeneity of Aristotelian cosmology and physics and in this way weakening the medieval Christian world-view which was closely linked with it, Mullā Ṣadrā, through his doctrine of substantial motion and through considering the science of the soul to be independent of physics, separated metaphysics to a large extent from medieval natural philosophy. This separation, although perhaps not of immediate significance in the eleventh/seventeenth-century Persia, which was still immune to European ideas, became of great importance in the later centuries. As the modern scientific world-view became more and more accepted in Persia during the Qajar period, the separation brought about by Ākhūnd between metaphysics and natural philosophy helped to preserve the traditional wisdom in the face of attacks by modernists whose only weapon was modern scientific theories connected with the world of matter. In this way also, Ākhūnd rendered great service to the Islamic intellectual sciences and helped their preservation until today.

There is no doubt that nearly the whole of the intellectual life of Persia during the past three centuries and a half has centred around Mullā Ṣadrā. Of his immediate students, Mullā Muḥsin Fayḍ, 'Abd al-Razzāq Lāhījī, and Qāḍī Sa'īd Qūmmī, all of whom are among the leading figures of Shi'ah Islam, we need say little here for they have already been discussed in the previous chapter.[73] It need only be added that these men in turn produced a generation of students who extended the teachings of Ākhūnd far and wide.[74] In the Qajar period, after a short interim of anarchy caused by the Afghan invasion, the school of Mullā Ṣadrā was once again revived, the most famous of its members being Ḥājjī Mullā Hādī Sabziwārī, Mullā 'Alī Nūrī, author of one of the most important commentaries upon the *Asfār*, Mullā Ismā'īl Khājū'ī also a teacher and commentator upon the *Asfar*, Mullā 'Alī Mudarris Zunūzī, author of a significant work *Badā'i' al-ḥikam* in Persian and glosses upon the *Asfār*, and Muḥammad Hīdajī, also the author of a commentary upon the *Asfār*.[75]

The influence of Ākhūnd is to be seen wherever the traditional school of *ḥikmat* is still preserved and taught in Persia and else where.[76] All the adherents of this school have regarded Mullā Ṣadrā as their master and it is no exaggeration to say that Ākhūnd stands along with Fārābī, Ibn Sīnā al-Ghazzālī, Naṣīr al-Dīn Ṭūsī, Suhrawardī, and Ibn 'Arabī among the principal intellectual figures of Islamic and that he, is no lesser a figure than his more famous predecessors.[77] In him the many spiritual streams of the earlier centuries met and united in a new river which has watered the intellectual soil of Persia during the past four centuries; his teachings are as alive today as they were at the time of their formulation.

NOTES

1. This chapter has been written with the invaluable help of Ḥājj Muḥammad Ḥusayn Ṭabāṭabā'ī, one of the leading authorities on the school of Mullā Ṣadrā in Iran today, the author of the twenty seven volume Quranic commentary *al-Mīzān* and the editor and commentator of the new edition of the *Asfār.*

2. Comte de Gobineau, one of the most observant of travellers to visit Persia during the past few centuries, was quite aware of Mullā Ṣadrā's significance although not quite well acquainted with his ideas, for in a well-known passage he writes: "Le vrai, l'incontestable merite de Mullā Ṣadrā reste celui que j'ai indiqué plus haut: e'est d'avoir raminé, rejeuni, pour le temps oú il vivait, la philosophie antique, en lui conservant les moins possible de ses formes avicenniques . . . ." Gobineau, *Les Religions et les philosophies dans l'Asie centrale,* les Editions G. Grés et Cie, Paris, 1923, p. 102.

3. The date of Mullā Ṣadrā's birth was unknown until quite recently when in preparing the new edition of the *Asfār*, Ạllāmah Tabāṭabā'ī collected a large number of handwritten manuscripts of the work. On the margin of one of the manuscripts dated 1197/1782 with marginal notes by Mullā Ṣadrā himself, the authenticity of which cannot be doubted, there appears this statment: "This truth was revealed to me on Friday, the 7th of Jumādī al-Ūlā 1037 A.Ḥ when 58 years had passed from (my life). . . ." Therefore, the date of his birth can be established as 979/1571 or 980/1572.

   For the traditional accounts of the life of Mullā Ṣadrā and his works, see M.B. Khunsārī, *Rawḍāt al-jannāt*, Tehran, lithographed edition, 1306/1888, Vol. II, pp. 331-32; M. A. Tabrīzī, *Rayḥānat al-adab*, Sa'dī Press, Tehran, 1331/1912, Vol. II, pp. 458-61; Mīr Khwand, *Rawḍāt al-Ṣafā'*, Tehran, lithographed edition, 1270/1853, Vol. VIII, p. 120; T. Tunikābunī, *Qiṣaṣ al-'ulamā',* 'Ilmī Press, Tehran, 1313/1895, pp. 329-33, and Āghā Buzurg Ṭihrānī, *al-Dharī'ah*, al-Gharrā' Press, Najaf, 1355/1936, on dealing with various writings of Ākhūnd.

   As for secondary sources, see M. Mudarrisī Chahārdahī, *Tārīkh-i falāsifa-yi islām*, 'Ilmī Press, Tehran, 1336 A.H. Solar, Vol. I, pp. 179ff.; A. A. Zanjāni, *al-Fīlsūf al-fārsī al-kabīr Ṣadr al-Dīn al-Shīrāzī,* al-Mufīd Press, Damascus, pp. 212-18, No. 3, 1951, pp. 318-27; J. 'Alī Yāsīn, *Ṣadr al-Dīn al-Shīrāzī mujaddid al-falsafat al-Islāmiyyah*, al-Ma'ārif Press, 1375/1956, and the introduction by M.Ṛ Muẓaffar, in the new edition of the *Asfār*, Dā'irat al-Ma'ārif al-Islāmiyyah, Qūm, 1378/1958.

For an account of the life and doctrines of Mullā Ṣadrā in European languages, see Gobineau, *op. cit*, pp. 91-103; E.G. Browne, *A Literary History of Persia,* University Press, Cambridge, 1924, Vol. IV, pp. 429-30; and M.Horten, *Die Philosophie des Islam*, Verlag Ernst Eheinhardt, München, 1924, pp. 57ff. Also Browne, *A Year Amongst the Persians*, Adam & Charles Black, London, 1950, pp. 141-43.

4. Concerning Bahā' al-Dīn 'Āmilī and Mīr Dāmād, see the preceding chapter.

   To know the names of the masters of a *ḥakīm* is important because learning *ḥikmat* from "within" is impossible without a master for the majority of even those who are gifted to pursue it. One can learn certain ideas from books alone but to understand what *ḥikmat* means and what the various authorities meant by various expressions there is need of a master who himself learnt the doctrines from another master and so one going back to the early masters. The *ḥakīm* is, therefore, as insistent upon the authenticity of his chain of masters as a verifier of *ḥadīth* is about the *isnād* of a tradition or a Sufi master about the *silsilah* or chain of his *ṭarīqah.*

5. We have alreay discussed in detail in previous chapters the meaning of this term as used here, i.e., a combination of gnosis, Illuminationist and Peripatetic philosophy which is neither theology nor philosophy as currently understood but theosophy in the proper and original sense of the term and not in its present usurpation by various pseudo-spiritualist groups.

6. The Khān school which is one of the most beautiful edifices of the Safavid period had fallen into ruins for some years when about ten years ago the Bureau of Archaeology of the Iranian Government undertook the task of repairing it. It is now operating once again as a *madrasah* for traditional learning.

7. He in fact criticizes Ibn Sīnā for having spent his time composing works on other sciences like mathematics and medicine.

8. The story is told in most of the traditional sources mentioned above that Mullā Ṣadrā once asked Mīr Dāmād why he was respected by all the religious authorities while Ākhūnd, despite his powerful family, was molested so much by some of the '*ulamā'*. Mīr Dāmād answered that although they were both saying the same thing, he hid his ideas within so many difficult expressions that only the *élite* would be able to understand them while Mullā Ṣadrā wrote so clearly that anyone with a knowledge of Arabic could detect the trend of his ideas.

9. See also *Rayḥānat al-adab,* pp. 458-61, where fifty works by him are mentioned, and A. A. Zanjānī, *op. cit.,* pp. 19-22 where he mentions twenty-six metaphysical and philosophical and seventeen religious works some of which are of doubtful authenticity. Refer also to J. 'Alī Yāsīn, *op. cit.,* pp. 58-62, where twenty-six works are named.

10. The *Kitāb al-hidāyah* dealing with a complete cycle of *ḥikmat,* i.e. logic, natural philosophy, and metaphysics, was composed by the seventh/thirteenth-century Persian author, Athīr al-Dīn Mufaḍḍal ibn 'Umar al-Abharī; it soon became one of the basic books of instruction in the *madrasahs.* The tenth/sixteenth century commentary upon it by Kamāl al-Dīn Mībudī was the best known before Mullā Ṣadrā composed his own commentary upon it.

11. The *Uṣūl al-kāfī* was also commented upon by Majlisī as we have mentioned in the previous chapter. The commentary of Mullā Ṣadrā which is of a more intellectual nature is one of the most important Shī'ah works wriṭten in the Safavid period and is perhaps his most significant religious composition along with Mafātiḥ al-ghayb.

12. This unpublished treatise the manuscript of which exists in the Majlis Library (MS.

103) in Tehran is the only known prose work of Mullā Ṣadrā in Persian, all the other above-mentioned writings being in Arabic.

13. The manuscript of the *Sharḥ al-hidāyah* in the Mishkāt Collection at Tehran University, MS. 254, is in Mullā Ṣadrā's own handwriting; several quatrains appear in the opening pages which are without doubt his own.
14. E. G. Browne, *op. cit.,* Vol. IV, p. 430.
15. The 1282/1865 Tehran lighographed edition with the commentaries of Sabziwārī on the margin runs over a 1,000 large pages and the new edition by 'Allāmah Ṭabāṭabā'ī with running commentary by himself and several other *ḥakīms* of the Qajar period including Sabziwārī and Mullā 'Alī Nūrī is planned in nine 400-page volumes of which three have appeared so far. The *Asfār* which is used in the graduate school of the theological faculty in Tehran University is taught over a five or six-year period and then only a certain parts of the book are covered. It is said that Ḥājjī Mullā Hādī Sabziwārī, the greatest Persian *ḥakīm* after Mullā Ṣadrā, taught the complete *Asfār* to his advanced disciples over a six-year period.
16. Mullā Ṣadrā, *Mafātīḥ al-ghayb, al-miftāḥ al-thālith, al-mashhad al-thāmin.*
17. See the preceding chapter in which the formative elements of Shī'ah intellectual life leading to Mullā Ṣadrā and other Safavid sages have been discussed.
18. See *Asfār*, Tehran, lithographed edition,1282/1865, Book II, Section IV. Mullā Ṣadrā writes that these pre-Socratic philosophers actually spoke in a symbolic language (*ramz*) and implied by their theory that the world was composed of a single element, the doctrine of the unity of Being or *waḥdat al-wujūd* which is the basis of the gnostic doctrines of Ibn 'Arabī. Mullā Ṣadrā in fact identifies the water of Thales with the *nafas al-Raḥmān* or the breath of the Compassionate which the Sufis consider to be the ultimate substance of the universe. These early Ionians who are considered by some today to be the founders of the modern quantitative sciences of nature appear to the Muslims in a different light as expositors of universal gnosis and those who, as Mullā Ṣadrā writes, "have adopted the light of *ḥikmat* from the lamp of prophecy".
19. For an account of the relation of Mullā Ṣadrā to Shi'ism and his success in unifying the three above-mentioned elements, see M. H. Ṭabāṭabā'ī, "Muṣāḥaba-yi Ustād 'Allāmah Ṭabāṭabā'ī bā Professor Henry Corbin dar Bāra-yi shi'ah," *Sālana-yi Maktab-i Tashayyu',* No. 2, 1339 Solar, pp. 61-64. This is one of the most important works written recently by a Shi'ah authority on the general perspective of Shi'ism and the various sciences developed by the Shi'ah, and is the result of a series of meetings between him and H. Corbin in which the latter posed several basic questions about the spiritual attitude of Shi'ism and the relation between Shi'ism and *ḥikmat* and Sufism. The book was written in answer to H. Corbin's questions and contains a wealth of precious knowledge about the intellectual life of Shi'ism.
20. It may at first seem surprising that Mulla Ṣadra wrote a treatise against those who called themselves Sufis. But if we consider the social and political conditions of the later Safavid period in which Sufism was greatly disdained by political authorities and much of it had become a body without a soul, we can perhaps understand some of the motifs for Mullā Ṣadrā's attack on it. However, the "Sufis" whom Mullā Ṣadrā attacked were not the Sufis proper but those who were seeking to destroy the exoteric truths and bring about social anarchy in the name of an esotericism that they themselves did not possess. Otherwise there is not the least doubt of Mullā Ṣadrā's connection with Sufism—although he preferred to use the name gnostic (*'ārif*) rather

than Sufi—nor can one doubt in any way the gnostic quality of his doctrines.

21. See the chapters on Suhrawardī in this volume.

22. If we have translated *ḥikmat* as philosophy in one case and as theosophy in the other, it is because the meaning of this term includes both the wisdom belonging to the rational and mental place or philosophy and the wisdom which transcends the level of the ordinary human mind and which, properly speaking, belongs to the angelic order and cannot be called philosophy as that term is currently understood in European languages.

23. See J. Muṣliḥ, *Falsafa-yi 'ālī yā ḥikmat-i Ṣadr al-Muta'allihīn,* Vol. I, University Press, Tehran, 1337 Solar, p. 3.

24. Ṣadr al-Dīn Shīrāzī, *Rasā'il,* Tehran, lithographed edition, 1302/1884, pp. 279-86.

25. Mullā Ṣadrā adds at the end of this discussion that the causes for the difference of view among various schools regarding different sciences are four in number:

    (i) differences in the science of unity leading to the creation of sects such as the atheists, etc.; (ii) the science of prophecy leading to separation between Muslims, Christians, Jews, and other religious groups; (iii) the science of Imamate leading to division between the Shi'ahs and Sunnis; and, finally, (iv) the science of jurisprudence leading to the creation of various schools and interpretations of Law. Mullā Ṣadrā adds that the main cause of multiplicity lies in misunderstanding the science of unity and the science of the soul or the science of the beginning and end of thing. *Rasā'il*, pp. 287-88.

26. J. Muṣliḥ, *op. cit.,* pp. 1-2.

27. See The chapter "Suhrawardī" in this volume.

28. Mullā Ṣadrā regards light as a perfect and intelligible example of the unity and gradation of Being and praises the Illuminationists on this point. See the first chapter of the *Asfār.*

29. See Seyyed Hossain Nasr, "The Polarisation of Being", *Pakistan Philosophical journal,* Vol. III, No. 2, October 1959, pp. 8-13.

30. The doctrine of the unity of Being in Mullā Ṣadrā is not new; it was expressed clearly five centuries before him by Ibn 'Arabī. Mullā Ṣadrā, however, was the first person to give it a logical dress and introduce it as a principle of *ḥikmat* as distinct from pure gnosis which does not concern itself with certain logical distinctions.

31. In dividing the hierarchies of universal existence into longitudinal and latitudinal orders Mullā Ṣadrā follows the scheme of *ishrāqī* angelology, which was discussed in the chapter on Suhrawardī.

32. What distinguishes the gnostics from the *ḥakīms* in this subject is that the former formulate the illuminations they receive which differ depending upon the degree of their inner realization. One gnostic in a certain state of contemplation (*ḥāl*) may have been aware of only the creatures or multiplicity as a reflection of unity, another of only God or Unity, and a third of unity in multiplicity. The *ḥakīms*, however, from a theoretical and more logical point of view, do not take the particular perspective of the traveller upon the path (*sālik*) into consideration and have even criticized some of the gnostics for considering multiplicity to be completely unreal.

33. By this latter distinction, Mullā Ṣadrā implies the difference which exists, or at least used to exist, in European languages between Being and existence. All creatures exist

but only in the case of God can one, properly speaking, say that He "is". See S. H. Nasr, "The Polarisation of Being", *op. cit.,* pp. 8-13.

34. See Ibn Sīnā, *Kitāb al-shifā' (tābī'īyyāt)*, Tehran, lithographed edition, pp. 291 ff.

35. The feature which distinguishes particulars from one another and determines all other qualities in them is, according to Mullā Ṣadrā, their degree of being.

36. Mullā Ṣadrā writes that it was Hermes who learnt about the truth of the "Platonic ideas" when he became illuminated by the light of the intelligible world and separated from the world of the senses. In this state Hermes met an illuminated figure in the spiritual world who taught him all the sciences and when he asked the figures who he was, the figure answered, "I am thy perfect nature (*anā ṭabā'uka'l-tāmm*)," *Asfār* p. 121. For a study of the rich symbolism of "perfect nature", which means the celestial or angelic part of the human soul, see H. Corbin, "Le récit d'initiation et l'hermétisme en Iran", *Eranos Jahrbuch*, Vol. 17, 1949, pp. 121-88.

37. For the general discussion on cause and effect, see J. Muṣliḥ, *op. cit.,* pp. 85 ff.

38. It is this "simple being" or the supreme intellect which the Sufis before Mullā Ṣadrā identified with the Reality of Muḥammad. See Ibn 'Arabī, *La Sagesse des prophètes*, tr. T. Burckhardt, Albin Michel, Paris, 1955, pp. 181 ff.

39. According to a principle—which is another of the well-known doctrines formulated by Mullā Ṣadrā and is called *basīṭ al-ḥaqīqah kull al-ashyā'*, i.e., Truth in its state of simplicity contains all things—the Divine Essence in its state of simplicity and "contraction" contains all realities within itself. This is indeed a direct consequence of the principle of the unity of Being; if there is but one Being and the whole universe is nothing but Being, the universe and all its realities are contained in a state of "contraction" in that One Being.

40. See J. Muṣliḥ, *op. cit.,* p. 100. This distinction may seem to differ from what was said previously. But it must be remembered that the Divine Essence cannot be limited to Being, which is its first determination as well as the principle of universal manifestation. It is this distinction to which Ākhūnd is referring here.

41. Mullā Ṣadrā placed so much emphasis upon this point that he discussed it not only in the First Book of the *Asfār* but in many other chapters of the work and in nearly all of his other books as well. See also H. A. Rāshid, *Du filsūf-i sharq wa gharb,* Parwīn Press Ispahan, 1334 A.H. Solar, pp. 50 ff., and J. Muṣliḥ, *op. cit.,* pp. 128 ff. Mullā Ṣadrā in the Second Book of the *Asfār* and other places insists that he is not the first among the *ḥakīms* to have introduced this idea but that the pre-Socratic philosophers had indicated although not explicitly the existence of substantial motion. Moreover, he gives the Quranic verses such as "Do ye create it or are We the Creator? We mete out death among you, and We are not to be outrun, that We may transfigure you and make you what ye know not" (lvi, 59-61, Pickthall's translation) in support of his view.

42. See Ibn Sīnā, *Dānish-nāma-yi 'alā'ī, (Ṭabī'iyyāt),* University Press, Tehran, 1331/1912, pp. 3ff. Aristotle also in *De Generatione et Corruptione* (319b, 31-320a, 2) divides motion into the four categories of quantity, quality, place, and substance, and speaks of substantial change as one of the processes which characterize the sublunary region. But by substaftial change Aristotle means only generation and corruption and for that reason later Muslim philosophers did not even apply the term "motion" to it and considered motion to belong only to the categories of quantity, quality, locomotion, and posture.

Mullā Ṣadrā, however, considers substantial motion to be an inner transformation of things somewhat in the alchemical sense in which there is not simply a coming into being and a passing away but a process through which a new state of being is reached. Moreoever, substantial change for the Aristotelians is sudden and instantaneous while for Ākhūnd it is gradual like other forms of motion. Also, substantial change in the Aristotelian sense is limited to the sublinary region, while for Mullā Ṣadrā the whole of gross and subtle manifestation partakes of substantial motion. Ākhūnd's conception change, therefore, cannot be identified with that of Aristotle and should not be confused with it because of similarity in terminology.

For an analysis of Aristotle's doctrine of motion, see also H. A. Wolfson, *Crescas' Critique of Aristotle,* Harvard University Press, Cambridge, 1929, pp. 512 ff.

43. Ibn Sīnā, *Shifā' (Ṭabī'iyyāt),* pp. 43-44.

44. The idea that God annihilates and re-creates the world at every moment is one that is shared by the majority of the Sufis. Jalāl al-Dīn Rūmī expresses it :

    Every moment the world is being renewed, and we
        unaware of its perpetual change.
    Life is ever pouring in afresh, though in the body
        it has the semblance of continuity.

    R.A. Nicholson, *Rūmī, Poet and Mystic,* George Allen & Unwin, London, 1950, p. 117. See also T. Burckhardt, *Introduction to Sufi Doctrine,* tr. D. M. Matheson, Shaykh Muhammad Ashraf, Lahore, 1959, Chap. IV.

45. Substantial motion is essentially a rebirth because it always means the attainment of a new state of being.

46. From what we have said above it is clear that in Mullā Ṣadrā's view motion is principial, for it is an inherent characteristic of corporeal and even subtle existence, and time is subservient to it contrary to the view of many previous philosophers who considered motion to be subservient to time. Mullā Ṣadrā's conception of time as the quantity of substantial motion, which is itself the renewal of cosmic existence, bears much resemblance to the doctrine of Abu'l-Barakāt al-Baghdādī For whom also time is the measure or dimension of existence. See S. Pines, *Nouvelles études sur Awḥad al-Zamān Abu'l-Barakāt al-Baghdādī,* Paris, Librairie Durlacher, 1955, Chap. II.

47. In *Faṣl* 33 of the first book of the *Asfār,* Ākhūnd writes that all bodies are limited within the four dimensions of length, breadth, depth, and time, and are differentiated by the division inherent in time, while their unity is preserved through their celestial archetypes or Platonic ideas.

48. See Chapter XLVII.

49. See Mullā Ṣadrā, *al-Wāridāt al-qalbiyyah, Rasā'il*, pp. 243-49.

50. The world of change here as in the case of Suhrawardī means the whole visible universe and not only the sublunary region of the Aristotelians. According ot Mulla Ṣadrā, the difference between the sublunary region composed of the four elements and the heavens composed of ether lies only in that the matter of the heavens is more subtle than the gross matter of the terrestrial environment and is governed by pure souls that are free from the passions of earthly souls.

51. The principle that the intellect, intelligence, and the intelligible are one (*ittiḥād al-'āqil wa'l-ma'qūl*) is another point in which Mullā Ṣadrā opposed the previous Muslim

philosophers. This principle, which was accepted by the Neoplatonists, was rejected by Ibn Sīnā (see *Ishārāt*, Ḥaydarī Press, Tehran, 1379/1959, Vol. III, pp. 292-93) and other Peripatetics. Ākhūnd, while acknowledging his debt to Porphyry and earlier Greek philosophers (see his *Rasā'il*, p. 319), considered himself the first among Muslims to have reinstated this principle which is made a cornerstone of his intellectual edifice. Actually Afḍal al-Dīn Kāshānī and before him Abu'l-Ḥasan 'Āmirī in his *Kitāb al-fuṣūl fi'l-ma'ālim al-ilāhiyyah* had accepted this principle (see M. Minovi, "Az khazā'in-i turkiyyah", *Revue de la Faculté des Lettres,* Université de Téhéran, Vol. IV, No. 3, Mars 1957, p. 59), but it was Mullā Ṣadrā who first systematized this principle and demonstrated it clearly.

For a discussion of the principle of the union of the intellect and the intelligible, see *Asfār*, pp. 277 ff.

52. "God's knowledge of things is identical with their being" (Mullā Ṣadrā, *al-Shawāhid al-rubūbiyyah*, Tehran, lithographed edition, 1236/1820, p. 36).

53. See Mullā Ṣadrā, *Sharḥ al-hidāyah al-athīriyyah*, Tehran lithographed edition, 1315/1897, pp. 308-09.

54. See his *Rasā'il*, p. 240, where he quotes the Quranic statement that "not a particle of dust in the heavens and earth is hidden from God's knowledge" as a support and consequence of his conception of Divine Knowledge.

55. Ākhūnd adds that in the case of prophets and saints, the creative power of the soul becomes so great that like God Himself it can even create objective and external forms.

56. The whole of the fourth book of the *Asfār* is devoted to the science of the soul where the soul takes on a meaning totally different from the quasi-material substance of the Aristotelians.

Mullā Ṣadrā often speaks of the complete science of things as *mabda' wa'l-ma'ād,* the origin and end, and has even a book by this name. He identifies the science of *mabda'* with theodicy and metaphysics and that of *ma'ād* with psychology and eschatology.

57. The view of Mullā Ṣadrā regarding the growth and perfection of the soul resembles the alchemical view in which the power to reach perfection is considered to lie within matter itself and not outside it.

58. Mullā Ṣadrā, *al-Shawāhid al-rubūbiyyah*, pp. 152 ff.

59. That is why Ākhūnd writes that "the first seed of the universe was the intellect and the last stage is also the intellect which is the fruit of that same tree" (*ibid.*, p. 165).

60. This principle which in Arabic is called *jismāniyat al-ḥudūth wa rūḥāniyyat al-baqā'* is another of the doctrines for which Mullā Ṣadrā is famous.

61. We have not enumerated these faculties in detail because Mullā Ṣadrā follows the earlier Muslim authors especially Ibn Sīnā on this point.

62. *Al-Shawāhid al-rubūbiyyah*, pp. 134 ff.

63. By emphasizing the immanent aspect of the development of the soul, Mullā Ṣadrā does not forget the transcendent factor, for in the treatise *Iksīr al-'ārifīn* he writes that the archangel Isrāfīl blows life into the body and gives it the power of sensation and motion, that Mīkā'īl enables the body to assimilate food and sends it its sustenance, that Jibra'īl gives it instruction regarding the revelation and acts of worship and finally that 'Izrā'īl enables the soul to abstract forms from matter and to separate itself from the body. *Rasā'il*, pp. 306-07.

64. Concerning the traditional conception of cosmic becoming, see A. K. Coomaraswamy, "Gradation and Evolution", *Isis,* XXXV, 1944, pp. 15-16 XXXVIII, 1947-48, pp. 87-94.

    As for the unity of the soul which from the gnostic point of view is identified with the Divine Essence or self, see A. K. Coomaraswamy, "On the One and Only Transmigrant", *Journal of the American Oriental Society,* June 1944, No. 3, pp. 19-43.

65. According to a famour *ḥadīth* of the Prophet, accepted by the Shī'ah and the Sunnis alike, the Quran has seven levels of meaning the last known only to God. It is from the esoteric interpretation of the revealed book that Mullā Ṣadrā and Sufis before him have drawn the gnostic doctrines inherent and hidden in the Islamic revelation as they are in all other revelations.

66. *Iksīr al-'ārifīn, Rasā'il,* p. 295. This terminology is a very old one in Islam; it was adopted by the early Sufis from the traditions of the prophets and Imams.

67. *Al-Shawāhid al-rubūbiyyah*, p. 140.

68. Mullā Ṣadrā, *Risālah fī'l-ḥashr, Rasā'il,* pp. 341-58.

69. In the case of animals, after death they join the masters of their species (*rabb al-naw'*) or archetypes except the higher animals who have the faculty of imagination developed in them. They have an independent existence in the world of cosmic imagination without however being distinct individually as in the case of man.

70. See Mullā Ṣadrā, *al-Mabdā' wa'l-ma'ād,* Tehran lithographed edition, 1314/1896, pp. 272 ff.

    He criticizes both the naturalists who deny the existence of the soul after death and the Peripatetics who accept only the resurrection of the soul but not of the body.

71. This esoteric view expressed in his commentary upon the *Uṣūl al-kāfī* as well as in the *Asfār* was one most attacked by the exoteric *'ulamā'*. The religious perspective which appeals essentially to the sentimental or passionate aspect of human nature must insist upon "eternal" punishment and reward in order to have its laws accepted in human society. Only the esoteric view meant for the saintly and appealing to the contemplative aspect of man, can take into consideration the relativity of heaven and hell with respect to the Divine Essence without in any way denying the reality or "eternity" or reward and punishment in the life hereafter with respect to human existence here.

72. For the background leading to Mullā Ṣadrā, see Chapter XLVII on "The School of Iṣpahān" in this work. See also Mullā Muḥsin Fayḍ, *al-Maḥajjat al-bayḍā'*. Vol. I, Islāmiyyah Press, Tehran, 1379/1959, introduction by Sayyid Muḥammad Mishkāt, pp. 10-23, in which the background leading to Mullā Ṣadrā as well as the distinguishing principles of his own doctrines are discussed.

73. It will be remembered that al-Ghazzālī in his *al-Munqidh min al-ḍalāl* considered the philosophers to be infidels on three points: their rejection of the resurrection of bodies, their limiting God's knowledge to universals, and their belief in the eternity of the world. See W. Montgomery Watt, *The Faith and Practice of al-Ghazālī*, George Allen & Unwin, London, 1953, p. 37.

    From what we have discussed of Mullā Ṣadrā's doctrine it is clear that he accepted the resurrection of bodies, God's knowledge of particulars, and creation of the world in time though not quite in the sense as that of the theologians.

74. Mullā Ṣadrā doctrines were especially influential in India to which country one of his disciples by the name of Muḥammad Ṣāliḥ Kāshānī migrated—after reaching a wild

state of ecstasy during one of Mullā Ṣadrā's lessons—and where he attracted many disicples. The works of Mullā Ṣadrā have continued to be taught in the Islamic schools of the Indian sub-continent, especially his *Sharḥ al-hidāyah* which came to be known by the author's name as *Ṣadrā.* Many glosses have been written on it by various philosophers and scholars in India such as Muḥammad Amjad al-Ṣādiqī (d. 1140/1727), Mullā Ḥasan al-Lakhnāwī (d. 1198/1783), Muḥammad A'lam al-Sindīlī (d. 1250/1834), and 'Abd al-'Alī Baḥr al-'Ulūm who lived in the thirteenth/ninteenth century. Numerous manuscripts of these and other glosses on the *Sharḥ al-hidāyah* are to be found in subH iÄ9̃0 JY ĩ17\ĩ H aza Library of Rampur and the Khuda Bakhsh Library in Patna (see *Catalogue of Arabic and Persian Manuscripts in the Oriental Library at Bankipur*, Ṽol. XX [Arabic MSS.], Bihar and Orissa, 1936, MSS. No. 2351 2368, 2371-78).

75. See Chapter XLVII on "The School of Iṣpahān".

76. For a list of the names of Mullā Ṣadrā's disciples in the Qajar period, see *Rayḥānat al-adab,* and Gobineau, *op. cit.* pp. 103 ff.

77. Iqbāl's statement that, "It is, moreover, the Philosophy of Ṣadrā which is the source of the metaphysics of early Bābism" (*Development of Metaphysics in Persia,* London, 1908, p. 175) is true only in a negative sense in the same way as the doctrine of the Rhenish mystics might be considered to be the source of the Protestant revolt during the Renaissance.

BIBLIOGRAPHY

Ja'far 'Alī Yāsīn, *Ṣadr al-Dīn al-Shirāzī mujaddid al-falsafat al-islāmiyyah,* al-Ma'ārif Press, Baghdad, 1375/1955; Sayyid Jalāl al-Dīn Āshtiyānī, *Hasti az naẓar-i falsafih wa 'irfān,* Khurāsān Press, Mashad, 1379/1959; Muḥammad Ḥusayn Fāḍil-i Tūnī, *Ilāhiyyāt,* University Press, Tehran, 1333 A.H. Solar; Comtde Gobineau, *Les Religions et les philosophies dans L'Asie centrale,* Les Editions G. Grés et Cie., Paris, 1923; M. al-Khuḍayrī, "Ṣadr al-Dīn al-Shirāzī," *Risālat al-Islām,* No. 2, 1950, pp. 212-18, No. 3, 1951, pp. 318-27; Murtaḍa Mudarrisi Chahārdihī, *Tārīkh-i Falāsifa-yi islām,* 2 Vols., 'Ilmī Press, Tehran, 1336 A.H. Solar; Jawād Muṣliḥ, *Falsafa-yi 'ālī yā ḥikmat-i Ṣadr al-Muta'allihīn,* Vol. I, University Press, Tehran, 1337 A. H. Solar onwards (this work is a translation and commentary of the *Asfār* in Persian of which only the first of the several volumes has appeared so far); Ḥusayn 'Alī Rāshid, *Du filsūf-i sharq wa gharb,* Parwīn Press, Ispahan, 1334 A. H. Solar; Ṣadr al-Dīn Shīrāzī, *al-Asfār al-arba'ah,* ed. Muḥammad Ḥusayn Ṭabāṭabā'ī, Vols. I and II, Dā'ir al-Ma'ārif al-Islāmiyyah, Qūm, 1378/1958 onwards (this is a projected nine-volume edition of the *Asfār* with various commentaries of which three have appeared so far); also Tehran, lithographed edition, 1282/1865; *Asrār al-āyāt,* Tehran, lithographed edition, 1322/1904; *Ḥāshiyah 'alā sharḥ ḥikmat al-ishrāq,* Tehran, lithographed edition, 1316/1898; *al-Mabda' al-ma'ād,* Tehran, lithographed edition, 1314/1896; *Mafātīḥ al-ghayb*, Tehran, lithographed edition; *al-Mashā'ir,* Tehran, lithographed edition, 1315/1897; *Sharḥ al-hidāyat al-athīriyyah,* Tehran, lithographed edition, 1313/1895; *Sharḥ ilāhiyāt al-shifā',* Tehran, lithographed edition, 1303/1885; *Sharḥ uṣūl al-kāfi,* Tehran, lithographed edition; *al-Shawāhid al-rubūbiyyah,* Tehran, lithographed edition, 1286/1869; *Kasr aṣnām al-jāhiliyyah,* ed. M. T. Danishpazhuh, University Press, Tehran, 1340 A.H. Solar; *Sih aṣl,* ed. S. H. Nasr, University Press, Tehran, 1340 A.H.Solar; *Mullā Ṣadrā Commemoration Volume,* (ed. S.H. Nasr) University Press, Tehran, 1340 A.H.Solar; S. J. Sajjādī, *The Philosophical Vocabulary of Ṣadr al-Dīn Shīrāzi,* University Press, Tehran, 1380/ 1960; S.H. Nasr, "Mullā Ṣadrā dar Hindustān," *Rāhnamā-yi kitāb,* Vol. IV, Day, 1340 A.H. Solar; Akbar Ṣayrafī, *Tārīkh-i falāsifa-yi islām,* Dānish Press, Tehran, 1315 A.H.Solar; Muḥammad Ḥusayn Ṭabāṭabā'i, "Muṣāḥaba-yi Ustād 'Allāmah Ṭabāṭabā'ī bā Professor Henry Corbin dar bāra-yi Shī'ah," *Sālāna-yi Maktab-i Tashayyu',* No. 2, Qum, 1339 Solar; Abū 'Abd Allāh al-Zanjānī, *al-Faylsūf al-fārsī al-kabīr Ṣadr al-Dīn al-Shīrāzī,* al-Mufīd Press, Damascus, 1936; M. Horten, *Das philosophische System des Schirazi,* Strassburg, 1913.

23

Ḥajjī Mullā Hādī Sabziwārī *

LIFE AND WORKS

After the death of Mullā Ṣadrā, the school established by him found its most famous interpreter and expositor in Ḥājjī Mullā Hādī Sabziwārī who was the greatest of the ḥakīms of the Qajar period in Persia. After a period to turmoil caused by the Afghan invasion, in which the spiritual as well as the political life of Persia was temporarily disturbed, traditional learning became once again established under the Qajars, and in the hands of Ḥājjī Mullā Hādī and his students the wisdom of Mullā Ṣadrā began once again to flourish through the Shi'ah world. This sage from Sabziwar gained so much fame that soon he became endowed with the simple title of *Ḥajjī* by which he is still known in the traditional *madrasahs,*[1] and his *Sharḥ-i manẓūmah* became the most widely used book on *ḥikmat* in Persia and has remained so until today.

Ḥājjī Mullā Hādī was born in 1212/1797-98 at Sabziwar in Khurasan, a city well known for its sufis and also for Shi'ah tendencies even before the ṣafavid period, where he completed his early education in Arabic gammar and language.[2] At the age of ten he went to Mashhad where he continued his studies in jurisprudence *(fiqh)*, logic, mathematics, and *ḥikmat* for another ten years. By now, his love for the intellectual sciences had become so great that the Ḥājjī left Mashhad as well and journeyed to Ispahan, as Mullā Ṣadrā had done two hundred and fifty years before him, to meet the greatest authorities of the day in *ḥikmat*. Ispahan in that period was still the major centre of learning, especially in *ḥikmat*. Ḥājjī spent eight years in this city studying under Mullā Ismā'īl Iṣpahānī and Mullā

---

* This essay originally appeared as "Renaissance in Iran-Ḥājjī Mullā Hādī Sabziwāri" in A History of Muslim Philosophy. Edited by M.M. Sharif. Vol. 2, pp. 1543-56.

'Ali Nūrī both of whom were the leading authorities in the school of Ākhūnd.

Ḥājjī Mullā Hādī, having completed his formal education, left Ispahan once again for Khurasan from where after five years of teaching he went on a pilgrimage to Mecca. Upon returning to Persia after three years of absence, he spent a year in Kirman where he married and then settled down in Sabziwar where he established a school of his own. His fame had by then become so great that disciples from all over Persia as well as from India and the Arab countries came to the small city of Sabziwar to benefit from his personal contact and to attend his classes. Nāṣir al-Dīn Shāh in his visit to Mashhad in 1274/1857-58 came specially to the city of Ḥājjī in order to meet him in person. In Sabziwar, away from the turmoil of the capital, Ḥājjī spent forty years in teaching, writing, and training disciples, of whom over a thousand completed the course on *ḥikmat* under his direction.

Ḥājjī's life was extremely simple and his spiritually resembled more that of a Sufi master than just of a learned *ḥakīm*. It is said that along with regular students whom he instructed in the *madrasah* he had also special disciples whom he taught the mysteries of Sufism and initiated into the Path.[3] He was not only called the "Plato of his time" and the "seal of the *Ḥukamā*' " *(Khātam al-ḥukamā'),* but was also considered by his contemporaries to possess the power of performing miracles of which many have been attributed to him in the various traditional sources. By the time he passed away in 1289/1878, Ḥājjī had become the most famous and exalted spiritual and intellectual figure in Persia and has ever since been considered one of the dominant figures in the intellectual life of the Persian world.

Unlike Mullā Ṣadrā all of whose writings with one exception were in Arabic, Ḥājjī wrote in Persian as well as in Arabic. Moreover, he composed a great deal of poetry collected in his *Dīwān* which consists of poems in Persian of gnostic inspiration and poems in Arabic on *ḥikmat* and logic. The writings of Ḥājjī, of which a complete list is available, are as follows: *Al-La'ālī*, Arabic poem on logic; *Ghurar al-farā'id* or the *Sharḥ-i manẓūmah,* Arabic poem with commentary on *ḥikmat; Dīwān* in Persian written under the pen name Asrār; commentary upon the prayer *Du'ā-yi kabīr;*[4] commentary upon the prayer *Du'ā-yi ṣabāḥ; Asrār al-ḥikam,* written at the request of Nāṣir al-Dīn Shāh, on *ḥikmat*; commentaries upon the *Asfār*, the *Mafātīḥ al-ghayb, al-Mabdā' wa'l -ma'ād,* and *al-Shawāhid al-rubūbiyyah* of Mullā Ṣadrā; glosses upon the commentary of Suyūtī upon the *Alfīyyah* of Ibn Mālik, on grammar; commentary upon the *Mathnawī* of Jalāl al-Dīn Rūmī; commentary upon the *Nibrās*, on the mysteries of worship; commentary upon the Divine Names; glosses upon the *Sharḥ-i tajrīd* of Lāhījī: *Rāḥ qarāḥ* and *Raḥīq* in rhetoric; *Hidāyat al-ṭālibīn*, as yet an unpublished treatise in Persian on prophethood and the Imamate; questions and answers regarding gnosis; and a treatise on the debate between Mullā Muḥsin Fayḍ and Shaykh Aḥmad Aḥsā'ī.[5]

Of these writings the most famous is the *Sharḥ-i manẓūmah,* which, along with the *Asfār* of Mullā Ṣadrā, the *Shifā'* of Ibn Sīnā, and the *Sharḥ al-ishārāt* of Naṣīr al-Dīn Ṭūsī, is the basic text on *ḥikmat.* This work consists of a series of poems on the essential questions of *ḥikmat* composed in 1239/1823 on which Ḥājjī himself wrote a commentary along with glosses in 1260/1844. The book contains a complete summary of *ḥikmat* in precise and orderly form. This work has been so popular that during the hundred years that have passed since its composition many commentaries have been written upon it including those of Muḥammad Hīdajī and the late Mīrzā Mahdī Āshtiyānī as well as that of Muḥammad Taqī Āmulī whose commentary called the *Durar al-fawā'id* is perhaps the most comprehensive of all. The other writings of Ḥājjī, especially the *Asrār al-ḥikam* which is of special interest because, as Ḥājjī himself writes in the introduction, it is a book concerned with the *ḥikmat* derived from the Islamic revelation (*ḥikmat-i īmānī*) and not just with Greek philosophy (*ḥikmat-i yūnānī*), and the commentary upon the *Mathnawī* are also of much importance, but the fame of Ḥājjī is due primarily to his *Sharḥ-i manẓūmah.*

SOURCES OF HĀJJĪ'S DOCTRINES AND THE CHARACTERISTICS OF HIS APPROACH

Ḥājjī cannot be considered to be the founder of a new school; rather, he expanded and clarified the teachings of Mullā Ṣadrā without departing from the basic features of Ākhūnd's doctrines. The sources of Ḥājjī's writings are, therefore, the same as those enumerated in our study of Mullā Ṣadrā, viz., gnostic doctrines drawn mostly from the teachings of Ibn 'Arabī, the teachings of the Shī'ah Imāms, *ishrāqī* theosophy, and Peripatetic philosophy.

In this writings the sage from Sabziwar drew mostly on the *Asfār* of Mullā Ṣadrā the *Qabasāt* of Mīr Dāmād, the commentary upon the *Ḥikmat al-ishrāq* of Suhrawardī by Quṭb al-Dīn Shīrāzī, the *Sharḥ al-ishārāt* of Naṣīr al-Dīn Ṭūsī, and the *Shawāriq* of Lāhījī. In general, Ḥājjī did not rely so much upon reading various texts as he did upon meditating and contemplating on the essential aspects of metaphysics. The major source of his knowledge, as with Mullā Ṣadrā, was his inner *imām* or the guardian angel through whom he was illuminated with the knowledge of the intelligible world. As to the formal sources of his doctrines, one must first of all mention Ākhūnd and, secondly, Ākhūnd's teachers and students some of whom have already been mentioned.[6]

Ḥājjī, following the path trodden by Mullā Ṣadrā, sought to combine gnosis, philosophy, and formal revelation; throughout his writings these three are present in a harmonious blend. He differed from Ākhūnd in that he was able to expound the gnostic elements of his doctrines much more explicitly than Ākhūnd and that he was not as much molested by the crities as the latter was. It was due to this fact that he was highly respected by the Qajars and the *'ulamā';* the Qajars were indeed not as opposed to Sufism and *ḥikmat* as were the Safavids. Possessed with the gift for poetry and eloquence and great intellectual intuition which sometimes even in the middle of a treatise on logic would draw him towards metaphysical expositions, Ḥājjī wrote openly on Sufism and appears more as a Sufi well versed in philosophy and theosophy than a ḥakīm interested in gnostic doctrines. He was, like Mullā Ṣadrā, among the few sages who were masters of both esoteric and exoteric doctrines, and of philosophy and gnosis.[7]

TEACHINGS

As already mentioned, Ḥājjī doctrines are in reality those of Mullā Ṣadrā's condensed and systematized into a more orderly form. Ḥājjī follows his master in all the essential elements of his teaching such as the unity and gradation of Being, substantial motion, and the union of the knower and the known. There are only two point on which Ḥājjī criticizes his master: first, on the nature of knowledge which in some of his writings Ākhūnd considers a quality of the human soul while Ḥājjī considers it to belong to its essence, like Being itself, above all the Aristotelian categories such as quality, quantity, etc.; and secondly, on Mullā Ṣadrā's doctrine of the union of the intellect and the intelligible which Ḥājjī accepts, criticizing, however, his method of demonstrating its validity. Otherwise, the principles of the teachings of Ḥājjī in *ḥikmat* are already to be found in the writings of Ākhūnd.

It must not be thought, however, that Ḥājjī Mullā Hādī simply repeated the teachings of his predecessor verbatim. It is enough to glance at the voluminous writings of Mullā Ṣadrā, in which one would surely be lost without a capable guide, and compare them with the precise form of *Sharḥ-i manẓūmah* to see what service Ḥājjī rendered to *ḥikmat* in general and to Mullā Ṣadrā's school in particular. Ḥājjī prepared the way for the study of Mullā Ṣadrā, and his writings may be considered to be an excellent introduction to the doctrines of his master.

The *Sharḥ-i manẓūmah* depicts a complete cycle of *ḥikmat*, containing in summary from all the basic elements of Mullā Ṣadrā's teaching on the subject. In discussing its contents, therefore, one becomes better acquainted with Mullā Ṣadrā as well as with Ḥājjī himself, and one gains a glimpse of traditional philosophy as it is taught in the Shi'ah *madrasahs* today.

The *Sharḥ-i manẓūmah,* excluding the part on logic, is divided into seven books each of which is divided into several chapters, and each chapter in turn into several sections. The seven books deal with Being and Non-Being, substance and accidents, the Divine Names and Qualities, natural philosophy, prophecy and dreams, eschatology, and ethics respectively.

The first book which is in a sense the basis of the whole work and is on general principles (*al-umūr al-'āmmah*) treats of the various aspects of Being, its positive and negative qualities, its unity and gradation, necessity and possibility, time and eternity, actuality and potentiality, quiddities, unity and multiplicity, and causality. Te second book treats of the definition of substance and accidents, and the third, which is called *al-ilāhiyyāt bi'l-ma'nī al-akhaṣṣ*, of the Divine Essence, the Divine Qualities and Attributes, and the Divine Acts. The fourth book contains a summary discussion of natural philosophy (*ṭabī'iyyāt*)—including the meaning of body (*jism*), motion, time and space—astronomy, physics (in the Aristotelian sense), psychology, and the science of heavenly souls. The fifth book treats of the cause of the truth and falsehood of dreams, the principles of miracles, the cause for strange happenings, and prophecy; and the sixth book of the resurrection of the soul and the body and questions pertaining to the Last Day. Finally, the last book treats of faith and infidelity and the various spiritual virtues such as repentance, truthfulness, surrender to the Divine Will, etc., which are usually discussed in the books on Sufi ethics such as the *Kitāb al-luma'* of Abu Naṣr al-Sarrāj.

Ḥājjī divides reality into three categories: the Divine Essence which is at once above all determinations including Being and is also the principle of all manifestations of Being Itself; extended being (*al-wujūd al-munbasiṭ)* which is the first act or word or determination of the Divine Essence and is identified with light; and particular beings which are the degrees and grades of extended being and from which the quiddities are abstracted.[8] All these stages of reality are unified so that one can say that reality is an absolute unity with gradations, of which the most intelligible symbol is light.

The first feature of Being which Ḥājjī discusses is that it is self-evident and undefinable. There is no concept more evident than Being, because all things, by virtue of their existence, are drowned in the ocean of Being.[9] Moreover, the definition of a species in logic involves its genus and specific difference, but there is no genus of which Being is the species. Therefore, from a logical point of view there is no definition of Being; Being is the most universal concept since the Divine Ipseity of which it is the first determination is, strictly speaking, above all concepts, yet the knowledge of the root or truth of Being, i.e., as It is in Itself and not in Its manifestation, is the most difficult to attain.

Existence, which is the extension or manifestation of Being, is principial with respect to the quiddities. This view, which we have already mentioned in previous chapters, is one of the major points of contention among Muslim *ḥakīms*. The Peripatetics gave priority to existence or Being over the quiddities, considering each being to be in essence different and distinct from other beings. Although Suhrawardī never speaks of the principiality of the quiddities as understood by the later *ḥakīms*, he can be interpreted to consider existence to have no reality independent of the quiddities. It was Mīr Dāmād who re-examined this whole question and reached the conclusion that either the quiddities or existence would have to be principial, and divided the philosophers before him into the followers either of the principiality of existence or Being (*aṣālat-i wujūd*), or of the principiality of the quiddites (*aṣālat-i māhiyyat*) while he himself sided with the latter group.[10] Mullā Ṣadrā in turn accepted his teacher's classification but sided with the followers of the principiality of existence. Ḥājjī, likewise, follows Ākhūnd in accepting the principiality of Being which he considers to be the source of all effects partaking of gradations.

Another question which arises concerning the concept of Being is whether It is just a verbal expression shared by particular beings or a reality which particular beings have in common. It is known that the Ash'arites considered the term "being" to be merely a verbal expression used for both the Creator and the creatures; otherwise, according to them, there would be an aspect common to both which is opposed to the idea of divine transcendence. Ḥājjī, like the other *ḥakīms*, rejects this reasoning and argues that in the statement "God is", by "is" we mean either non-being in which case we have denied God or something other than what we mean in the statement "man is" in which case we have denied our intelligence the ability to attain a knowledge of God. Since both of these conclusions are untenable, "is" in the case of God must share a meaning in common with "is" in the case of this or that creature.[11] The truth is that Being is one reality with degrees of intensity and not many realities from which the mind abstracts the concept of Being.[12]

Another point on which Ḥājjī criticizes the Ash'arites is that of the existence of the images of things in the mind which is one of the important aspects of his doctrines. The Ash'arites believe that in the mind the quiddity and existence of an object are one and the same; when we think of man, the quiddity of the conception of man in our mind is the same as its existence in our mind. Ḥājjī opposes this view and distinguishes between quiddity and existence even in the mind. The world of the mind is similar to the external world with the same quiddity in each case. The difference between the two comes in their existence; each has an existence proper to itself. If external existence becomes mental existence, then the object as it exists externally becomes the image of that object in the mind. For example, when we think of fire, the concept of fire exists in our mind. It is the same quiddity as the objective fire that burns but its mode of existence differs. It has a mental existence which, although deprived of the power which makes fire burn and give off heat, is nevertheless a mode of being.[13]

Reality, then, is a unity comprising stages or grades of intensity[14] the source of which is the Divine Essence that we may consider to be the principle of Pure Being which is without quiddity if by quiddity we mean the answer to the question *quid est*— "what is it?"—or idetical with its quiddity if by quiddity we understand that by which a thing is what it is. Being has certain negative and positive qualities, the first such as the qualities of being neither substance nor accident, having no opposite, having no like, not being a compound and having no genus, species, and specific difference, etc.; and the second, the attributes of power, will, knowledge, and the like.

The quiddities, which accompany all stages of universal existence below Pure Being Itself, are abstracted by the mind from particular beings and are in fact the limitations of Being in each state of manifestation in all the vertical (*ṭūlī*) and horizontal (*'arḍī*) stages in which Being manifests Itself. It is, therefore, by the quiddities that we can distinguish between various beings and different levels of existence. Ḥājjī divides the quiddities according to their association with matter or potentiality. Quiddities are either free from matter in which case they are called the world of the spirits, or combined with matter and are then called the world of bodies. In the world of spirits, if the quiddities are by essence and in actuality free from all matter, they are the intelligences (*'uqūl*), and if they are free but have need of matter to become actualized, they are the souls (*nufūs*). And in the world of bodies, if the quiddities possess a subtle form of matter, they belong to the world of inverted forms (*'ālam al-mithāl*), which is the same as that of cosmic imagination, and if they possess a gross form of matter, they belong to the physical world. All of these worlds are distinguished in this manner by their quiddities, but all of them are in reality stages of the same Being which manifests Itself in different manners according to the conditions at each stage of manifestation.

After a discussion of the various aspects of Being and the quiddities, Ḥājjī turns to a study of substance and accidents.[15] There are three substances, the intelligences, souls and bodies, and the nine categories of accidents as outlined by Aristotle and Porphyry. Of special interest in this discussion is the category of quality (*kayf*) which is closely connected with that of knowledge. Dawānī, the ninth/fifteenth-century philosopher and jurist, had considered knowledge (*'ilm*) to be in essence of the category of the known (*ma'lūm*) and in accident of the category of the quality of the soul. Mullā Ṣadrā, on the contrary, believed that knowledge belongs in essence to the category of quality and in accident to that of the known. Ḥājjī adds and modifies these views, considering knowledge to be an accident of the category of the known as well as that of quality but in essence beyond all categories like Being Itself.[16]

The third chapter of the *Sharḥ-i manẓūmah* concerns the Names and Qualities, i.e., what pertains to the Divine Being. His Names, Attributes, and Acts.[17] Ḥājjī, after emphasizing the transcendence, unity, and simplicity of the Divine Essence, begins his discussion about the Divine Qualities and Attributes, which are mentioned in the Quran and interprets each following the tradition of the *ḥakīms* and Sufis before him. Of special interest is his account of the epithet "Knower" (*al-'Alīm*) in which Ḥājjī discusses Divine Knowledge mentioning that knowledge is in the Essence of God and God is in Essence the Knowner of all things. He knows all things by knowing His own Essence.[18]

The Knowledge of God consists of knowledge of beings at several stages which Ḥajjī enumerates as follows:[19] *'ilm-i 'inānī,* the heavenly science, which is the knowledge of God that creatures have no being of their own; *'ilm-i qalamī,* the science of the Pen, the knowledge that God has of all beings in the world of multiplicity before their manifestation;[20] *'ilm-i lawḥī,* the science of the Tablet, which consists of the knowledge of the universals as they are issued forth from the First Intellect or the Pen; *'ilm-i qaḍā'ī,* the science of predestination, which is the knowledge of the archetypes or masters of species of the realities of this world; and, finally *'ilm-i qadarī,* the science of fate which consists of the knowledge of particulars whether they be of the world of cosmic imagination or the psyche or of the world of the elements which is the physical world. God, therefore, has knowledge of all things, and all degrees of existence are included in His knowledge.

Following the study to God's Essence and his Attributes, Ḥājjī turns to His Acts[21] which in reality mean the stages of Being in which God's signs are made manifest. God's Acts are of many kinds and from them the hierarchy of creatures comes into being. This hierarchy consists of seven stages: the longitudinal intelligences, horizontal intelligences which are the same as the celestial archetypes,[22] the universal soul and the soul of the heavenly spheres, the inverted forms of the world of imagination, nature, form, and matter. These stages, altother distinct from one another, do not destroy the unity of God's Acts. God's Essence, Attributes, and Acts all possess unity, each in its own degree. The lowest stage of unity is the unity of the Acts, the highest that of the Essence, the realization of which comes at the end of the spiritual journey.

In the chapter on natural philosophy, Ḥājjī briefly outlines the physics of the Muslim Peripatetics as contained in detail in the *Shifā'* of Ibn Sīnā and other similar texts, and the Ptolemaic astronomy of epicycles as perfected by Muslim astronomers with the modifications made in it by Mullā Ṣadrā and the other later *ḥakīms*. The most important of these modifications is the introduction of the idea of substantial motion according to which the whole of the cosmic substance is in a state of becoming and the quantity of change is comprised in the measure of time. Ḥājjī also displays the tendency to interpret various aspects of the natural and mathematical sciences symbolically; for instance, the water of Thales which he, like Mullā Ṣadrā, identifies with the breath of the Compassionate (*nafas al-Raḥmān*) or the *tetractys* of Pythagoras which he regards as the symbol for the four principial stages of Being, intellect, soul, and nature.

After the discussion of natural philosophy, Ḥājjī turns to the soul and its faculties and stages of development. These are three types of souls: vegetative, animal, and rational, the last of which comprises the human soul as well as the soul of the heavenly spheres. The vegetative soul has the three faculties of feeding, growth, and reproduction; and the animal soul, the five external senses, the five internal senses, and the power of motion.[23] In man all of these faculties are developed to their fullness, but they are no more than the tools and instruments of the human soul which Ḥājjī calls the *ispahbad* light[24] and which is of the family of the lights of heaven.

The perfection of the soul is attained by treading the stages of the intellect and finally unifying itself with God. The soul is given essentially two powers, theoretical and practical, for each of which there are four degrees of perfection. The theoretical intellect is comprised of the potential intellect which has the capacity merely of receiving knowledge, the habitual intellect by which acquaintance is made with simple truth, the active intellect by which knowledge is gained without the aid of the senses, and finally the acquired intellect by which the spiritual essences can be contemplated directly.[25]

As for the practical intellect, it too consists of four stages: *tajliyah,* which consists in following the divine Laws revealed through the prophets; *takhliyah*, purifying the soul of evil traits; *taḥliyah*, embellishing the soul with spiritual virtues, and, finally, *fanā'* or annihilation, which has the three degrees: annihilation in the Divine Acts, in the Divine Attributes, and finally in the Divine Essence.[26]

In the chapter on prophecy[27] Ḥājjī discusses the qualifications and characteristics which distinguish a prophet from ordinary men. The prophet is the intermediary between this world and the next, between the world of the senses and the spiritual essences, so that his being is necessary to maintain the hierarchy of Being. The prophet is distinguished by the fact that he has knowledge of all things which he has acquired by the grace of God and not through human instruction, by his power of action which is such that the matter of this world obeys him as if it were his body, and by his senses which are such that he sees and hears through them what is hidden to others. He is also marked by his immunity from sin and error (*'iṣmah*) in all his acts and deeds.

Sainthood (*wilāyah*) is in one aspect similar to prophecy in that the saint, like the prophet, has knowledge of the spiritual world. Yet every prophet is a saint while every saint is not a prophet. The prophet, in addition to his aspect of sainthood, has the duty of establishing laws in society and guiding the social, moral, and religious life of the people to whom he is sent. Among the prophets themselves, a distinction is to be made between the *nabī* and the *rasūl*, the latter being distinguished by the fact that he bring a divine Book in addition to his prophetic mission. Among those who are called *rasūl* there is a further distinction to be made between the *ūlu'l-'azm,* i.e., those whose *Sharī'ah* abrogates the *Sharī'ah* before theirs, and those with whom this is not the case.[28] Finally, there is the Seal of the Prophets (*Khātam al-anbiyā'*) the Prophet who envelops all these stages within himself.[29]

The mission of the Prophet Muḥammad—upon whom be peace—by virture of his being the Seal of Prophets is the summation of all previous prophetic missions; his spirit is the Universal Intellect which is the first theophany of the Divine Essence and which made the body of the Prophet so subtle that he was able to make the Nocturnal Ascent (*mi'rāj*) to the highest heaven. That is why his light filled all directions and also that to whatever direction he turned he had no shadow. The direction of prayer (*qiblah*) of Moses was in the the West or in the world of multiplicity and that of Jesus in the East or the world of unity. The *qiblah* of the Prophet Muḥammad, on the other hand, is neither in the East nor in the West,[30] but between them because, being the centre as well as the totality of existence, he brought a prophetic message based upon unity in multiplicity and multiplicity in unity.[31]

As a Shi'ah, Ḥājjī was greatly concerned with the question of the Imamate in addition to that of prophecy and, therefore, discusses the political and religious differences which distinguish the Shi'ah conception of the Imamate from that of the Sunnis. For the Shi'ahs, as Ḥājjī writes, the spirit of 'Alī is in essence one with that of the Prophet. It is the Universal Soul as the spirit of the Prophet is the Universal Intellect. Moreover, the light of 'Alī is passed on to his descendants until the last and twelfth Imam who is the invisible guardian and protector of the world and without whom all religion and social as well as the cosmic order will be disturbed. Just as there are twelve signs of the Zodiac, so are there twelve Imams of whom the last is like *Pisces* for all the stars of the Imamate and sainthood.[32] The Last Day which means the end of the longitudinal hierarchy of existence is also the day of the manifestation of the twelfth Imam who is himself the last stage of the hierarchy which extends upwards to the Divine Essence or Light of lights (*nūr al-anwār*).

On the question of eschatology,[33] Ḥājjī follows closely the teachings of Mullā Ṣadrā in considering the soul to have come into being with the body but to have a life independent of the body after death. He also rejects the argument of earlier philosophers against bodily resurrection and defends the idea of the resurrection of the soul and the body together on the Last Day. There are two resurrections, the first at death which is the minor and the other on the Last Day which is the major resurrection. In the first case all the faculties of the soul are absorbed in the *ispahbadī* Light and in the second all the lights of all universe are absorbed in the divine source of all being. He mentions the events which are to take place at the time of resurrection and discusses the symbolic as well as the literal meaning of the Scale (*mīzān*), the Bridge (*ṣirāṭ*), and the Account-taking (*ḥisāb*) of good and evil. The physical *ṣirāṭ* is that which, as the Quran mentions, covers the chasm over the inferno, but the spiritual *ṣirāṭ* is the path which the Universal Man treads towards the Truth (*Ḥaqq*) and which connects him with the Truth.

In the final chapter on ethics Ḥājjī outlines the degrees of faith (*īmān*) from simple acceptance to demonstration and from that to spiritual vision. This last degree can be reached only through the purification of the soul and the acquisition of spiritual virtues such as purity, truthfulness, reliance upon God, surrender to the Divine Will, etc. When man acquires all of these virtues his soul becomes simple and pure; he then becomes the receptor of the divine effusions which illuminate his being and finally unify him with the Centre which is at once his own source of being and the origin of cosmic existence.

POST-SABZIWĀRIAN ḤIKMAT

The doctrines of Ḥājjī which we have outlined and his influence are still very much alive in Persia. The school of those whose teachers learnt the mysteries of *ḥikmat* from Ḥājjī Sabziwārī himself and narrated stories about his life to them has been able to preserve itself in Persia, despite the anticontemplative attitude encouraged by the spirit of excessive modernism, chiefly because of the life which Ḥājjī and to a certain extent some of the others Qajar *ḥakīms* infused into it.[34]

Of the famous masters of *ḥikmat* in Persia during the last century, we may name Abu'l-Ḥasan Jilwah, Muḥammad Riḍā' Qumsha'ī, Jahāngīr Khān Qashqā'ī, Mullā 'Alī Zunūzī, the author of *Badāyi' al-ḥikam,* and Mīrzā Ṭāhir Tunikābunī, all of whom were contemporaries of Ḥājjī, and those of a later date such as the late Mīrzā Mahdī Āshtiyānī, the author of *Asās al-tawḥīd,* who passed away only recently. Of the masters living today there are several who are worthy of special attention such as Sayyid Muḥammad Kāẓim 'Aṣṣār,[35] Ḥājj Muḥammad Ḥusayn Ṭabāṭabā'ī, the most prolific writer among the present *ḥakīms* of Persia,[36] and Sayyid Abu'l-Ḥasan Rafī'ī Qazwīnī, a man who is a true master of all the traditional sciences and perhaps the greatest living authority on *ḥikmat* and who lives in Qazwin in meditation and training of a few disciples away from the turmoils of modern life. One should also mention Muḥyī al-Dīn Qumsha'ī, the author of *Ḥikmat-i ilāhī* and a large *Dīwān* of Sufi poetry and the holder of the chair of Mullā Ṣadrā in the Theological

Faculty of Tehran University; Mirzā Raḥīm Arbāb who lives in Ispahan, the old centre of *ḥikmat* in Persia; Ḥā'irī Māzandarānī, now residing in Simnan, the author of *Ḥikmat-i Bū 'Alī* and one of the most erudite of the living *ḥakīms*; Jawād Muṣliḥ, the author of a commentary upon the *Asfār* and its translator into Persian; Murtiḍā Muṭahharī, Muḥammad 'Alī Ḥakīm, Ḥusayn 'Alī Rāshid, and Maḥmūd Shibāhī, all with the exception of Mīrzā Raḥīm Arbāb and Ḥā'irī Māzandarānī being professors at the Theological Faculty of Tehran University; Aḥmad Āshtīyānī, the author of several works on *ḥikmat* and gnosis; Fāḍil-i Tūni, the commentator of the *Fuṣūṣ al-ḥikam* of Ibn 'Arabī and many other treatises and a professor at the Faculty of Letters of Tehran University; and Muḥammad Taqī Āmulī, the author of the commentary *Durar al-fawā'id* upon the *Sharḥ-i manẓūmah*.

One cannot discuss the intellectual history of Islam fully without taking into account this long tradition the roots of which go back to the early civilizations of the Middle East and which has been preserved in Persia and in the bosom of Shi'ism to this day.[37] The outstanding figure of Ḥājjī Mullā Hādī was able to revive and strengthen this tradition in the Qajar period as Mullā Ṣadrā had done two centuries before him, and to make this wisdom to continue as a living spiritual and intellectual tradition till today.

NOTES

1. Only the most eminent figures in the intellectual life of Islam have come to receive such simple designations. In Persia one can name only a few such luminaries, Ibn Sīnā being called Shaykh; Naṣīr al-Dīn Ṭūsī, Khwājah: Jalāl al-Dīn Rūmī, Mullā: Ibn 'Arabī, Shaykh al-Akbar; and Mullā Ṣadrā, Ākhūnd. In view of these designations it is casy to see what an exalted position has been accorded to Ḥājjī in Persia.
2. There is an account of the life of Ḥājjī by himself on which we have drawn much for our information. See M. Mudarrisī Chahārdihī, *Tārikh-i falāsafa-yi islām*, 'Ilmī Press, Tehran, 1336-37 A.H. Solar, Vol. II, pp. 131ff: and also by the same author, *Life and Philosophy* of *Ḥājjī Mullā Hādī Sabziwarī*, Ṭahūrī Bookshop, Tehran, 1955. The story of the life of Ḥājjī as related by his son as well as a summary of some of Hājjī's doctrines not all of which, however, can be considered to the authentic is given by E.C. Browne, in his *A Year Amongst the Persians,* Adam & Charles Black, London, 1950 pp. 143-58. Accounts of his life are also found in the usual sources such as the *Qiṣaṣ al-'ulamā', Maṭla' al-shams*, and *Riyāḍ al'ārifīn.* When Gobineau visited Persia, Ḥājjī was alive and at the height of his fame; he is montioned with great respect in Gobineau's writings; see Comte de Gobineau, *Les Religions et les philosophics dans l'asie centrale*, G. Grés et Cie, Paris, 1923, pp. 113-16. There are also references to Ḥājjī in A. M. A. Shushtery, *Oulines of Islamic Culture*, Bangalore, 1938, Vol. II, pp. 452-54; and in M. Iqbāl, The *Development of Metaphysics in Persia*, Luzac & Co., London, 1908, pp. 175ff.

3. Among his special disciples one may name Sulṭān 'Alī Shāh Gunābādī who later became the founder of the Gunābādī brotherhood of Sufis which is one of the most widely expanded brotherhoods in Persia today. For the stages through which Ḥājjī's students had to pass being able to participate in his courses on *ḥikmat*, see E.G. Browne, *op. cit.*, pp. 147-48.

4. There are many prayers composed by the various Shi'ah Imams, especially the fourth Imam Zayn al-'Ābidīn, like the *Du'ā-yi kubrā, Miṣbāḥ,* and the *Ṣaḥifa-yi sajjādiyyah* (Sajjād being the title of the fourth Imam) which are read and chanted throughout the year, especially during Ramaḍān, as devotional prayers. Many of them, however, are not simply prayers of devotion but are replete with gnostic and metaphysical doctrines of highest inspiration and have been, therefore, commented upon many of the ḥukamā' and gnostics, who like Ḥājjī, have drawn out their inner meaning by the light of their own inspiration.

5. See M. Mudarrisī Chahārdihī, op. *cit.,* pp. 63ff.

6 It is difficult to understand Iqbāl's statement made in his *Development of Metaphysics in Persia* that with Sabziwārī Persian thought went back to pure Platonism and abandoned the Neoplatonic theory of emanation. Actually, Ḥājjī, like other Muslim *ḥakīms* before him, accepts the multiple states of Being each of which has issued forth from the state above through effusion or theophany. It is true that Plato was a definite source of Ḥājjī's doctrines as he was for nearly all the later Persian *ḥakīms* after Suhrawardī, but this is not to deny Ḥājjī's affinity to the doctrines of Plotinus and his commentators, especially the hierarchy of the intelligences.

7. See the chapter on Suhrawardī .

8. The relation of particular beings to Extended Being is like that of knots to the chord in which they are tied. See *Sharḥ-i manẓūmah*, Tehran, lithographed edition, 1298/1880, section on *Ilāhiyyāt*, pp. i ff.; and M.R. Ṣāliḥī Kirmānī, *Wujūd az naẓar-i falāsafa-yi islām*, Pīrūz Press, Qum, 1336/1917, pp. 55 ff.

9. See S. H. Nasr, "The Polarisation of Being," *Pakistan Philosophical Journal*, Vol. III, No. 2, Oct. 1959, pp. 8-13.

10. We can, therefore, justlysay that this issue as understood by the later *ḥakīms* is one of the distinguishing features of *ḥikmat* in the Safavid period and that the earlier schools, the Peripatetics as well as the Illuminationists, did not interpret this question in the same manner as the later *ḥakīms.*

11. The whole discussion concerning Being occupies the first section of the *Ilāhiyyāt of Sharḥ-i manẓūmah,* pp. 1-131.

12. The theologians (*mutakallimūn*) believed that each creature in the objective world is a quiddity including the Divine Essence which is an unknowable quiddity. Although this view is diametrically opposed to the view of the *ḥakīms*, in certain passages Ḥājjī interprets the view of the theologians symbolically to mean the same as the view of the Illuminationists and, therefore, defends them even though attacking them for their literalism.

13. For this view Ḥājjī is indebted partly to Mullā Ṣadrā and partly to Jalāl al-Dīn Dawānī.

14. In his commentary upon the *Mathnawī*, Tehran, lithographed edition, 1285/1868, p. 8, Ḥājjī names these stages as the Divine Essence or Ipseity; its first determination; the archetypes (*al-a'yān al-thābitah*); the world of the spirits (*arwāḥ*); the world of inverted forms or simlitudes (*amthāl*); the world of bodies (*ajsām*); and, finally, the stage which is the summation of all those before it, i.e. the sage of the Perfect or

Universal Man (*al-insān al-kāmil*). In other places Ḥājjī considers the seven stages of universal existence to be Divine Essence which is the Principle, the world of Divinity, of the intelligences, of the angels, of the archetypes, of forms and of matter. This descending hierarchy is also mentioned in E.G. Browne, *op. cit.*, p. 150; A. M. A. Shushtery, *op. cit.*, 454.

15. *Sharḥ-i manẓūmah,* pp. 131-40.

16. Mullā 'Ali Zunūzī, a contemporary of the sage of Sabziwar, in his *Badāyi' al-ḥikam* criticizes Ḥājjī' view and defends Mullā Ṣadrā against his criticism. The view of Mullā Ṣadrā as mentioned above appears in some of his works, while in others he also considers knowledge to be, like Being, above the categories.

17. *Sharḥ-i manẓūmah,* pp. 140-51.

18. *Ibid.,* p. 157. M.T. Āmulī, *Durar al-fawā'id,* Muṣṭafawī Press, Tehran, Vol. I, pp. 480ff. It is in this discussion that Ḥājjī criticizes Mullā Ṣadrā for having proved the identity of the knower and the known in the *mashā'ir* through the argument of relation *(taḍāyuf)* which Ḥājjī considers to be insufficient.

19. *Asrār al-ḥikam*, Tehran, lithographed edition, 1286/1869, pp. 83ff.

20. This knowledge, Ḥājjī compares to the point of the Pen before writing which contains all the letters of the alphabet before they become distinct on paper. The Pen is the same as the reality of Muḥammad (*al-ḥaqīqat al-Muḥammadiyyah*) and the first victorial light (*nūr al-qāhir*) to the Illuminationists.

21. *Sharḥ-i manẓūmah*, pp. 183-84.

22. Refer to the chapter on Suhrawardi. This seven-fold hierarchy is essentially the same as mentioned above with only a change in terminology which occurs often in the *hakīms* works of later *ḥakims*.

23. *Sharḥ-i manẓūmah,* pp. 284ff.; *Asrār al-ḥikam*, pp. 152ff. These faculties are also outlined in Iqbāl, op. cit., and Browne, *op. cit.,* p. 157.

24. For the meaning of this expression which is taken from the terminology of the Illuminationists, see the chapter on Suhrawardī.

25. See Iqbāl, *op. cit.,* pp. 185-86.

26. These stages have already been discussed in the chapter on Mullā Ṣadrā whose terminology Ḥājjī has adopted directly. See also A.M.A., Shushtery, *op. cit.,* p. 454.

27. *Sharḥ-i manẓūmah,* pp. 318-29; also *Asrār al-ḥikam*, pp. 307ff.

28. Regarding the question of the relation of Islam to previous religious and abrogation of older religions, see. F. Schuon, *The Transcendent Unity of Religions,* Pantheon Co., New York, 1953, Chaps. V to VII.

29. Ḥājjī considers the greatest miracle of the Prophet Muḥammad, who is the Seal of Prophecy, to be the Quran which in the beauty of language has no match in Arabic literature. He adds that in each period God gives those miracles to His prophets which conform to the mentality of the people of that age. That is why the miracle of the Quran lies in its language as the Arabs considered eloquence to be of such great importance; likewise, in the case of Moses his miracle was in magic which was at his time one of the basic arts, and in the case of Christ raising the dead to life because medicine occupied at that time an exalted position among the sciences.

30. This is with reference to the verse of Light in the Quran (xxiv, 35), in which the olive treee, from the oil of which the Divine Light emanates, is said to be neither of the East nor of the West.

31. By this symbolism Ḥājjī implies that the message of Moses was essentially the exoteric aspect of the Abrahamic tradition, and the message of Jesus its esoteric aspect, while Islam, being a totality, is the summation of the two, at once esoteric and exoteric. See also F. Schuon, *op. cit.,* chap.VI

32. *Asrār al-ḥikmah,* p. 369.

33. *Sharḥ-i manẓūmah,* pp. 326ff.; *Asrār al-hikam,* pp. 261 ff.

34. A list of some of these *ḥakīms* is given by Gobineau, *op. cit.,* pp. 116-20. See also I'timād al-Salṭanih Muḥammad Ḥusayn Khān, *Kitāb al-ma'āthir wa'l āthār,* Tehran, lithographed edition, 1306/1888, pp. 131-226.

35. This great authority on *ḥikmat* and gnosis has trained a generation of students in Tehran University and the Sepahsālār *madrasah* but had not written extensively on these subjects.

36. This sage whom we mentioned in the chapter on Mullā Ṣadrā is the author of many important works in Arabic and Persian including the commentary *al-Mīzān, Uṣūl-i falsafah wa Rawish-i ri'ālism* with commentary by Murtiḍā Muṭahharī, a book on the principles of Shi'ism which came as answers to a set of questions posed by Henry Corbin and published as the *Sālāna-yi Maktab-i Tashayyu'*, No. 2; commentary upon the *Asfār*, etc. Ṭabāṭabā'ī has revived the study of *ḥikmat* in Qum which is the most important centre of Shi'ah studies today and has trained many scholars who have themselves become authorities on the intellectual sciences.

37. It is for this reason that with great obstinacy and despite some awkwardness we have refused to translate *hikmat* and *ḥakīm* simply as philosophy and philosopher even if in Persia too *hikmat* is often called *falasfaḥ*. Philosophy in Western languages is alomost synonymous with one form or another of rationalism, and recently irrationalism has been divcorced from *sapientia* which *hikmat* and even *falsafah* imply in Arabic and Persian.

BIBLIOGRAPHY

Muḥammad Taqī Āmulī, *Durar al-fawā'id,* Vols., Muṣṭafawī Press, Tehran, 1377-78/1957-58; E.G. Browne, *A Year Among the Persians,* Adam & Charles Black, London, 1950; Comte de Gobineau, *Les Religions et les philosophies dans l'Asie centrale*, G. Grés et Cie, Paris, 1923; Ḥājjī Mullā Hādī Sabziwārī, *Asrār al-ḥikam,* Tehran, lithographed edition, 1286/1869; *Dīwān-i asrār,* Tehran, lithographed edition, Teheran, 1300/1882; *Sharḥ-i du'ā-yi jawshan-i kabīr wa sabāḥ,* lithographed edition, 1267/1850' *Sharḥ-i manẓūmah,* Tehran, lithographed edition, 1298/1880 and many later editions *Sharḥ-i Mathnawī,* Tehran, lithographed edition, 1285/1868; Muḥammad Iqbāl, *The Development of Metaphysics in Persia,* Luzae & Co., London, 1908; Murtiḍā Mudarrisī Chahārdihī, *Life and Philosophy of Ḥājjī Mullā Hādī Sabziwārī*, Ṭahūrī Bookshop, Tehran, 1955; *Tārīkh-i falāsafa-yi islām,* 2 Vols., 'Ilmī Press, Tehran 1336-37 A.H. Solar; Muḥammad Riḍā' Ṣāliḥī Kirmānī, *Wujūd az naẓari falāsafā-yi islām,* Pīrūz Press, Qum, 1336, A.H. Solar; A.M.A. Shushtery, *Outlines of Islamic Culture,* 2 Vols., Bangalore, 1938.

PART VI

ISLAMIC THOUGHT IN MODERN IRAN

24

Islamic Philosophy in Modern Persia: A Survey of Activity in the 50's and 60's*

One of the unfortunate shortcomings of modern Western scholarship concerning the Islamic world is that while serious studies are often made of the intellectual and spiritual life of what is usually called the ''medieval'' period, when it comes to the contemporary era most of the studies are limited to the social, economic and political fields. A picture of the contemporary Islamic world is usually drawn depicting it as if it contained nothing of intellectual interest. Even the studies made in art and literature are usaully limited only to those individuals or trends that seek to innovate and break existing traditions while the surviving tradition is laid aside as if it did not exist, not matter how vital and active it might be. The bias inherent in most techniques and methods of current research to measure only change ignores permanence by definition no matter how significant the permanent and continuing traditions may be in reality. This *a priori* judgment of the significance of change and ''evolution'' vis-á-vis the permanent background of things,[1] combined with the still widely accepted image of the Islamic intellectual tradition as nothing more than a bridge between the Hellenistic world and medieval 'Europe,[2] have prevented for the most part serious studies from being made about Islamic intellectual life in its more current phase.[3]

In this survey we wish partially to redress this neglect by describing recent activity in Persia in the domain of Islamic philosophy (*ḥikmat),* thus drawing the attention of the Western audience to one of the main arenas of Islamic intellectual life which has remained especially neg-

* This essay was originally presented in summery form at Columbia University in 1971 at the International Conference on Islamic Philosophy and Sciences. It later appeared as ''Islamic Philosophy in Contemporay Persia: A Survey of Activity During the Past Two Decades'', Research Monograph No. 3, Middle East Center, University of Utah Press, 1972.

lected until now. There are altogether three groups of people who concern themselves with philosophy in Persia today: the completely traditionally educated men who have kept alive the traditions of Islamic philosophy to this day: the scholars who have had both a traditional and a modern education and who combine often the traditional approach with modern techniques of research and exposition; and finally, those who are primarily concerned with secular, modern European philosophy. Here we are concerned only with the first two groups and not with the third, whose very subject matter differs completely in character from traditional Islamic philosophy,[4] although even among this group a few of the better translator have a firm background in the Islamic sciences.[5]

THE COMPLETELY TRADITINALLY TRAINED SCHOLARS

Among the traditional masters of Islamic philosophy most active during the past two decades may be mentioned ‘Allāmah Sayyid Muḥammad Ḥusayn Ṭabāṭabā’ī, who is the author of numerous works including the twenty seven-volume Quranic commentary *al-Mīzān,* the *Uṣūl-i falsafah* with the commentary of Murtaḍā Muṭahharī,[6] and *‘Alī wa'l-ḥikmat al-ilāhiyyah,* and who is also responsible for the new edition of the *Asfār* of Mullā Ṣadrā,[7] Sayyid Abu’l-Ḥasan Rafī‘ī Qazwīnī, the great master of Mullā Ṣadrā’s school who has written only a few treatises[8] but has trained many outstanding students such as Sayyid Jalāl al-Dīn Āshtiyānī, who has studies with both him and ‘Allāmah Ṭabāṭabā’ī; Sayyīd Muḥammad Kāẓim ‘Aṣṣār, former professor of Islamic philosophy at Tehran University and the Sipahsālār *madrasah* and the author of *Thalāth rasā’il fi'l-ḥikmat al-islāmiyyah,*[9] and numerous scattered works now being printed together under the direction of S. J. Āshtiyānī; Mīrzā Aḥmad Āshtiyānī, known especially for his mastery of ethics and gnosis and the author of *Nāma-yi rahbarān-i āmūzish-i kitāb-i takwīn;*[10] Mahdī Ilāhī Qumsha’ī former professor of Tehran University and author of the well-known two-volume *Ḥikmat-i ilāhī khāṣṣ wa ‘āmm,* which has been printed several times; ‘Allāmah Muḥammad Ṣāliḥ Ḥā’irī Simnānī, the most loyal follower of Peripatetic philosophy in Persia today, standing ‘‘opposed’’ to the school of Mullā Ṣadrā and the author of *Ḥikmat-i Bū ‘Alī;*[11] Ḥājjī Āqā Raḥīm Arbāb, the last grand master of the school of Isfahan who, although he has not written much on Islamic philosophy, has trained many fine students;[12] ‘Abd al-Wahhāb Sha‘rānī, the editor of Sabziwāzī’s *Asrār al-ḥikam;*[13] Jalāl Humā’ī, one of the most outstanding literary figures and scholars of contemporary Persia who, in addition to his numerous works on Persian literature and the Islamic sciences, has also produced the finest modern study on Ghazzālī in Persian, the *Ghazzālī nāmah;*[14] Maḥmūd Shihābī,[15] both jurisprudent and traditional philosopher, author of a study of Ibn Sīnā's *al-Ishārāt wa'l-tanbīhāt;* Jawād Muṣliḥ, known especially for his partial translation of the *Asfār* of Mullā Ṣadrā into Persian as *Falsafa-yi 'ālī;*[16] Ḥusayn Qulī Rāshid,[17] famous Khurāsānī preacher who has written *Du filsūf-i sharq wa gharb,* comparing Mullā Ṣadrā's theory of motion with Einstein's theory of relativity; Sayyid Muḥammad Mishkāt, the editor of many important philosophical treatises by Ḥillī, Kāshānī, Ibn Sīnā, Quṭb al-Dīn Shīrāzī and others and the author of several independent treatises written before the period under consideration in this essay; and finally a lady of Isfahan who usually signs her works as "a Persian lady" *(Yak bānū-yi īrānī)* and who has written a dozen works on ethics, gnosis, eschatology and religious sciences including *Ma'ād yā ākhirīn sayr-i bashar,*[18] and a commentary upon the Quran.

The younger traditional scholars who have been most active recently in Islamic philosophy include Mīrzā Mahdī Ḥā'irī, the only one of the traditional class of *ḥakīms* with an extensive experience of the West and the author of *'Ilm-i kullī,*[19] and *Kāwishhā-yi 'aql-i naẓarī,*[20] which marks an important phase in the encounter of traditional Islamic philosophy and Western thought; Murtaḍā Muṭahharī, a prolific author whose philsophical studies include the commentary upon 'Allāmah Ṭabāṭabā'ī's *Uṣūl-i falsafah* and the recent edition of Bahmanyār's *Kitāb al-taḥṣīl;*[21] and finally Sayyid Jalāl al-Dīn Āshtiyānī, the most prolific of the contemporary traditional philosophers whose incredible output during the past decade includes *Hastī az naẓar-i falsafah wa 'irfān,*[22] an edition of Mullā Ṣadrā's *al-Maẓāhir al-ilāhiyyah,*[23] an edition of Mullā Muḥammad Ja'far Lāhījānī's commentary *(Sharḥ al-mashā'ir)* upon Mullā Ṣadrā's *Mashā'ir,*[24] *Sharḥ-i ḥāl wa ārā-yi falsafī-yi Mullā Ṣadrā,*[25] *Sharḥ bar muqaddamah-i Qayṣarī dar taṣawwuf-i islāmī,*[26] an edition of Mullā Ṣadrā's *al-Shawāhid al-rubūbiyyah* with the commentary of Sabziwārī,[27] and an edition of Sabziwārī's *Majmū'a-yi rasā'l.*[28] He is currently writing and editing an anthology of Islamic philosophy in Persia from Mīr Dāmād to the present with the collaboration of H. Corbin.

THE SCHOLARS WITH BOTH TRADITIONAL AND MODERN TRAINING

As for the second group, some of the more active among them are Yaḥyā Mahdawī, Ghulām Ḥusayn Ṣadīqī, Mehdi Mohaghegh, S. H. Nasr, 'Alī Murād Dāwūdī, Sayyīd Abu'l-Qāsim Pūr-Ḥusaynī, Riḍā Dāwarī, Sayyid

Ja'far Sajjādī, Muḥammad Taqī Danechepazhuh, Aḥmad Fardīd, Muḥammad Khwansārī, Fatḥallāh Mujtabī'ī, Ḥasan Malikshāhī, Sayyid 'Alī Mūsawī Bihbahānī, and Ibrāhīm Dībājī, all of Tehran University; Akbar Dānāsirisht, an independent scholar of Tehran, Ghulām Ḥusayn Āhanī and Ismā'īl Wā'iz Jawādī of Isfahan University, Karāmat Ra'nā Ḥusaynī of the Department of Culture and Fine Arts of Shiraz, 'Abd al-Muḥsin Mishkāt al-Dīnī and Zayn al-Dīn Zāhidī (Jūrabchī) of Mashhad University (who could also be included in the first group), and Muḥammad Jawād Falāṭūrī now teaching at the University of Köln in Germany. To this list must of course be added the scholars in the field of Arabic and Persian such as Dhabīḥallāh Ṣafā, Mojtaba Minovi, Ghulām Ḥusayn Yūsufī and Sayyid Ja'far Shahīdī who, although not technically in the field of Islamic philosophy, have made important contributions to it through editorial works and scholarly studies.

CENTERS FOR THE STUDY OF ISLAMIC PHILOSOPHY

Islamic philosophy as taught and studied by the first two group mentioned above has its center in either the traditional *madrasahs,* especially those of Qum, Tehran, Mashhad, and Isfahan as well as Najaf in Iraq, or in universities and institutes, or finally in private circles where much of traditional philosophical instruction is still carried out. As to universities, by far the most important until now has been Tehran, where in both the Faculty of Theology and the philosophy department of the Faculty of Letters and Humanities many courses are offered in Islamic philosophy, both on the undergraduate and graduate levels. But also of importance are the Faculties of Letters and Humanities of Tabriz and Isfahan Universities. Those Institutes that have played an active role in the publication of Islamic philosphical works include: *Anjuman-i āthār-i millī,Bunyād-i farhang-i Īrān, Anjuman-i tarjumah wa nashr-i kitāb,* and two supported by sources from abroad: the French Institut Franco-Iranien, and the Tehran branch of the McGill Institute. The first, which is more precisely the department of Iranian Studies of the Institut Franco-Iranian, has played a very important role in making works of Islamic philosophy known to both East and West as well as in arousing interest among Persians themselves in their own intellectual tradition. Directed for over twenty years by the celebrated French orientalist and philosopher, Henry Corbin, the Institute has published seventeen works which include:

1. Abū Ya'qūb Sijistānī, *Kashf al-maḥjūb,* ed. H. Corbin, 1949.
2. Suhrawardī, *Oeuvres philosophiques et mystiques,* ed. H. Cordin, 1951.

3. Nāṣir-i Khusraw, *Jāmi' al-ḥikmatayn,* ed. H. Corbin and M. Mo'in, 1953.
4-5. Ibn Sīnā, *Avicenne et le récit visionnaire,* 1954.
6. Muḥammad Surkh of Nayshāpūr, *Commentaire de la Qasida Ismaéliénne d'Abu'l-Haitham Jorjani,* 1955.
7. J. Aubin, *Materiaux pour la biographie de Shah Ni'matullah Wali Kirmani,* 1956.
8. Rūzbihān Baqlī Shīrāzī, *'Abhar al-'āshiqīn (Le Jasmin des Fidèles d'amour),* ed. H. Corbin and Mo'in, 1958.
9. H. Corbin, *Trilogie ismaélienne,* 1961.
10. Mullā Ṣadrā Shīrāzī, *Kitāb al-mashā'ir (Le Livre des pénétrations métaphysiques),* ed. H. Corbin, 1964.
11. 'Azīz al-Dīn Nasafī, *Kitāb al-insān al-kāmil (Le Livre de l'homme parfait)*, ed. M. Molé, 1962.
12. Rūzbihān Baqlī Shīrāzī, *Sharḥ-i shaṭḥīyyāt (Commentaire sur les paradoxes des Soufis)*, ed. H. Corbin, 1966.
13. G. Lazard, *Les Premiers poètes persans*, 1964.
14. H.N.M. Mokrī, *Shāh-nāma-yi ḥaqīqat (Le Livre des rois de vérités),* ed. M. Mokrī, 1966.
15. Notes to vol. n. 14, to follow.
16. Sayyid Ḥaydar Āmulī, *Jāmi' al-asrār* and *Risālah fī ma'rifat al-wujūd* ed. H. Corbin and O. Yahya, 1969.
17. Suhrawardī, *Majmū'a-yi āthār-i fārsī (Oeuvres en persan)*, ed. S.H. Nasr, 1970.

The Institute also possesses one of the best libraries anywhere on Islamic philosophy. Professor Corbin himself has conducted many seminars at Tehran University during this period, the past decade usually in collaboration with S.H. Nasr. Corbin has also participated over the years in many private discussions and study groups mostly with 'Allāmah Sayyid Muḥammad Ḥusayn Ṭabāṭabā'ī. These encounters, during which often many other noteworthy scholars such as the late Badī' al-Zamān Furūzānfar and M. Muṭahharī have been present,[29] represent one of the most interesting intellectual encounters between East and West in recent years. They have influenced the writings of Corbin as well as those of the Persian scholars present. In fact a volume entitled *Muṣāḥaba-yi 'Allāmah Tabātabā'ī bā ustād Corbin*[30] has been produced based upon the discussions which have taken place during these gatherings.

The activities of the second foreign Institute, the Tehran Branch of the McGill Institute of Islamic Studies, is of much more recent origin. It began two years ago in 1969 when Professor T. Izutsu came to Tehran to co-direct the Institute with M. Mohaghegh of Tehran University. Since then many scholars and students have visited it. Despite its short life, however, the Institute has already produced a major work in its "Persian Wisdom Series," the *Ghurar al-farā'id* or *Sharḥ-i manẓūmah*[31] of Sabziwārī, with an extensive English analysis of his metaphysics by Izutsu. There have also been regular lectures by eminent scholars at the Institute and the first number of its bulletin, entitled *Collected Papers on Islamic Philosophy and Mysticism,* has just appeared. The scholars in the Institute are now busy with the first critical edition of the *Qabasāt* of Mīr Dāmād, the glosses of Mīrzā Mahdī Āshtiyānī upon Sabziwārī's *Sharḥ-i manẓūmah,* and the *Kāshif al-asrār* of Isfarā'inī which are all to appear shortly.

CENTENARY CELEBRATIONS AND COMMEMORATIONS

Activities that have helped a great deal in the dissemination of interest in Islamic philosophy and in the publication of relevant material are the various centenary celebrations held during the past two decades in Persia. Of these the most important was certainly the millenary of Ibn Sīnā held at Tehran University in 1951. This celebration brought a large number of international scholars to Persia and many works of the master of Muslim Peripatetics were published at that time mostly under the auspices of *Anjuman-āthār-i millī*. Also a series of commemorative volumes, edited by Dh. Safā and S. Naficy, was brought out[32] containing many studies on him. This celebration was followed by that of the seven hundredth anniversary of Naṣīr al-Dīn al-Ṭūsī during which again many works and studies on the philosopher-astronomer were published along with a commemorative volume, *Yādbūd-i haftṣadumīn sāl-i Khwājah Naṣīr-i Ṭūsī*.[33]

The year 1961 marked the four hundredth anniversary of the birth of Mullā Sadrā. At the same time the intellectual climate of Persia was ready for a revival of his teachings. As a result this ocasion triggered off a burst of activity which has continued unabated until now so that Mullā Ṣadrā may be considered (along with Ibn Sīnā and Suhrawardī) to be the most thoroughly studied *ḥakīm* in Persia during recent years. *The Mullā Ṣadrā Commemoration Volume*[34] was published on this occasion by the Faculty of Theology of Tehran University along with three other volumes. Mashhad University also participated through the works of S.J. Āshtiyānī, and the University of Isfahan through those of Gh. Āhanī.

A more limited celebration of the eleven hundredth anniversary of Myḥammad ibn Zakariyyā' al-Rāzī was held at Tehran University in 1965. Although most of the studies were devoted to his scientific and medical achievements, some studies were made also of his philosophy including M. Mohaghegh's publication of the text, with a translation as well as an extensive introduction of Rāzī's *al-Sīrat al-falsafiyyah.*[35]

In 1969 the hundredth anniversary celebration of the death of Ḥājjī Mullā Hādī Sabziwārī was held and again several of his works were published by Mashhad University whose Faculty of Theology also devoted a special number of its *Bulletin* to this *ḥakīm*. S. J. Āshtiyānī of this University published for the occasion the commentary of Sabziwārī upon Mullā Ṣadrā's *al-Shawāhid al-rubūbiyyah* as well as the collection of the *Rasā'il* of Sabziwārī. The publication of his *Sharḥ al-manẓūmah* by the McGill Institute was also in connection with this anniversary celebration.

In 1970 two important celebrations were held which touch indirectly upon Islamic philosophy: the millenary of Shaykh Muḥammad al-Ṭūsī at Mashhad University and the six hundred and fifieth year celebration of the birth of Rashīd al-Dīn Faḍlallāh at Tehran University. Both have provided the occasion for the publication of a number of books touching upon Islamic intellectual life. The proceedings of the Rashīd al-Dīn colloquium[36] are to appear soon and contain several studies that touch upon Islamic philosophy and science, and the papers of the Ṭūsī colloquium are also to follow shortly. These special colloquia in addition to the first International Congress of Iranologists (Tehran, 1966) and the First National Congress of Iranian Studies (Tehran, 1970) - both of which had sections devoted especially to Islamic philosophy - have helped to arouse interest in Islamic philosophy and to focus the interest of various scholars on specific persons, themes or periods.

PUBLISHED WORKS ON ISLAMIC PHILOSOPHY

Publications in the field of Islamic philosophy in Persia can be classified under seven categories as follows: (1) catalogues of manuscripts: (2) editions of texts of Islamic philosophy in both Arabic and Persian; (3) translation of Arabic philosophical works into Persian; (4) explanation of traditional themes and doctrines; (5) writings concerning various Islamic philosophers and schools; (6) encyclopedias and dictionaries of philosophical as well as Sufi and gnostic technical terminology; and (7) criticism of Western thought from the point of view of Islamic philosophy along with "comparative philosophy."[37]

1. The movement underfoot during the past two decades to catalogue the major manuscript libraries in Persia had made a major contribution to the spread of our knowledge about Islamic philosophy and has uncovered some very important texts belonging especially to later

Islamic history. Among the manuscript collections that are particularly rich in philosophical works may be mentioned the holdings of the Library of the Shrine of Imām Riḍā in Mashhad; the several collections of Tehran University, the Sipahsālār Mosque School, the Malik, the National and the Majlis libraries, all in Tehran; and several private collections in Tabriz, Isfahan and Shiraz. The Majlis library is particularly rich in Islamic philosophy and theology and contains the private libraries of several of the most famous *ḥakīms* of the past century.

The catalogues of most of these libraries have now been printed, many by fine scholars who have included in their accounts a wealth of information on the history of Islamic thought as well as on particular Islamic philosophers and their works. Especially important for Islamic philosophy among these catelogues are those of M.T. Danechepazhuh and M. Munzawī for the Central Library and the Library of the Faculty of Letters of Tehran University, 'A. Ḥī'irī of the Majlis Library, 'A. Anwār of the National Library and A. Gulchīn Ma'ānī of the Shrine Library at Mashhad.

2. A large number of texts of Islamic philosophy along with introductions and explanations have been published during the pst two decades, some by traditional scholars in Tehran, Qum, Isfahan, Mashhad and a few other cities, and others by scholars trained in modern methods of compiling a critical text with the appropriate introductions, indices, etc. In both categories are to be found well-edited as well as faulty texts. Some of the more important of these texts include the following works by Ibn Sīnā or attributed to him: *Dānish-nāma-yi 'alā'ī* (Logic),[38] (Physics),[39] (Metaphysics);[40] *Mi'rāj-nāmah;*[41] *Risālah dar ḥaqīqat wa kayfiyyat-i silsila-yi mawjūdāt wa tasalsul-i asbāb wa musabbabāt;*[42] *Risāla-yi nafs;*[43] *Ishārāt wa tanbīhāt* (Persian translation);[44] *Panj risālah;*[45] *'Uyūn al-ḥikmah;*[46] *Qurāḍa-yi ṭabī'iyyāt;*[47] *al-Tanbīhāt wa'l-ishārāt bi inḍimām-i lubāb al-ishārāt* (of Fakhr al-Dīn Rāzī):[48] *Īḍāḥ al-ishārāt;*[49] *Ẓafar-nāmah.*[50]

Works of Nāṣir-i Khusraw include: *Khwān al-ikhwān;*[51] *Zād al-musāfirīn,*[52] *Gushāyish wa rahāyish;*[53] and the *Jāmi' al-ḥikmatayn* mentioned above.

Included in the works of Aḥmad Ghazzāli and 'Ayn al-Quḍāt Hamadānī are: *Risāla-yi sawāniḥ;*[54] *Muṣannafāt* (including *Zubdat al-ḥaqā'iq, Tamhīdāt* and *Shakwa'l-gharīb*);[55] and *Nāmahhā-yi 'Ayn al-Quḍāt.*[56]

Abū Ḥāmid Ghazzālī's works include *Faḍā'il al-inām fi rasā'il Ḥujjat al-islām* (Collection of his letters);[57] *Kimiyā-yi sa'ādat,*[58] and *Naṣīḥat al-mulūk;*[59] *Makātīb-i fārsī-yi Ghazzālī.*[60]

Writings of Suhrawardī comprise *Manṭiq al-talwīḥāt;*[61] several of his Persian treatises published individually by Mahdī Bayānī and Sayyid Muḥammad Bāqir Sabziwārī as well as the collected Persian works and the *Ḥikmat al-ishrāq* mentioned above.

Works of Afḍal al-Dīn Kāshānī are *Muṣannafāt* (including his collected treatises),[62] and *Risāla-yi nafs-i Arisṭūṭālīs.*[63]

Naṣīr al-Dīn Ṭūsī's works include *Āghāz wa anjām;*[64] *Fuṣūl,*[65] *Majmū'a-yi rasā'il;*[66] *Sharḥ mas'alat al-'ilm;*[67] *Si guftār-i Khwāja-yi Ṭūsī;*[68] *Awṣāf al-ashraf;*[69] *Sharḥ al-ishārāt wa'l-tanbīhāt;*[70] *Akhlāq-i muḥtashamī wa si risāla-yi dīgar;*[71] *Gushāyish-namah* attributed to him published along with Raḍī al-Dīn Nayshābūrī's *Makārim al-akhlāq;*[72] *Jabr wa ikhtiyār;*[73] and *Akhlāq-i nāṣirī.*[74]

In addition to the editions of Āshtiyānī, Ṭabāṭabā'ī and Corbin mentioned above, the works of Ṣadr al-Dīn Shīrāzī include *Kasr aṣnām al-jāhiliyyah;*[75] *Risāla-yi jabr wa tafwīḍ* (*Khalq al-a' māl*);[76] *Sih aṣl;*[77] and *'Arshiyyah* (text with Persian translation).[78]

Mullā Muḥsin Fayḍ Kāshānī has written *Majmū'a-yi sih risālah;*[79] *al-Maḥajjat al-bayḍā' fī iḥyā' al-iḥyā'*[80] and *Kalimāt-i maknūnah.*[81]

Works by Ḥājjī Mullā Hādī Sabrziwārī include several facsimile editions of the old lithographed edition of the *Sharḥ-i manẓūmah,* as well as the editions of A. Sha'rānī, S.J. Āshtiyānī and Izutsu and Mohaghegh mentioned above.

In addition to these authors to whose writings the contemporary schools of Persia have devoted special attention, a few other Muslim philosophers have been the subject of recent study. For example several logical and philosophical treatises of 'Umar ibn Sahlān Sāwajī have been edited by M.T. Danechepazhuh;[82] also Abu'l Ḥasan al-'Āmirī, *al-Sa'ādah wa'l-is'ād;*[83] several editions of 'Abd al- Razzāq Lāhījī's *Gawhar-murād; Asrār al-ṣalāh* of Qāḍī Sa'īd Qummī;[84] Ḥasan ibn Yūsuf al-Ḥillī, *Īḍāḥ al-maqāṣid;*[85] Ibn Muqaffa', *al-Adab al-wajīz li'l-walad al-ṣaghīr* with the Persian translation of Naṣīr al-Dīn Ṭūsī;[86] Abū Isḥāq Quhistānī, *Haft bāb-i Abū Isḥāq;*[87] and finally the *Rasā'il of Khayyām*[88] and *Kulliyyāt-i āthār-i fārsī-yi Ḥakīm 'Umar Khayyām.*[89] Many works in the fields of Sufism, theology (*kalām*), principles of jurisprudence (*uṣūl al-fiqh*) and science which touch closely upon the domain of traditional philosophy could be added to this list.

3. Consistent With the rise of the modern educational system and its emphasis upon Persian along with the encouragement of the spread of modern foreign languages there has been a notable decline in the knowledge of Arabic among the educated classes save for the *'ulamâ'* and

a few exceptional people. Arabic continues to be taught extensively in high schools and the universities, but relatively speaking fewer people are able to read philosophical texts in Arabic today than before. As a result there has not only been a noticeable effort made to edit classical Persian texts of Islamic philosophy but also to translate Arabic works into Persian. Interestingly enough this movement goes back to the 4th (A.D. 10th) and 5th (A.D. 11th) centuries and is not totally new; but today it is perhaps more intensified and more crucial for the future of Islamic philosophy itself in Persia than before. In fact there was a concerted effort in this direction during the Qajar period which must be considered as the historical background of the present movement to translate philosophical writings into Persian. This produced some fine Persian translations of earlier Arabic works such as that of Mullā Ṣadrā's *Kitāb al-mashā' ir* by Badī' al-Mulk.[90]

During the past two decades both older translations have been printed and new translations made. In the history of Islamic philosophy there might be mentioned the edition of the 11th (A.D. 17th) century translation of Ibn al-Qifṭī's *Ta'rīkh al-ḥukamā'*.[91] the new translation of the *'Uyūn al-anbā' fī ṭabaqāt al-aṭibbā'* of Ibn Abī Uṣaybi'ah;[92] and Ibn Juljul's *Ṭabaqāt al-aṭibbā' wa'l-ḥukamā'*.[93] Other translations include Aristotle, *Nakhustīn maqāla-yi mā ba'd al-ṭabī 'ah mawsūm bi maqālat al-alif al-ṣughrā* (the Arabic Translation of Isḥāq ibn Ḥunayn with the commentaries of Yaḥyā ibn 'Adī and Ibn Rushd);[94] Fārābī, *Fuṣūs al-ḥikmah*;[95] Ibn Sīnā, *Tarjama-yi rawānshināsī-yi shifā,*[96] his *Tarjumah wa tawḍīḥ-i du risālah az Ibn Sīnā*,[97] and his *al-Ishārāt wa'l-tanbīhāt namaṭ-i nuhum (maqāmāt al-'arifīn)* with the commentaries of Fakhr al-Dīn Rāzī and Naṣīr al-Dīn Ṭūsī;[98] Ibn Muskūyah (Miskawayh), *Akhlāq wa rāh-i sa'ādat* (from *Ṭahārat al-a'rāq*);[99] Abū Ḥāmid Ghazzālī, *I'tirāfāt* (translation of *al-Munqidh min al-ḍalāl*)[100] and *Khud āmūz-i ḥikmat-i mashshā'* (trans. of *Maqāṣid al-falāsifah)*;[101] Ibn Ṭufayl, *Zindah bīdār* (*Ḥayy ibn Yaqẓān)*;[102] Ṣadr al-Dīn Shīrāzī, *Mashā'ir,*[103] his *Manṭiq-i nuwīn* (*al-Lama'āt al-mashriqiyyah*);[104] the *Falsafa-yi ālī* (translation and summary of the *Asfār*), by J. Muṣliḥ, alluded to above, as well as the translation of the *'Arshiyyah,* mentioned above; and Mullā Muḥsīn Kāshānī, *Ḥaqā'iq*.[105] Recently the two English works of Iqbāl on Islamic philosophy, the *Reconstruction of Religious Thought in Islam* and *the Development of Metaphysics in Persia,* have also been translated respectively as *Iḥyā-yi fikr-i dīnī dar Islām*[106] and *Sayr-i falsafah dar Īrān.*[107]

Some of these translations are of high quality, such as that of B. Furūzānfar which is written in masterly Persian, but few can compare with the best translations of the older periods, not only that of the Qajars but also those of the early Pahlavi period such as the translation of *Fann-i samā'-i tabī'ī* from the *Shifā'* of Ibn Sīnā by the late M. Furūghī. A great deal more needs to be done in this field, both in making new translations and in editing and publishing Persian translations made in the past. The need for this type of scholarly work felt everywhere in Persia should in the future make this category of writings on Islamic philosophy among the most important in the Persian-speaking world. The general interest in Islamic philosophy and its influence in Persia will depend to a large extent upon this endeavor.

4. Consistent In addition to the works of individual scholars and the collected works cited above several other books have appeared during the past two decades which concern different doctrines and teachings of Islamic philosophy and their development throughout history, although most of the important doctrinal studies are by the traditional scholars cited above. Other works of interest in this category, including logic, are: Gh. Āhanī, *Naqd-i falsafah*;[108] M. Ḥusaynī Māzandarānī, *Sharḥ-i nafis-i ḥāshiya-yi Mullā 'Abdallāh;*[109] M.T. Sibṭ Shīrāzī, *Shifā'al-maraḍ fi'l-jabr wa'l-tafwīḍ*;[110] M.T. Fāḍil-i Tūnī, *Ḥāshiyysāt;*[111] J. Tārā, *Tanbīhāt wa ishārāt*;[112] M.J. Qāḍī Kamari'ī, *Tuḥfa-yi sulṭānī;*[113] I. Wā' iẓ Jawādī, *Hudūth wa qidam;*[114] S.H. Nasr, *Naẓar-i mutajakkirān islāmī dar bāra-yi ṭabī'at;*[115] M.I. Āyatī, *Maqūlāt wa ārā-yi marbūṭ-i bi ān;*[116] M. Riḍā Ilāhī, *Dībāchah bar falsafa-yi wujūd*;[117] 'A. Mishkāt al-Dīnī, *Taḥqīq dar ḥaqīqat-i 'ilm*;[118] H. Malikshāhī, *Ḥarakat wa istīfa-yi aqsām-i ān;*[119] and 'A. M. Dā'ūdī *ql dar ḥikmat-i mashshā'*.[120] In this category of writings it might be added that, while the traditional authors have discussed various themes as independent intellectual subjects in the traditional method, most of the scholars trained in the modern method have taken the historical perspective and discussed various topics in the light of their development during a particular period.

5. Strangely enough, during the past two decades most of the works on particular intellectual figures have been devoted to a few men like Ibn Sīnā, Suhrawardī, Mullā Ṣadrā and Sabziwārī, while many figures, some of great importance such as al-Kindī and al-Fārābī, have received far less attention than in many other Muslim countries. Besides the works devoted to Ibn Sīnā, Ṭūsī, Rāzī, Mullā Ṣadrā, Sabziwārī and others for whom special celebrations were held and series of works published, some of the recent writings devoted to particular figures include: A. Dānāsirisht, *Khulāṣa-yi afkār-i Suhrawardī wa Mullā Ṣadrā;*[121] D. Rasā'ī and M. Mihrīn, *Falsafa-yi Abū Naṣr-i Fārābī*;[122] 'A. Mishkāt al-Dīnī, *Ta'thīr wa mabādī-yi ān yā kulliyyāt-i falsafa-yi ṭabī'ī-yi Ṣadr al-Dīn Shīrāzī;*[123] A.

Mishkāt al-Dīnī, *Naẓar-ī bi falsafa-yi Ṣadr al-Dīn Shīrāzī*;[124] A. Zanjānī, *al-Faylasūf al-fārsī al-kabīr Ṣadr al-Dīn al-Shīrāzī.*[125] M. Mohaghegh, *Fīlsūf-i Rayy*,[126] M.R. Ṣāliḥī Kirmānī, *Wujūd az naẓar-i falāsifa-yi islām yā rāhnamā-yi sharḥ-i manẓūmah-i Sabziwārī*,[127] A.A. Siassi, *'Ilm al-nafs-i ibn-i Sīnā;*[128] R. Farmanish, *Aḥwāl wa āthār-i 'Ayn al-Quḍāt;*[129] M. Mudarrisī Zanjānī, *Sargudhasht wa' aqā 'id-i falsafī-yi Khwājah Naṣīr al-Dīn Ṭūsī;*[130] and Z. Zāhidī, *Khudāmūz-i manẓūmah.*[131]

6. During the past two decades several encyclopedias and philosophical dictionaries have appeared that have enhanced the study of Islamic philosophy. Besides the new editions of such classical works on the history of Islamic philosophy as the *Rawḍāt al-jannāt, Nāma-yi dānishwarān* and *Rayḥānat al-adab* which have appeared recently, the *Lughat-nāma-yi Dihkudā* (ed. M. Mo'in and later by S.J. Shahīdī) and the *Dā'irat al-ma'ārif-i fārsī* (ed. Gh. H. Muṣāḥab) must be mentioned as important new works. Both are still unfinished and are planned for completion during the next two years. But even in their present state they contain a wealth of information on various Islamic philosophers, their works and their ideas.

In the field of technical dictionaries of philosophical and gnostic terminology there is still much to be done to make all the existing terms available not to speak of coming new ones for modern concepts. Four dictionaries by S.J. Sajjādī are of much utility: *Muṣṭalaḥāt-i falsafī-yi Ṣadr al-Dīn Shīrāzī*;[132] *Farhang-i lughāt wa iṣṭilāḥāt-i falsafī;*[133] *Farhang-i 'ulūm-i 'aqlī*;[134] and *Farhang-i muṣṭalaḥāt-i 'urafā.'*[135] The new, standard five volume *Farhang-i Mu'īn* also has much that can help students of Islamic philosophy. There are several projects also underway to produce more extensive works devoted particularly to philosophical terminology. A. Fardīd has been working on this subject for a quarter of a century and hopes soon to bring out in writing the fruit of this research. M. Khwānsārī is now preparing a dictionary of technical terms dealing with logic. The Iranian Academy is also working in this domain as is the *Bunyād-i farhang-i Īrān*, which has already produced a useful dictionary for scientific terms.

7. Consistent Finally something must be said of the writings of the few men who have been working on what might be called, for want of a better term, "comparative studies" of Eastern and Western philosophies and also critical appraisals of Western thought from the point of view of traditional Islamic doctrines. People in this group have been until now very limited. They include from the class of the traditional *ḥakīms*, 'Allāmah Ṭabāṭabā'ī whose *Uṣūl-i falsafah*, already mentioned, was one of the first in this field in Persia, M. Muṭahharī who has devoted

mentioned, was one of the first in this field in Persia, M. Ḥa'irī, now residing in the West, whose *Kāwishhā-yi 'aql-i naẓarī*, mentioned above, is particularly pertinent from this point of view and M.T. Ja'farī, a prolific author, some of whose works include: *Jabr wa ikhtiyār,*[136] *Wujdān az naẓar-i akhlāqī,*[137] *Ṭabī'at wa mā warā'-i ṭabī'at,* and a commentary upon the *Mathnawī* of Rūmī which he has just begun and of which three volumes have already appeared. Among those belonging to university circles may be mentioned A. Fardīd who has written several penetrating essays in this field, and S.H. Nasr. A few scholars have also been working on the question of relations between Islamic and Hindu metaphysics and mysticism, foremost among them S.J. Nā'īnī who has edited many texts of Dārā Shukūh in Persian including the *Sirr-i akbar* (translation of the Upanishads edited with Tara Chand),[138] F. Mujtabā'ī who has been working on Mīr Findiriskī's commentary upon the *Yoga Vaiśistha*, and D. Shayegan who has made a study of Dārā Shukūh comparing Sufism and Hinduism and is also the author of *Adyān wa maktabhā-yi falsafī-yi Hind.*[139] A few Persian scholars have also been working in "comparative studies" abroad such as A. J. Falāṭūrī who has been living in Germany for many years.

Until now most studies in this field have suffered from insufficient knowledge in depth of the real nature of Western philosophy, and many superficial comparisons have been made along with a few serious studies. But with the growth of a more profound knowledge of the West and also acquaintance with the works of such authors as R. Guénon, F. Schuon, T. Burckhardt, and A. Coomaraswamy among the intellectual elite and also, on another level, familiarity with the comparative studies of H. Corbin and T. Izutsu, there is no doubt that such studies will grow in both depth and number in the future.

Besides the list of works on Islamic philosophy already mentioned, which is not by any means meant to be exhaustive, numerous articles have appeared on Islamic philosophy during the past two decades, the complete list of which can be found in Ī. Afshār's *Index Iranicus*. The journals that have been especially important in the field of Islamic philosophy during this period are the *Reviews* of the Faculties of Letters and Humanities of Tehran, Tabriz and Mashhad Universities *Ma'ārif-i islāmī* (the foremost journal in Persia today devoted to Islamic culture, edited by M. Bakhtiyār), *Maktab-i Tashayyu', Sukhan, Rāhnamā-yi Kitāb, Talāsh, Yaghmā, Maqālāt wa Barrasīhā-yi Dānishkadah-i Ilāhiyyāt-i Tehrān, Mihr* and *Majalla-yi Taḥqīq dar Mabda'i Āfarīnish.*

CONCLUSION

Islamic philosophy continues today as a living tradition in Persia. It is in fact one of the most precious aspects of the intellectual heritage of Islam in Persia, one which can aid it in preserving its traditions and preventing it from becoming completely drawned in the flood of modernism, whose profound failure is only hidden by a shining veneer of apparent success. Scholarly activity in the field of Islamic philosophy in Persia can be a great aid to Western scholars of the subject who have for the most part not been sufficiently acquainted with it until now. It can also serve the scholars of other Muslim lands to know better an as yet neglected aspect of the Islamic heritage. In the same way the efforts of other Muslim scholars can aid Persian scholars and the intellectual elements in Persian society in general in charting a course which will certainly be shared to a large extent by all the Muslim countries, whose destiny of necessity lies together. In finding the path for the future the intellectual leaders of Islamic society must look toward Islam itself as the most important determining factor, and within it the intellectual heritage contained in the teachings of Islamic philosophy can play a crucial role in preventing the Muslims from committing intellectual suicide. In this important task of bringing back to life through clear and penetrating scholarship the perennial truths contained within Islamic philosophy, and at the same time making better known the percennial truths contained within Is lamic philosophy and also making better know the part which has established the pattern of thinking of contemporary Muslims, the scholars of Persia can both learn from the works of others and make their own important contributions in collaboration with them. Insofar as Western scholarship is concerned closer collaboration in the field of Islamic philosophy between Muslim and Western scholars can not only immeasurably enrich scholarship itself, but can also bring to light once again an intellectual heritage which the East and the West once shared profoundly together, a heritage which can still act as an important bridge for true intellectual understanding, without which no other form of understanding is possible.

NOTES

1. See S.H. Nasr, ''Man in the Universe—Permanence amids Apparent Change'' in *Sufi Essays,* Albany (N.Y.) 1991
2. We have dealt extensively with this theme in the introduction to S.H. Nasr, *Science and Civilization in Islam;* Cambridge (U.S.A.), 1968.
3. A few people such as H. Corbin, T. Izutsu and S.H. Nasr have sought during the past few years to make available in Western language this until now unknown phase of

Islamic intellectual life. Despite their many writing, however, their views have not as yet penetrated fully into all the scholarly circles in the West. See also M. Hodgson, "The Role of Islam in World History," *International Journal of Middle East Studies,* vol. I (1970), pp. 99-123, especially pp. 101-2.

4. See S. H. Nasr, "The Comparison of Philosophy East and West," *Philosophy East and West,* January 1972.
5. We have in mind such fine translators of European philosophical works into Persian as M. Furūghī, Riḍā-zādah Shafaq and Ṃ Buzurgmihr.
6. 3 vols.; Qum, 1332 A.H. Solar. All publication dates cited hereafter are based on the Islamic Persian solar calendar unless otherwise indicated. Ṭabāṭabā'ī now lives in Qum.
7. We have given an account of his life and works in our introduction to the English translation of his *Shi'ite Islām* Albany (N.Y.), 1975
8. See S. H. Nasr (ed.) *Mullā Ṣadrā Commemoration Volume,* Tehran, 1340, and *Indo-Iranica,* A.D. December 1961. Qazwīnī resides in Tehran and Qazwin.
9. Translated into Arabic by Ṣalāḥ al-Ṣāwī, Tehran, 1349.
10. Tehran, 1374 (A.H. Lunar). Āshtiyānī lives in Mashhad.
11. 3 vols.; Tehran, 1335-37. Simnānī lives in Simnān.
12. The account of his life as well as many of the other traditional masters mentioned above is to be found in the numbers of the journal *Ma'ārif-i islāmī,* which began publication three years ago.
13. Tehran, 1380 (A.Ḥ Lunar). Sha'rānī is presently of Islamic philosphy at Tehran University.
14. Tehran, 1342. Humā'ī is a professor at Tehran University.
15. Professor at Tehran University and author of several works on logic.
16. 2 vols.; Tehran 1337, 1339 Muṣliḥ, originally from Shiraz, is now a professor at Tehran University.
17. Former professor at Tehran University who has taught the *Asfār* for many years.
18. Isfahan, 1342.
19. Tehran, 1334.
20. Tehran, 1347
21. Tehran, 1349. Muṭahharī is a professor at Tehran University.
22. Mashhad, 1380 (A.H. Lunar). Āshtiyānī is a professor at Mashhad University.
23. Mashhad, 1382 (A.H. Lunar).
24. *Ibid.*
25. *Ibid.*
26. Mashhad, 1345.
27. Mashhad, 1346.
28. Mashhad, 1348.
29. The gap in language as well as thought patterns has been bridged during most of these sessions by S.H. Nasr and sometimes D. Shayegan.

30. *Maktab-i tashayyu'*, Tehran, 1339.

31. Tehran, 1348.

32. *Yadnāma-yi Ibn Sīnā,* Tehran, 1335.

33 Ed. Muḥammad Taqī Mudarris Raḍawī, Tehran, 1335.

34 Ed. S.H. Nasr, Tehran, 1341.

35 Tehran, 1343.

36 Ed. Īraj Afshār, Tehran, 1350.

37. We do not intend to give an extensive list of all the works in these categories. A complete bibliography of books published in Persia can be found in Kh. Mushār, *Fihrist-i kitābhā-yi chāppi-yi fārsī,* 2 vols.; Tehran, 1337-42; Afshār and H. Banī Ādam, *Kitābshināsī-yi dahsāla-yi (1333-1342) kitābhā-yi Īrān,* Tehran, 1346; the *Rāhnamā-yi kitāb* and the annual bibliography published by the National Library *(Kitābkhāna-yi millī).*

38. Ed. S.M. Mishkāt, Tehran, 1330.

39. *Ibid.*, 1331.

40. Ed. M. Mo'in, Tehran, 1331.

41. Ed. Gh. Ṣadīqī, Tehran, 1331.

42. Ed. M. 'Amīd, Tehran, 1331.

43. *Ibid.*

44. Ed. E. Yarshater, Tehran, 1332.

45. *Ibid.*

46. Ed. M. Minovi, Tehran, 1333.

47 Ed. Gh. Ṣadīqī, Tehran, 1334.

48. Ed. M. Shihābī, Tehran, 1339.

49. Ed. and trans. M. Jūrābchī, Mashhad, 1341.

50. Ed. Gh. Ṣadīqī, Tehran, 1348.

51. Ed. 'A. Qawīm, Tehran, 1338.

52. *Ibid.*, 1339, also ed. Badhl al-Raḥmān, Tehran, 1339.

53. Ed. S. Naficy, Tehran, 1340.

54. Ed. R. Farmanish, Tehran, 1341.

55. Ed. 'A. 'Uṣayrān, Tehran, 1341.

56. Ed. 'A. Munzawī and 'A. 'Uṣayrān, Tehran, 1348.

57. Ed. Mu'ayyad Thābitī, Tehran, 1333.

58. Ed. A. Ārām, Tehran, 1333.

59. Ed. J. Humā'ī (new edition in press).

60. Ed. 'A. Iqbāl, Tehran, 1333.

61. Ed. 'Alī Akbar Fayyāḍ, Tehran, 1334.

62. 2 vols.; ed. M. Minovi and Y. Mahdawī, Tehran, 1331 and 1337.

63. Ed. M.T. Bahār, Isfahan, 1333.
64. Ed. I. Afshār, Tehran, 1335.
65. Ed. M. T. Danechepazhuh, Tehran, 1335.
66. Ed. M. Mudarris Raḍawī, Tehran, 1335.
67. Ed. 'A. Nūrā'ī, Mashhad, 1335.
68. Ed. M.T. Danechepazhuh, Tehran, 1335.
69. Ed. S.N. Taqawī, Tehran, 1336.
70. 3 Vols.; Tehran, 1378 (A.H. lunar).
71. Ed. M.T. Danechepazhuh, Tehran, 1339.
72. *Ibid.,* 1341.
73. Qum, 1341.
74. Ed. I. Waḥīd Dāmghānī, Tehran, 1346.
75. Ed. M.T. Danechpazhuh, Tehran, 1340.
76. Ed. M. 'A. Rawḍātī, Isfahan, 1340.
77. Ed. S.H. Nasr, Tehran, 1340.
78. Ed. and trans. Gh. Āhanī, Isfahan, 1341.
79. Ed. I. Miyānjī, Tehran, 1378 (A.H. Lunar).
80. 4 vols.; ed. S.M. Mishkāt, Tehran, 1339.
81. Ed. 'A. 'Uṭārudī, Tehran, 1342.
82. Tehran, 1337. twice.
83. Ed. M. Minovi, Tehran, 1336.
84. Ed. S.M.B. Sabziwārī, Tehran, 1339.
85. Ed. S.M. Mishkāt, Tehran, 1337.
86. Ed. Gh. Āhanī, Isfahan, 1340.
87. Text with English trans. V. Ivanow, Tehran, 1336.
88. Ed. M. Awistā, Tehran, 1338.
89. Ed. M. 'Abbāsī, Tehran, 1338.
90. See Corbin's edition of the *Kitāb al-mashā'ir*, which contains this Persian translation also.
91. Ed. B. Dārābī Tehran, 1347.
92. Trans. Dj. Ghazbān and M. Nadjmābādī, Vol. I, Tehran, 1349.
93. Trans. S. M.K. Īmān, Tehran, 1971.
94. Trans. S.M. Mishkāt, Tehran, 1346.
95. Trans. Gh. Āhanī, Isfahan, 1339.
96. Trans. A. Dānāsirisht, Tehran, 1348.
97. Trans. T. Anṣārī, Tehran, 1343.
98. Trans. S.A. Pūr Ḥusaynī, Tehran, 1347.

99. Trans. Bānū-yi Irānī, Isfahan, 1339.
100. Trans. Z. Kiyā'ī Nizhād, Tehran, 1338.
101. Trans. M. Khazā'ilī, Tehran, 1338.
102. Trnas. B. Furuzānfar, Tehran, 1343.
103. Trans. Gh. Āhanī, Isfahan, 1340.
104. Trans. A. Mishkāt al-Dīnī, Tehran, n.d.
105. Trans. M. B. Sā'idī, Tehran, 1340.
106. Trans. A. Ārām, Tehran, 1346.
107. Trans. A.H. Āryānpūr, Tehran, 1347.
108. Isfshan, 1340.
109. Vol. I, Qum, 1337.
110. Tehran, 1335.
111. Tehran, 1333.
112. Tehran, 1385 (A.H. Lunar).
113. Tehran, 1339.
114. Tehran, 1347.
115. Tehran, 1341.
116. Tehran, 1343.
117. Tehran, 1344.
118. *Ibid.*
119. *Ibid.*
120. Tehran, 1349.
121. Tehran, 1348.
122. Tehran, 1388 (A.H. Lunar).
123. Mashhad, 1347.
124. Tehran, 1345.
125. Tehran, 1348.
126. Tehran, 1349.
127. Qum, 1337.
128. Tehran, 1338.
129. Tehran, 1335.
130. Mashhad, 1344.
131. Mashhad, 1344.
132. Tehran, 1340.
133. Tehran, 1338.
134. Tehran, 1341.
135. Tehran, 1339.
136. Tehran, 1347.
137. *Ibid.*
138. Tehran, 1340.
139. 2 vols., Tehran, 1346.

Index